Fundamentals of Organizational Behavior

Fundamentals of Organizational Behavior

MANAGING PEOPLE AND ORGANIZATIONS

Ricky W. Griffin
TEXAS A&M UNIVERSITY

Gregory Moorhead
ARIZONA STATE UNIVERSITY

Houghton Mifflin Company Boston   New York

For Professor Gavril Ilizarov and Dr. Joseph Gugenheim for "thinking outside the box"
　—*Ricky Griffin*

This book is dedicated to my fellow cancer survivors—Live Strong!
　—*Greg Moorhead*

V.P, Editor-in-Chief: *George Hoffman*
Senior Sponsoring Editor: *Lisé Johnson*
Associate Editor: *Julia Perez*
Senior Project Editor: *Fred Burns*
Editorial Assistant: *Brett Pasinella*
Senior Manufacturing Coordinator: *Marie Barnes*
Senior Art and Design Coordinator: *Jill Haber*
Senior Composition Buyer: *Sarah Ambrose*
Executive Marketing Manager: *Steven W. Mikels*
Marketing Associate: *Lisa E. Boden*
Cover image: ©Getty Images

Photo Credits: Page 8: ©Michael Grimm; p. 17: ©Katherine Lambert; p. 19: ©Russ Quackenbush; p. 32: © Juliana Sohn/M.S. Logan Ltd.; p. 39: ©Greg Girard/Contact Press Images; p. 43: ©Gene Puskar/AP/Wide World; p. 64: ©Peter Cosgrove/AP/Wide World; p. 69: Courtesy Lockheed-Martin;. p. 76: ©France Ruffenach; p. 93: ©Alessandra Sanguinetti; p. 97: ©Clive Brunskill/Getty Images; p. 101: ©Saureb Das/AP/Wide World; p. 123: ©Peter M. Fisher/Corbis; p. 126: ©Taro Yamasak/People Weekly/Time, Inc.; p. 133: ©Christina Caturano; p. 145: Dorothy Low; p. 154: ©Dennis Brack/Bloomberg/Landov; p. 176: ©Robert Burroughs; p. 179: ©Robert Brenner/PhotoEdit; p. 185: Chris Mueller/Redux Pictures; p. 201: ©John Russell/AP/Wide World; p. 208: ©Barbel Schmidt; p. 214: ©Erica Berger/Corbis Outline; p. 229: ©John R. Boehm; p. 236: © Thomas Broening; p. 240: © Pablol Bartholomew/MediaWeb India; p. 262: Jose Azel/Aurora & Quanta Productions; p. 266: ©Michele Asselin; p. 268: ©Margaret Salmon; p. 281: ©Peter Serling. All Rights Reserved; p. 284: ©Axel Koester; p. 286: AP/Wide World Press; p. 315: ©David McLean/Aurora & Quanta Productions; p. 321: ©Laura Pedrick/The New York Times; p. 326: ©Corbis; p. 345: ©Robert Semeniuk; p. 350 (left): ©Robert Laberge/Getty Images; p. 350 (right) ©AP; p. 359: ©Mark Richards; p. 371: ©Michael L. Abramson; p. 379: ©Greg Miller; p. 381: ©Andrew Garn; p. 395: ©Mark Ralston/SCMP; p. 402: ©Everett Collection; p. 409: ©Beth Claggett/Bloomberg/Landov

Copyright © 2006 by Houghton Mifflin Company. All rights reserved.

No part of this work may be reproduced or transmitted in any form or by any means, electronic or mechanical, including photocopying and recording, or by any information storage or retrieval system without the prior written permission of Houghton Mifflin Company unless such copying is expressly permitted by federal copyright law. Address inquiries to College Permissions, Houghton Mifflin Company, 222 Berkeley Street, Boston, MA 02116-3764.

Printed in the U.S.A.

Library of Congress Control Number: 2004116804

ISBN: 0-618-49270-4

1 2 3 4 5 6 7 8 9—DOW—09 08 07 06 05

CONTENTS

Preface xv

Part One Introduction to Organizational Behavior 1

1 An Overview of Organizational Behavior and Management 2

What Is Organizational Behavior? 4

The Historical Roots of Organizational Behavior 5
The Scientific Management Era 5 Classical Organization Theory 6

The Emergence of Organizational Behavior 7
Precursors of Organizational Behavior 7 The Hawthorne Studies 7 The Human Relations Movement 8 Toward Organizational Behavior: The Value of People 9

Contemporary Organizational Behavior 10
The Situational Perspective 11 The Interactional Perspective 12

The Role of Organizational Behavior in Management 13
■ *Business of Ethics 14* Fundamental Managerial Functions 14 Basic Managerial Roles 15 Critical Managerial Skills 17

Contemporary Managerial Challenges 18
Workforce Rightsizing 18 New Ways of Organizing 19 Globalization 19 Ethics and Social Responsibility 20

Managing for Effectiveness 20
Individual-Level Outcomes 21 Group- and Team-Level Outcomes 21 Organization-Level Outcomes 22

Organizational Behavior Case for Discussion: *Yellow Rules the Road* 23

Experiencing Organizational Behavior: *Relating OB and Popular Culture* 24

Self-Assessment Exercise: *Assessing Your Own Theory X and Theory Y Tendencies* 25

OB Online 25

Building Managerial Skills 25

2 Global and Workforce Diversity 29

The Nature of Diversity in Organizations 31
What Is Workforce Diversity? 31 Who Will Be the Workforce of the Future? 33 Global Workforce Diversity 34 The Value of Diversity 35

v

The Emergence of International Management 37

The Growth of International Business 37 Trends in International Business 38 Cross-Cultural Differences and Similarities 39

Dimensions of Diversity 41

Primary Dimensions of Diversity 42 ■ *World View* 44 Secondary Dimensions of Diversity 46

Managing the Multicultural Organization 46

Managerial Behavior Across Cultures 46 Multicultural Organization as Competitive Advantage 47 Creating the Multicultural Organization 48

Organizational Behavior Case for Discussion: *UPS Delivers Diversity to a Diverse World* 51

Experiencing Organizational Behavior: *Understanding Your Own Stereotypes and Attitudes Toward Others* 52

Self-Assessment Exercise: *Cross-Cultural Awareness* 54

OB Online 54

Building Managerial Skills 55

Part One Video Case: *Karen Sand: Manager in Action* 58

Part Two Individual Processes in Organizations 59

3 Foundations of Individual Behavior 60

Understanding Individuals in Organizations 62

The Psychological Contract 62 The Person-Job Fit 63 The Nature of Individual Differences 64

Personality and Individual Behavior 64

■ *Mastering Change* 65 The "Big Five" Personality Traits 65 The Myers-Briggs Framework 67 Other Personality Traits at Work 68 Emotional Intelligence 69

Attitudes and Individual Behavior 70

Work-Related Attitudes 70 Affect and Mood in Organizations 71

Perception and Individual Behavior 72

Stress and Individual Behavior 73

Causes and Consequences of Stress 74 Managing Stress 75

Creativity in Organizations 76

Types of Workplace Behavior 78

Performance Behaviors 78 Withdrawal Behavior 78 Dysfunctional Behaviors 79 Organizational Citizenship 79

Organizational Behavior Case for Discussion: *Valuing Employees at the World's Largest Firm* 80

Experiencing Organizational Behavior: *Matching Personalities and Jobs* 82

Self-Assessment Exercise: *Assessing Your Locus of Control* 82

Contents

OB Online 83

Building Managerial Skills 83

4 Motivation in Organizations 86

The Nature of Motivation 88

The Importance of Motivation 88   The Motivational Framework 88   Historical Perspectives on Motivation 89   ■ *Business of Ethics* 90

Need-Based Perspectives on Motivation 91

Hierarchy of Needs Theory 91   ERG Theory 93   Dual-Structure Theory 94   Other Important Needs 96

Process-Based Perspectives on Motivation 98

Equity Theory of Motivation 98   Expectancy Theory of Motivation 100

Learning-Based Perspectives on Motivation 104

How Learning Occurs 105   Reinforcement Theory and Learning 105   Social Learning in Organizations 109   Organization Behavior Modification 109

Organizational Behavior Case for Discussion: *When Employees Are Owners* 113

Experiencing Organizational Behavior: *Understanding the Dynamics of Expectancy Theory* 115

Self-Assessment Exercise: *Assessing Your Equity Sensitivity* 115

OB Online 116

Building Managerial Skills 116

5 Job Design and Work Structures 119

Motivation and Employee Performance 121

Job Design in Organizations 122

Job Specialization 122   Early Alternatives to Job Specialization 123   Job Enrichment 124   Job Characteristics Theory 125

Participation, Empowerment, and Motivation 128

Early Perspectives on Participation and Empowerment 128   Areas of Participation 128   Techniques and Issues in Empowerment 129

Alternative Work Arrangements 130

■ *Business of Ethics* 130   Variable Work Schedules 131   Flexible Work Schedules 131   Job Sharing 132   Telecommuting 133

Organizational Behavior Case for Discussion: *Employee Participation at Chaparral Steel* 134

Experiencing Organizational Behavior: *Learning About Job Design* 136

Self-Assessment Exercise: *The Job Characteristics Inventory* 136

OB Online 138

Building Managerial Skills 139

6 Goal Setting, Performance Management, and Rewards 142

Goal Setting and Motivation 144
Goal-Setting Theory 144 Broader Perspectives on Goal Setting 146 Evaluation and Implications 147

Performance Management in Organizations 147
The Nature of Performance Management 148 Purposes of Performance Management 148 Performance Measurement Basics 149 ■ *Mastering Change* 151

Individual Rewards in Organizations 152
Roles, Purposes, and Meanings of Rewards 152 Types of Rewards 153

Managing Reward Systems 156
Linking Performance and Rewards 156 Flexible Reward Systems 157 Participative Pay Systems 158 Pay Secrecy 158 Expatriate Compensation 158

Organizational Behavior Case for Discussion: *Rewarding the Hourly Worker* 161

Experiencing Organizational Behavior: *Using Compensation to Motivate Workers* 162

Self-Assessment Exercise: *Diagnosing Poor Performance and Enhancing Motivation* 163

OB Online 164

Building Managerial Skills 164

Part Two Video Case: *Motivating the Salesforce at Wheelworks* 168

Part Three Interpersonal Processes in Organizations 169

7 Communication in Organizations 170

The Nature of Communication in Organizations 172
Purposes of Communication in Organizations 172 ■ *Mastering Change* 173

Methods of Communication 174
Written Communication 174 Oral Communication 175 Nonverbal Communication 175

The Communication Process 176
Source 176 Encoding 177 Transmission 177 Decoding 178 Receiver 178 Feedback 179 Noise 179

Electronic Information Processing and Telecommunications 179

Communication Networks 181
Small-Group Networks 181 Organizational Communication Networks 183

Managing Communication 186
Improving the Communication Process 186 Improving Organizational Factors in Communication 189

Organizational Behavior Case for Discussion: *A Tale of Two Companies* 192

Experiencing Organizational Behavior: *The Importance of Feedback in Oral Communication* 193

Self-Assessment Exercise: *Diagnosing Your Listening Skills*   194

OB Online   195

Building Managerial Skills   195

8 Group Dynamics   198

The Nature of Groups   200
■ *Mastering Change*   202

Types of Groups   202
Formal Groups 202   Informal Groups 203

Stages of Group Development   204
Mutual Acceptance 204   Communication and Decision Making 206   Motivation and Productivity 206   Control and Organization 206

Group Performance Factors   207
Composition 207   Size 209   Norms 210   Cohesiveness 210

Intergroup Dynamics   212

Conflict in Groups and Organizations   213
Reactions to Conflict 213   Managing Conflict 216

Managing Group and Intergroup Dynamics in Organizations   217

Organizational Behavior Case for Discussion: *Using Groups to Get Things Done*   219

Experiencing Organizational Behavior: *Learning the Benefits of a Group*   221

Self-Assessment Exercise: *Group Cohesiveness*   221

OB Online   222

Building Managerial Skills   223

9 Using Teams in Organizations   226

Differentiating Teams from Groups   227
Job Categories 229   Authority 230   Reward Systems 230

Benefits and Costs of Teams in Organizations   231
Enhanced Performance 231   Employee Benefits 231   Reduced Costs 232   Organizational Enhancements 232   ■ *Mastering Change* 233   Costs of Teams 233

Types of Teams   234
Quality Circles 234   Work Teams 234   Problem-Solving Teams 235   Management Teams 235   Product Development Teams 235   Virtual Teams 236

Implementing Teams in Organizations   236
Planning the Change 236   Phases of Implementation 239

Essential Team Issues   242
Team Performance 242   Start at the Top 243

Organizational Behavior Case for Discussion: *None of Us Is as Smart as All of Us*   244

Experiencing Organizational Behavior: *Using Teams* 245

Self-Assessment Exercise: *Understanding the Benefits of Teams* 246

OB Online 247

Building Managerial Skills 247

Part Three Video Case: *Denver Broncos: Teamwork in Action* 250

Part Four Leadership and Decision-Making Processes in Organizations 253

10 Leadership Models and Concepts 254

The Nature of Leadership 256
The Meaning of Leadership 256   Leadership Versus Management 256

Early Approaches to Leadership 257
Trait Approaches to Leadership 258   ■ *World View* 259   Behavioral Approaches to Leadership 259

The LPC Theory of Leadership 262
Task Versus Relationship Motivation 262   Situational Favorableness 263   Evaluation and Implications 265

The Path-Goal Theory of Leadership 265
Basic Premises 265   Evaluation and Implications 267

Vroom's Decision Tree Approach to Leadership 267
Basic Premises 267   Evaluation and Implications 270

Other Contemporary Approaches to Leadership 271
The Leader-Member Exchange Model 271   The Hersey and Blanchard Model 271

Organizational Behavior Case for Discussion: *How Do You Manage Magic?* 274

Experiencing Organizational Behavior: *Understanding Successful and Unsuccessful Leadership* 275

Self-Assessment Exercise: *Applying Vroom's Decision Tree Approach* 275

OB Online 276

Building Managerial Skills 276

11 Leadership and Influence Processes 279

Leadership as Influence 280

Influence-Based Approaches to Leadership 281
Transformational Leadership 281   Charismatic Leadership 282

Leadership Substitutes: Can Leadership Be Irrelevant? 283
Workplace Substitutes 283   Superleadership 284

Power in Organizations 284
The Nature of Power 284   Types of Power 285   The Uses of Power in Organizations 287

Contents

Organizational Politics   291
The Pervasiveness of Political Behavior 292 ■ *Business of Ethics* 292   Managing Political Behavior 294

Impression Management   298

Organizational Behavior Case for Discussion: *A Corporate Marriage Made in Heaven (Not!)* 299

Experiencing Organizational Behavior: *Learning About Ethics and Power*   301

Self-Assessment Exercise: *Are You a Charismatic Leader?*   301

OB Online   303

Building Managerial Skills   303

12 Decision Making and Negotiation   306

The Nature of Decision Making   308
Types of Decisions 308   Information Required for Decision Making 310

The Decision-Making Process   311
The Rational Approach 311   The Behavioral Approach 315   The Practical Approach 316   The Personal Approach 317

Related Behavioral Aspects of Decision Making   320
Ethics and Decision Making 320   Escalation of Commitment 321 ■ *Business of Ethics* 322

Group Decision Making   322
Group Polarization 323   Groupthink 323   Participation 325   Group Problem Solving 326

Negotiation in Organizations   328
Approaches to Negotiation 328   Win-Win Negotiation 330

Organizational Behavior Case for Discussion: *The Most Stressful Conditions*   332

Experiencing Organizational Behavior: *Programmed and Nonprogrammed Decisions*   333

Self-Assessment Exercise: *Rational Versus Practical Approaches to Decision Making*   334

OB Online   334

Building Managerial Skills   334

Part Four Video Case: *The Baker's Best Story*   338

Part Five   Organizational Processes and Characteristics   339

13 Organization Design   340

Essential Elements of Organization Structure   342
Organization Structure 342 ■ *Mastering Change* 343   Division of Labor 343   Coordinating the Divided Tasks 345   Authority, Responsibility, and Decision Making 350

Classic Views of Structure: The Universal Approach   352

Ideal Bureaucracy 352   The Classic Principles of Organizing 353   Human Organization 353

Contingency Approaches to Organization Design   354
Strategy 354   Structural Imperatives 354

Organization Designs   357
Mechanistic and Organic Designs 357   Mintzberg's Designs 357   Matrix Organization Design 359

Organizational Behavior Case for Discussion: *Restructuring at Cisco*   362

Experiencing Organizational Behavior: *Understanding Organization Structure in a Real-World Organization*   363

Self-Assessment Exercise: *Diagnosing Organization Structure*   364

OB Online   365

Building Managerial Skills   365

14 Organizing Culture   368

The Nature of Organization Culture   369
Historical Foundations 370   Culture Versus Climate 372

Creating the Organization Culture   373
Establish Values 373   Create Vision 373   Initiate Implementation Strategies 374   Reinforce Cultural Behaviors 374

Describing Organization Culture   374
The Ouchi Framework 374   The Peters and Waterman Approach 377

Emerging Issues in Organization Culture   378
Innovation 378   Procedural Justice 380

Managing Organization Culture   380
Taking Advantage of the Existing Culture 380   Teaching the Organization Culture: Socialization 381   ■ *Business of Ethics 382*   Changing the Organization Culture 382

Organizational Behavior Case for Discussion: *Southwest Airlines: Flying High with Culture*   385

Experiencing Organizational Behavior: *Culture of the Classroom*   386

Self-Assessment Exercise: *Assessing Your Preference for Organization Culture*   387

OB Online   388

Building Managerial Skills   388

15 Organization Change and Development   391

Forces for Change   393
People 393   Technology 394   ■ *World View 394*   Information Processing and Communication 395   Competition 396

Planned Organization Change   396
Lewin's Process Model 396   The Continuous Change Process Model 397

Organization Development 399
Systemwide Organization Development 399   Task and Technological Organization Development 400   Group and Individual Organization Development 401

Resistance to Change 405
Organizational Sources of Resistance 405   Individual Sources of Resistance 407

Managing Successful Organization Change and Development 408
Take a Holistic View 408   Start Small 409   Secure Top Management Support 409   Encourage Participation 409   Foster Open Communication 409   Reward Contributors 409

Organizational Behavior Case for Discussion: *Change of Direction at Schwab* 411

Experiencing Organizational Behavior: *Planning a Change at the University* 413

Self-Assessment Exercise: *Support for Change* 413

OB Online 414

Building Managerial Skills 414

Part Five Video Case: *Organization Structure and Design* 417

Endnotes 419

Answers to Test Preppers 433

Index 435

PREFACE

Organizational behavior is the study of human behavior in organizations, of the interface between human behavior and the organization, and of the organization itself. Hence, it reflects an exciting but challenging part of every manager's work—dealing with people. As the field of organizational behavior has grown, however, so too has the length of survey textbooks traditionally used in organizational behavior courses.

As we prepared this first edition of *Fundamentals of Organizational Behavior*, we carefully considered what material could be viewed as "fundamental" in nature—that is, what material simply had to be discussed in any course in organizational behavior. We chose to provide detailed coverage of that material, but to not include other material that, while interesting and important, was not as essential.

This book reflects this differentiation between essential and non-essential material. Traditional survey books today tend to have twenty or more chapters; we have been able to cover the fundamental material from the field, though, in only fifteen chapters and far fewer pages than you might see in a comprehensive book. But that does not mean that the book is a superficial or "discount" treatment of the field. As you will see, our text covers the fundamentals in detail and is presented in a dynamic and contemporary fashion; it also makes full use of bold visual features such as color and photographs that are generally preferred by today's readers.

We believe that *Fundamentals of Organizational Behavior* will prepare and energize managers of the future for the complex and challenging tasks of the new century while preserving the past contributions of the classics. Even though this text focuses only on the fundamentals, it is comprehensive in its presentation of practical perspectives, backed by the research and teachings of the experts. We expect each reader to be inspired by the most exciting task of the new century: managing people in organizations.

Content and Organization

Part One discusses the managerial context of organizational behavior. In Chapter 1 we introduce the field of organizational behavior and relate it to the manager's job. Chapter 2 provides a thorough treatment of two increasingly important contextual perspectives on organizational behavior, global issues and workforce diversity.

Part Two includes four chapters that focus on key aspects of individual processes in organizations. Chapter 3 presents the foundations for understanding individual behavior in organizations by discussing the psychological nature of people, elements of personality, individual attitudes, perceptual processes, and creativity. Chapter 4 discusses employee motivation. Chapters 5 and 6 focus on specific methods, techniques, and strategies used by managers to affect individual performance in organizations.

were that people respond to their social environment, motivation depends more on social needs than on economic needs, and satisfied employees work harder than unsatisfied employees. This perspective represented a fundamental shift away from the philosophy and values of scientific management and classical organization theory.

The works of Douglas McGregor and Abraham Maslow perhaps best exemplified the early values of the human relations approach to management.[10] McGregor is best known for his classic book *The Human Side of Enterprise*, in which he identified two opposing perspectives that he believed typified managerial views of employees. Some managers, McGregor said, subscribed to what he labeled Theory X. **Theory X** takes a pessimistic view of human nature and employee behavior. In many ways, it is consistent with the premises of scientific management. In contrast, McGregor's **Theory Y** takes a much more optimistic and positive view of employees. Theory Y, which is generally representative of the human relations perspective, was the approach McGregor himself advocated. Table 1.1 lists the basic assumptions of Theory X and Theory Y.

In 1943, Abraham Maslow published a pioneering theory of employee motivation that became well known and widely accepted among managers. Maslow's theory, which we describe in Chapter 4, assumes that motivation arises from a hierarchical series of needs. As the needs at each level are satisfied, the individual progresses to the next higher level.

The Hawthorne studies and the human relations movement played major roles in developing the foundations for the field of organizational behavior. Some of the early theorists' basic premises and assumptions were incorrect, however. For example, most human relationists believed that employee attitudes such as job satisfaction are the major causes of employee behaviors such as job performance. As we will see later, however, this usually is not the case. Also, many of the human relationists' views were unnecessarily limited and situation specific. Thus, there was still plenty of room for refinement and development in the emerging field of human behavior in organizations.

Theory X, described by Douglas McGregor, is an approach to management that takes a negative and pessimistic view of workers.

Theory Y, also described by McGregor, is an approach to management that offers a more positive and optimistic perspective on workers.

Toward Organizational Behavior: The Value of People

Organizational behavior began to emerge as a mature field of study in the late 1950s and early 1960s.[11] That period witnessed the field's evolution from the simple

As the field of organizational behavior began to emerge, managers came to better appreciate the importance of human behavior at work. This view does not imply, of course, that the social environment is the only thing that matters. If a manager took the approach reflected here, the firm probably would not survive very long. Enlightened managers should remember that a variety of factors, including technology, profitability, and the social environment, are all important. Successful organizations are usually those that optimize these and other imperatives in an effective manner.

"You know what I think, folks? Improving technology isn't important. Increased profits aren't important. What's important is to be warm, decent human beings."

© The New Yorker Collection 1987 J.B. Handelsman from cartoonbank.com. All Rights Reserved.

TABLE 1.1

Theory X and Theory Y

Theory X Assumptions	Theory Y Assumptions
1. People do not like work and try to avoid it.	1. People do not naturally dislike work; work is a natural part of their lives.
2. People do not like work, so managers have to control, direct, coerce, and threaten employees to get them to work toward organizational goals.	2. People are internally motivated to reach objectives to which they are committed.
3. People prefer to be directed, to avoid responsibility, to want security; they have little ambition.	3. People are committed to goals to the degree that they receive personal rewards when they reach their objectives.
	4. People will seek and accept responsibility under favorable conditions.
	5. People have the capacity to be innovative in solving organizational problems.
	6. People are bright, but under most organizational conditions, their potentials are underutilized.

Reference: Douglas McGregor, *The Human Side of Enterprise* (New York: McGraw-Hill, 1960), pp. 33–34, 47–48.

assumptions and behavioral models of the human relationists to the concepts and methodologies of a true scientific discipline. Since that time, organizational behavior as a scientific field of inquiry has made considerable strides, although there have been occasional steps backward as well. Overall, however, managers increasingly recognize the value of human resources and strive to better understand people and their roles in complex organizations and competitive business situations.[12] Many of the ideas discussed in this book have emerged over the past two or three decades. We turn now to contemporary organizational behavior.

Contemporary Organizational Behavior

LEARNING OBJECTIVE

Characterize contemporary organizational behavior.

Researchers and managers who use concepts and ideas from organizational behavior must recognize that the field has an interdisciplinary focus and a descriptive nature; that is, it draws from a variety of other fields and attempts to describe behavior (rather than examine how behavior can be changed in consistent and predictable ways). The central concepts of organizational behavior can be grouped into three basic categories: (1) individual processes, (2) interpersonal processes, and (3) organizational processes and characteristics. As Figure 1.2 shows, these categories provide the basic framework for this book.

Part Two of the book addresses individual processes, starting with foundations of individual behavior and then moving to popular motivational theories and techniques organizations use to increase the motivation of their employees. Part Three addresses such interpersonal processes as communication, groups, and teams. Part Four covers related interpersonal processes such as leadership, decision making, and negotiation. Finally, Part Five focuses on the organizational processes of organization design, culture, and change and development.

Chapter 1 An Overview of Organizational Behavior and Management

FIGURE 1.2

The Framework for Understanding Organizational Behavior

Organizational behavior is an exciting and complex field of study. The specific concepts and topics that constitute the field can be grouped into three categories: individual, interpersonal, and organizational processes and characteristics. Here these concepts and classifications are used to provide an overall framework for the organization of this book.

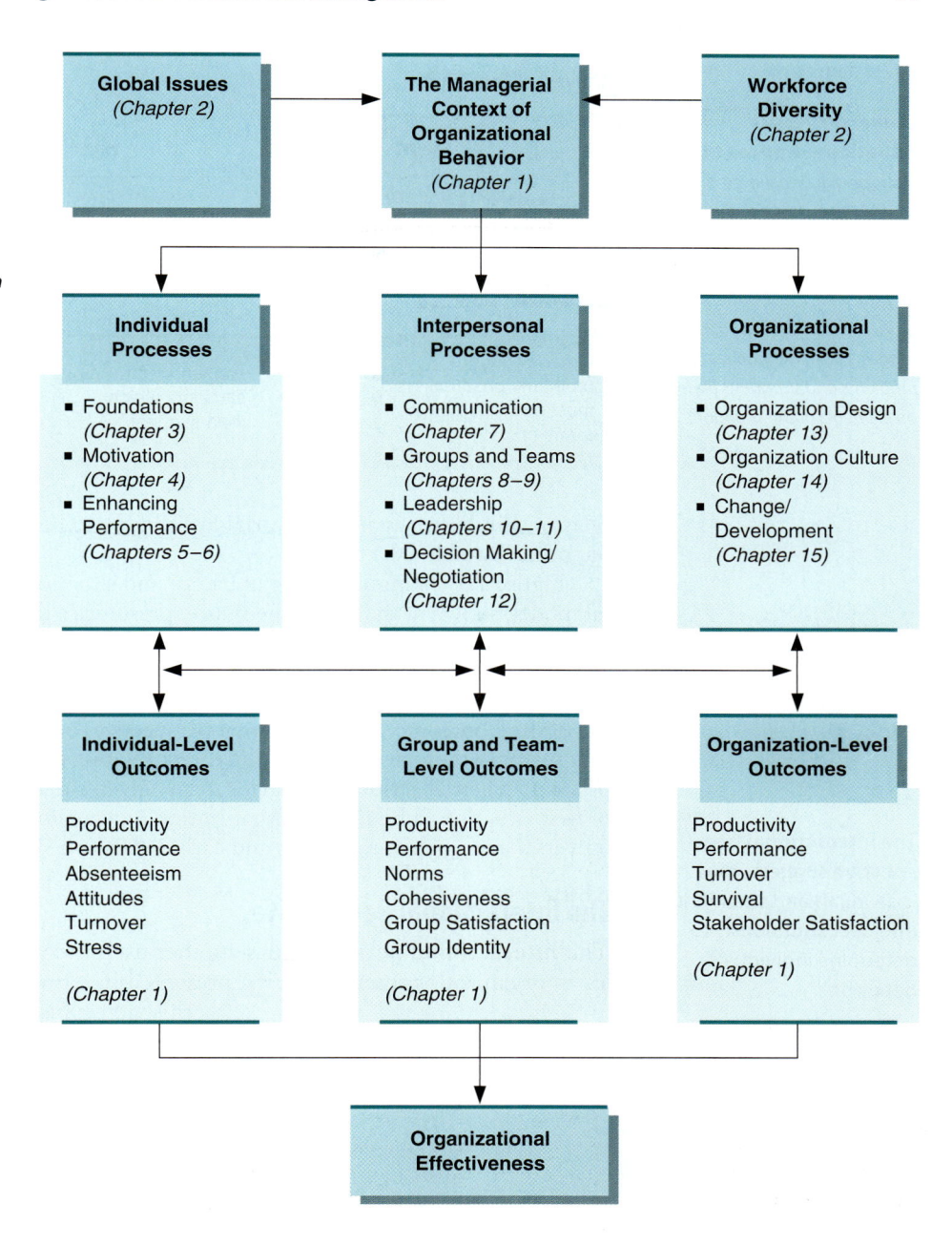

Global Issues (Chapter 2) → **The Managerial Context of Organizational Behavior** (Chapter 1) ← **Workforce Diversity** (Chapter 2)

Individual Processes
- Foundations (Chapter 3)
- Motivation (Chapter 4)
- Enhancing Performance (Chapters 5–6)

Interpersonal Processes
- Communication (Chapter 7)
- Groups and Teams (Chapters 8–9)
- Leadership (Chapters 10–11)
- Decision Making/ Negotiation (Chapter 12)

Organizational Processes
- Organization Design (Chapter 13)
- Organization Culture (Chapter 14)
- Change/ Development (Chapter 15)

Individual-Level Outcomes
Productivity
Performance
Absenteeism
Attitudes
Turnover
Stress
(Chapter 1)

Group and Team-Level Outcomes
Productivity
Performance
Norms
Cohesiveness
Group Satisfaction
Group Identity
(Chapter 1)

Organization-Level Outcomes
Productivity
Performance
Turnover
Survival
Stakeholder Satisfaction
(Chapter 1)

Organizational Effectiveness

The Situational Perspective

The **situational perspective** suggests that in most organizations, situations and outcomes are contingent on, or influenced by, other variables.

One fundamental viewpoint essential for understanding behavior in organizations comes from the **situational perspective.** In the earlier days of management studies, managers searched for universal answers to organizational questions. They sought prescriptions, the "one best way" that could be used in any organization under any conditions—searching, for example, for forms of leadership behavior that would always lead employees to be more satisfied and to work harder. Eventually, however, researchers realized that the complexities of human behavior and organizational settings make universal conclusions virtually impossible. They discovered that in organizations, most situations and outcomes are situational; that is, the

FIGURE 1.3

Universal Versus Situational Approach
Managers once believed they could identify the "one best way" to solve problems or react to situations. Here we illustrate a more realistic view, the situational approach. The situational approach suggests that approaches to problems and situations depend on elements of the situation.

Universal Approach

Organizational problems or situations determine . . . → the one best way of responding.

Situational Approach

Organizational problems or situations must be evaluated in terms of . . . → elements of the situation, which then suggest . . . → contingent or situational ways of responding.

relationship between any two variables is likely to be contingent on, or to depend on, other variables.[13]

Figure 1.3 distinguishes the universal and situational perspectives. The universal model, shown at the top of the figure, presumes a direct cause-and-effect linkage between variables. For example, it suggests that whenever a manager encounters a certain problem or situation (such as motivating employees to work harder), a universal approach is used (such as raising pay or increasing autonomy) that will lead to the desired outcome. The situational perspective, on the other hand, acknowledges that several other variables alter the direct relationship. In other words, the appropriate managerial action or behavior in any given situation depends on the elements of that situation. The field of organizational behavior gradually has shifted from a universal approach in the 1950s and early 1960s to a situational perspective today.

The Interactional Perspective

The **interactional perspective** is another useful way to better understand behavior in organizational settings. First presented in terms of interactional psychology, this view, illustrated in Figure 1.4, assumes individual behavior results from a continuous and multidirectional interaction between the characteristics of the person and the characteristics of the situation. More specifically, the interactional perspective attempts to explain how people select, interpret, and change various situations.[14]

The interactional view implies that simple cause-and-effect descriptions of organizational phenomena are not enough. For example, one set of research studies may suggest that job changes lead to improved employee attitudes, whereas another set may propose that attitudes influence how people perceive their jobs in the first place. Both positions are probably incomplete: Employee attitudes may influence job perceptions, but these perceptions may in turn influence future attitudes.

The **interactional perspective** suggests that individuals and situations interact continuously to determine individuals' behavior.

Individual ↔ Situation → Behavior

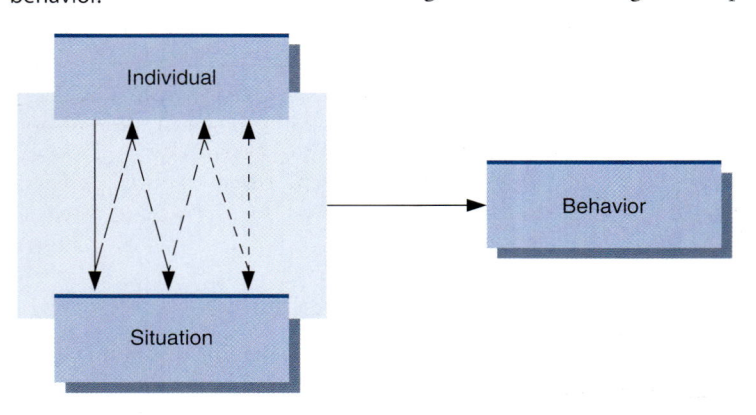

FIGURE 1.4

The Interactionist Perspective on Behavior in Organizations
When people enter an organization, their own behaviors and actions shape that organization in various ways. Similarly, the organization itself shapes the behaviors and actions of each individual who becomes a part of it. This interactionist perspective can be useful in explaining organizational behavior.

The Role of Organizational Behavior in Management

LEARNING OBJECTIVE
Discuss the role of organizational behavior in management

Virtually all organizations have managers with titles such as chief financial officer, marketing manager, director of public relations, vice president for human resources, and plant manager. But probably no organization has a position called "organizational behavior manager." The reason is simple: Organizational behavior is not a designated function or area; rather, an understanding of organizational behavior is a fundamental perspective or set of tools that all managers can use to carry out their jobs more effectively.[15]

An appreciation and understanding of organizational behavior help managers better recognize why others in the organization behave as they do.[16] For example, most managers in an organization are directly responsible for the work-related behaviors of a set of other people: their immediate subordinates. Typical managerial activities in this realm include motivating employees to work harder, ensuring that employees' jobs are properly designed, resolving conflicts, evaluating performance, and helping workers set goals to achieve rewards. The field of organizational behavior abounds with models and research relevant to each of these functions.[17]

Unless they happen to be chief executive officers (CEOs), managers also report to others in the organization (and even the CEO reports to the board of directors). In dealing with these individuals, an understanding of basic issues associated with leadership, power and political behavior, decision making, organization structure and design, and organization culture can be extremely beneficial. Again, the field of organizational behavior provides numerous valuable insights into these processes. Managers can also use their knowledge of organizational behavior to better understand their own needs, motives, behaviors, and feelings, which will help them improve their decision-making capabilities, control stress, communicate better, and comprehend how career dynamics unfold. The study of organizational behavior provides insights into all of these concepts and processes.

Managers interact with a variety of colleagues, peers, and coworkers inside the organization. An understanding of attitudinal processes, individual differences, group and intergroup dynamics, organization culture, and power and political behavior can help managers handle such interactions more effectively. Organizational behavior provides a variety of practical insights into these processes. Virtually all of the behavioral processes already mentioned are also valuable in interactions with people outside the organization: suppliers, customers, competitors, government officials, representatives of citizens' groups, union officials, and potential joint venture partners. In addition, a special understanding of the environment, technology, and global issues is valuable. Again, organizational behavior offers managers numerous insights into how and why things happen as they do. The Business of Ethics box provides an unfortunate illustration of how management and organizational behavior can also be related.

Finally, these patterns of interactions hold true regardless of the type of organization. Whether a business is large or small, domestic or international, growing or stagnating, its managers perform their work within a social context. The same can be said of managers in health care, education, government, and student organizations such as fraternities, sororities, and professional clubs. We can see, then, that it is essentially impossible to understand and practice management without considering the numerous areas of organizational behavior. Hence we now look at the nature of the manager's job in more detail. There are many different ways to conceptualize the job of a contemporary manager.[18] The most widely accepted approaches, however, are from the perspectives of basic managerial functions, common managerial roles, and fundamental managerial skills.[19]

BUSINESS OF ETHICS

Putting a Price on Talent Can Be a Slippery Slope

In 2003, American corporations paid their top managers more money than ever before in U.S. history and more than in any other nation. The high level of compensation can be partly explained by the nature of the job: Executives deserve large salaries because their jobs are difficult and require specialized skills. Another explanation is the economic principle of supply and demand: Because few individuals possess the experience and training necessary to head a major corporation, high demand for executive talent leads to high compensation.

For companies with financial difficulties or impending bankruptcies, however, there is a third explanation: the need to retain managerial talent. Top managers are likely to look for employment elsewhere when bankruptcy threatens, but companies in dire circumstances often hope to retain their most experienced managers to help them through the difficult period. Thus, troubled firms often rely on bonuses as additional compensation intended to discourage top managers from "jumping ship."

But what seems like a sound business policy can have severe negative consequences for other interested parties. For example, Enron reportedly paid more than $55 million in bonuses to about five hundred key personnel after beginning bankruptcy proceedings. That money could have been used instead to pay employees, retirees, investors, and suppliers of the failed firm. Investors and employees have often reacted to this practice by seeking to overthrow retention bonus plans in bankruptcy court before the compensation can be paid. This has happened in cases involving steelmaker LTV; Polaroid, manufacturer of cameras and film; and clothing manufacturer Burlington Industries.

Groups opposed to the bonus plans claim that such bonuses reward the managers who are most directly re-

"By definition, bankruptcy is a world inhabited by companies that have trouble keeping promises." —Stephen Bobo, bankruptcy attorney with the Chicago law firm D'Ancona & Pflaum

sponsible for the company's current problems. They also assert that such payments are unfair to lower-level employees, who are least able to find another job and have the fewest personal resources to sustain them through a period of unemployment. Personal finance advisers counsel employees of companies facing bankruptcy to seek other employment, demand a retention bonus, and even hire a lawyer. "By definition, bankruptcy is a world inhabited by companies that have trouble keeping promises. It's a world where promises aren't kept and there isn't enough to go around," says Stephen Bubo, a bankruptcy attorney with the Chicago law firm D'Ancono and Pflaum. Workers and investors of failed companies, who have been stripped of their jobs and billions of investment dollars, would surely agree.

References: "Use of Retention Bonuses Draws Fire: Select Few Get Cash While Others Face Financial Ruin," *USA Today*, February 14, 2002; Victoria Zunitch, "What If Your Company Fails?: Five Ways to Protect Your Finances and Career When Your Employer Goes Bankrupt," CNN/Money online, January 23, 2002, www.money.cnn.com on February 25, 2002; "Polaroid Retirees Lose Benefits," *USA Today*, January 14, 2002.

Fundamental Managerial Functions

Managers in all organizations engage in four basic functions, generally referred to as planning, organizing, leading, and controlling. All organizations also use four kinds of resources: human, financial, physical, and information. As Figure 1.5 illustrates, managers combine these resources through the four basic functions, with the ultimate purpose of efficiently and effectively attaining the goals of the organization. That is, the figure shows how managers apply the basic functions across resources to advance the organization toward its goals.

Planning is the process of determining an organization's desired future position and the best means of getting there.

Planning Planning, the first managerial function, is the process of determining the organization's desired future position and deciding how best to get there. The planning process at Sears, for example, includes studying and analyzing the envi-

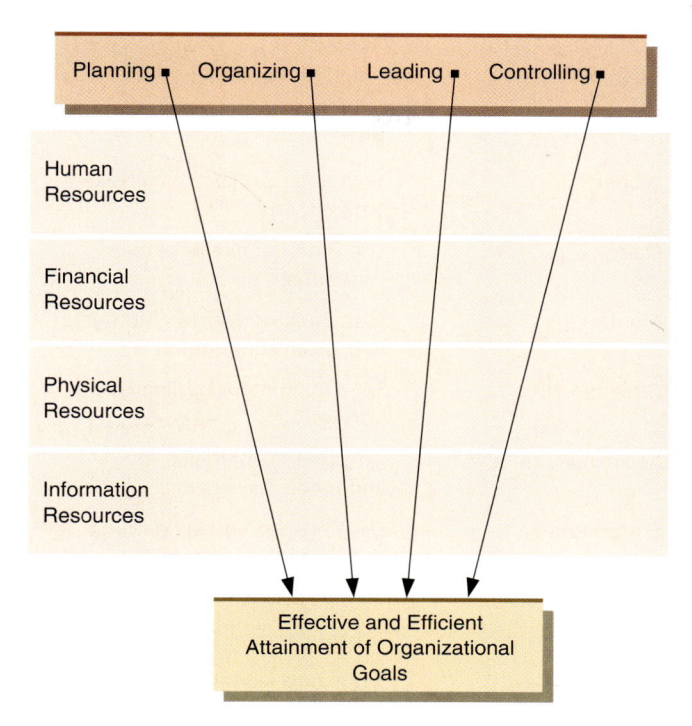

FIGURE 1.5

Basic Managerial Functions

Managers engage in the four basic functions of planning, organizing, leading, and controlling. These functions are applied to human, financial, physical, and information resources, with the ultimate purpose of attaining organizational goals efficiently and effectively.

Organizing is the process of designing jobs, grouping jobs into units, and establishing patterns of authority between jobs and units.

Leading is the process of getting the organization's members to work together toward achieving the organization's goals.

Controlling is the process of monitoring and correcting the actions of the organization and its members to keep them directed toward their goals.

ronment, deciding on appropriate goals, outlining strategies for achieving those goals, and developing tactics to help execute the strategies. Behavioral processes and characteristics pervade each of these activities. Perception, for instance, plays a major role in environmental scanning, and creativity and motivation influence how managers establish goals, strategies, and tactics for their organization. Larger corporations, such as General Electric and IBM, usually rely on their top management teams to handle most planning activities. In smaller firms, the owner usually takes care of planning.

Organizing The second managerial function is **organizing,** the process of designing jobs, grouping jobs into manageable units, and establishing patterns of authority among jobs and groups of jobs. This process produces the basic structure, or framework, of the organization. For large organizations such as Sears, that structure can be extensive and complicated. Smaller firms can often function with a relatively simple and straightforward form of organization. As noted earlier, the processes and characteristics of the organization itself are a major theme of organizational behavior.

Leading Leading, the third managerial function, is the process of motivating members of the organization to work together toward achieving the organization's goals. A Sears manager, for example, must hire people, train them, and motivate them. Major components of leading include motivating employees, managing group dynamics, and the actual process of leadership. These are all closely related to major areas of organizational behavior. All managers, whether they work in a huge multinational corporation or a small neighborhood business, must understand the importance of leading.

Controlling The fourth managerial function, **controlling,** is the process of monitoring and correcting the actions of the organization and its people to keep them headed toward their goals. A Sears manager has to control costs, inventory, and so on. Again, behavioral processes and characteristics are a key part of this function. Performance evaluation, reward systems, and motivation, for example, all apply to control. Control is important to all businesses, but it may be especially critical to smaller ones. General Motors, for example, can withstand a loss of several thousand dollars due to poor control, but the same loss may be devastating to a small firm.

Basic Managerial Roles

In an organization, as in a play or a movie, a role is the part a person plays in a given situation. Managers often play a number of different roles. The traditional model of managerial roles, summarized in Table 1.2, identifies ten basic roles clustered into three general categories: interpersonal, informational, and decision-making roles.[20]

TABLE 1.2

Important Managerial Roles

Category	Role	Example
Interpersonal	Figurehead	Attend employee retirement ceremony
	Leader	Encourage workers to increase productivity
	Liaison	Coordinate activities of two committees
Informational	Monitor	Scan *BusinessWeek* for information about competition
	Disseminator	Send out memos outlining new policies
	Spokesperson	Hold press conference to announce new plant
Decision-making	Entrepreneur	Develop idea for new product and convince others of its merits
	Disturbance handler	Resolve dispute
	Resource allocator	Allocate budget requests
	Negotiator	Settle new labor contract

Key **interpersonal roles** are the figurehead, the leader, and the liaison.

Interpersonal Roles **Interpersonal roles** are primarily social in nature; that is, they are roles in which the manager's main task is to relate to other people in certain ways. The manager sometimes may serve as a *figurehead* for the organization. Taking visitors to dinner and attending ribbon-cutting ceremonies are part of the figurehead role. In the role of *leader*, the manager works to hire, train, and motivate employees. Finally, the *liaison* role consists of relating to others outside the group or organization. For example, a manager at Intel might be responsible for handling all price negotiations with a key supplier of electronic circuit boards. Obviously each of these interpersonal roles involves behavioral processes.

Key **informational roles** are the monitor, the disseminator, and the spokesperson.

Informational Roles The three **informational roles** involve some aspect of information processing. The *monitor* actively seeks information that might be of value to the organization in general or to specific managers. The manager who transmits this information to others is carrying out the role of *disseminator*. The *spokesperson* speaks for the organization to outsiders. A manager chosen by Dell Computer to appear at a press conference announcing a new-product launch or other major deal, such as a recent decision to undertake a joint venture with Microsoft, would be serving in this role. Again, behavioral processes are part of each of these roles because information is almost always exchanged between people.

Important **decision-making roles** are the entrepreneur, the disturbance handler, the resource allocator, and the negotiator.

Decision-Making Roles Four **decision-making roles** exist. The *entrepreneur* voluntarily initiates change, such as innovations or new strategies, in the organization. The *disturbance handler* helps settle disputes between various parties, such as other managers and their subordinates. The *resource allocator* decides who will get what: how the organization's resources will be distributed among various individuals and groups. The *negotiator* represents the organization in reaching agreements with other organizations, such as when settling contracts between management and labor unions. Again, behavioral processes clearly are crucial in each of these decisional roles.

Chapter 1   An Overview of Organizational Behavior and Management   17

Technical skills are the skills necessary to accomplish specific tasks within the organization.

The manager uses **interpersonal skills** to communicate with, understand, and motivate individuals and groups.

The manager uses **conceptual skills** to think in the abstract.

The manager uses **diagnostic skills** to understand cause-and-effect relationships and to recognize the optimal solutions to problems.

Management involves four basic functions, ten roles, and four fundamental skills. The work of Claire Fraser, president of the Institute for Genomic Research, clearly illustrates several of these. Her current challenges include supervising research leading to new scientific breakthroughs, managing the institute's most talented employees, keeping abreast of all current developments in her field, and managing several ongoing applied and basic research programs.

Critical Managerial Skills

Another important element of managerial work involves the skills necessary to carry out basic functions and fill fundamental roles. In general, most successful managers have a strong combination of technical, interpersonal, conceptual, and diagnostic skills.[21]

Technical Skills   **Technical skills** are abilities necessary to accomplish specific tasks within the organization. Designing a new network card for IBM, developing a new formula for a frozen-food additive for Conagra, and writing a press release for Exxon require technical skills. Hence, these skills are generally associated with the operations the organization employs in its production processes. For example, Bill Hewlett and David Packard, founders of Hewlett-Packard, began their careers as engineers. They still work hard today to keep abreast of new technology; their technical skills are an important part of their success. Other examples of managers with strong technical skills include H. Lee Scott (president and CEO of Wal-Mart, who started his career as a store manager) and Gordon Bethune (retired CEO of Continental Airlines, a former pilot).

Interpersonal Skills   A manager uses **interpersonal skills** to communicate with, understand, and motivate individuals and groups. As we noted, managers spend a large portion of their time interacting with others, so clearly it is important that they get along with other people. During his tenure as CEO of Continental Airlines, Gordon Bethune became one of the most admired business leaders in America. Part of his success was attributable to how he dealt with people in the firm; he treated them with dignity and respect, and was always open and direct when he talked to them. For example, he referred to everyone in the firm, from baggage handlers to pilots to executives, as his coworkers, and he was candid when he had to relay bad news.

Conceptual Skills   **Conceptual skills** involve the manager's ability to think in the abstract. A manager with strong conceptual skills is able to see the "big picture"; that is, she or he can see opportunity where others perceive roadblocks or problems. For example, after Steve Wozniak and Steve Jobs built a small computer of their own design in a garage, Wozniak saw merely a new toy that could be tinkered with. Jobs, however, saw far more and convinced his partner that they should start a company to make and sell the computers. Thus was born Apple Computer.

Diagnostic Skills   Most successful managers also bring diagnostic skills to the organization. **Diagnostic skills** allow managers to better understand cause-and-effect relationships and to recognize the optimal solutions to problems. For example, when Gordon Bethune took over Continental, he immediately began searching for ways to turn the failing company around. It was his diagnostic skills that enabled him to first recognize the enormous costs incurred because of late departures and arrivals, then identify the reasons for this problem, and, finally, determine how to most effectively change things to solve the problem.

Contemporary Managerial Challenges

LEARNING OBJECTIVE
Identify and discuss contemporary managerial challenges.

Organizational behavior has several implications for various organizational and managerial challenges. In this section, we identify some of the challenges and opportunities facing managers today and note their relevance to organizational behavior.

Workforce Rightsizing

Rightsizing is the process of optimizing the size of an organization's workforce through downsizing, expanding, and/or outsourcing.

One important challenge involves workforce **rightsizing,** achieving and maintaining the optimal workforce in terms of size and location. Since 1990 alone, for instance, many organizations have had to first reduce their workforces during the economic slowdown in the early 1990s, then expand by hiring new employees during the boom period of the late 1990s, and then reduce them once again as a result of another economic downturn that began in 2001. In 2004, hiring began to increase once again.

Downsizing *Downsizing* means purposely becoming smaller by reducing the size of the workforce or by shedding entire divisions or businesses. Downsizing became common in the mid-1980s. For example, IBM and AT&T underwent major downsizing efforts involving thousands of employees. Because of declining sales of Western-style boots, Justin Industries closed two of its factories, putting 260 people out of work. Growing international competition recently compelled Kellogg Company to shut down much of its oldest factory, cutting 550 jobs. Organizations undergoing such downsizing must strive to manage the effects of these cutbacks, not only for those employees who are let go but also for those who continue—albeit with reduced security. Of course, downsizing sometimes has positive results. The firm that cuts staff presumably lowers its costs. But the people who leave may find they are happier as well. Many start their own businesses, and some find employment with companies that better meet their needs and goals. Unfortunately, others suffer the indignities of unemployment and financial insecurity.

Expansion During boom periods, such as the late 1990s, downsizing gives way to *expansion*. Indeed, some sectors, especially those involving high-technology and intensive knowledge work, sometimes experience such severe labor shortages that firms may have to pay hefty signing bonuses and provide an array of benefits and perks. A clear understanding of organizational behavior can help managers in this situation in a variety of ways. These include attracting new workers in sufficient numbers and with necessary skills and abilities, retaining both newer and older workers in the face of alternative work options, and blending newer and older workers into a harmonious and effective workforce.

Simultaneously, even during the best of times, managers should be somewhat cautious to avoid expanding too quickly. If an organization hires more workers than it can sustain, managers may once again find themselves having to reduce their workforce as soon as economic growth slows or the firm's fortunes stall. To help buffer against this possibility, many firms, especially larger ones, rely on adding temporary workers to their workforce to meet expansion needs without incurring a substantial commitment to providing those workers with long-term job security. Here again, organizational behavior concepts help managers deal with issues arising from blending permanent and temporary workers in a single job setting.

Outsourcing A related element of rightsizing is *outsourcing*, contracting some organizational functions to other firms. This practice has been common for years. For instance, many larger firms routinely outsource such activities as office maintenance and food service operations to other firms specializing in those areas. By focusing its workforce on its essential activities, a business can presumably maintain a more stable workforce and be more competitive. In recent years, however, outsourcing has become more and more controversial as organizations have started sending more of their work to foreign firms. For instance, if a domestic manufacturing firm employing 10 people on its cleaning crew outsources that work to a domestic janitorial services firm, the manufacturing firm may eliminate 10 jobs but the janitorial services firm creates 10 new ones. In contrast, if the janitorial work is outsourced abroad, domestic jobs are eliminated with no corresponding increase in the foreign firm.

New Ways of Organizing

Another challenge today is dealing with the complex array of new ways to organize.[22] Recall from our earlier discussion that theorists such as Max Weber advocated "one best way" of organizing. These organizational prototypes generally resembled pyramids—tall structures with power controlled at the top and rigid policies and procedures governing most activities. Today, however, many organizations seek greater flexibility and the ability to respond more quickly to their environment by adopting flat structures. These structures are characterized by few levels of management; broad, wide spans of management; and fewer rules and regulations. The increased use of work teams also goes hand in hand with today's approach to organizing.

Globalization

The world economy is becoming increasingly global in character.[23] Managing in a global economy poses many different challenges and opportunities. For example, at a macro level, property ownership arrangements vary widely. So does the availability of natural resources and components of infrastructure, as well as the role of government in business. For our purposes, a very important consideration is how behavioral processes vary widely across cultural and national boundaries. Values, symbols, and beliefs differ sharply among cultures. Different work norms and the role work plays in a person's life influence patterns of both work-related behavior and attitudes toward work. They also affect the nature of supervisory relationships, decision-making styles and processes, and organizational configurations. Group and intergroup processes, responses to stress, and the nature of political behaviors also differ from culture to culture.

The modern competitive environment and globalization combine to make competition increasingly complex for today's managers. Harley-Davidson has faced increasingly stiff competition in recent years from BMW, Honda, and Kawasaki. While Harley has an almost cultlike following among its current owners, the firm must look to the future. Harley has initiated a new program called Rider's Edge, a two-and-a–half-day training program to introduce potential customers to motorcycle ownership. This first-time Harley rider is learning from Rider's Edge instructor Paul Lessard.

Ethics and Social Responsibility

Another challenge that has taken on renewed importance concerns ethics and social responsibility. An individual's **ethics** are his or her beliefs about what is right and wrong or good and bad. **Social responsibility** is the organization's obligation to protect and contribute to the social environment in which it functions. Thus, the two concepts are related, but they are also distinct from each other.

Both ethics and social responsibility have taken on new significance in recent years. Scandals in organizations ranging from Royal Caribbean Cruise Lines (improper dumping of waste) to Tyco (improper use of company assets for the benefit of senior managers) to various Olympics committees (bribery of government officials) have made headlines around the world. The fallout from the Enron scandal will no doubt continue for years. From the social responsibility angle, pollution and the obligation of businesses to help clean up our environment, business contributions to social causes, and similar issues are receiving increasing attention.

Leadership, organization culture, and group norms—all important organizational behavior concepts—are relevant in managing these processes.[24] For example, Enron's collapse has been partly attributed to a work culture that promoted overly aggressive competition among the firm's own employees, group norms that made it acceptable to take risks that others would deem unacceptable, and top management leadership that continued to encourage questionable business practices.

> Individual **ethics** are personal beliefs about what is right and wrong or good and bad.
>
> An organization's **social responsibility** is its obligation to protect or contribute to the social environment in which it functions.

Managing for Effectiveness

LEARNING OBJECTIVE
Discuss the role of organizational behavior in managing for effectiveness.

Earlier in this chapter, we noted that managers work toward various goals. We will now look at the nature of these goals in detail. In particular, as Figure 1.6 shows, goals, or outcomes, exist at three specific levels in an organization: individual-level, group-level, and organizational-level outcomes. Of course, it may sometimes be necessary to make tradeoffs among these three types of outcomes, but in general each is seen as a critical component of organizational effectiveness. The sections that follow elaborate on these levels in more detail.

FIGURE 1.6

Managing for Effectiveness

Managers work to optimize a variety of individual-level, group- and team-level, and organization-level outcomes. Sometimes it is necessary to make tradeoffs among the different types and levels of outcomes, but each is an important determinant of organizational effectiveness.

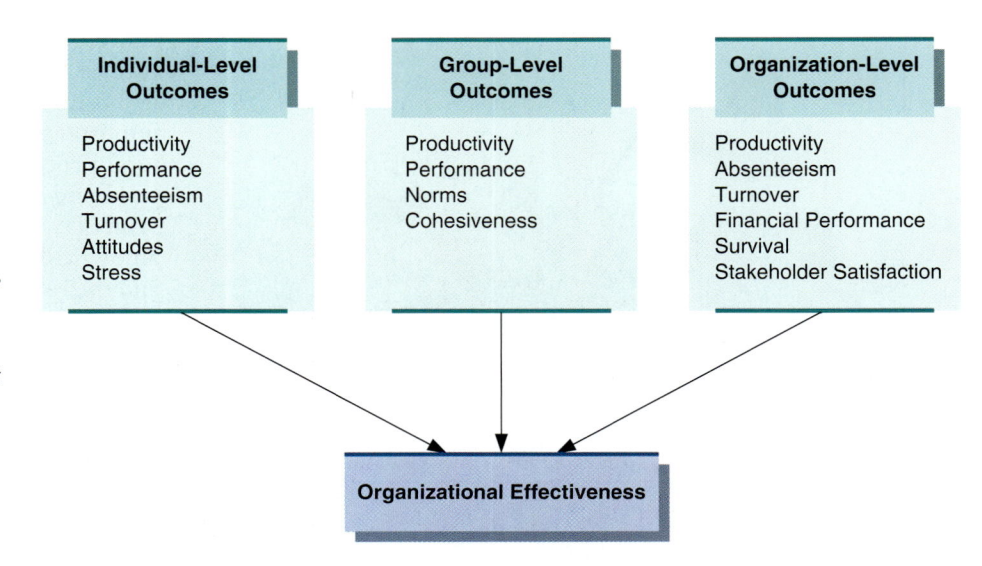

Individual-Level Outcomes	Group-Level Outcomes	Organization-Level Outcomes
Productivity	Productivity	Productivity
Performance	Performance	Absenteeism
Absenteeism	Norms	Turnover
Turnover	Cohesiveness	Financial Performance
Attitudes		Survival
Stress		Stakeholder Satisfaction

→ **Organizational Effectiveness**

Individual-Level Outcomes

Several different outcomes at the individual level are important to managers. Given the focus of the field of organizational behavior, it should not be surprising that most of these outcomes are directly or indirectly addressed by various theories and models.

Individual Behaviors First, several individual behaviors result from a person's participation in an organization. One important behavior is productivity. A person's productivity is an indicator of his or her efficiency and is measured in terms of the products or services created per unit of input. For example, if Bill makes 100 units of a product in a day and Sara makes only 90 units in a day, then, assuming that the units are of the same quality and that Bill and Sara earn the same wages, Bill is more productive than Sara.

Performance, another important individual-level outcome variable, is a somewhat broader concept. It is made up of all work-related behaviors. For example, even though Bill is highly productive, he may also refuse to work overtime, express negative opinions about the organization at every opportunity, and do nothing that does not fall precisely within the boundaries of his job. Sara, on the other hand, may always be willing to work overtime, is a positive representative of the organization, and goes out of her way to make as many contributions to the organization as possible. Based on the full array of behaviors, then, we might conclude that Sara actually is the better performer.

Two other important individual-level behaviors are absenteeism and turnover. Absenteeism is a measure of attendance. Although virtually everyone misses work occasionally, some people miss far more than others. Some look for excuses to miss work and call in sick regularly just for some time off; others miss work only when absolutely necessary. Turnover occurs when a person leaves the organization. If the departing individual is a good performer or if the organization has invested heavily in training the person, turnover can be costly.

Individual Attitudes and Stress Another set of individual-level outcomes influenced by managers consists of individual attitudes. (We discuss attitudes more fully in Chapter 3.) Levels of job satisfaction or dissatisfaction, organizational commitment, and organizational involvement all play an important role in organizational behavior. Stress, also discussed in Chapter 3, is another important individual-level outcome variable. Given its costs, both personal and organizational, it is evident that stress is becoming an increasingly important topic for both researchers in organizational behavior and practicing managers.

Group- and Team-Level Outcomes

Another set of outcomes exists at the group and team level. Some of these outcomes parallel the individual-level outcomes just discussed. For example, if an organization makes extensive use of work teams, team productivity and performance are important outcome variables. On the other hand, even if all the people in a group or team have the same or similar attitudes toward their jobs, the attitudes themselves are individual-level phenomena. Individuals, not groups, have attitudes. But groups or teams can also have unique outcomes that individuals do not share. For example, as we will discuss in Chapter 8, groups develop norms that govern the behavior of individual group members. Groups also develop different levels of cohesiveness. Thus, managers need to assess both common and unique outcomes when considering the individual and group levels.

Organization-Level Outcomes

Finally, a set of outcome variables exists at the organization level. As before, some of these outcomes parallel those at the individual and group levels, but others are unique. For example, we can measure and compare organizational productivity. We can also develop organization-level indicators of absenteeism and turnover. Profitability, however, is generally assessed only at the organizational level. Organizations are also commonly assessed in terms of financial performance: stock price, return on investment, growth rates, and so on. They are also evaluated in terms of their ability to survive and the extent to which they satisfy important stakeholders such as investors, government regulators, employees, and unions.

Clearly, then, the manager must balance different outcomes across all three levels of analysis. In many cases, these outcomes appear to contradict one another. For example, paying workers high salaries can enhance satisfaction and reduce turnover, but it may also detract from bottom-line performance. Similarly, exerting strong pressure to increase individual performance may boost short-term profitability but increase turnover and job stress. Thus, the manager must look at the full array of outcomes and attempt to balance them in an optimal fashion. The manager's ability to do this is a major determinant of the organization's success.

Synopsis

Organizational behavior is the study of human behavior in organizational settings, of the interface between human behavior and the organization, and of the organization itself. The study of organizational behavior is important because organizations have a powerful influence over our lives. Serious interest in the study of management first developed around the beginning of the twentieth century. Two of the earliest approaches were scientific management (best represented by the work of Frederick Taylor) and classical organization theory (exemplified by the work of Max Weber).

Organizational behavior began to emerge as a scientific discipline as a result of the Hawthorne studies. Douglas McGregor and Abraham Maslow led the human relations movement that grew out of those studies. The basic concepts of the field fall into three categories: individual processes, interpersonal processes, and organizational processes and characteristics. Those categories form the framework for the organization of this book. Important contextual perspectives on the field of organizational behavior are the situational and interactional perspectives.

By its very nature, management requires an understanding of human behavior to help managers better comprehend those at different levels in the organization, those at the same level, those in other organizations, and themselves. The manager's job can be characterized in terms of four functions, three sets of roles, and four skills. The basic managerial functions are planning, organizing, leading, and controlling. The roles consist of three interpersonal roles, three informational roles, and four decision-making roles. The four basic skills necessary for effective management are technical, interpersonal, conceptual, and diagnostic skills.

Several challenges confront managers today. Among the most important are workforce rightsizing, new ways of organizing, globalization, and ethics and social responsibility. Managing for effectiveness involves balancing a variety of individual-level, group- and team-level, and organization-level outcome variables.

Discussion Questions

1. Some people have suggested that understanding human behavior at work is the single most important requirement for managerial success. Do you agree or disagree with this statement? Why?

2. In what ways is organizational behavior comparable to functional areas such as finance, marketing, and production? In what ways does it differ from these areas? Is it similar to statistics in any way?

3. Identify some managerial jobs that are highly affected by human behavior and others that are less affected. Which would you prefer? Why?

4. Besides those cited in the text, what reasons can you think of for the importance of organizational behavior?
5. Suppose you are hiring a new manager. One candidate has outstanding technical skills but poor interpersonal skills. The other has exactly the opposite mix of skills. Which would you hire? Why?
6. Some people believe individuals working in an organization have a basic human right to satisfaction with their work and to the opportunity to grow and develop. How would you defend this position? How would you argue against it?
7. Many universities offer a course in industrial or organizational psychology. The content of those courses is quite similar to the content of this course. Do you think behavioral material is better taught in a business or in a psychology program, or is it best to teach it in both?
8. Get a recent issue of a popular business magazine such as *BusinessWeek* or *Fortune*, and scan its major articles. Do any articles reflect concepts from organizational behavior? Describe.
9. The text identifies four basic managerial functions. Based on your own experiences or observations, provide examples of each function.
10. Which managerial skills do you think are among your strengths? Which are among your weaknesses? How might you improve the latter?
11. Are there any kinds of businesses that have not been affected by globalization? Explain.
12. What individual-level, group- or team-level, or organization-level outcome variables can you identify beyond those noted in the text?

Organizational Behavior Case for Discussion

Yellow Rules the Road

Since its founding in 1923, Yellow Corporation (formerly Yellow Freight Corporation) has led the transportation industry by using its trucks to haul large, heavy items between major shipping centers in the United States, Canada, and Mexico. For decades the firm focused on ways to increase its efficiency, such as ensuring that all trucks were full before they left the warehouse and using an inflexible delivery schedule to reduce last-minute changes. But Yellow was the victim of its own success: As operational efficiency increased, customer service received less attention, allowing newer and more responsive companies to lure away many of the firm's customers. Further, the customers most likely to seek a more service-oriented transportation provider were the very ones that were willing to pay premium prices for the extra service.

Bill Zollars, who assumed the role of chief executive officer (CEO) of Yellow in 1996, was intrigued by the opportunity to revitalize the carrier. James Welch, president and chief operating officer, recollects, "We were a defensive company—a follower, not a leader. We were yearning for leadership. This company was ready for change." Zollars understood that successful organizational transformation would need to be profound, altering the attitudes, behaviors, and performance of each of the firm's 30,000 employees.

Communication was one key to Zollars' management revolution at Yellow. The CEO spent eighteen months traveling to the company's several hundred locations to talk face to face with customers and employees at all levels. He repeatedly put forth his message of the need for enhanced customer service, but the meetings consisted of more than promises and motivational speeches. Zollars was the first Yellow manager to accurately report the true defect rate: the percentage of shipments that were late, wrong, or damaged. Yellow employees were stunned to learn that their defect rate was a whopping 40 percent, but that knowledge was necessary to provide motivation and a benchmark for improvement. Zollars also instituted the company's first ongoing program for surveying customer satisfaction and reporting the results openly throughout the company.

Zollars' leadership created a sense of motivation and pride among employees, which in turn led to continuing high levels of productivity and performance. He made a great effort to listen to his employees, entertain their suggestions, and give them additional authority to make decisions. He earned an enviable reputation for honesty and commitment, attempting to "walk the walk" as well as "talk the talk." Zollars asserts, "If people doing the work don't believe what's coming from the leadership, it doesn't get implemented. Period."

Technology also played an important role in Yellow's success. The firm implemented a variety of automated systems to improve customer service and satisfaction. The systems provide up-to-the-minute information about a shipment's progress via the Internet, maintain a customer database that enables faster scheduling, and develop truck-loading procedures and routes to ensure on-time delivery. However, the real technology success story at Yellow isn't merely the innovative and efficient use of technology but also the savvy application of those systems to support employees and customers.

Perhaps the most challenging yet most important change at Yellow was the re-envisioning of the company's mission from delivery of freight to customer service. When employees saw their primary goal as the efficient movement of cargo, the firm focused on one set of processes. Today, thanks to the efforts of Zollars and other managers, employees realize that supporting customers by meeting their delivery needs is their paramount task. This shift in perspective enables the firm to provide better service to its customers, develop innovative new products and services, improve its performance, and, ultimately, compete successfully in an increasingly tough industry. As Bill Zollars says in the firm's 2000 annual report, "Our business really isn't about moving freight. It's about earning the trust of the consumers of our services."

Case Questions

1. What role has organizational behavior played at Yellow?
2. Identify examples of management functions, roles, and skills as reflected by Bill Zollars' actions at Yellow.
3. What measures of effectiveness are most relevant for a firm like Yellow? How might behavioral processes affect each measure?

References: Matthew Boyle, "America's Most Admired Companies: The Right Stuff," *Fortune*, March 4, 2002, www.fortune.com on March 6, 2002; Chuck Salter, "Fresh Start 2002: On the Road Again," *Fast Company*, January 2002, pp. 50–58 (quotation on p. 57), www.fastcompany.com; "Yellow Corporation 2000 Annual Report," March 2001, www.yellowcorp.com on March 6, 2002.

Experiencing Organizational Behavior

Relating OB and Popular Culture

Purpose: This exercise will help you appreciate the importance and pervasiveness of organizational behavior concepts and processes in both contemporary organizational settings and popular culture.

Format: Your instructor will divide the class into groups of three to five. Each group will be assigned a specific television program to watch before the next class meeting.

Procedure: Arrange to watch the program as a group. Each person should have a pad of paper and a pencil handy. As you watch the show, jot down examples of individual behavior, interpersonal dynamics, organizational characteristics, and other concepts and processes relevant to organizational behavior. After the show, spend a few minutes comparing notes. Compile one list for the entire group. (It is advisable to turn off the television set during this discussion!)

During the next class meeting, have someone in the group summarize the plot of the show and list the concepts it illustrated. The following television shows are especially good for illustrating behavioral concepts in organizational settings:

Network Shows	Syndicated Shows
Survivor	*Seinfeld*
The West Wing	*Cheers*
N.Y.P.D. Blue	*Star Trek*
The Apprentice	*Home Improvement*
24	*L.A. Law*
CSI	*Gilligan's Island*

Follow-up Questions

1. What does this exercise illustrate about the pervasiveness of organizations in our contemporary society?
2. What recent or classic movies might provide similar kinds of examples?
3. Do you think television programs from countries other than the United States would provide more or fewer examples of shows set in organizations?

Self-Assessment Exercise
Assessing Your Own Theory X and Theory Y Tendencies

The following questions aim to provide insights into your tendencies toward Theory X or Theory Y management styles. Answer each question on the scale by circling the number that best reflects your feelings. For example, circle a 5 for a statement if you strongly agree with it or a 2 if you disagree with it.

1. Most employees today are lazy and have to be forced to work hard.
2. People in organizations are motivated only by extrinsic rewards such as pay and bonuses.
3. Most people do not like to work.
4. Most people today generally avoid responsibility.
5. Many employees in big companies today do not accept the company's goals but instead work only for their own welfare.
6. Most people are not innovative and are not interested in helping their employer solve problems.
7. Most people need someone else to tell them how to do their job.
8. Many people today have little ambition, preferring to stay where they are and not work hard for advancement.
9. Work is not a natural activity for most people; rather, it is something they feel they have to do.
10. Most employees today are not interested in utilizing their full potential and capabilities.

Instructions: Add up your responses. If you scored 40 or above, you have clear tendencies toward the Theory X view of management. If you scored 20 or below, you have clear tendencies toward the Theory Y view of management. If you scored between 20 and 40, your tendencies fall in between the extreme Theory X and Y viewpoints, and you have a more balanced approach. (*Note:* This brief instrument has not been scientifically validated and is to be used for classroom discussion purposes only.)

OB Online

1. Find a company website that stresses the firm's history. What role, if any, does that history seem to play in the way the firm is currently managed?
2. Do a web search using the key word *bureaucracy*. Based on a representative sample of sites identified by your search, what is the prevailing meaning most people seem to attach to this term?
3. Do a web search for the key term *Hawthorne studies*. What information beyond that provided in the chapter do these sites contain?
4. Visit Amazon.com or another Internet book retailer and identify the top ten best-selling business books today. What, if anything, do they seem to have in common?

Building Managerial Skills

Exercise Overview: Conceptual skills involve the ability to think in the abstract; diagnostic skills focus on responses to situations. Managers must frequently use these skills together to better understand the behavior of others in the organization, as this exercise illustates.

Exercise Background: Human behavior is a complex phenomenon in any setting, but is especially so in organizations. Understanding how and why people choose particular behaviors can be difficult and frustrating, but also very important. Consider the following scenario.

Sandra Buckley has worked in your department for several years. Until recently, she was a model employee. She always arrived on time, or even early, to work and stayed late whenever necessary to get her assignments done. She was upbeat and cheerful, and worked very hard. She frequently said the company was the best place she had ever worked and you were the perfect boss.

About six months ago, you began to notice changes in Sandra's behavior. She has come in late occasionally, and you cannot remember the last time she agreed to work past 5:00 P.M. She also complains a lot. Other workers have started to avoid her because she is so negative all the time. You also suspect she may be looking for a new job.

Exercise Task: Using the preceding scenario as background, do the following:

1. Assume you have done some background work to find out why Sandra's behavior has changed. Write a brief case that includes possible reasons for these changes (e.g., your case might include the fact that you recently promoted someone else to a position that Sandra may have expected to get). Make the case as descriptive as possible.
2. Relate elements of your case to the various behavioral concepts discussed in the chapter.
3. Decide whether or not you might be about to resolve things with Sandra to overcome whatever issues have arisen from your case. For example, if Sandra is upset because she was passed over for a promotion, how might you attempt to straighten things out?
4. Which behavioral process or concept discussed in the chapter is easiest to change? Which is the most difficult to change?

TEST PREPPER

ACE self-test

You have read the chapter and studied the key terms, and the exam is any day now. Think you're ready to ace it? Take this sample test to gauge your comprehension of chapter material. You can check your answers at the back of the book. Want more test questions? Visit the student website at http://college.hmco.com/business/students/ (select Griffin/Moorhead, Fundamentals of Organizational Behavior 1e) and take the ACE quizzes for more practice.

1. **T F** Southwest Airlines claims its most significant advantages come from its employees.
2. **T F** Fredrick Taylor developed ways for employees to work at a pace slower than their capabilities.
3. **T F** Scientific management, developed in the early 1900s, is no longer used today.
4. **T F** Sociologist Max Weber described "bureaucracies" as inefficient, inflexible organizations.
5. **T F** Hawthorne studies identified a strong relationship between lighting and employee productivity.
6. **T F** The human relations movement supported the idea that a satisfied employee will work harder than an unsatisfied employee.
7. **T F** "Universal" models suggest that certain management solutions will work in all situations.
8. **T F** An example of the controlling function is monitoring the actions of employees.
9. **T F** Jack manages a group of software programmers and is an excellent programmer himself. From this you know Jack has strong conceptual skills.
10. **T F** One of the main issues surrounding outsourcing is whether the net number of domestic jobs is decreased.
11. **T F** Managers who are interested in successfully achieving company goals should focus primarily on individual-level outcomes.
12. **T F** Performance is a broader outcome than productivity.
13. **T F** Attitudes can be measured at the group level.
14. **T F** Attempting to positively influence outcomes at the individual level can negatively influence outcomes at the organization level.
15. Jim is a manager who is taking a class in organizational behavior. Jim will likely learn about all of the following in his class except
    a. human behavior in organizational settings.
    b. some employees' decision to leave a company while others decide to stay.
    c. the interface between human behavior and the organization.
    d. competition and how it affects the stock prices of publicly held firms.
    e. organizations themselves.
16. At Quiktire, Inc., managers have determined the most efficient method for installing customers' tires. Employees are required to follow these methods and are paid based on the number of tires they install each day. Quicktire's technique is similar to which of these management approaches?
    a. Bureaucracy
    b. System 4 management
    c. Unionization
    d. Soldiering
    e. Scientific management
17. The primary difference between scientific management and classical organization theory is that
    a. scientific management focuses on profits rather than losses.
    b. scientific management emphasizes individual efficiency rather than organizational efficiency.
    c. scientific management was developed outside rather than within the United States.
    d. scientific management is a more recent approach.
    e. scientific management failed rather than succeeded.
18. Early writers suggested all of the following as ways to improve management practices except
    a. improve working conditions.
    b. become more democratic in dealing with employees.
    c. accommodate employee needs.
    d. adjust lighting to enhance employee interaction.
    e. use psychology to understand employee motivation.
19. Scientific management predicts that each individual will produce as much as possible to increase personal income, but the Hawthorne researchers discovered
    a. the work group as a whole may establish acceptable levels of output.
    b. employees work only as hard as their supervisors.
    c. employees' efforts decline over the course of the five-day workweek.
    d. employees' efforts increase over the course of the five-day workweek.
    e. managers produce as much as possible, but to satisfy their egos rather than earn more income.

20. One basic premise of the human relations movement was that
    a. Theory X management is more effective than Theory Y management.
    b. "chiseling" and "rate busting" are unavoidable facts of work life.
    c. singling out workers for special treatment may actually decrease productivity.
    d. most employees work better alone than in groups.
    e. a satisfied employee will work harder than an unsatisfied employee.

21. If you were a manager, would you try to increase employees' performance by increasing their satisfaction?
    a. Yes, because a more satisfied worker is a more productive worker.
    b. No, because job satisfaction is not a major influence on job performance.
    c. Yes, but only for new workers.
    d. No, because the cost of satisfying workers outweighs the benefits of higher performance.
    e. Yes, but once workers were satisfied, I would stop trying to satisfy them.

22. Which of the following best illustrates the situational perspective of management?
    a. Science can determine the "one best way" to manage under any conditions.
    b. Management principles are universal and therefore apply in all situations.
    c. The appropriate way to manage depends on the nature of the particular situation.
    d. Simple cause-and-effect linkages between two variables are common.
    e. A manager can easily fix a problem in one situation with a solution that has worked in another situation.

23. Organizational behavior concepts apply
    a. in domestic but not international companies.
    b. in large but not small companies.
    c. in growing but not stable companies.
    d. in for-profit but not nonprofit organizations.
    e. in virtually all organizations.

24. Recently the managers at Practicum Unlimited, a firm that develops educational materials, redesigned its jobs, established new reporting and authority relationships, and grouped jobs into different departments. Which managerial function did they perform?
    a. Planning
    b. Organizing
    c. Leading
    d. Controlling
    e. Decision making

25. The president of a university regularly attends graduation ceremonies, but her role there is not to plan, organize, lead, or control. Rather, in handing out diplomas, she is acting as a
    a. figurehead.
    b. resource allocator.
    c. disseminator.
    d. monitor.
    e. decision maker.

26. If you were hiring a new manager to help you see the "big picture" of how your organization might become more effective, you would consider applicants with strong
    a. technical skills.
    b. interpersonal skills.
    c. conceptual skills.
    d. diagnostic skills.
    e. decision-making skills.

27. Which is not a way to rightsize an organization?
    a. Downsizing
    b. Outsourcing
    c. Expansion
    d. Eliminating an entire division or business
    e. Retaining the full number of employees during economic slowdowns

28. Which of the following are you least likely to see in modern organizations?
    a. Flat, flexible structures
    b. Power centralized at the top
    c. Wide spans of management
    d. Fewer rules and regulations
    e. Increased teamwork

29. Productivity is defined as
    a. the number of products or services created per unit of input.
    b. the combination of all work-related behaviors.
    c. the time a person spends at work.
    d. the number of days an employee is not absent in a given period.
    e. the quality of the products or services an employee produces.

30. Profitability is generally assessed only at which level?
    a. Individual
    b. Industry
    c. Organization
    d. Group
    e. Team

CHAPTER 2

Managing Global and Workforce Diversity

MANAGEMENT PREVIEW

Both the world of business and the workforces in organizations are becoming increasingly global and diverse. These developments affect our lives as workers and managers and pose numerous challenges. In some organizations, increasing workforce diversity is due to changing demographics among the general population of society; in others, it is the result of the globalization of the organization's products, services, suppliers, customers, and employees. Regardless of the cause of workforce diversity management must deal with diversity and develop ways to manage it. In this chapter, we explore how to manage these cross-cultural issues. First, we examine the different types and sources of diversity affecting organizations today. We then trace the emergence of international management issues and describe the dimensions and complexities of organizational diversity. Next, we discuss the primary and secondary dimensions of diversity. We also examine cross-cultural factors that affect individual, interpersonal, and organizational issues. Finally, we look at managing multicultural and multinational organizations.

After you have studied this chapter, you should be able to:
- [ ] *Describe the nature of diversity in organizations.*
- [ ] *Discuss the emergence of international management.*
- [ ] *Identify and explain key dimensions of diversity.*
- [ ] *Describe the fundamental issues in managing the multicultural organization.*

We start by describing the diversity programs in operation at Procter & Gamble.

Procter & Gamble (P&G) produces a wide variety of items, including such popular U.S. brand names as Tide, Crest, Always, Pampers, Cover Girl, Olay, Secret, Scope, Charmin, Ivory, Folgers, and Pringles. With more than 250 brands, P&G is the largest producer of products for the home, products that are purchased primarily by women. A recent survey by P&G found that women control 80 percent of family purchasing decisions. As a result, P&G, long known for its effective marketing campaigns, now focuses on attracting and retaining more women to match the diversity represented by its customers.

Managing this diversity was not always a priority at P&G. Many female employees were leaving the company, with few remaining to be promoted to top management ranks. Even meetings to discuss products such as a diaper or makeup brand often failed to include a single female participant. The solution was clear: find out why women were leaving the company and respond. Today some of the new initiatives at P&G include local task forces for each facility, diversity specialists in the human resources departments, flexible work arrangements, generous family leave policies, and sabbaticals. A companywide survey identified areas of concern among female employees, and another survey gathered insights from those who had recently quit. The "Careers" page of the company website lists "We show respect for all individuals" as the firm's number one principle, supported by the statements "We believe that all individuals can and want to contribute" and "We value differences."

One-third of P&G vice presidents today are women, up from 5 percent in 1992, and two members of its board of directors are female, up from none in 1992. Women head some of P&G's most important brands, including Tide, the firm's bestseller. P&G was recognized by *Business Ethics* as number five among the one hundred best corporate citizens, in part for its diversity programs. P&G's website states, "Of the approximately 700 firms [being evaluated for this distinction], P&G is the only company that has ranked within the top 5 for all years of this ranking."

Business Ethics found that companies on its "100 Best" list had significantly higher financial performance than did comparable firms not on the list. P&G management also equates diversity with success. "Our success as a global company is a direct result of our diverse and talented workforce. Our ability to develop new consumer insights and ideas and to execute in a superior way across the world is the best possible testimony to the power of diversity that any organization could ever have," says John E. Pepper, P&G chairman.

> "Our success as a global company is a direct result of our diverse and talented workforce." —John Pepper, chairman, Procter & Gamble

References: "Careers," "Diversity," "Purpose, Values, Principles," Procter & Gamble websites, www.pg.com and www.pgcareers.com, on April 23, 2004; *2001 Annual 10-K Report*, Procter & Gamble, p. 38; Mary Miller, "The 100 Best Corporate Citizens for 2002," *Business Ethics*, March–April 2001, www.business-ethics.com on April 23, 2004; Tara Parker-Pope, "P&G Retools to Keep More Female Employees," *Cincinnati Post*, September 14, 1998, p. 7B.

More and more organizations are developing and expanding their internal and external programs in the areas of diversity, and most are finding that doing so makes good business sense. Organizations such as Procter & Gamble, AT&T, Denny's (Advantica), Ernst and Young, the Anderson School at UCLA, Pitney Bowes, and Pfizer are using innovative ways to manage an increasingly diverse workforce through various diversity initiatives, including roundtables and seminars on diversity, and diversity marketing to reach new employees, suppliers, and customers that make a difference on the bottom line. It is essential that managers be aware of the different aspects of diversity, the wide range of diversity programs in use, and the impact of diversity on corporate performance. We start this chapter with a more detailed discussion of the meaning and nature of diversity in organizations.

The Nature of Diversity in Organizations

LEARNING OBJECTIVE
Describe the nature of diversity in organizations.

You have no doubt heard the term *diversity* many times, but what does it mean in the workplace today? Usually when we speak of diversity, we think only of the gender, racial, and ethnic differences in the workforce. More broadly, the term refers to a mixture of items, objects, or people characterized by differences and similarities.[1] The similarities can be as important as the differences. After all, none of us are exactly alike. We may be similar but never the same. Thus, although two employees may have the same gender, ethnicity, and even university education, they are different individuals who may act differently and react differently to various management styles. Managers have to deal simultaneously with similarities and differences among people in organizations.[2] They must deal with diversity within their own organizations and in the organizations they encounter all over the world. The opportunities and difficulties inherent in managing multicultural organizations will be a key management challenge in the twenty-first century.

The increasing diversity of the workforce is due to four trends. First, as the job market changes in response to economic conditions, it becomes increasingly important to find the best workers and then utilize them to best serve the organization. Layoffs are costly, as are recruiting and hiring new employees. During economic downturns, companies such as Silicon Graphics struggle to ensure that no one group of employees is disproportionately affected by layoffs, for example.[3] Second, more companies are focusing their marketing efforts on the increasing buying power in the minority markets. A diverse, or segmented, marketing effort requires a marketing team that represents the markets being targeted. As an example, McDonald's, highly ranked on *Fortune*'s list of the fifty best companies for minorities, is diversifying what it buys as well as what it sells by buying $3 billion a year from minority-owned firms.[4] Third, more companies are seeking to expand their markets around the world, requiring more diverse thinking to effectively reach global markets. Finally, companies seeking to achieve a global presence via expansion, acquisitions, and mergers inevitably go through a period of consolidation to reduce duplication of efforts around the world and to capitalize on the synergies of cross-border operations. Typically, consolidation means grouping employees from around the world together into newly streamlined units, resulting in more diverse groups. These four trends, then, are the drivers behind the increasing diversity in the workforce.[5]

What Is Workforce Diversity?

Workforce diversity is the similarities and differences in such characteristics as age, gender, ethnic heritage, physical abilities and disabilities, race, and sexual orientation among the employees of organizations.

Workforce diversity refers to the similarities and differences in such characteristics as age, gender, ethnic heritage, physical abilities and disabilities, race, and sexual orientation among the employees of organizations. 3M defines its goals regarding workforce diversity as "valuing uniqueness, while respecting differences, maximizing individual potentials, and synergizing collective talents and experiences for the growth and success of 3M."[6] In a diverse workforce, managers are compelled to recognize and handle the similarities and differences among the organization's people.

Employees' conceptions of work, expectations of rewards from the organization, and practices in relating to others are all influenced by diversity.[7] Managers of diverse work groups need to understand how the social environment affects employees' beliefs about work, and they must have the communication skills to

Coca-Cola CEO Douglas Daft (second from left) is shown with some of the employees who represent the company's drive to diversify its workforce. At Coca-Cola, 40 percent of new hires are minorities. This comes after a racial discrimination suit in 2000 that cost the company $192 million. And minorities are not only at the lower levels of the organization; they now make up 30 percent of the executive committee of the board of directors.

develop confidence and self-esteem in members of diverse work groups. Many people tend to stereotype others in organizations. A **stereotype** is a generalization about a person or a group of people based on certain characteristics or traits. Many managers fall into the trap of stereotyping workers as being like themselves and sharing a managerial orientation toward work, rewards, and relating to coworkers. However, if workers do not share those views, values, and beliefs, problems can arise. A second situation involving stereotyping occurs when managers characterize workers according to a particular attribute, such as age, gender, race, or ethnic origin. It is often easier for managers to group people based on easily identifiable characteristics and treat those groups as "different." Managers who stereotype workers based on assumptions about the characteristics of the work group tend to ignore individual differences, which leads to making rigid judgments about others that do not take into account the specific person and the current situation.[8]

Stereotypes tend to become rigid judgments about others that ignore the specific person and the current situation. Acceptance of stereotypes can lead to the dangerous process of prejudice toward others.

Prejudices are judgments about others that reinforce beliefs about superiority and inferiority.

Stereotypes can lead to the even more dangerous process of prejudice toward others. **Prejudices** are judgments about others that reinforce beliefs about superiority and inferiority. They can lead to an exaggerated assessment of the worth of one group and a diminished assessment of the worth of other groups.[9] When managers prejudge employees, they make assumptions about the nature of those individuals that may or may not be true, and they manage them accordingly. In other words, managers build job descriptions, reward systems, performance appraisal systems, and management systems and policies that fit their stereotypes of employees.

Management systems built on stereotypes and prejudices do not meet the needs of a diverse workforce. An incentive system may offer rewards that people do not value, job descriptions that do not fit the jobs and the people who do them, and performance evaluation systems that measure the wrong things. In addition, managers who engage in prejudice and stereotyping fail to recognize employees' distinctive individual talents, which often leads to lower self-esteem and possibly lower levels of job satisfaction and performance among those employees. Stereotypes can also become self-fulfilling prophecies.[10] If we assume someone is incompetent and treat the person as such, over time the employee may begin to share the same belief. This can lead to reduced productivity, lower creativity, and lower morale.

Of course, managers caught in this counterproductive cycle can change. As a first step, they must recognize that diversity exists in organizations. Only then can they begin to manage it appropriately. Managers who do not recognize diversity may face an unhappy, disillusioned, and underutilized workforce.

Who Will Be the Workforce of the Future?

Employment statistics can help us understand just how different the workforce of the future will be. Figure 2.1 compares the workforce composition of 1990 to projections for 2010. All workforce segments will increase as a percentage of the total workforce except the white male segment, which will decline from 47.4 to 43.2 percent. This may not seem very dramatic, but it follows decades in which white males have dominated the workforce by well over 50 percent. When one considers that the total U.S. workforce is expected to be more than 150 million people in 2010, a 4 percent drop represents a significant decline.[11]

Figure 2.2 shows the percentage of the growth attributable to each segment from 2000 to 2010. Although the overall workforce growth is expected to be 12 percent, the growth rate for white males is expected to be only 6.7 percent. The number of females in the workforce is predicted to increase by 15.1 percent; thus, more than 62 percent of women in the United States are expected to be working in 2010.

Examining the age ranges of the workforce gives us another view of the changes. In contrast to its standing in earlier decades, the sixteen-to-twenty-four age group will grow more rapidly than the overall population—an increase of 3.4 million (14.8 percent) between 2000 and 2010. The number of workers in the twenty-five-to-fifty-four age group is expected to increase by 5 million (5.0 percent), and the number of workers in the fifty-five and older group is expected to rise by 8.5 million (46.6 percent).[12]

FIGURE 2.1

Workforce Composition: 1990–2010

In the period between 1990 and 2010, all workforce segments are expected to increase as a percentage of the total workforce except the white male segment, which will decline from 47.4 to 43.2 percent.

Reference: Bureau of Labor Statistics, *Monthly Labor Review*, November 2001.

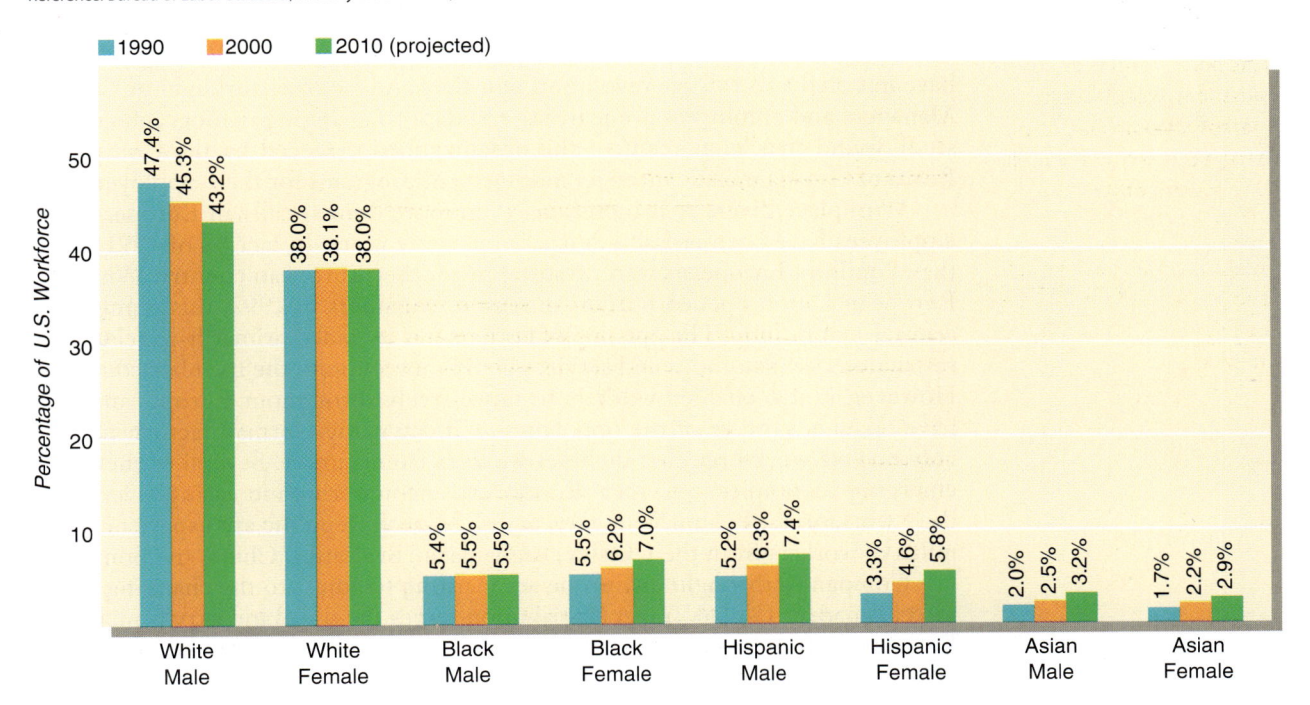

Segment	1990	2000	2010 (projected)
White Male	47.4%	45.3%	43.2%
White Female	38.0%	38.1%	38.0%
Black Male	5.4%	5.5%	5.5%
Black Female	5.5%	6.2%	7.0%
Hispanic Male	5.2%	6.3%	7.4%
Hispanic Female	3.3%	4.6%	5.8%
Asian Male	2.0%	2.5%	3.2%
Asian Female	1.7%	2.2%	2.9%

FIGURE 2.2

Expected Percentage of Growth in Workforce: 2000–2010

There is no question that the composition of the U.S. workforce is changing. For the period from 2000 to 2010, the growth rate in all segments is higher for women than for men and higher for non-whites than for whites.

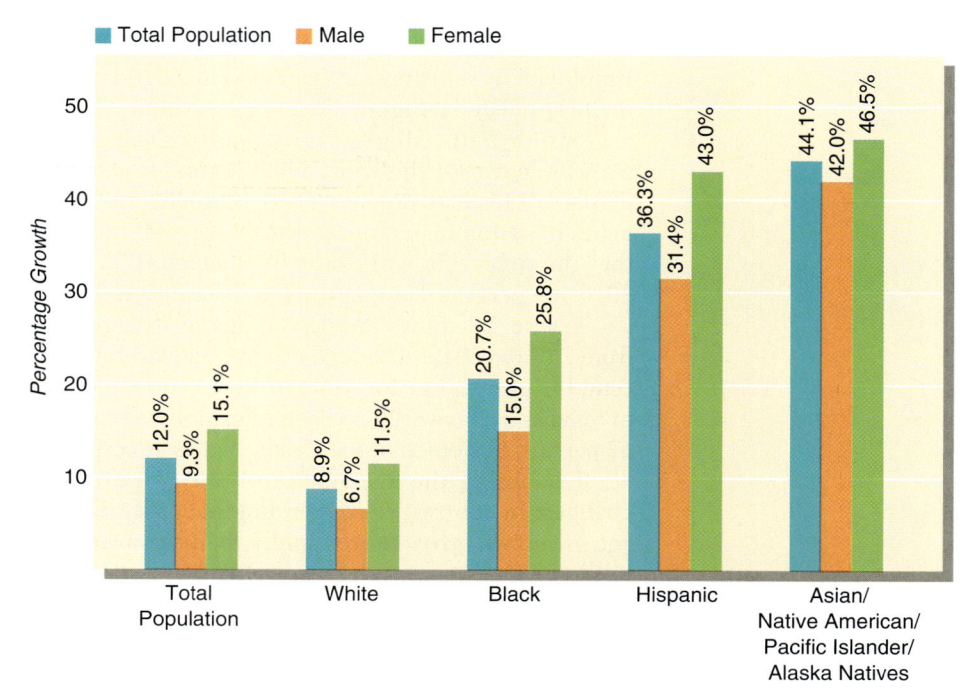

Bar chart showing Percentage Growth by demographic group (Total Population, Male, Female):

Group	Total Population	Male	Female
Total Population	12.0%	9.3%	15.1%
White	8.9%	6.7%	11.5%
Black	20.7%	15.0%	25.8%
Hispanic	36.3%	31.4%	43.0%
Asian/Native American/Pacific Islander/Alaska Natives	44.1%	42.0%	46.5%

Reference: Bureau of Labor Statistics, *Monthly Labor Review,* November 2001.

Global Workforce Diversity

Diversity in the workforce is more than a U.S. phenomenon. Similar statistics on workforce diversity are found in other countries. In Canada, for instance, minorities are the fastest-growing segment of the population and the workforce. In addition, women make up two-thirds of the growth in the Canadian workforce, increasing from 35 percent in the 1970s to 45 percent in 1991.[13] These changes have initiated a workforce revolution in offices and factories throughout Canada. Managers and employees are learning to adapt to changing demographics. One study found that 81 percent of the organizations surveyed by the Conference Board of Canada include diversity management programs for their employees.[14]

Workplace diversity is increasing even more dramatically in Europe, where employees have been crossing borders for many years. In fact, as of 1991, more than 2 million Europeans were working in another European country. When the European Union opened borders among its members in 1992, this number increased significantly. The opening of borders was intended primarily to relax trade restrictions so that goods and services could move among the member countries. However, it also enabled workers to move freely throughout Europe, and they have taken advantage of the opportunity. Today many German factories have a very diverse workforce that includes workers from Turkey. Several of the newly emerging economies in Central Europe are encountering increasing diversity in their workforces. Poland, Hungary, and the Czech Republic are experiencing an influx of workers from the Ukraine, Afghanistan, Sri Lanka, China, and Somalia.[15]

Companies throughout Europe are learning to adjust to the changing workforce. Amadeus Global Travel Distribution serves the travel industry primarily in Europe, but its staff of 650 is composed of individuals from thirty-two countries. Amadeus developed a series of workshops to teach managers how to lead multicultural teams. Such seminars also teach them how to interact more effectively with peers, subordinates, and superiors who come from a variety of countries.[16] Other companies experiencing and responding to the same phenomenon in Europe include Mars, Hewlett-Packard Spain, Fujitsu in Spain, and BP. Companies in Asia are also encountering increasing diversity. In Thailand, where rapid industrialization and slow population growth have created a shortage of skilled and unskilled workers, demand for foreign workers to fill the gap is growing, creating problems integrating local and foreign workers.[17] Thus, the issues created by workforce diversity are prevalent throughout the globe. We discuss the emergence of international management in the next major section of this chapter. First, we need to look at why it is important to value diversity rather than just tolerate it.

The Value of Diversity

The United States has historically been seen as a "melting pot" of people from many different countries, cultures, and backgrounds. For centuries, it was assumed that people who came from other countries should assimilate themselves into the existing cultural context. Although equal employment opportunity and accompanying affirmative action legislation have had significant effects on diversifying workplaces, they sometimes focused on bringing into the workplace people from culturally different groups and fully assimilating them into the existing organization. In organizations, however, integration proved to be difficult. People were usually resistant to the change and slow to adopt it. Substantive career advancement opportunities rarely materialized for those who were "different."

Workforce diversity has become an increasingly important issue in the last few years as employees, managers, consultants, and the government finally recognize that the composition of the workforce affects organizational productivity. Today, instead of a melting pot, the U.S. workplace is regarded more as a "tossed salad" made up of a delightful mosaic of flavors, colors, and textures. Rather than trying to assimilate those who are different into a single organizational culture, the current view holds that organizations need to celebrate the differences and utilize the variety of talents, perspectives, and backgrounds of all employees.

Benefits of Valuing Diversity Valuing diversity means giving up the assumption that everyone who is not a member of the dominant group must assimilate. This is not easily accomplished in most organizations. Truly valuing diversity is not merely giving lip service to an ideal, putting up with a necessary evil, promoting a level of tolerance for those who are different, or tapping into the latest fad. It is an opportunity to develop and utilize all of the human resources available to the organization for the benefit of the workers as well as the organization. Later in this chapter, we discuss the benefits of creating a multicultural organization.

Valuing diversity is not just the right thing to do for workers; it is the right thing to do for the organization, financially and economically. One of the most important benefits of diversity is the richness of ideas and perspectives it makes available to the organization. Rather than relying on one homogeneous dominant group for new ideas and alternative solutions to increasingly complex problems, companies that value diversity have access to more perspectives on a problem. These fresh perspectives may lead to development of new products, opening of new markets, or improving service to existing customers.

Overall, the organization wins when it truly values diversity. A worker whom the organization values is more creative and productive. Valued workers in diverse organizations experience less interpersonal conflict because employees understand

Valuing diversity means putting an end to the assumption that everyone who is not a member of the dominant group must assimilate.

Assimilation is the process through which members of a minority group are forced to learn the ways of the dominant group.

Assimilation   Assimilation is the process through which members of a minority group are forced to learn the ways of the majority group. In organizations, this entails hiring people from diverse backgrounds and attempting to mold them to fit into the existing organizational culture. One way companies attempt to make people fit in is to require that employees speak only one language. In Chicago, Carlos Solero was fired three days after he refused to sign a work agreement that included a policy of English-only at a suburban manufacturing plant. Management said the intent of the English-only policy was to improve communication among workers at the plant. In response, Solero and seven other Spanish speakers filed lawsuits against the plant.[18] Attempts to assimilate diverse workers by imposing English-only rules can lead to a variety of organizational problems. Most organizations develop systems such as performance evaluation and incentive programs that reinforce the values of the dominant group. (Chapter 14 discusses organizational culture as a means of reinforcing organizational values and controlling workers' behavior.) By universally applying the values of the majority group throughout the organization, assimilation tends to perpetuate false stereotypes and prejudices. Workers who are different are expected to meet the standards for dominant-group members.[19]

Dominant groups tend to be self-perpetuating. Majority-group members may avoid people who are "different" simply because they find communication with them difficult. Moreover, informal discussions over coffee and lunch and during after-hours socializing tend to be limited to people in the dominant group. Those who are not in the dominant group miss out on informal communications regarding office politics, company policies, and other issues; as a result, they often do not understand more formal communications. For example, informal discussions may provide background and explanations; a subsequent formal memorandum may then be clear to those "in the know," but less clear to those not in the dominant group. The dominant group likewise remains unaware of opinions from "the outside."

Similarly, since the dominant group makes decisions based on their values and beliefs, the minority group has little say in decisions regarding compensation, facility location, benefit plans, performance standards, and other work issues that pertain directly to all workers. Workers who differ from the majority very quickly get the idea that to succeed in such a system, one must be like the dominant group in terms of values and beliefs, dress, and most other characteristics. Since success depends on assimilation, differences are driven underground.

Most organizations have a fairly predictable dominant group. Table 2.1 shows the results of interviews with members of several organizations who were asked to list the attributes reinforced by their organization's culture. Typically, white organization members view themselves as quite diverse. Others in the organization, however, view them as quite homogeneous, having attributes similar to those listed in the table. Also, dominant-group members tend to be less aware of the problems homogeneity can cause. Generally, those not in the dominant group feel the effects more keenly.

Failure to heed cultural diversity can be very costly to the organization. In addition to blocking minority involvement in communication and decision making, it can result in tensions among workers, lower productivity, rising costs due to increasing absenteeism, higher employee turnover, increased equal employment opportunity and harassment suits, and lower worker morale.[20]

TABLE 2.1

Attributes Reinforced by the Culture in Typical Organizations

- Rational, linear thinker
- Impersonal management style
- Married with children
- Quantitative
- Adversarial
- Careerist
- Individualistic
- Experience in competitive team sports
- In control
- Military veteran

- Age 35–49
- Competitive
- Protestant or Jewish
- College graduate
- Tall
- Heterosexual
- Predictable
- Excellent physical condition
- Willing to relocate

Reference: Marilyn Loden and Judy B. Rosener, *Workforce America! Managing Employee Diversity as a Vital Resource* (Homewood, IL: Business One Irwin, 1991), p. 43. Copyright © 1991 by Business One Irwin. Used with permission.

The Emergence of International Management

LEARNING OBJECTIVE

Discuss the emergence of international management.

A primary source of diversity in organizations is the increasing globalization of organizations and management. However, in many ways, international management is nothing new. Centuries ago, the Roman army was forced to develop a management system to deal with its widespread empire.[21] Likewise, the Olympic Games, the Red Cross, and many similar organizations have international roots. From a business standpoint, however, international management is relatively new, at least in the United States.

The Growth of International Business

In 2000, the volume of international trade in current dollars was almost forty times greater than the amount in 1960, and the figures are projected to continue escalating. What has led to this dramatic increase? As Figure 2.3 shows, four major factors account for much of the momentum.

First, communication and transportation have advanced dramatically over the past several decades. Telephone service has improved, communication networks span the globe and can interact via satellite, and once remote areas have become accessible. Telephone service in some developing countries is now based almost entirely on cellular phone technology rather than land-based wired telephone service. Fax machines and electronic mail allow managers to send documents around the world in seconds as opposed to the days it took in years past. In short, it is far easier to conduct international business today.

Second, businesses have expanded internationally to increase their markets. Companies in smaller countries, such as Nestlé in Switzerland, recognized long ago that their domestic markets were too small to sustain much growth and therefore moved into international activities. Many U.S. firms, on the other hand, had all the business they could handle until recently; hence, they are just beginning to consider international opportunities. As U.S. companies grow internationally, they confront many differences in the ways various countries conduct business. Differences in laws, local customs, tariffs, and exchange rates are only a few of these

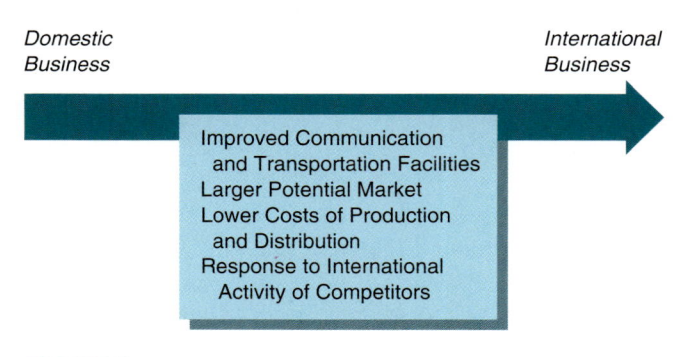

FIGURE 2.3

Forces That Have Increased International Business

Movement along the continuum from domestic to international business is due to four forces. Businesses subject to these forces are becoming more international.

Domestic Business → International Business

- Improved Communication and Transportation Facilities
- Larger Potential Market
- Lower Costs of Production and Distribution
- Response to International Activity of Competitors

challenges. In spite of the Foreign Corrupt Practices Act in the United States, some companies are having difficulty finding legal ways to do business, and individuals are still getting into legal difficulties. For example, Saybolt, Inc., pled guilty to paying a $50,000 bribe to Panamanian government officials within the Panamanian Ministry of Commerce and Industries to obtain a government lease for a laboratory site adjacent to the Panama Canal. David H. Mean, then president of Saybolt, was convicted of conspiracy, violation of the Foreign Corrupt Practices Act, and interstate travel to promote bribery.[22] Companies in the tobacco industry that have significantly increased their global efforts are currently embroiled in a global controversy over the ethics of marketing tobacco products around the world.

Third, more and more firms are moving into the international realm to control costs, especially labor costs. Plans to cut costs in this way do not always work out as planned, but many firms are successfully using inexpensive labor in Asia and Mexico.[23] In searching for lower labor costs, some companies have discovered well-trained workers and built more efficient plants that are closer to international markets.[24]

Finally, many organizations have become international in response to competition. If an organization starts gaining strength in international markets, its competitors often must follow suit to avoid falling too far behind in sales and profitability. Exxon Mobil Corporation and Texaco realized they had to increase their international market share to keep pace with foreign competitors such as BP and Royal Dutch/Shell.

Trends in International Business

The most striking trend in international business is obvious: growth. More and more businesses are entering the international marketplace, including many smaller firms. We read a great deal about the threat of foreign companies. For example, for many years successful Japanese automobile firms such as Toyota and Nissan produced higher-quality cars for lower prices than did U.S. firms. What is often overlooked, however, is the success of U.S. firms abroad. Ford, for example, has long had a successful business in Europe and today employs less than half its total workforce on U.S. soil. Further, U.S. firms make dozens of products better than any other company in the world.[25] General Motors Europe has had strong sales in Europe since 1985, rising to a 13 percent market share, the second best in Europe, behind Volkswagen.[26] In addition, many foreign firms, such as BMW and Mercedes, are now producing their products in the United States because of the lower wage rates, more favorable tax rates, and improved quality.

Business transactions are also becoming increasingly blurred across national boundaries. Ford owns 25 percent of Mazda, General Motors and Toyota have a joint venture in California, Ford and Volkswagen have one in Argentina, and Honda and British Sterling have one worldwide. Mergers are also taking place all over the globe. Ford owns Jaguar and Volvo, Daimler-Benz merged with Chrysler to form DaimlerChrysler, and Renault and Nissan share ownership.

PART TWO

Individual Processes in Organizations

CHAPTER 3

Foundations of Individual Behavior

CHAPTER 4

Motivation in Organizations

CHAPTER 5

Job Design and Work Structures

CHAPTER 6

Goal Setting, Performance Management, and Rewards

CHAPTER 3

Foundations of Individual Behavior

MANAGEMENT PREVIEW

Think about human behavior as a jigsaw puzzle. Puzzles consist of various pieces that fit together in precise ways. And, of course, no two puzzles are exactly alike. They have different numbers of pieces, the pieces are of different sizes and shapes, and the pieces fit together in different ways. The same can be said of human behavior and its determinants. Each of us is a whole picture, like a fully assembled jigsaw puzzle, but the puzzle pieces that define us and the way those pieces fit together are unique. Thus, every person in an organization is fundamentally different from everyone else. To be successful, managers must recognize that these differences exist and attempt to understand how they affect behavior. In this chapter, we explore some of the key characteristics that differentiate people from one another in organizations. First, we investigate the psychological nature of individuals in organizations. We then look at elements of people's personalities that can influence behavior and consider individual attitudes and their role in organizations. In subsequent sections we examine perception, stress, and creativity. Finally, we examine various kinds of workplace behaviors that affect organizational performance.

After you have studied this chapter, you should be able to:
- ☐ *Explain the nature of the individual-organization relationship.*
- ☐ *Define* personality *and describe personality attributes that affect behavior in organizations.*
- ☐ *Discuss individual attitudes in organizations and how they affect behavior.*
- ☐ *Describe basic perceptual processes and the role of attributions in organizations.*
- ☐ *Discuss the causes and consequences of stress and describe how stress can be managed.*
- ☐ *Describe creativity and its role in organizations.*
- ☐ *Explain how workplace behaviors can directly or indirectly influence organizational effectiveness.*

We begin by looking at healthy and unhealthy connections that people may develop within their workplace.

You can love your job, but will it love you back? Psychologists and other experts who study job-related mental health report a disturbing trend: More and more workers say they prefer long hours. Many employees routinely put in 12-hour days or work from home every weekend. It's an ironic twist in a society where "formerly, personal success was evinced by the ability to not work, to be a part of a leisure class, to be idle," says psychotherapist and author Ilene Philipson. "Today, we measure our success by how *much* we work," she adds.

Philipson's book *Married to the Job: Why We Live to Work and What We Can Do About It* contains numerous examples. One high-performing manager fell out of favor after asking for a raise. The lack of subsequent praise caused deep depression and anxiety attacks. Philipson says this client is typical of the career-obsessed worker: "What [these workers] have done is to transfer all of their unmet emotional needs to the workplace." Many of these employees believe work is the most important thing in their life, to which Philipson responds, "Your boss is not your friend. Your colleagues are not your family. Workplaces are intensely political environments. If you bring your heart and soul there, you're likely setting yourself up for feeling betrayed."

Professor Benjamin Hunnicutt, an expert on work, claims, "Work has become how we define ourselves. It is now answering the traditional religious questions: Who am I? How do I find meaning and purpose? Work is no longer just about economics; it's about identity." Most of Philipson's patients have few social relationships outside of work. Many use work to help them through tough times. Yet the praise they receive at work is powerfully addictive, and that can also be dangerous. Yolanda Perry-Pastor, a patient of Philipson's, kept assuming more job duties until she suffered a nervous breakdown. She says, "I've been though a lot in my life," referring to domestic abuse and single parenthood, "but that was nothing compared with this."

Another contributing factor is companies that "ensnare" workers by offering a homelike environment, personal services, or just encouraging workers to consider their coworkers as family. For example, Houston-based BMC Software offers hammocks, a gym, sports leagues, a movie theater, live piano music, free gourmet meals, massages, banking, hairstyling services, oil changes and car washes, child care, elder care, pet care, medical exams, and even bedrooms for those who can't make it home. BMC's chief of human resources claims, "I know this is hard to believe, but . . . [i]t gives you a balanced life without having to leave." Psychologist Maynard Brusman disagrees: "The workplace has become [a workers'] community. They come to me anxious, and they don't know why. They've become caught up in the culture. The question is, 'Is that healthy?' From what I've seen, it isn't."

Workers who are obsessed with their careers find that work consumes all their passion and time, leaving nothing for other relationships. Perry-Pastor says of her two children during the time she was overworking, "They were never allowed to be sick. . . . I would pay for baby-sitters, lessons, tutors, whatever they needed. I thought they were taken care of." Work relationships become more rewarding than relationships at home. Sociologist Arlie Hochschild theorizes that dual-income couples work long hours to escape their hectic home lives. "At home, you don't always get a pat on the back," says Karin Hanson, formerly of Microsoft. "In your office, you can hear, 'Hey, good work.'" Some managers may believe that an all-consuming interest in work is acceptable and even desirable, but the quality and quantity of work drop and incidences of absence, turnover, accidents, and workplace violence all increase with stress. Many workers drop out of the workforce entirely—a loss for families and for society.

Philipson claims that career-obsessed individuals are not weak or insecure. "These people are in the same boat with all of the rest of us who work longer hours, take fewer vacations, and wake up and go to sleep thinking about work," she asserts. So how can one avoid becoming over-involved in work? The psychotherapists recommend that you start by defining yourself and your worth in nonwork terms. Look to religion, family, or community for praise and comfort. Develop compelling interests and strong friendships outside of work. Take "real" nights, weekends, vacations—no work allowed. Focus less on praise, which can put you under someone else's control, and more on developing your own sense of self-worth. And, yes, miss work every now and then. Play hooky. Take an occasional day off and just relax.

"[F]ormerly, personal success was evinced by the ability to not work....Today, we measure our success by how much we work."—Psychotherapist and author Ilene Philipson

References: Andrea Sachs, "Wedded to Work," *Time*, September 2002, p. A21; Ilene Philipson,"Work Is Life," PsychotherapistResources.com website, April 22, 2004; Jerry Useem, "Welcome to the New Company Town," *Fortune*, February 13, 2004, pp. 76–84; Pamela Kruger, "Betrayed by Work," *Fast Company*, February 1, 2003.

People and the organizations where they work are continually defining and redefining their relationships. In much the same way, relationships between people evolve and change over time. To do so, they must assess how well their respective needs and capabilities match each other. As the opening vignette indicates, some people risk developing a dependence on their work. Others develop and maintain a healthy and productive relationship with their employer. A variety of unique characteristics possessed by each and every employee affects how these individuals feel about the organization, how they will alter their future attitudes about the firm, and how they perform their jobs. These characteristics reflect the basic elements of individual behavior in organizations.

Understanding Individuals in Organizations

LEARNING OBJECTIVE

Explain the nature of the individual-organization relationship.

As a starting point in understanding human behavior in the workplace, we consider the basic nature of the relationship between individuals and organizations. We also explore the nature of individual differences.

The Psychological Contract

Most people have a basic understanding of a contract. Whenever we buy a car or sell a house, for example, both buyer and seller sign a contract that specifies the terms of the agreement. A psychological contract is similar in some ways to a standard legal contract, but is less formal and clearly defined. In particular, a **psychological contract** is the overall set of expectations an individual holds with respect to what he or she will contribute to the organization and what the organization will provide in return.[1] Thus, a psychological contract is not written on paper, nor are all of its terms explicitly negotiated.

Figure 3.1 illustrates the essential nature of a psychological contract. The individual makes a variety of **contributions** to the organization: effort, skills, ability, time, loyalty, and so forth. These contributions presumably satisfy various needs and requirements of the organization. That is, since the organization may have hired the person because of her skills, it is reasonable for the organization to expect the employee to subsequently display those skills in performing her job.

In return for these contributions, the organization provides **inducements** to the individual. Some inducements, such as pay and career opportunities, are tangible rewards. Others, such as job security and status, are more intangible. Just as the contributions the individual makes must satisfy the organization's needs, the inducements the organization offers must serve the individual's needs. That is, if a person accepts employment with an organization because he thinks he will earn an attractive salary and have an opportunity to advance, he will subsequently expect those rewards will actually be forthcoming.

If both the individual and the organization perceive that the psychological contract is fair and equitable, they will be satisfied with the relationship and will likely continue it. On the other hand, if either party sees an imbalance or inequity

A **psychological contract** is a person's set of expectations regarding what he or she will contribute to the organization and what the organization will provide in return.

An individual's **contributions** to an organization include such things as effort, skills, ability, time, and loyalty.

Organizations provide **inducements** to individuals in the form of tangible and intangible rewards.

Chapter 3 Foundations of Individual Behavior

Contributions from the Individual
- Effort
- Ability
- Loyalty
- Skills
- Time
- Competencies

Inducements from the Organization
- Pay
- Job Security
- Benefits
- Career Opportunities
- Status
- Promotion Opportunities

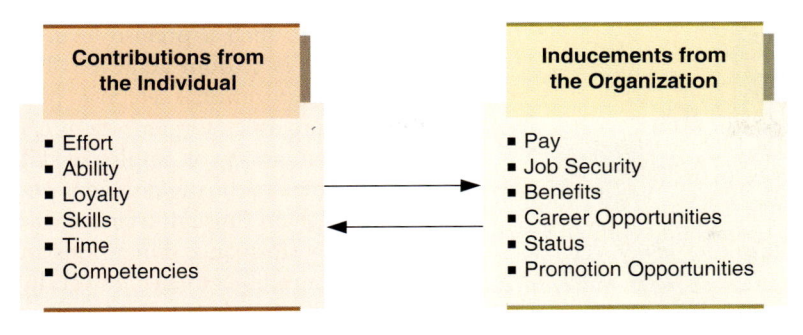

FIGURE 3.1

The Psychological Contract

Psychological contracts govern the basic relationship between people and organizations. Individuals contribute such things as effort and loyalty. Organizations, in turn, offer such inducements as pay and job security.

in the contract, it may initiate a change. For example, the individual may request a pay raise or promotion, decrease her contributed effort, or look for a better job elsewhere. The organization can also initiate change by requesting that the individual improve his skills through training, transfer him to another job, or terminate his employment altogether.

A basic challenge the organization faces, then, is to manage psychological contracts. The organization must ensure that it is getting value from its employees. At the same time, it must ensure that it is providing employees with appropriate inducements. If the organization is underpaying its employees for their contributions, for example, they may perform poorly or leave for better jobs elsewhere. On the other hand, if they are being overpaid relative to their contributions, the organization is incurring unnecessary costs.[2]

The Person-Job Fit

Person-job fit is the extent to which the contributions the individual makes match the inducements the organization offers.

One specific aspect of managing psychological contracts is managing the person-job fit. **Person-job fit** is the extent to which the contributions the individual makes match the inducements the organization offers. In theory, each employee has a specific set of needs that he or she wants fulfilled and a set of job-related behaviors and abilities to contribute. Thus, if the organization can take perfect advantage of those behaviors and abilities and exactly fulfill the employee's needs, it will have achieved a perfect person-job fit.

Psychological contracts play an important role in the relationship between an organization and its employees. As long as both parties agree that the contributions an employee makes and the inducements the organization provides are balanced, both parties are satisfied and will likely maintain their relationship. But if a serious imbalance occurs, one or both parties may attempt to change the relationship. As illustrated here, an employee who is sufficiently dissatisfied may even resort to using company assets for his or her personal gain.

DILBERT reprinted by permission of United Feature Syndicate, Inc.

Understanding and managing person-job fit is an important element in effective psychological contracts. For example, consider the crew members for the *Atlantis* space shuttle. Each had demonstrated both the technical skills to perform in space and the emotional strength to withstand the rigors of space travel. Further, they have also demonstrated the ability to work together as a team both in training and in actual space missions. Clearly, then, each crew member has an advanced level of person-job fit.

Of course, such a precise level of person-job fit is seldom achieved. For one thing, organizational selection procedures are imperfect. Organizations can make approximations of employee skill levels when making hiring decisions and can improve them through training. But even simple performance dimensions are hard to measure objectively and validly. Second, as discussed in the Mastering Change box, both people and organizations change. An individual who finds a new job stimulating and exciting may find the same job boring and monotonous after a few years of performing it. Similarly, when the organization adopts new technology, it has changed the skills it needs from its employees. Third, each individual is unique. Measuring skills and performance is difficult enough; assessing needs, attitudes, and personality is far more complex. Therefore, each of these individual differences makes matching individuals with jobs a challenge.

The Nature of Individual Differences

Individual differences are personal attributes that vary from one person to another.

Individual differences are personal attributes that vary from one person to another. Individual differences may be physical, psychological, and emotional. Taken together, all of the individual differences that characterize any specific person serve to make that individual unique from everyone else. We devote much of the remainder of this chapter to individual differences. Before proceeding, however, we must note the importance of the situation in assessing the behavior of individuals.

Are specific differences that characterize a given individual good or bad? Do they contribute to or detract from performance? The answer, of course, is that it depends on the circumstances. One person may be very dissatisfied, withdrawn, and negative in one job setting but very satisfied, outgoing, and positive in another. Working conditions, coworkers, and leadership are all important ingredients.

Thus, whenever an organization attempts to assess or account for individual differences among its employees, it must also be sure to consider the situation in which behavior occurs. Individuals who are satisfied, productive workers in one context may prove to be dissatisfied, unproductive workers in another. Attempting to consider both individual differences and contributions in relation to inducements and contexts, then, is a major challenge for organizations as they attempt to establish effective psychological contracts with their employees and achieve optimal fits between people and jobs.

> **LEARNING OBJECTIVE**
>
> Define *personality* and describe personality attributes that affect behavior in organizations.

Personality and Individual Behavior

Personality traits represent some of the most fundamental sets of individual differences in organizations. **Personality** is the relatively stable set of psychological

MASTERING CHANGE

Changing the Way Companies Change

After many years of improving organizational technology and work processes, some managers are now concentrating on changing the way people think. For instance, many corporate leaders are coming to realize that internal mental processes such as attitudes, perception, and creativity are the fundamental sources of individual behavior. And the most thoughtful plans, the most remarkable innovations, and the most appealing products are worth very little without the support that comes from the sum of thousands of individual actions. "[W]hat I [previously] failed to recognize was that the way people think is far more important than the tools they use," says Dennis Pawley, a former Chrysler executive, now head of Lean Learning, a change consulting firm.

"Learning" has become the new corporate rallying cry. Corporations and consulting firms are developing training programs to teach workers how to learn. But many are finding that teaching people how to learn is much harder than teaching them specific skills. Peter Senge, a noted management expert, claims that organizations need to develop an increased sensitivity to human relationships at work. He explains, "[To change companies], we keep bringing in mechanics—when what we need are gardeners. We keep trying to drive change—when what we need to do is cultivate change." Senge agrees with a concept also articulated by Pawley: "The people who do the work should be the ones to improve the work." Senge asserts that in his extensive experience as a management consultant, he has "never seen a successful organizational-learning program rolled out from the top [of the organization]. Not a single one."

So if change requires learning, and learning requires that organizations become more humane and experimen-

> "We keep trying to drive change—when what we need to do is cultivate change."—*Peter Senge, management expert*

tal, how exactly can training programs get workers to learn better? Most effective programs begin by selecting a motivated team, usually at the middle-management level. Then students receive training through a variety of media, including case studies, role playing, teaching, reading, and lectures. Next, students are asked to take their "book knowledge" and apply it in simulated environments. Lean Learning, for example, assigns students the task of reworking a toy-airplane assembly line to make it more efficient. To reinforce the lessons learned mentally and physically, students are asked to use journals and dialogues to express their feelings and reflections. Finally, students who have been transformed are themselves now ready to transform by spreading their learning throughout their organizations.

References: Lean Learning Center website, "How You Will Learn," www.leanlearningcenter.com on April 11, 2004; Fara Warner, "Think Lean," *Fast Company*, February 2003, pp. 40–42; Alan M. Webber, "Will Companies Ever Learn?," *Fast Company*, October 2002; Alan M. Webber, "Learning for a Change," *Fast Company*, May 1999 (quotation), www.fastcompany.com on April 11, 2002.

Personality is the relatively stable set of psychological attributes that distinguish one person from another.

The **"big five" personality traits** are a set of fundamental traits that are especially relevant to organizations.

attributes that distinguish one person from another.[3] Managers should strive to understand basic personality attributes and the ways they can affect people's behavior in organizational situations, as well as their perceptions of and attitudes toward the organization.

The "Big Five" Personality Traits

Psychologists have identified literally thousands of personality traits and dimensions that differentiate one person from another. But in recent years, researchers have identified five fundamental personality traits that are especially relevant to organizations. Because these five traits are so important and currently receive much attention, they are commonly referred to today as the **"big five" personality traits**.[4] Figure 3.2 illustrates these traits.

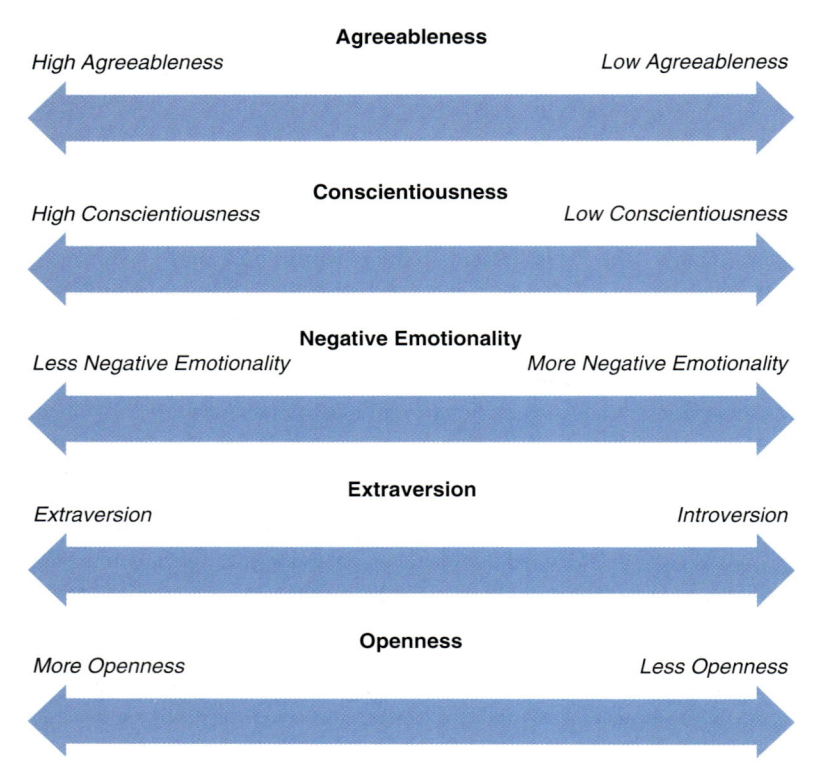

FIGURE 3.2

The "Big Five" Personality Framework

Agreeableness
High Agreeableness ←————————→ Low Agreeableness

Conscientiousness
High Conscientiousness ←————————→ Low Conscientiousness

Negative Emotionality
Less Negative Emotionality ←————————→ More Negative Emotionality

Extraversion
Extraversion ←————————→ Introversion

Openness
More Openness ←————————→ Less Openness

The "big five" personality framework is currently very popular among researchers and managers. These five dimensions represent fundamental personality traits presumed to be important in determining the behaviors of individuals in organizations. In general, experts agree that personality traits closer to the left end of each dimension are more positive in organizational settings, whereas traits closer to the right are less positive.

Agreeableness is the ability to get along with others.

Conscientiousness refers to the number of goals on which a person focuses.

Negative emotionality is characterized by moodiness and insecurity.

Extraversion is the quality of being comfortable with relationships; the opposite extreme, introversion, is characterized by more social discomfort.

Agreeableness is a person's ability to get along with others. Highly agreeable people tend to be gentle, cooperative, forgiving, understanding, and good-natured in their dealings with others. Disagreeable people are usually irritable, short-tempered, uncooperative, and generally antagonistic toward others. While research has not yet fully investigated the effects of agreeableness, it is likely that highly agreeable people are better able to develop good working relationships with coworkers, subordinates, and managers, whereas less agreeable people have less positive working relationships. The same pattern may extend to relationships with customers, suppliers, and other key organizational constituents.

Conscientiousness refers to the number of goals on which a person focuses. People who focus on relatively few goals at one time are likely to be organized, systematic, careful, thorough, responsible, and self-disciplined as they work to pursue those goals. Others tend to take on a wider array of goals and, as a result, to be more disorganized, careless, and irresponsible, as well as less thorough and self-disciplined. Research has found that more conscientious people tend to be higher performers than less conscientious people across a variety of jobs. This pattern seems logical, of course, since more conscientious people will take their jobs seriously and perform them in a responsible fashion.

Negative emotionality is characterized by moodiness and insecurity. People with less negative emotionality tend to be relatively poised, calm, resilient, and secure, whereas people with more negative emotionality are usually more excitable, insecure, reactive, and subject to extreme mood swings. People with less negative emotionality are better able to handle job stress, pressure, and tension. Their stability may also lead them to be seen as more reliable than their less stable counterparts.

Extraversion refers to a person's comfort level with relationships. People considered to be extraverts are sociable, talkative, assertive, and open to new relationships. In contrast, introverts are uncomfortable in social situations and less open to new relationships. Research suggests that extraverts tend to be higher overall job performers than introverts and are also more likely to be attracted to jobs based on personal relationships, such as sales and marketing positions.

Openness is the capacity to entertain new ideas and to change as a result of learning new information.

Finally, **openness** refers to a person's rigidity of beliefs and range of interests. People with high levels of openness are willing to listen to new ideas and change their own ideas, beliefs, and attitudes as a result of new information. They also tend to have broad interests and to be curious, imaginative, and creative. People with low levels of openness tend to be less receptive to new ideas and less willing to change their views, to have fewer and narrower interests, and to be less curious and creative. People with more openness are likely to be better performers, owing to their flexibility and their tendency to be better accepted by others in the organization. Openness may also encompass an individual's willingness to accept change. For example, people with high levels of openness are generally more receptive to change, whereas people with low levels of openness are more likely to resist change.

The "big five" framework continues to appeal to both researchers and managers. The potential value of this framework is that it encompasses an integrated set of traits that appear to be valid predictors of certain behaviors in particular situations. Thus, managers who can develop both an understanding of the framework and the ability to assess these traits in their employees will be in a good position to understand how and why employees behave as they do.[5] On the other hand, managers must also be careful not to overestimate their ability to assess the "big five" traits in others. Even assessment using the most rigorous and valid measures is likely to be somewhat imprecise. Another limitation of the "big five" framework is that it is based primarily on research conducted in the United States. Thus, questions about its generalizability to other cultures remain unanswered. Even within the United States, a variety of other factors and traits are also likely to affect behavior in organizations.

The Myers-Briggs Framework

Another interesting approach to understanding personalities in organizations is the Myers-Briggs framework. This framework, based on the classical work of Carl Jung, differentiates people in terms of four general dimensions, defined as follows:

- *Extroversion (E) Versus Introversion (I)*. Extroverts get their energy from being around other people; Introverts feel worn out by others and need solitude to recharge their energy.
- *Sensing (S) Versus Intuition (N)*. Sensing individuals prefer concrete ideas; Intuitives prefer abstract concepts.
- *Thinking (T) Versus Feeling (F)*. Thinking individuals base their decisions more on logic and reason; Feeling individuals base their decisions more on feelings and emotions.
- *Judging (J) Versus Perceiving (P)*. People who are the Judging type enjoy completion or being finished with tasks or activities; Perceiving individuals enjoy the process and open-ended situations.

To use this framework, the organization has people complete a questionnaire designed to measure their personalities on each dimension. Higher or lower scores on each dimension are used to classify people into one of sixteen different personality categories.

The Myers-Briggs Type Indicator (MBTI) is one popular questionnaire some organizations use to assess personality types. Indeed, it is among the most popular selection instruments used today, with as many as 2 million people participating each year. Research suggests that the MBTI is a useful method for determining communication styles and interaction preferences. In terms of personality attributes, however, questions exist about both the validity and the stability of the MBTI.

Other Personality Traits at Work

Besides the personality dimensions used in the "big five" and Myers-Briggs frameworks, several other personality traits influence behavior in organizations. Among the most important are locus of control, self-efficacy, authoritarianism, Machiavellianism, self-esteem, and risk propensity.

Locus of control is the extent to which people believe their behavior has a real effect on what happens to them.[6] Some people, for example, believe that if they work hard, they will succeed. They also may believe that people who fail do so because they lack ability or motivation. People who believe individuals are in control of their lives are said to have an *internal locus of control*. Other people think fate, chance, luck, or others' behavior determines what happens to them. For example, an employee who fails to get a promotion may attribute that failure to a politically motivated boss or just bad luck rather than to her or his own lack of skills or poor performance record. People who think forces beyond their control dictate what happens to them are said to have an *external locus of control*.

Self-efficacy is a related but subtly different personality characteristic. Self-efficacy is a person's beliefs about his or her capabilities to perform a task.[7] People with high self-efficacy believe they can perform well on a specific task, whereas people with low self-efficacy tend to doubt their ability to perform a particular task. While self-assessments of ability contribute to self-efficacy, so does the individual's personality. Some people simply have more self-confidence than others. As a result of their belief in their ability to perform a task effectively, they are more self-assured and better able to focus their attention on performance.

Another important personality characteristic is **authoritarianism,** the extent to which an individual believes power and status differences are appropriate within hierarchical social systems such as organizations.[8] A person who is highly authoritarian may accept directives or orders from someone with more authority purely because the other person is "the boss." On the other hand, while a person who is not highly authoritarian may still carry out appropriate and reasonable directives from the boss, she or he is also more likely to question things, express disagreement with the boss, and even refuse to carry out orders believed to be objectionable. A highly authoritarian manager may be autocratic and demanding, and highly authoritarian subordinates will be more likely to accept this behavior from their leader. On the other hand, a less authoritarian manager may allow subordinates a bigger role in making decisions, and less authoritarian subordinates will respond positively to this behavior.

Machiavellianism is another important personality trait, named after Niccolo Machiavelli, a sixteenth-century author. In his book *The Prince*, Machiavelli explained how the nobility could more easily gain and use power. Machiavellianism is now used to describe behavior directed at gaining power and controlling the behavior of others. Research suggests that Machiavellianism is a personality trait that varies from person to person. More Machiavellian individuals tend to be rational and nonemotional, may be willing to lie to attain personal goals, put little weight on loyalty and friendship, and enjoy manipulating others' behavior. Less Machiavellian individuals are more emotional, less willing to lie to succeed, value loyalty and friendship highly, and get little personal pleasure from manipulating others. By all accounts, Dennis Kozlowski, the indicted former CEO of Tyco International, had a high degree of Machiavellianism. He apparently came to believe his position of power in the company gave him the right to do just about anything he wanted with company resources.[9]

Locus of control is the extent to which people believe their circumstances are a function of either their own actions or external factors beyond their control.

Self-efficacy is a person's beliefs about his or her capabilities to perform a task.

Authoritarianism is the belief that power and status differences are appropriate within hierarchical social systems such as organizations.

People who possess the personality trait of **Machiavellianism** behave to gain power and control the behavior of others.

Chapter 3 Foundations of Individual Behavior

Self-esteem is the extent to which a person believes he or she is a worthwhile and deserving individual.

A person's **risk propensity** is the degree to which she or he is willing to take chances and make risky decisions.

Emotional intelligence (EQ) is the extent to which people are self-aware, can manage their emotions, can motivate themselves, express empathy for others, and possess social skills.

Self-esteem is the extent to which a person believes she or he is a worthwhile and deserving individual.[10] A person with high self-esteem is more likely to seek higher-status jobs, be more confident in his ability to achieve higher levels of performance, and derive greater intrinsic satisfaction from his accomplishments. A person with less self-esteem may be more content to remain in a lower-level job, be less confident of her abilities, and focus more on extrinsic rewards. Among the major personality dimensions, self-esteem has been the most widely studied in other countries. While more research is clearly needed, the published evidence suggests that self-esteem as a personality trait indeed exists in a variety of countries and that its role in organizations is reasonably important across different cultures.[11]

Risk propensity is the degree to which an individual is willing to take chances and make risky decisions. A manager with a high risk propensity, for example, might be expected to experiment with new ideas and gamble on new products. She may also lead the organization in new and different directions. This manager may also be a catalyst for innovation. On the other hand, the same individual could also jeopardize the continued well-being of the organization if her risky decisions prove to be bad ones. A manager with low risk propensity may lead to a stagnant and overly conservative organization. On the other hand, he may help the organization successfully weather turbulent times by maintaining stability and calm. Thus, the potential consequences of risk propensity to an organization depend heavily on that organization's environment.

Risk propensity is the degree to which a person is willing to take chances and make risky decisions. Top managers at Lockheed Martin demonstrated strong risk propensity in their quest to earn a $200 billion contract to build the Joint Strike Fighter shown here. No less than three times did they essentially risk the company's future to help it remain the leader in the bidding. Had they ultimately failed, Lockheed Martin would have suffered the consequences for years.

Emotional Intelligence

The concept of emotional intelligence has been identified in recent years and provides some interesting insights into personality. **Emotional intelligence,** or **EQ,** refers to the extent to which people are self-aware, can manage their emotions, can motivate themselves, express empathy for others, and possess social skills.[12] These various dimensions can be described as follows:

Self-awareness. This is the basis for the other components. It refers to one's capacity for being aware of how one is feeling. In general, greater self-awareness allows people to more effectively guide their own lives and behaviors.

Managing emotions. This refers to one's capacity to balance anxiety, fear, and anger so they do not overly interfere with getting things accomplished.

Motivating oneself. This dimension refers to the ability to remain optimistic and continue striving in the face of setbacks, barriers, and failure.

Empathy. Empathy is a person's ability to understand how others are feeling even without being explicitly told.

Social skill. This refers to a person's ability to get along with others and to establish positive relationships.

The **human resource approach** to motivation assumes employees want and are able to make genuine contributions to the organization.

decision would be. The symbolic gesture of seeming to allow participation was expected to enhance motivation, even though no real participation took place.

The Human Resource Approach The **human resource approach** to motivation carries the concepts of needs and motivation one step further. Whereas the human relationists believed the illusion of contribution and participation would enhance motivation, the human resource view assumes the contributions themselves are valuable to both individuals and organizations. It asserts that people want to contribute and are able to make genuine contributions. Management's task, then, is to encourage participation and create a work environment that makes full use of the human resources available. This philosophy guides most contemporary thinking about employee motivation. At Ford, Westinghouse, Texas Instruments, and Hewlett-Packard, for example, work teams are being called on to solve a variety of problems and make substantive contributions to the organization.

Need-Based Perspectives on Motivation

LEARNING OBJECTIVE
Describe the need-based perspectives on motivation.

Need-based theories of motivation assume that need deficiencies cause behavior.

Need-based perspectives represent the starting point for most contemporary thought on motivation, although these theories also attracted critics.[8] The basic premise of **need-based theories** and models, consistent with our motivation framework introduced earlier, is that humans are motivated primarily by deficiencies in one or more important needs or need categories. Need theorists have attempted to identify and categorize the needs that are most important to people. (Some observers call these *content theories* because they deal with the content, or substance, of what motivates behavior.) The best-known need theories are the hierarchy of needs, ERG, and dual-structure theories.

Hierarchy of Needs Theory

Maslow's **hierarchy of needs theory** assumes human needs are arranged in a hierarchy of importance.

The **hierarchy of needs theory,** developed by psychologist Abraham Maslow in the 1940s, is the best-known need theory.[9] Influenced by the human relations school, Maslow argued that human beings are "wanting" animals: They have innate desires to satisfy a given set of needs. Furthermore, Maslow believed these needs are arranged in a hierarchy of importance, with the most basic needs at the foundation.

Figure 4.2 shows Maslow's hierarchy of needs. The three sets of needs at the bottom of the hierarchy are called *deficiency needs*, because they must be satisfied for the individual to be fundamentally comfortable. The top two sets of needs are termed *growth needs* because they focus on personal growth and development.

The most basic needs in the hierarchy are *physiological needs*. They include the needs for food, sex, and air. Next in the hierarchy are *security needs:* things that offer safety and security, such as adequate housing and clothing, and freedom from worry and anxiety. *Belongingness needs,* the third level in the hierarchy, are primarily social. Examples include the need for love and affection and the need to be accepted by peers. The fourth level, *esteem needs*, actually encompasses two slightly different kinds of needs: the need for a positive self-image and self-respect and the need to be respected by others. At the top of the hierarchy are *self-actualization needs*. These involve realizing one's full potential and becoming all that one can be.

Maslow believed each need level must be satisfied before the level above it can become important. Thus, once physiological needs have been satisfied, their importance diminishes, and security needs emerge as the primary sources of motivation. This escalation up the hierarchy continues until the self-actualization needs become the primary motivators. Suppose, for example, that Jennifer Wallace earns

FIGURE 4.2

The Hierarchy of Needs

Maslow's hierarchy of needs consists of five basic categories of needs. Of course, each individual has a wide variety of specific needs within each category.

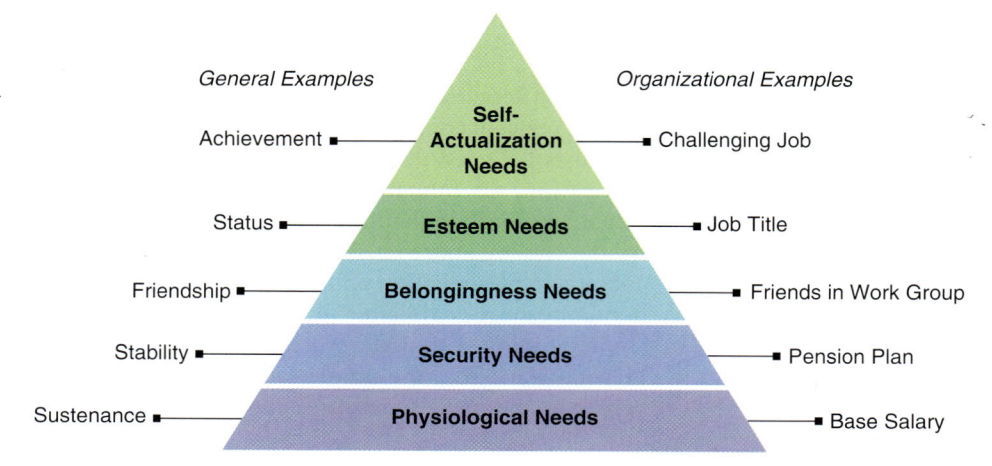

General Examples | *Organizational Examples*

- Achievement — **Self-Actualization Needs** — Challenging Job
- Status — **Esteem Needs** — Job Title
- Friendship — **Belongingness Needs** — Friends in Work Group
- Stability — **Security Needs** — Pension Plan
- Sustenance — **Physiological Needs** — Base Salary

all the money she needs and is very satisfied with her standard of living. Additional income may have little or no motivational impact on her behavior. Instead, Jennifer will strive to satisfy other needs, such as a desire for higher self-esteem.

However, if a previously satisfied lower-level set of needs becomes deficient again, the individual returns to that level. For example, suppose Jennifer unexpectedly loses her job. At first, she may not be too worried because she has savings and is confident she can find another good job. As her savings dwindle, however, she will become increasingly motivated to seek new income. Initially, she may seek a job that both pays well and satisfies her esteem needs. But as her financial situation grows increasingly grim, she may lower her expectations regarding esteem and instead focus almost exclusively on simply finding a job with a reliable paycheck.

In most businesses, physiological needs are probably the easiest to evaluate and to meet. Adequate wages, toilet facilities, ventilation, and comfortable temperatures and working conditions are measures taken to satisfy this most basic level of needs. Security needs in organizations can be satisfied by such things as job continuity (no layoffs), a grievance system (to protect against arbitrary supervisory actions), and an adequate insurance and retirement system (to guard against financial loss from illness and ensure retirement income).

Most employees' belongingness needs are satisfied by family ties and group relationships both inside and outside the organization. In the workplace, people usually develop friendships that provide a basis for social interaction and can play a major role in satisfying social needs. Managers can help satisfy these needs by fostering a sense of group identity and interaction among employees. At the same time, managers can be sensitive to the probable effects on employees (such as low performance and absenteeism) of family problems or lack of acceptance by coworkers. Esteem needs in the workplace are met at least partly by job titles, choice offices, merit pay increases, awards, and other forms of recognition. Of course, to be sources of long-term motivation, tangible rewards such as these must be distributed equitably and be based on performance.

Self-actualization needs are perhaps the hardest to understand and the most difficult to satisfy. For example, it is difficult to assess how many people completely meet their full potential. In most cases, people who are doing well on Maslow's hierarchy will have satisfied their esteem needs and will be moving toward self-actualization. Working toward self-actualization, rather than actually achieving it, may be the ultimate motivation for most people.

Research shows that the need hierarchy does not generalize very well to other countries. For example, in Greece and Japan, security needs may motivate employees more than self-actualization needs. Likewise, belongingness needs are especially important in Sweden, Norway, and Denmark. Research has also found differences in the relative importance of various needs in Mexico, India, Peru, Canada, Thailand, Turkey, and Puerto Rico.[10]

Maslow's need hierarchy makes a certain amount of intuitive sense. In addition, because it was the first motivation theory to become popular, it is also one of the best known among practicing managers. However, research has revealed a number of deficiencies in the theory. For example, five levels of needs are not always present, the actual hierarchy of needs does not always conform to Maslow's model, and need structures are more unstable and variable than the theory would lead us to believe.[11] Furthermore, managers' attempts to use a theory such as this one are often awkward or superficial. Thus, the theory's primary contribution seems to lie in providing a general framework for categorizing needs.

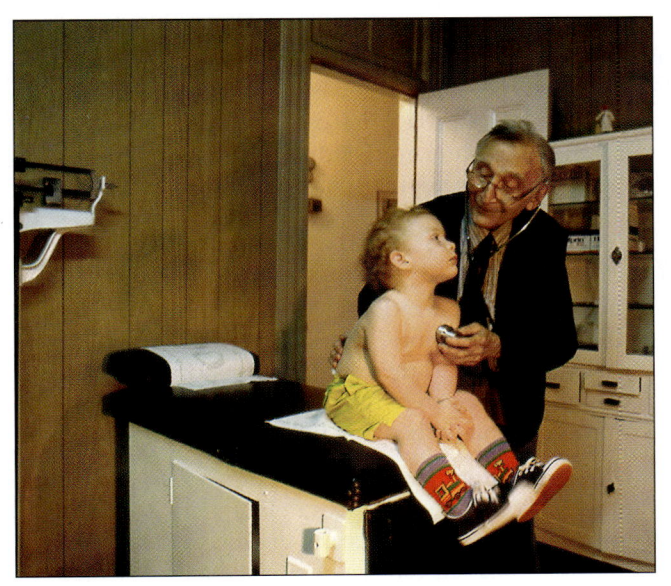

Need theories of motivation assume that need deficiencies cause behavior. Maslow's need hierarchy culminated with self-actualization needs, involving potential and fulfillment. For example, Dr. Salvator Altchek practiced medicine in Brooklyn for 67 years. For more than sixty of those years, he continued to make house calls and charged only $5 per visit for his services. Dr. Altchek clearly had all of the material possessions he needed and so chose to devote his life to helping others. Clearly, the needs that motivated this behavior had nothing to do with material things.

ERG Theory

ERG theory describes existence, relatedness, and growth needs.

ERG theory, developed by Yale psychologist Clayton Alderfer, is another historically important need theory of motivation.[12] In many respects, **ERG theory** extends and refines Maslow's needs hierarchy concept, although there are also several important differences between the two. The *E*, *R*, and *G* stand for three basic need categories: existence, relatedness, and growth. *Existence needs*, those necessary for basic human survival, roughly correspond to the physiological and security needs of Maslow's hierarchy. *Relatedness needs*, those involving the need to relate to others, are similar to Maslow's belongingness and esteem needs. Finally, *growth needs* are analogous to Maslow's needs for self-esteem and self-actualization.

In contrast to Maslow's approach, ERG theory suggests that more than one kind of need—for example, relatedness and growth needs—may motivate a person at the same time. A more important difference from Maslow's hierarchy is that ERG theory includes a satisfaction-progression component and a frustration-regression component. The satisfaction-progression concept suggests that after satisfying one category of needs, a person progresses to the next level. On this point, the need hierarchy and ERG theories agree. The need hierarchy model, however, assumes the individual remains at the next level until the needs at that level are satisfied. In contrast, the frustration-regression component of ERG theory suggests that a person who is frustrated by trying to satisfy a higher level of needs eventually will regress to the preceding level.[13]

Suppose Nick Hernandez has satisfied his basic needs at the relatedness level and now is trying to satisfy his growth needs. That is, he has many friends and social relationships, and now wants to learn new skills and advance in his career. For a variety of reasons, such as organizational constraints (few challenging jobs, a glass ceiling, etc.) and lack of opportunities to advance, he is unable to satisfy those needs. No matter how hard he tries, he seems stuck in his current position. According to ERG theory, frustration of his growth needs will cause Nick's relatedness needs to once again become dominant motivators. As a result, he will put renewed effort into making friends and developing social relationships.

Dual-Structure Theory

The **dual-structure theory** identifies motivation factors, which affect satisfaction, and hygiene factors, which determine dissatisfaction.

Another important need-based theory of motivation is the **dual-structure theory**, which in many ways is similar to the need theories just discussed. This theory was originally called the "two-factor theory," but the more contemporary name used here is more descriptive. Although few researchers today accept the theory, it has become widely known and accepted among practicing managers.

Development of the Theory
Frederick Herzberg and his associates developed the dual-structure theory in the late 1950s and early 1960s.[14] Herzberg began by interviewing approximately two hundred accountants and engineers in Pittsburgh. He asked them to recall times when they felt especially satisfied and motivated by their jobs and times when they felt particularly dissatisfied and unmotivated. He then asked them to describe what caused the positive and negative feelings. The responses to the questions were recorded by the interviewers and later subjected to content analysis. (In a content analysis, the words, phrases, and sentences respondents used are analyzed and categorized according to their meanings.)

To his surprise, Herzberg found that entirely different sets of factors were associated with the two kinds of feelings about work. For example, a person who indicated "low pay" as a source of dissatisfaction would not necessarily identify "high pay" as a source of satisfaction and motivation. Instead, people associated entirely different causes, such as recognition or achievement, with satisfaction and motivation. The findings led Herzberg to conclude that prevailing thinking about satisfaction and motivation was incorrect. As Figure 4.3 shows, at that time job satisfaction was viewed as a single construct ranging from satisfaction to dissatisfaction. If this were the case, Herzberg reasoned, one set of factors should influence movement back and forth along the continuum. But because his research had identified differential influences from two different sets of factors, Herzberg argued that two different dimensions must be involved. Thus, he saw motivation as a dual-structured phenomenon.

Figure 4.3 also illustrates the dual-structure concept that there is one dimension ranging from satisfaction to no satisfaction and another ranging from dissatisfaction to no dissatisfaction. The two dimensions presumably must be associated with the two sets of factors identified in the initial interviews. Thus, this theory proposed, employees might be either satisfied or not satisfied and, at the same time, dissatisfied or not dissatisfied.[15]

Motivation factors are intrinsic to the work itself and include factors such as achievement and recognition.

Hygiene factors are extrinsic to the work itself and include factors such as pay and job security.

In addition, Figure 4.3 lists the primary factors identified in Herzberg's interviews. **Motivation factors,** such as achievement and recognition, were often cited as primary causes of satisfaction and motivation. When present in a job, these factors apparently could cause satisfaction and motivation; when they were absent, the result was feelings of no satisfaction rather than dissatisfaction. The other set of factors, **hygiene factors**, came out in response to the question about dissatisfaction and lack of motivation. The respondents suggested that pay, job security, supervisors, and working conditions, if seen as inadequate, could lead to feelings of dissatisfaction. When these factors were considered acceptable, however, the person still was not

Chapter 4 Motivation in Organizations

The Traditional View

Satisfaction ←——————————————→ Dissatisfaction

Herzberg's View

Satisfaction ←——————————————→ No Satisfaction

Motivation Factors
- Achievement
- Recognition
- The Work Itself
- Responsibility
- Advancement and Growth

Dissatisfaction ←——————————————→ No Dissatisfaction

Hygiene Factors
- Supervision
- Working Conditions
- Interpersonal Relationships
- Pay and Job Security
- Company Policies

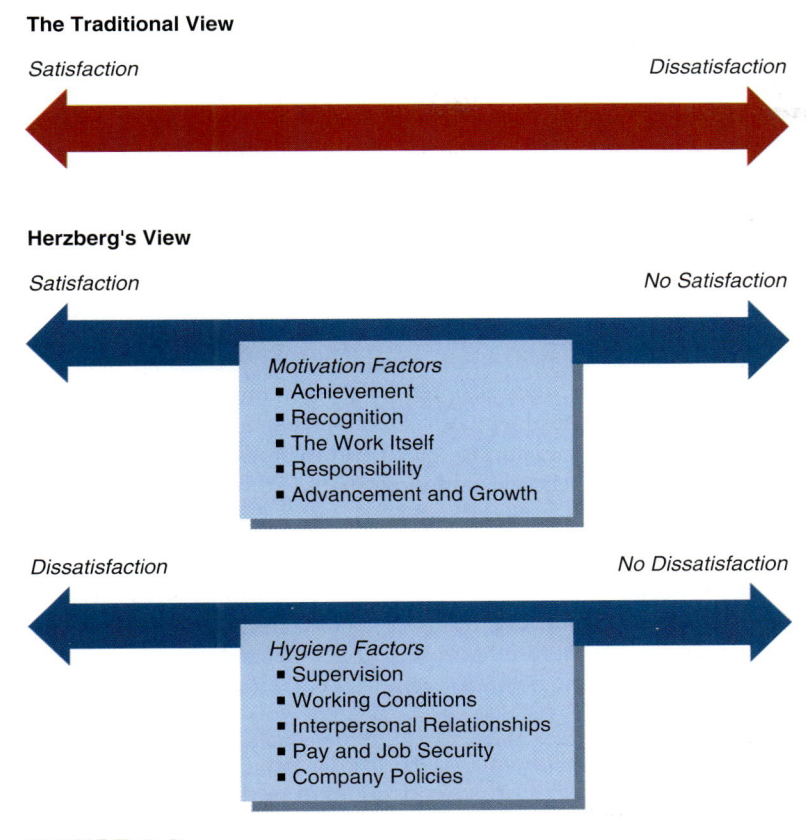

FIGURE 4.3

The Dual-Structure Theory of Motivation

The traditional view of satisfaction suggested that satisfaction and dissatisfaction are on opposite ends of a single dimension. Herzberg's dual-structure theory found evidence of a more complex view. In this theory, motivation factors affect one dimension, ranging from satisfaction to no satisfaction. Other workplace characteristics, called hygiene factors, *are assumed to affect another dimension, ranging from dissatisfaction to no dissatisfaction.*

necessarily satisfied; rather, he or she was simply not dissatisfied.[16]

To use the dual-structure theory in the workplace, Herzberg recommended a two-stage process. First, the manager should try to eliminate situations that cause dissatisfaction, which Herzberg assumed to be the more basic of the two dimensions. For example, suppose Susan Kowalski wants to use the dual-structure theory to enhance motivation in the group of seven technicians she supervises. Her first goal would be to achieve a state of no dissatisfaction by addressing hygiene factors. Imagine, for example, she discovers that their pay is a bit below market rates and a few are worried about job security. Her response would be to secure a pay raise for them and to allay their concerns about job security.

According to the theory, once a state of no dissatisfaction exists, trying to further improve motivation through hygiene factors is a waste of time.[17] At that point, the motivation factors enter the picture. Thus, when Susan is sure she has adequately dealt with hygiene issues, she should try to increase opportunities for achievement, recognition, responsibility, advancement, and growth. As a result, she would be helping her subordinates feel satisfied and motivated.

Unlike many other theorists, Herzberg described explicitly how managers could apply his theory. In particular, he developed and described a technique called *job enrichment* for structuring employee tasks.[18] (We discuss job enrichment in Chapter 5.) Herzberg tailored this technique to his key motivation factors. This unusual attention to application may explain the widespread popularity of the dual-structure theory among practicing managers.

Evaluation of the Theory Because it gained popularity so quickly, the dual-structure theory has been scientifically scrutinized more closely than almost any other organizational behavior theory.[19] The results have been contradictory, to say the least. The initial study by Herzberg and his associates supported the basic premises of the theory, as did a few follow-up studies.[20] In general, studies that use the same methodology Herzberg did (content analysis of recalled incidents) tend to support the theory. However, this methodology has itself been criticized, and studies that use other methods to measure satisfaction and dissatisfaction frequently obtain results quite different from Herzberg's.[21] If the theory is "method bound," as it appears to be, its validity is therefore questionable.

Several other criticisms have been directed against the theory. Critics say the original sample of accountants and engineers likely does not represent the general working population. Furthermore, they maintain the theory fails to account for individual differences. Also, subsequent research has found that a factor such as pay may affect satisfaction in one sample and dissatisfaction in another, and that the effect of a given factor depends on the individual's age and organizational level. In addition, the theory does not define the relationship between satisfaction and motivation.

Research has also suggested that the dual-structure framework varies across cultures. Only limited studies have been conducted, but findings suggest that employees in New Zealand and Panama assess the impact of motivation and hygiene factors differently than U.S. workers.[22] It is not surprising, then, that the dual-structure theory is no longer held in high esteem by organizational behavior researchers. Indeed, the field has since adopted far more complex and valid conceptualizations of motivation, most of which we discuss later in this chapter. However, because of its initial popularity and its specific guidance for application, the dual-structure theory merits a special place in the history of motivation research.

Other Important Needs

Each theory discussed so far describes interrelated sets of important individual needs within specific frameworks. Several other key needs have been identified that are not allied with any single integrated theoretical perspective. The three most frequently mentioned needs are the needs for achievement, affiliation, and power.

The Need for Achievement   The **need for achievement** is most frequently associated with the work of David McClelland.[23] This need arises from an individual's desire to accomplish a goal or task more effectively than in the past. Individuals who have a high need for achievement tend to set moderately difficult goals and to make moderately risky decisions. Suppose Mark Cohen, a regional manager for a national retailer, sets a sales increase goal for his stores of either 1 percent or 50 percent. The first goal is probably too easy, and the second is probably impossible to reach; either would suggest a low need for achievement. But a mid-range goal of, say, 15 percent might present a reasonable challenge but also be within reach. Setting this goal may more accurately reflect a high need for achievement.

High-need achievers also want immediate, specific feedback on their performance. They want to know how well they did something as quickly after finishing it as possible. For this reason, high-need achievers frequently take jobs in sales, where they get almost immediate feedback from customers, and avoid jobs in areas such as research and development, where tangible progress is slower and feedback comes at longer intervals. If Mark Cohen asks his managers for their sales performance only on a periodic basis, he may not have a high need for achievement. But if he constantly calls each store manager in his territory to ask about their sales increases, this activity indicates a high need for achievement on his part.

Preoccupation with work is another characteristic of high-need achievers. They think about it on their way to the workplace, during lunch, and at home. They find it difficult to put their work aside, and they become frustrated when they must stop working on a partly completed project. If Mark Cohen seldom thinks about his business in the evening, he may not be a high-need achiever. However, if work is always on his mind, he may indeed be a high-need achiever.

Finally, high-need achievers tend to assume personal responsibility for getting things done. They often volunteer for extra duties and find it difficult to delegate part of a job to someone else. Accordingly, they derive a feeling of accomplishment

> The **need for achievement** is the desire to accomplish a task or goal more effectively than in the past.

The need for achievement is the desire to accomplish a task or meet a goal more effectively than in the past. During the height of her tennis career, Martina Navratilova was the best and most feared player on earth. Her strong competitive drive recently prompted her to make a comeback at Wimbledon. Even though she did not fare well in her comeback attempt, her actions nevertheless reflect her strong need for achievement.

when they have done more work than their peers without the assistance of others. Suppose Mark Cohen visits a store one day and finds the merchandise is poorly displayed, the floor is dirty, and sales clerks don't seem motivated to help customers. If he has a low need for achievement, he may point the problems out to the store manager and then leave. But if his need for achievement is high, he may well stay in the store for a while, personally supervising the necessary changes.

Although high-need achievers tend to be successful, they often do not achieve top management posts. The most common explanation is that although high need for achievement helps these people advance quickly through the ranks, the traits associated with the need often conflict with the requirements of high-level management positions. Because of the amount of work they are expected to do, top executives must be able to delegate tasks to others. In addition, they seldom receive immediate feedback, and they often must make decisions that are either more or less risky than those with which a high-need achiever would be comfortable.[24] High-need achievers tend to do well as individual entrepreneurs with little or no group reinforcement. Steve Jobs, cofounder of Apple Computer, and Bill Gates, cofounder of Microsoft, are both recognized as being high-need achievers.

The **need for affiliation** is the need for human companionship.

The Need for Affiliation Individuals also experience the **need for affiliation**, the need for human companionship.[25] Researchers recognize several ways in which people with a high need for affiliation differ from those with a lower need. Individuals with a high need tend to want reassurance and approval from others and usually are genuinely concerned about others' feelings. They are likely to act and think as they believe others want them to, especially those with whom they strongly identify and desire friendship. As we might expect, people with a strong need for affiliation most often work in jobs with a lot of interpersonal contact, such as sales and teaching positions.

Suppose Watanka Jackson is seeking a job as a petroleum field engineer, a job that will take her into remote areas for long periods of time with little interaction with coworkers. Aside from her academic training, one reason for the nature of her job search might be that she has a low need for affiliation. In contrast, a classmate of hers, William Pfeffer, may be seeking a job in the corporate headquarters of a petroleum company. His preferences might be dictated, at least in part, by a desire to be around other people in the workplace; he thus has a higher need for affiliation.

The **need for power** is the desire to control the resources in one's environment.

The Need for Power A third major individual need is the **need for power,** the desire to control one's environment, including financial, material, informational, and human resources.[26] People vary greatly along this dimension. Some individuals spend much time and energy seeking power; others avoid power whenever possible. People with a high need for power can be successful managers if three conditions are met. First, they must seek power for the betterment of the organization rather than for their own interests. Second, they must have a fairly low need for affiliation, because fulfilling a personal need for power may alienate others in the workplace. Third, they need a great deal of self-control to curb their desire for power when it threatens to interfere with effective organizational or interpersonal relationships.[27]

Process-Based Perspectives on Motivation

LEARNING OBJECTIVE

Explain the major process-based perspectives on motivation.

Process-based perspectives on motivation focus on how people behave in their efforts to satisfy their needs.

Equity theory focuses on people's desire to be treated with what they perceive as equity and to avoid perceived inequity.

Equity is the belief that one is being treated fairly in relation to others; inequity is the belief that one is being treated unfairly in relation to others.

Process-based perspectives on motivation deal with how motivation occurs. Rather than attempting to identify motivational stimuli, process perspectives focus on why people choose certain behavioral options to satisfy their needs and how they evaluate their satisfaction after they have attained those goals. Three useful process perspectives on motivation are the equity, expectancy, and goal-setting theories. We discuss the equity and expectancy theories here. Because of its much more applied focus, we cover goal-setting theory in Chapter 6.

Equity Theory of Motivation

The **equity theory** of motivation is based on the relatively simple premise that people in organizations want to be treated fairly.[28] The theory defines **equity** as the belief that one is being treated fairly in relation to others and *inequity* as the belief that one is being treated unfairly compared with others. Equity theory is just one of several theoretical formulations derived from social comparison processes. Social comparisons involve evaluating our own situation in terms of others' situations. In this chapter, we focus mainly on equity theory because it is the most highly developed of the social comparison approaches and the one that applies most directly to the work motivation of people in organizations.

Forming Equity Perceptions
People in organizations form perceptions about the equity of their treatment through a four-step process. First, they evaluate how they are being treated by the firm. Second, they assess how a "comparison-other" is being treated. The comparison-other might be a person in the same work group, someone in another part of the organization, or even a composite of several people throughout the organization.[29] Third, they compare their own circumstances with those of the comparison-other and use this comparison as the basis for forming an impression of either equity or inequity. Fourth, depending on the strength of this feeling, they may choose to pursue one or more of the alternatives discussed in the next section.

Equity theory describes the equity comparison process in terms of an input-to-outcome ratio. Inputs are an individual's contributions to the organization: such factors as education, experience, effort, and loyalty. Outcomes are what the person receives in return: pay, recognition, social relationships, intrinsic rewards, and similar things. In effect, then, this part of the equity process is essentially a personal assessment of one's psychological contract. A person's assessments of inputs and outcomes for both self and others are based partly on objective data (for example, the person's own salary) and partly on perceptions (such as the comparison-other's level of recognition). The equity comparison thus takes the following form:

$$\frac{\text{Outcome (self)}}{\text{Inputs (self)}} \text{ compared with } \frac{\text{Outcomes (other)}}{\text{Inputs (other)}}$$

If the two sides of this psychological equation are comparable, the person experiences a feeling of equity; if the two sides do not balance, a feeling of inequity results. We should stress, however, that a perception of equity does not require that the perceived outcomes and inputs be equal, only that their ratios be the same. A person may believe his comparison-other deserves to make more money because she works harder, thus making her higher ratio of outcome to input acceptable. Only if her outcomes seem disproportionate to her inputs does the comparison provoke a perception of inequity.

Responses to Equity and Inequity Figure 4.4 summarizes the results of an equity comparison. If a person feels equitably treated, she is generally motivated to maintain the status quo. For example, she will continue to provide the same level of input to the organization as long as her outcomes do not change and the inputs and outcomes of the comparison-other do not change. But a person who is experiencing inequity, real or imagined, is motivated to reduce it. Moreover, the greater the inequity, the stronger the level of motivation.

There are six common methods to reduce inequity.[30] First, we may change our own inputs. Thus, we may put more or less effort into the job, depending on which way the inequity lies, as a way to alter our ratio. If we believe we are being underpaid, for example, we may decide not to work as hard.

Second, we may change our own outcomes. We might, for example, demand a pay raise, seek additional avenues for growth and development, or even resort to stealing as a way to "get more" from the organization. Or we might alter our perceptions of the value of our current outcomes, perhaps by deciding our present level of job security is greater and more valuable than we originally thought.

A third, more complex response is to alter our perceptions of ourselves and our behavior. After perceiving an inequity, for example, we may change our original self-assessment and decide we are really contributing less but receiving more than we originally believed. For example, we might decide we are not really working as many hours as we first thought—for instance, that some of our time spent in the office is really just socializing and not really contributing to the organization.

Fourth, we may alter our perception of the comparison-other's inputs or outcomes. After all, much of our assessment of other people is based on perceptions, and perceptions can be changed. For example, if we feel underrewarded, we may decide our comparison-other is working more hours than we originally believed—say, by coming in on weekends and taking work home at night.

Fifth, we may change the object of comparison. We might conclude, for instance, that the current comparison-other is the boss's personal favorite, is unusually lucky, or has special skills and abilities. A different person would thus provide a more valid basis for comparison. Indeed, we might change comparison-others fairly often.

FIGURE 4.4

Responses to Perceptions of Equity and Inequity

People form equity perceptions by comparing their situation with that of someone else. If they perceive equity, they are motivated to maintain the current situation. If they perceive inequity, they are motivated to use one or more of the strategies shown here to reduce the inequity.

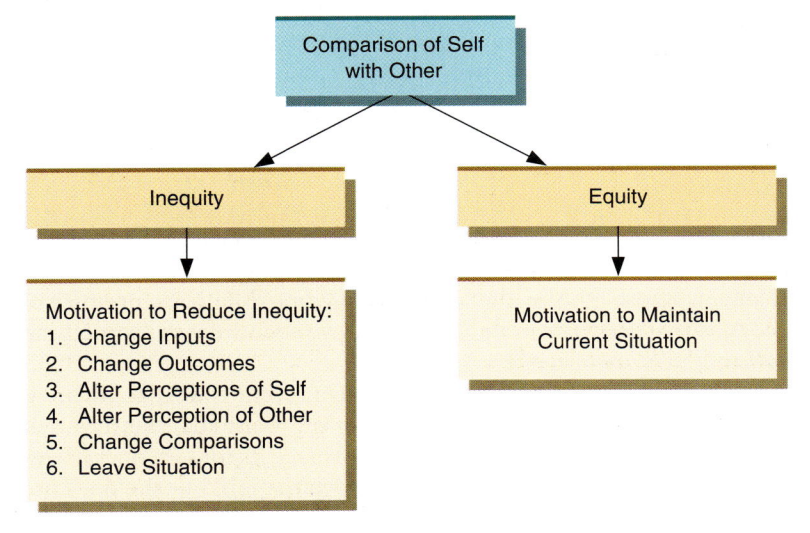

Comparison of Self with Other
→ Inequity
  Motivation to Reduce Inequity:
  1. Change Inputs
  2. Change Outcomes
  3. Alter Perceptions of Self
  4. Alter Perception of Other
  5. Change Comparisons
  6. Leave Situation
→ Equity
  Motivation to Maintain Current Situation

Finally, as a last resort, we may simply leave the situation; that is, we might decide that the only way to feel better about things is to be in a different situation altogether. Transferring to another department or seeking a new job may be the only way to reduce the inequity.

Evaluation and Implications Most research on equity theory has been narrowly focused, dealing with only one ratio: between pay (hourly and piece-rate) and the quality or quantity of worker output given overpayment and underpayment.[31] Findings support the predictions of equity theory quite consistently, especially when the worker feels underpaid. When people being paid on a piece-rate basis experience inequity, they tend to reduce their inputs by decreasing quality and to increase their outcomes by producing more units. When a person paid by the hour experiences inequity, the theory predicts an increase in quality and quantity if he feels overpaid and a decrease in quality and quantity if he feels underpaid. Research provides stronger support for responses to underpayment than for responses to overpayment, but overall, most studies appear to uphold the basic premises of the theory. One interesting recent twist on equity theory suggests that some people are more sensitive than others to perceptions of inequity. That is, some people pay a good deal of attention to their relative standing within the organization. Others focus more on their own situation without considering others' situations.[32]

Social comparisons clearly are a powerful factor in the workplace. For managers, the most important implication of equity theory concerns organizational rewards and reward systems. Because "formal" organizational rewards (pay, task assignments, etc.) are more easily observable than "informal" rewards (intrinsic satisfaction, feelings of accomplishment, etc.), they are often central to a person's perceptions of equity.

Equity theory offers managers three messages. First, everyone in the organization needs to understand the basis for rewards. If people are to be rewarded more for high-quality work than for quantity of work, for instance, that fact needs to be clearly communicated to everyone. Second, people tend to take a multifaceted view of their rewards; they perceive and experience a variety of rewards, some tangible and others intangible. Finally, people base their actions on their perceptions of reality. If two people make exactly the same salary, but each thinks the other makes more, each will base his or her experience of equity on the perception, not the reality. Hence, even if a manager believes two employees are being fairly rewarded, the employees themselves may not necessarily agree if their perceptions differ from the manager's.

Expectancy Theory of Motivation

Expectancy theory is a more inclusive model of motivation than equity theory. Over the years since its original formulation, the theory's scope and complexity have continued to grow.

The Basic Expectancy Model Victor Vroom is generally credited with first applying the theory to motivation in the workplace.[33] The theory attempts to determine how individuals choose among alternative behaviors. The basic premise of **expectancy theory** is that motivation depends on how much we want something and how likely we think we are to get it.

A simple example illustrates this premise. Suppose a recent college graduate is looking for her first managerial job. While scanning the want ads, she sees that Shell Oil is seeking a new executive vice president to oversee its foreign operations. The starting salary is $600,000. The student would love the job, but she does not

Expectancy theory suggests that people are motivated by how much they want something and the likelihood they perceive of getting it.

Chapter 4 Motivation in Organizations

The expectancy theory of motivation suggests that people are motivated to pursue outcomes that they value and believe they have a reasonable chance to attain. Rock star Bono and Treasury Secretary Paul O'Neil toured impoverished areas of Africa together. The publicity generated by the odd couple—the anti-establishment rocker and the conservative government official—helped bring renewed attention to the poverty issue. In a nutshell, the two individuals saw a problem, decided how they could help address it, and then worked together to accomplish their goal.

bother to apply because she recognizes that she has no chance of getting it. Reading on, she sees a position that involves scraping bubble gum from underneath desks in college classrooms. The starting pay is $5.85 an hour, and no experience is necessary. Again, she is unlikely to apply; even though she assumes she could get the job, she does not want it.

Then she comes across an advertisement for a management training position with a large company known for being an excellent place to work. No experience is necessary, the primary requirement is a college degree, and the starting salary is $37,000. She will probably apply for this position because (1) she wants it and (2) she thinks she has a reasonable chance of getting it. (Of course, this simple example understates the true complexity of most choices. Job-seeking students may have strong geographic preferences, have other job opportunities, and also be considering graduate school. Most decisions of this type, in fact, are quite complex.)

Figure 4.5 summarizes the basic expectancy model. The model's general components are effort (the result of motivated behavior), performance, and outcomes. Expectancy theory emphasizes the linkages among these elements, which are described in terms of expectancies and valences.

Effort-to-Performance Expectancy Effort-to-performance expectancy is a person's perception of the probability that effort will lead to successful performance. If we believe our effort will lead to higher performance, this expectancy is very strong, perhaps approaching a probability of 1.0, where 1.0 equals absolute certainty that the outcome will occur. If we believe our performance will be the same

Effort-to-performance expectancy is a person's perception of the probability that effort will lead to performance.

FIGURE 4.5

The Expectancy Theory of Motivation

The expectancy theory is the most complex model of employee motivation in organizations. As shown here, the key components of expectancy theory are effort-to-performance expectancy, performance-to-outcome expectancy, and outcomes, each of which has an associated valence. These components interact with effort, the environment, and the ability to determine an individual's performance.

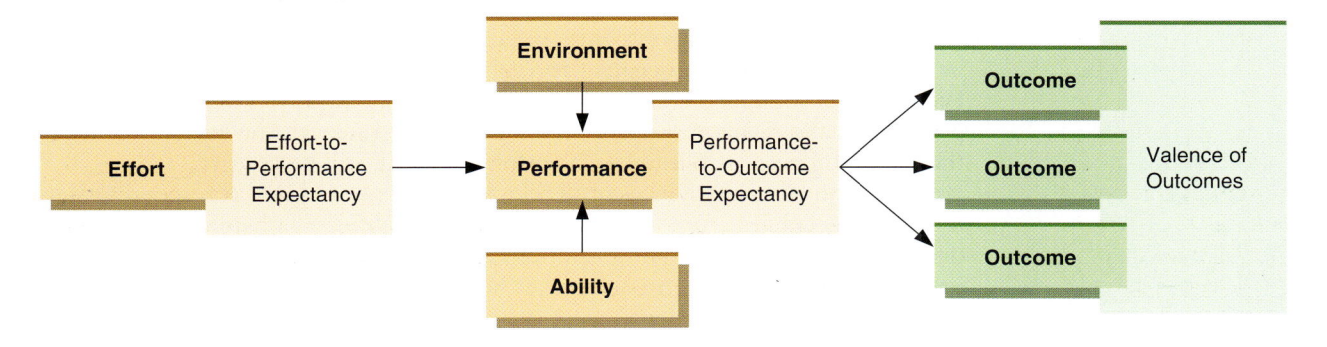

no matter how much effort we make, our expectancy is very low—perhaps as low as 0, meaning there is no probability that the outcome will occur. A person who thinks there is a moderate relationship between effort and subsequent performance—the normal circumstance—has an expectancy somewhere between 1.0 and 0. Mia Hamm, a star soccer player who believes she has a great chance of scoring higher than any opponent when she puts forth maximum effort, clearly sees a link between her effort and her performance.

Performance-to-Outcome Expectancy Performance-to-outcome expectancy is a person's perception of the probability that performance will lead to certain other outcomes. If a person thinks a high performer is certain to get a pay raise, this expectancy is close to 1.0. At the other extreme, a person who believes raises are entirely independent of performance has an expectancy close to 0. Finally, if a person thinks performance has some bearing on the prospects for a pay raise, his or her expectancy is somewhere between 1.0 and 0. In a work setting, several performance-to-outcome expectancies are relevant because, as Figure 4.5 shows, several outcomes might logically result from performance. Each outcome, then, has its own expectancy. Green Bay quarterback Brett Favre may believe that if he plays aggressively all the time (performance), he has a great chance of leading his team to the playoffs. Playing aggressively may win him individual honors such as the Most Valuable Player award, but he may also experience more physical trauma and throw more interceptions. (All three anticipated results are outcomes.)

Outcomes and Valences An **outcome** is anything that might potentially result from performance. High-level performance conceivably might produce such outcomes as a pay raise, a promotion, recognition from the boss—as well as fatigue, stress, or less break time—among others. The **valence** of an outcome is the relative attractiveness or unattractiveness—the value—of that outcome to the person. Pay raises, promotions, and recognition may all have positive valences, whereas fatigue, stress, and less break time may all have negative valences.

The strength of outcome valences varies from person to person. Work-related stress may be a significant negative factor for one person but only a slight annoyance to another. Similarly, a pay increase may have a strong positive valence for someone desperately in need of money; a slight positive valence for someone interested mostly in getting a promotion; or, for someone in an unfavorable tax position, even a negative valence!

The basic expectancy framework suggests that three conditions must be met before motivated behavior occurs. First, the effort-to-performance expectancy must be well above zero. That is, the worker must reasonably expect that exerting effort will produce high levels of performance. Second, the performance-to-outcome expectancies must be well above zero. Thus, the person must believe performance will realistically result in valued outcomes. Third, the sum of all the valences for the potential outcomes relevant to the person must be positive. One or more valences may be negative as long as the positives outweigh the negatives. For example, stress and fatigue may have moderately negative valences, but if pay, promotion, and recognition have very high positive valences, the overall valence of the set of outcomes associated with performance will still be positive.

Conceptually, the valences of all relevant outcomes and the corresponding pattern of expectancies are assumed to interact in an almost mathematical fashion to determine a person's level of motivation. Most people do assess likelihoods of and preferences for various consequences of behavior, but they seldom approach them in such a calculating manner.

Performance-to-outcome expectancy is an individual's perception of the probability that performance will lead to certain outcomes.

An **outcome** is anything that results from performing a particular behavior.

Valence is the degree of attractiveness or unattractiveness a particular outcome has for a person.

Chapter 4 Motivation in Organizations

The Porter-Lawler Model   The original presentation of expectancy theory placed it squarely in the mainstream of contemporary motivation theory. Since then, the model has been refined and extended many times. Most modifications have focused on identifying and measuring outcomes and expectancies. An exception is the variation of expectancy theory developed by Lyman Porter and Edward Lawler. These researchers used expectancy theory to develop a novel view of the relationship between employee satisfaction and performance.[34] Although the conventional wisdom was that satisfaction leads to performance, Porter and Lawler argued the reverse: If rewards are adequate, high levels of performance may lead to satisfaction.

The Porter-Lawler model appears in Figure 4.6. Some of its features are quite different from the original version of expectancy theory. For example, the extended model includes abilities, traits, and role perceptions. At the beginning of the motivational cycle, effort is a function of the value of the potential reward for the employee (its valence) and the perceived effort-reward probability (an expectancy). Effort then combines with abilities, traits, and role perceptions to determine actual performance.

Performance results in two kinds of rewards. Intrinsic rewards are intangible: a feeling of accomplishment, a sense of achievement, and so forth. Extrinsic rewards are tangible outcomes such as pay and promotion. The individual judges the value of his or her performance to the organization and uses social comparison processes (as in equity theory) to form an impression of the equity of the rewards received. If the rewards are regarded as equitable, the employee feels satisfied. In subsequent cycles, satisfaction with rewards influences the value of the rewards anticipated, and actual performance following effort influences future perceived effort-reward probabilities.

FIGURE 4.6

The Porter-Lawler Model

The Porter-Lawler expectancy model predicts that satisfaction is determined by the perceived equity of intrinsic and extrinsic rewards for performance. That is, rather than satisfaction causing performance, which many people might predict, this model argues that it is actually performance that eventually leads to satisfaction.

REFERENCE: Figure from Porter, Lyman W., and Edward E. Lawler, *Managerial Attitudes and Performance*. Copyright © 1968. Reproduced by permission of Edward E. Lawler III.

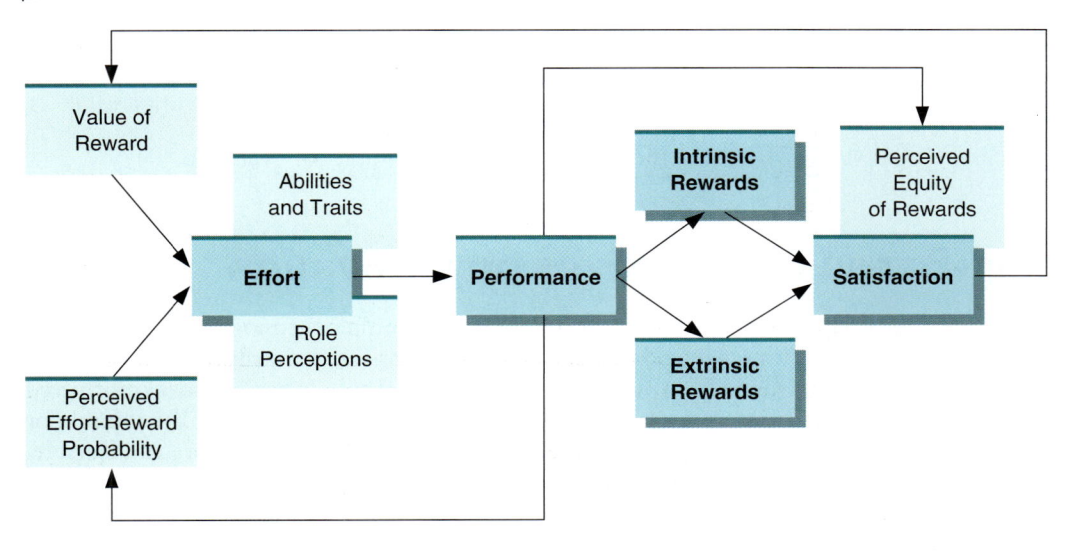

Evaluation and Implications Expectancy theory has been tested by many researchers in a variety of settings and using a variety of methods.[35] As noted earlier, the complexity of the theory has been both a blessing and a curse.[36] Nowhere is this double-edged quality more apparent than in the research undertaken to evaluate the theory. Several studies have supported various parts of the theory. For example, both kinds of expectancy and valence have been found to be associated with effort and performance in the workplace.[37] Research has also confirmed expectancy theory's claims that people will not engage in motivated behavior unless they (1) value the expected rewards, (2) believe their efforts will lead to performance, and (3) believe their performance will result in the desired rewards.[38]

However, expectancy theory is so complicated that researchers have found it difficult to test. In particular, the measures of various parts of the model may lack validity, and the procedures for investigating relationships among the variables have often been less scientific than researchers would like. Moreover, people are seldom as rational and objective in choosing behaviors as expectancy theory implies. Still, the logic of the model, combined with the consistent, albeit modest, research support for it, suggests the theory has much to offer.

Research also suggests that expectancy theory is more likely to explain motivation in the United States than in other countries. People in the United States tend to be very goal oriented and to believe they can influence their own success. Thus, under the right combinations of expectancies, valences, and outcomes, they will be highly motivated. Different patterns may exist in other countries. For example, many people from Moslem countries believe God determines the outcome of every behavior; thus, the concept of expectancy is not applicable.[39]

Because expectancy theory is so complex, it is difficult to apply directly in the workplace. A manager would need to figure out what rewards each employee wants and how valuable those rewards are to each person, measure the various expectancies, and finally adjust the relationships to create motivation. Nevertheless, expectancy theory offers several important guidelines for the practicing manager. Following are some of the more fundamental guidelines:

1. Determine the primary outcomes each employee wants.
2. Decide what levels and kinds of performance are needed to meet organizational goals.
3. Make sure the desired levels of performance are possible.
4. Link desired outcomes and desired performance.
5. Analyze the situation for conflicting expectancies.
6. Make sure the rewards are large enough.
7. Make sure the overall system is equitable for everyone.[40]

Learning-Based Perspectives on Motivation

LEARNING OBJECTIVE
Describe learning-based perspectives on motivation.

Learning is another key component in employee motivation. In any organization, employees quickly learn which behaviors are rewarded and which are ignored or punished. Thus, learning plays a critical role in maintaining motivated behavior. **Learning** is a relatively permanent change in behavior or behavioral potential that results from direct or indirect experience. For example, we can learn to use a new software application program by practicing and experimenting with its various functions and options.

Chapter 4 Motivation in Organizations

Learning is a relatively permanent change in behavior or behavioral potential resulting from direct or indirect experience.

How Learning Occurs

Our understanding of how learning occurs has evolved from a simple and straightforward process to a much richer and more sophisticated one. The former is best represented by the traditional view, also called classical conditioning, while the latter is reflected in the contemporary view of learning as a cognitive process.

The Traditional View: Classical Conditioning The most influential historical approach to learning is classical conditioning, developed by Ivan Pavlov in his famous experiments with dogs.[41] **Classical conditioning** is a simple form of learning that links a conditioned response with an unconditioned stimulus. In organizations, however, only simple behaviors and responses can be learned in this manner. For example, suppose an employee receives bad news one day from his boss. The employee could come to associate, say, the color of the boss's suit on that day with bad news. Thus, the next time the boss wears that suit to the office, the employee may experience dread.

Classical conditioning is a simple form of learning that links a conditioned response with an unconditioned stimulus.

This form of learning, however, is obviously simplistic and not directly relevant to motivation. Learning theorists soon recognized that although classical conditioning offered some interesting insights into the learning process, it was inadequate as an explanation of human learning. For one thing, classical conditioning relies on simple cause-and-effect relationships between one stimulus and one response; it cannot deal with the more complex forms of learned behavior that typify human beings. For another, classical conditioning ignores the concept of choice; it assumes behavior is reflexive, or involuntary. Therefore, this perspective cannot explain situations in which people consciously and rationally choose one course of action from among many. Because of these shortcomings of classical conditioning, theorists eventually moved on to other approaches that seemed more useful in explaining the processes associated with complex learning.

The Contemporary View: Learning as a Cognitive Process Although not tied to a single theory or model, contemporary learning theory generally views learning as a cognitive process; that is, it assumes people are conscious, active participants in how they learn.[42]

First, the cognitive view suggests that people draw on their experiences and use past learning as a basis for their present behavior. These experiences represent knowledge, or cognitions. For example, an employee faced with a choice of job assignments will use previous experiences in deciding which one to accept. Second, people make choices about their behavior. The employee recognizes that she has two alternatives and chooses one. Third, people recognize the consequences of their choices. Thus, when the employee finds the job assignment rewarding and fulfilling, she will recognize that the choice was a good one and will understand why. Finally, people evaluate those consequences and add them to prior learning, which affects future choices. Faced with the same job choices next year, the employee will probably be motivated to choose the same one. As implied earlier, several perspectives on learning take a cognitive view. Perhaps foremost among them is reinforcement theory. Although reinforcement theory per se is not really new, it has been applied to organizational settings only in the last few years.

Reinforcement Theory and Learning

Reinforcement theory is based on the idea that behavior is a function of its consequences.

Reinforcement theory (also called *operant conditioning*) is generally associated with the work of B. F. Skinner.[43] In its simplest form, **reinforcement theory** suggests that behavior is a function of its consequences.[44] Behavior that results in pleasant consequences is more likely to be repeated (the employee will be motivated to repeat the current behavior), and behavior that results in unpleasant consequences is less likely to be repeated (the employee will be motivated to engage in different behaviors). Reinforcement theory also suggests that in any given situation, people explore a variety of possible behaviors. Future behavioral choices are affected by the consequences of earlier behaviors. Cognitions, as already noted, also play an important role. Therefore, rather than assuming the mechanical stimulus-response linkage suggested by the traditional classical view of learning, contemporary theorists believe people consciously explore different behaviors and systematically choose those that result in the most desirable outcomes.

Suppose a new employee at Monsanto in St. Louis wants to learn the best way to get along with his boss. At first, the employee is very friendly and informal, but the boss responds by acting aloof and, at times, annoyed. Because the boss does not react positively, the employee is unlikely to continue this behavior. In fact, he then starts acting more formal and professional, and finds the boss much more receptive to this posture. The employee will probably continue this new set of behaviors because they have resulted in positive consequences.

Types of Reinforcement in Organizations The consequences of behavior are called **reinforcement.** Managers can use various kinds of reinforcement to affect employee behavior. There are four basic forms of reinforcement: positive reinforcement, avoidance, extinction, and punishment.

Positive reinforcement is a reward or other desirable consequence that follows behavior. Providing positive reinforcement after a particular behavior motivates employees to maintain or increase the frequency of that behavior. A compliment from the boss after an employee has completed a difficult job and a salary increase following a worker's period of high performance are examples of positive reinforcement. This type of reinforcement has been used at Corning's ceramics factory in Virginia, where workers receive bonuses for pulling blemished materials from assembly lines before they go into more expensive stages of production.[45]

Avoidance, also known as **negative reinforcement,** is another means of increasing the frequency of desirable behavior. Rather than receiving a reward following a desirable behavior, the person is given the opportunity to avoid an unpleasant consequence. For example, suppose a boss habitually criticizes employees who dress casually. To avoid criticism, an employee may routinely dress to suit the supervisor's tastes. The employee is thus motivated to engage in desirable behavior (at least from the supervisor's viewpoint) to avoid an unpleasant, or aversive, consequence.

Extinction decreases the frequency of behavior, especially behavior that was previously rewarded. If rewards are withdrawn for behaviors that were previously reinforced, the behaviors will probably become less frequent and eventually die out. For example, a manager with a small staff may encourage frequent visits from subordinates as a way to keep in touch with what is going on. Positive reinforcement might include cordial conversation, attention to subordinates' concerns, and encouragement to come in again soon. As the staff grows, however, the manager may find that such unstructured conversations make it difficult to get her own job done. She then might begin to brush off casual conversation and reward only to-the-point, "business" conversations. Withdrawing the rewards for casual chatting will probably extinguish that behavior. We should also note that if managers, inadvertently or otherwise, stop rewarding valuable behaviors such as good performance, those behaviors also may become extinct.

Reinforcement is the consequences of behavior.

Positive reinforcement is a reward or other desirable consequence that a person receives after exhibiting behavior.

Avoidance, or negative reinforcement, is the opportunity to avoid or escape from an unpleasant circumstance after exhibiting behavior.

Extinction decreases the frequency of behavior by eliminating a reward or desirable consequence that follows that behavior.

weaker needs for personal growth and development are less likely to be motivated by the core job characteristics.

Figure 5.3 expands the basic job characteristics theory by incorporating general guidelines to help managers implement it.[13] Managers can use such means as forming natural work units (that is, grouping similar tasks together), combining existing tasks into more complex ones, establishing direct relationships between workers and clients, increasing worker autonomy through vertical job loading, and opening feedback channels. Theoretically, such actions should enhance the motivational properties of each task. Using these guidelines, sometimes in adapted form, several firms, including 3M, Volvo, AT&T, Xerox, Texas Instruments, and Motorola, have successfully implemented job design changes.[14]

Much research has been devoted to this approach to job design.[15] This research has generally supported the theory, although performance has seldom been found to correlate with job characteristics.[16] Several apparent weaknesses in the theory have also come to light. First, the measures used to test the theory are not always as valid and reliable as they should be. Further, research has frequently failed to support the role of individual differences. Finally, guidelines for implementation are not specific; hence, managers usually must tailor them to their own particular circumstances. Still, the theory remains a popular perspective on studying and changing jobs.[17]

FIGURE 5.3

Implementing the Job Characteristics Theory

Managers should use a set of implementation guidelines when applying the job characteristics theory to their organizations. This figure shows some of these guidelines. For example, managers combine tasks, form natural work units, establish client relationships, vertically load jobs, and open feedback channels.

Source: J. R. Hackman, G. R. Oldham, R. Janson, and K. Purdy. "A New Stage for Job Enrichment." which appears in *The California Management Review,* vol. 17, no. 4. Copyright © 1975, by The Regents of the University of California. By permission of The Regents.

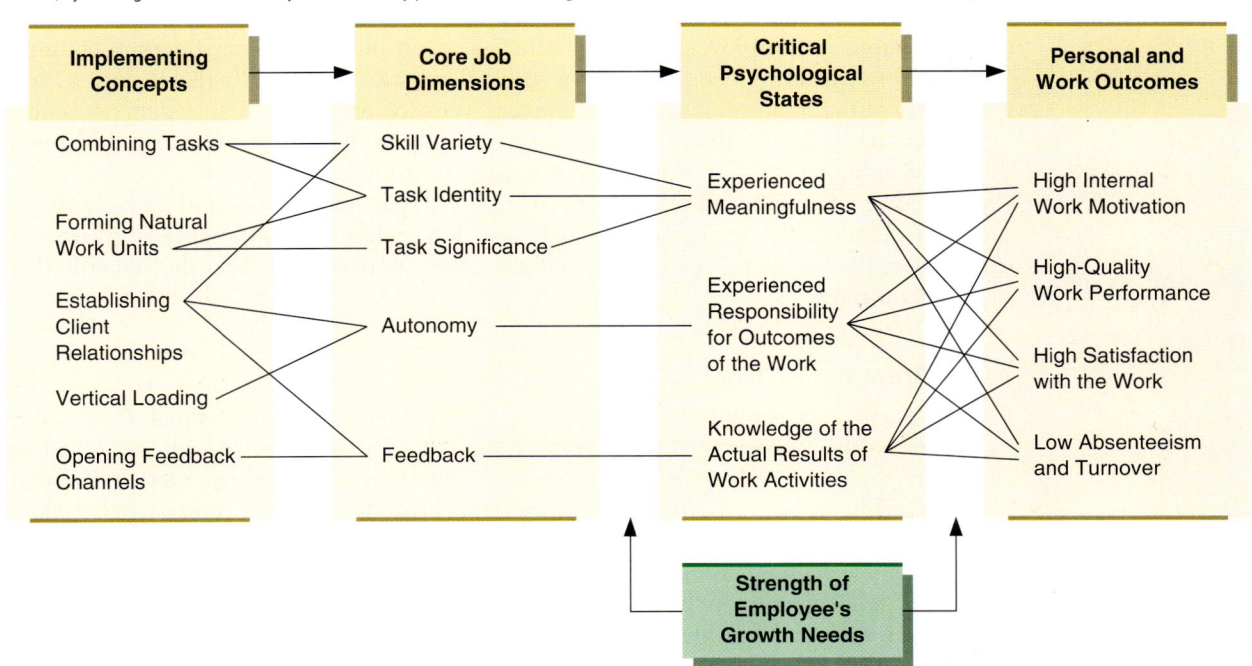

Implementing Concepts	Core Job Dimensions	Critical Psychological States	Personal and Work Outcomes
Combining Tasks	Skill Variety	Experienced Meaningfulness	High Internal Work Motivation
Forming Natural Work Units	Task Identity		High-Quality Work Performance
Establishing Client Relationships	Task Significance	Experienced Responsibility for Outcomes of the Work	High Satisfaction with the Work
Vertical Loading	Autonomy		
Opening Feedback Channels	Feedback	Knowledge of the Actual Results of Work Activities	Low Absenteeism and Turnover

Strength of Employee's Growth Needs

Participation, Empowerment, and Motivation

LEARNING OBJECTIVE

Discuss the relationship among participation, empowerment, and motivation.

Participative management and empowerment are two more important methods managers can use to enhance employee motivation. In a sense, participation and empowerment are extensions of job design because each fundamentally alters how employees in an organization perform their jobs. **Participation** occurs when employees have a voice in decisions about their own work. (One important model that helps managers determine the optimal level of employee participation, the Vroom-Yetton-Jago model, is discussed in Chapter 10.) **Empowerment** is the process of enabling workers to set their own work goals, make decisions, and solve problems within their spheres of responsibility and authority. Thus, empowerment is a somewhat broader concept that promotes participation in a wide variety of areas, including but not limited to the work itself, the work context, and the work environment.[18]

Participation entails giving employees a voice in making decisions about their own work.

Empowerment is the process of enabling workers to set their own work goals, make decisions, and solve problems within their sphere of responsibility and authority.

Early Perspectives on Participation and Empowerment

The human relations movement in vogue from the 1930s through the 1950s (see Chapter 1) assumed employees who are happy and satisfied will work harder. This view stimulated management interest in having workers participate in a variety of organizational activities. Managers hoped that if employees had a chance to participate in decision making concerning their work environment, they would be satisfied, and this satisfaction would supposedly result in improved performance. However, managers tended to see employee participation merely as a way to increase satisfaction rather than as a source of potentially valuable input. Eventually managers began to recognize that employee input was useful in itself, apart from its presumed effect on satisfaction. In other words, they came to see employees as valued human resources who can contribute to organizational effectiveness.[19]

The role of participation and empowerment in motivation can be expressed in terms of both the need-based perspectives and the expectancy theory discussed in Chapter 4. Employees who participate in decision making may be more committed to executing decisions properly. Furthermore, successfully making a decision, executing it, and then seeing the positive consequences can help satisfy one's need for achievement, provide recognition and responsibility, and enhance self-esteem. Simply being asked to participate in organizational decision making may also enhance an employee's self-esteem. In addition, participation should help clarify expectancies; that is, participating in decision making should enable employees to better understand the linkage between their performance and the rewards they want most.

Areas of Participation

At one level, employees can participate in addressing questions and making decisions about their own jobs. Instead of just telling them how to do their jobs, for example, managers can ask employees to make their own decisions about how to do them. Based on their own expertise and experience with their tasks, workers may be able to improve their own productivity. In many situations, they may also be well qualified to make decisions about what materials to use, what tools to use, and so forth.

Managers might also let workers make decisions about administrative matters, such as work schedules. If jobs are relatively independent of one another, employees might decide when to change shifts, take breaks, go to lunch, and so forth. A

Chapter 5 Job Design and Work Structures

"DON'T FORGET TO EMPTY THE SUGGESTION BOX."

Participation and empowerment can play powerful roles in motivating employees. But for these benefits to have any hope of fruition, managers must ensure their efforts to involve employees in decision making are sincere. For example, if employees sense that their manager is asking for their opinion only for symbolic purposes and has already made a decision, things can backfire in unfortunate ways.
©Harley Schwadron.

work group or team might also be able to schedule vacations and days off for all its members. Furthermore, employees are getting increasing opportunities to participate in broader issues of product quality. Participation of this type has become a hallmark of successful Japanese and other international firms, and many U.S. companies have followed suit.[20]

Techniques and Issues in Empowerment

In recent years, many organizations have actively sought ways to extend participation beyond the traditional areas. Simple techniques such as suggestion boxes and question-and-answer meetings allow a certain degree of participation, for example. The basic motive has been to better capitalize on the assets and capabilities inherent in all employees. Thus, many managers today prefer the term *empowerment* to *participation* because it implies a more comprehensive involvement.

One method some firms use to empower their workers is the use of work teams. This method grew out of early attempts to use what Japanese firms call *quality circles*. A quality circle is a group of employees who voluntarily meet regularly to identify and propose solutions to problems related to quality. This use of quality circles quickly grew to encompass a wider array of work groups, now generally called *work teams*. These teams are groups of employees empowered to plan, organize, direct, and control their own work. Their supervisor plays the role of a "coach" rather than a traditional "boss." We discuss work teams more fully in Chapter 9.

Another method some organizations use to facilitate empowerment is to change their overall method of organizing. The basic pattern is for an organization to eliminate layers from its hierarchy, thereby becoming much more decentralized. Power, responsibility, and authority are delegated as far down the organization as possible, putting control of work squarely in the hands of those who actually do it.

Regardless of the specific technique used, however, empowerment enhances organizational effectiveness only if certain conditions exist. First, the organization must be sincere in its efforts to spread power and autonomy to lower levels; token efforts to promote participation in just a few areas are unlikely to succeed. This point is clearly illustrated in the cartoon. Second, the organization must be committed to maintaining participation and empowerment. Workers will be resentful if they are given more control only to later have it reduced or taken away altogether. Third, the organization must be systematic and patient in its efforts to empower workers. Turning over too much control too quickly can spell disaster. Finally, the organization must be prepared to increase its commitment to training. Employees receiving more freedom concerning how they work are likely to need additional training to help them exercise that freedom most effectively.

Alternative Work Arrangements

LEARNING OBJECTIVE
Identify and describe key alternative work arrangements.

Beyond the actual redesigning of jobs and the use of participation and empowerment, many organizations today are experimenting with a variety of alternative work arrangements. These arrangements are generally intended to enhance employee motivation and performance by giving workers more flexibility regarding how and when they work. Among the more popular alternative work arrangements are variable work schedules, flexible work schedules, job sharing, and telecommuting.[21] As the Business of Ethics box points out, adopting any of these techniques is not necessarily a straightforward decision.

BUSINESS OF ETHICS

Safety Starts at Home

It's an interesting convergence of legal and social trends. Under pressure from both workers and employers, the Occupational Safety and Health Administration (OSHA) recently changed the way it protects workers who work for their employers at home.

Prior to the new ruling, employers who asked workers to work from home—for example, by telecommuting or doing home manufacturing—were legally liable for ensuring that employees had a safe and hazard-free working environment at all times. That meant employers had to inspect workers' homes to ensure that all safety requirements were being met. For example, the employer had to verify that there were two external exits, no lead paint had been used on the walls, the employee's chairs were ergonomically sound, and the indoor air quality met OSHA standards. This stipulation led to somewhat absurd decisions, such as corporations allowing employees to use home telephones but not home computers if the employees' monitors did not meet low-radiation requirements. An employer could also be held accountable for employees' unsafe behaviors, such as plugging too many electrical devices into one power outlet or standing on a chair rather than on a ladder to change a light bulb.

The OSHA ruling was very broad, requiring employers to take a proactive stance on home safety. "Even when the workplace is in a designated area in an employee's home, the employer retains some degree of control over the conditions of the 'work at home' agreement. Employers should exercise reasonable diligence to identify in advance the possible hazards associated with particular home work assignments... [This] may necessitate an on-site examination of the working environment by the employer," according to a 1999 OSHA publication for employers. Employers found the requirements burdensome, especially as more workers began telecommuting. Employees, too, thought the requirements were too intrusive, invading the privacy of their homes.

"If you would be liable for your employees on-site, then you wouldn't be less liable just because you have someone working off-site."—Nicole Goluboff, attorney and specialist in the legal implications of telecommuting

Consequently, in 2000, OSHA backed down from its position on requirements, and the new policy became law in January 2001. However, it's still not clear how much responsibility a company has if a worker is injured at home. And a new area of growing concern has emerged: cybercrime. Is a company liable if a client's confidential information is stolen because an employee's home computer didn't have hacker protection? What if the employee uses a home computer for business and also peddles online pornography? Nicole Goluboff, an attorney specializing in the legal implications of telecommuting, says, "If you would be liable for your employees on-site, then you wouldn't be less liable just because you have someone working off-site." Who knows where all this will lead? Only time—and the courts, no doubt—will tell.

References: Jeremy Quittner, "OSHA Won't Come Knockin' on the Home Office Door," *BusinessWeek*, March 3, 2000, pp. 96–98; "Occupational Injury and Illness Recording and Reporting Requirements," Occupational Health and Safety Administration website, January 19, 2001, www.osha.gov on May 6, 2004; Chris Sandlund, "Telecommuting: A Legal Primer," *BusinessWeek*, March 20, 2000 (quotation), pp. 42–43.

Variable Work Schedules

Many exceptions exist, of course, but the traditional work schedule in the United States has long been days that start at 8:00 or 9:00 in the morning and end at 5:00 in the evening, five days a week (and, of course, managers often work many additional hours outside of this time period). Although exact starting and ending times vary, most companies in other countries have also used a well-defined work schedule. Such a schedule, however, makes it difficult for workers to attend to routine personal business: going to the bank, seeing a doctor or dentist for a checkup, attending a parent-teacher conference, getting an automobile serviced, and so forth. Employees locked into this work schedule may find they need to take a sick day or vacation day to handle these activities. On a more psychological level, some people may feel so powerless and constrained by their job schedules that they grow resentful and frustrated.

To help counter these problems, one alternative some businesses use is a compressed workweek schedule.[22] An employee following a **compressed workweek schedule** works a full forty-hour week in fewer than the traditional five days. Typically this schedule involves working ten hours a day for four days, leaving an extra day off. Another alternative is for employees to work slightly less than ten hours a day but complete the forty hours by lunchtime on Friday. A few firms have tried having employees work twelve hours a day for three days, followed by four days off. Firms that have used these forms of compressed workweeks include John Hancock, ARCO, and R. J. Reynolds. One problem with this schedule is that if everyone in the organization is off at the same time, the firm may have no one on duty to handle problems or deal with outsiders on the off day. On the other hand, if a company staggers days off across the workforce, people who don't get the more desirable days off (Monday and Friday, for most people) may be jealous or resentful. Another problem is that when employees put in too much time in a single day, they tend to tire and perform at a lower level later in the day.

A popular schedule some organizations are beginning to use is called a "nine-eighty" schedule. Under this arrangement, an employee works a traditional schedule one week and a compressed schedule the next, getting every other Friday off. That is, the employee works eighty hours (the equivalent of two weeks of full-time work) in nine days. By alternating the regular and compressed schedules across half of its workforce, the organization is staffed at all times but still gives employees two additional full days off each month. Shell Oil and Amoco Chemicals currently use this schedule.

In a **compressed workweek**, employees work a full forty-hour week in fewer than the traditional five days.

Flexible Work Schedules

Another promising alternative work arrangement is **flexible work schedules,** sometimes called **flextime.** With the compressed workweek schedules previously discussed, employees get time off during normal working hours, but they must still follow a regular and defined schedule on the days they do work. Although flextime usually gives employees less say about what days they work, it also allows them more personal control over the times when they work on those days.[23]

Figure 5.4 illustrates how flextime works. The workday is broken down into two categories: flexible time and core time. All employees must be at their workstations during core time, but they can choose their own schedules during flexible time. Thus, one employee may choose to start work early in the morning and leave in mid-afternoon, another to start in the late morning and work until late afternoon, and a third to start early in the morning, take a long lunch break, and work until late afternoon.

Flexible work schedules, or **flextime**, give employees more personal control over the hours they work each day.

6:00 A.M.	9:00 A.M. – 11:00 A.M.		1:00 P.M. – 3:00 P.M.		6:00 P.M.
Flexible Time	Core Time	Flexible Time	Core Time	Flexible Time	

FIGURE 5.4

Flexible Work Schedules

Flexible work schedules are an important new work arrangement used in some organizations today. All employees must be at work during "core time." In the hypothetical example shown here, core time is from 9 to 11 A.M. and 1 to 3 P.M. The other time, then, is flexible: Employees can come and go as they please during that time, as long as the total time spent at work meets organizational expectations.

The major advantage of this approach, as already noted, is that workers get to tailor their workday to fit their personal needs. A person who needs to visit the dentist in the late afternoon can just start work early; a person who stays out late one night can start work late the next day; and an employee who needs to run some errands during lunch can take a longer midday break. On the other hand, flextime is more difficult to manage because others in the organization may not be sure when a person will be available for meetings other than during the core time. Expenses such as utilities will also be higher since the organization must remain open for a longer period each day.

Some organizations have experimented with a plan in which workers set their own hours but then must follow that schedule each day. Others allow workers to modify their own schedule each day. Organizations that have used the flexible work schedule method include Control Data Corporation, DuPont, Metropolitan Life, Chevron Texaco, and some offices of the U.S. government.

Job Sharing

In **job sharing**, two or more part-time employees share one full-time job.

Yet another potentially useful alternative work arrangement is job sharing. In **job sharing**, two part-time employees share one full-time job. Job sharing may be desirable for people who want to work only part-time or when job markets are tight. For its part, the organization can accommodate the preferences of a broader range of employees and may benefit from the talents of more people. Perhaps the simplest job-sharing arrangement to visualize is that of a receptionist. To share this job, one worker would staff the receptionist's desk from, say, 8:00 A.M. to noon each day, the office might close from noon to 1:00 P.M., and a second worker would staff the desk from 1:00 P.M. until 5:00 P.M. To the casual observer or visitor to the office, the fact that two people serve in one job is essentially irrelevant. The responsibilities of the job in the morning and the afternoon are not likely to be interdependent. Thus, the position can easily be broken down into two or perhaps even more components.

Organizations sometimes offer job sharing to entice more workers to the organization. If a particular kind of job is difficult to fill, a job-sharing arrangement may make it more attractive to more people. There are also cost benefits for the organization. Since the employees may be working only part-time, the organization does not have to give them the same benefits that full-time employees receive. The organization can also tap into a wider array of skills when it provides job-sharing arrangements. The firm gets the advantage of the two sets of skills from one job.

Job sharing is an alternative work arrangement in which two part-time employees share one full-time job. Amy Frank (left) and Denise Brown share the job of vice president of fixed-income sales at Fleet Boston. Frank works all day Monday and Tuesday, and Wednesday morning; Brown works Wednesday afternoon and all day Thursday and Friday. This arrangement allows each to pursue a career, earn a reasonable income, and spend time at home with their children.

Some workers like job sharing because it gives them flexibility and freedom. Certain workers, for example, may want only part-time work. Stepping into a shared job may also give them a chance to work in an organization that otherwise wants to hire only full-time employees. When the job sharer isn't working, she or he may attend school, take care of the family, or simply enjoy leisure time.

Job sharing does not work for every organization, and it isn't attractive to all workers, but it has produced enough success stories to suggest it will be around for a long time. Among the organizations particularly committed to job-sharing programs are the Bank of Montreal, United Airlines, and the National School Board Association. Each of these organizations, and dozens more, reports that job sharing has become a critical part of its human resource system. Although job sharing has not been scientifically evaluated, it appears to be a useful alternative to traditional work scheduling.

Telecommuting

Telecommuting is a work arrangement in which employees spend part of their time working off-site.

A relatively new approach to alternative work arrangements is **telecommuting,** in which employees spend part of their time working off-site, usually at home. By using email, computer networks, and other technology, many employees can maintain close contact with their organizations and do as much work at home as they could in their offices. The increased power and sophistication of modern communication technology is making telecommuting easier and easier.

Many employees like telecommuting because it gives them added flexibility. By spending one or two days a week at home, for instance, they have the same kind of flexibility to manage personal activities as by flextime or compressed schedules allow. Some employees also believe they get more work done at home because they are less likely to be interrupted. Organizations may benefit for several reasons as well: They can reduce absenteeism and turnover since employees will need to take less "formal" time off, and they can save on facilities such as parking spaces because fewer people will be at work on any given day.

On the other hand, many employees do not thrive under this arrangement. Some feel isolated and miss the social interaction of the workplace. Others simply lack the self-control and discipline to walk from the breakfast table to their desk and start work. As noted in the Business of Ethics box on page 130, another concern for some organizations is the safety and health of their employees who work at home. Managers may also encounter coordination difficulties in scheduling meetings and other activities that require face-to-face contact. Still, given the boom in communication technology and the pressures for flexibility, many more organizations will no doubt use telecommuting in the years to come.[24]

Synopsis

Managers seek to enhance employee performance by capitalizing on the potential for motivated behavior to improve performance. Methods often used to translate motivation into performance involve job design, employee participation and empowerment, alternative work arrangements, performance management, goal setting, and rewards.

Job design is how organizations define and structure jobs. Historically there was a general trend toward increasingly specialized jobs, but more recently the movement has consistently been away from extreme specialization. Two early alternatives to specialization were job rotation and job enlargement. Job enrichment approaches stimulated considerable interest in job design.

The job characteristics theory grew from early work on job enrichment. One basic premise of this theory is that jobs can be described in terms of a specific set of motivational characteristics. Another is that managers should work to enhance the presence of those motivational characteristics in jobs but also take individual differences into account.

Participative management and empowerment can help improve employee motivation in many business settings. New management practices, such as the use of various kinds of work teams and of flatter, more decentralized methods of organizing, are intended to empower employees throughout the organization. Organizations that want to empower their employees need to understand a variety of issues as they implement participation.

Alternative work arrangements are commonly used today to enhance motivated job performance. Among the more popular alternative arrangements are compressed workweeks, flexible work schedules, job sharing, and telecommuting.

Discussion Questions

1. What are the primary advantages and disadvantages of job specialization? Were they the same in the early days of mass production?
2. Under what circumstances might job enlargement be especially effective? Especially ineffective? What about job rotation?
3. What trends today might suggest a return to job specialization?
4. What are the strengths and weaknesses of job enrichment? When might this approach be useful?
5. Do you agree or disagree that individual differences affect how people respond to their jobs? Explain.
6. What are the primary similarities and differences between job enrichment and the job characteristics approach?
7. What are the motivational consequences of participative management from the perspective of expectancy and equity theories?
8. What motivational problems might result from an organization's attempt to set up work teams?
9. Which form of alternative work schedule might you prefer?
10. Do you think you would like telecommuting? Why or why not?

Organizational Behavior Case for Discussion

Employee Participation at Chaparral Steel

Chaparral Steel enjoys a stellar reputation as one of the most effective firms in the steel industry. Chaparral was founded in 1973 in a small town near Dallas and today enjoys annual sales of more than $500 million. In earlier times, most steel companies, such as U.S. Steel (now USX) and Bethlehem Steel, were large, bureaucratic operations. However, increased competition from low-cost foreign steel firms, especially in Japan and Korea, has caused major problems for these manufacturers with their high overhead costs and inflexible modes of operation.

These competitive pressures, in turn, have also led to the formation of so-called minimills such as Chaparral. These minimills are consciously designed to be much smaller and more flexible than the traditional steel giants. Because of their size, technology, and flexibility, these firms are able to maintain much lower production costs and respond more quickly to customer requests. Today Chaparral is recognized as one of the best of this new breed of steel companies. For example, whereas most mills produce 1 ton of steel with an average of 3 to 5 hours of labor, Chaparral produces a ton with fewer than 1.2 hours of labor. Chaparral has also successfully avoided all efforts to unionize its employees.

Since its inception, Chaparral has been led by Gordon Forward. Forward knew that if Chaparral was going to succeed with what was then a new strategic orientation in the industry, it would also need to be managed in new and different ways. One of the first things he decided to do as part of his new approach was to systematically avoid the traditional barriers that tend to arise between management and labor, especially in older industries such as steel. For example, he mandated that there would be neither reserved parking spaces in the parking lot nor a separate dining area inside the plant for managers. Today everyone dresses casually at the work site, and people throughout the firm are on a first-name basis with one another. Workers take their lunch and coffee breaks whenever they choose, and coffee is provided free for everyone.

Forward also insisted that all employees be paid on a salary basis—no time clocks or time sheets for anyone, from the president down to the custodians. Workers are organized into teams, and each team selects its own "leader." The teams also interview and select new members as needed and are responsible for planning their own work, setting their own work schedules, and even allocating vacation days among themselves. Teams are also responsible for implementing any necessary disciplinary actions toward a member. Finally, no one has a monotonous, narrowly defined job to be performed on a continuous basis. Instead, each team is responsible for an array of tasks and functions; the teams themselves are encouraged to ensure that all members know how to perform all the assigned tasks and functions and to rotate people across them regularly.

Forward clearly believes in trusting everyone in the organization. For example, when the firm recently needed a new rolling mill lathe, it budgeted $1 million for its purchase, then put the purchase decision in the hands of an operating machinist. The machinist, in turn, investigated various options, visited other mills in Japan and Europe, and then recommended an alternative piece of machinery costing less than half of the budgeted amount. Forward also helped pioneer an innovative concept called "open-book management": Any employee at Chaparral can see any document, record, or other piece of information at any time and for any reason.

Chaparral also recognizes the importance of investing in and rewarding people. Continuous education is an integral part of the firm's culture, with a variety of classes offered all the time. For example, one recent slate of classes included metallurgy, electronics, finance, and English. The classes are intended to benefit both individual workers and the organization as a whole. The classes are scheduled on-site and in the evening. Some include community college credit (tuition is charged for these classes, although the company pays for half the costs), while others are noncredit only (there are no charges for these classes). Forward has a goal that at any given time, at least 85 percent of Chaparral's employees will be enrolled in at least one class.

Everyone also participates in the good—and the bad—times at Chaparral. For example, all workers have a guaranteed base salary that is adequate but, by itself, is below the standard market rate. However, in addition to their base pay, employees get pay-for-performance bonuses based on their individual achievements. Finally, companywide bonuses are paid to everyone on a quarterly basis. These bonuses are tied to overall company performance. The typical bonuses increase an employee's total compensation to a level well above the standard market rate. Thus, hard work and dedication on everyone's part means all employees can benefit.

Case Questions

1. Describe how managers at Chaparral Steel appear to be implementing various need- and process-based theories of motivation.
2. Discuss the apparent role and nature of job design at Chaparral.
3. Describe how Chaparral uses participation and empowerment to motivate its workers.

References: "Chaparral Steel," Foundation for Enterprise Development website (reporting the U.S. Department of Labor, Office of the American Workplace, "best practices" winners), www.fed.org on April 27, 2004; John Case, "HR Learns How to Open the Books," *HRMagazine*, May 1998, pp. 70–76; John Case, "Opening the Books," *Harvard Business Review*, March–April 1997, pp. 118–129; Brian Dumaine, "Chaparral Steel: Unleash Workers and Cut Costs," *Fortune*, May 18, 1992, p. 88.

Experiencing Organizational Behavior

Learning About Job Design

Purpose: This exercise will help you assess the processes involved in designing jobs to make them more motivating.

Format: Working in small groups, you will diagnose the motivating potential of an existing job, compare its motivating potential to that of other jobs, suggest ways to redesign the job, and then assess the effects of your redesign suggestions on other aspects of the workplace.

Procedure: Your instructor will divide the class into groups of three or four. In assessing the characteristics of jobs, use a scale value of 1 ("very little") to 7 ("very high").

1. Using the scale values, assign scores on each core job dimension used in the job characteristics theory (see page 125) to the following jobs: secretary, professor, food server, auto mechanic, lawyer, short-order cook, department store clerk, construction worker, and newspaper reporter.
2. Researchers often assess the motivational properties of jobs by calculating their motivating potential score (MPS). The usual formula for MPS is

$$(\text{Variety} + \text{Identity} + \text{Significance})/3 \times \text{Autonomy} \times \text{Feedback}$$

Use this formula to calculate the MPS for each job in step 1.
3. Your instructor will now assign your group one of the jobs from the list. Discuss how you might reasonably go about enriching the job.
4. Calculate the new MPS score for the redesigned job, and check its new position in the rank ordering.
5. Discuss the feasibility of your redesign suggestions. In particular, look at how your recommended changes might necessitate changes in other jobs, in the reward system, and in the selection criteria used to hire people for the job.
6. Briefly discuss your observations with the rest of the class.

Follow-up Questions

1. How might your own preexisting attitudes explain some of your own perceptions in this exercise?
2. Are some jobs simply impossible to redesign? Explain.

Self-Assessment Exercise

The Job Characteristics Inventory

The questionnaire below was developed to measure the central concepts of the job characteristics theory. Answer the questions in relation to the job you currently hold or the job you most recently held.

Characteristics from Hackman and Oldham's Job Diagnostic Survey

Reference: *Work Design* by Hackman/Oldham, © Adapted by permission of Pearson Education, Inc., Upper Saddle River, NJ.

Skill Variety

1. How much *variety* is there in your job? That is, to what extent does the job require you to do many different things at work, using a variety of your skills and talents?

1	2	3	4	5	6	7
Very little; the job requires me to do the same routine things over and over again.			Moderate variety			Very much; the job requires me to do many different things, using a number of different skills and talents.

2. The job requires me to use a number of complex or high-level skills.

How accurate is the statement in describing your job?

1	2	3	4	5	6	7
Very inaccurate	Mostly inaccurate	Slightly inaccurate	Uncertain	Slightly accurate	Mostly accurate	Very accurate

Chapter 5 Job Design and Work Structures

3. The job is quite simple and repetitive.*

How accurate is the statement in describing your job?

1	2	3	4	5	6	7
Very inaccurate	Mostly inaccurate	Slightly inaccurate	Uncertain	Slightly accurate	Mostly accurate	Very accurate

Task Identity

1. To what extent does your job involve doing a *"whole" and identifiable piece of work*? That is, is the job a complete piece of work that has an obvious beginning and end? Or is it only a small *part* of the overall piece of work, which is finished by other people or by automatic machines?

1	2	3	4	5	6	7
My job is only a tiny part of the overall piece of work; the results of my activities cannot be seen in the final product or service.			My job is a moderate-sized "chunk" of the overall piece of work; my own contribution can be seen in the final outcome.			My job involves doing the whole piece of work, from start to finish; the results of my activities are easily seen in the final product or service.

2. The job provides me a chance to completely finish the pieces of work I begin.

How accurate is the statement in describing your job?

1	2	3	4	5	6	7
Very inaccurate	Mostly inaccurate	Slightly inaccurate	Uncertain	Slightly accurate	Mostly accurate	Very accurate

3. The job is arranged so that I do *not* have the chance to do an entire piece of work from beginning to end.*

How accurate is the statement in describing your job?

1	2	3	4	5	6	7
Very inaccurate	Mostly inaccurate	Slightly inaccurate	Uncertain	Slightly accurate	Mostly accurate	Very accurate

Task Significance

1. In general, how significant or important is your job? That is, are the results of your work likely to significantly affect the lives or well-being of other people?

1	2	3	4	5	6	7
Not very significant; the outcomes of my work are *not* likely to have important effects on other people.			Moderately significant			Highly significant; the outcomes of my work can affect other people in very important ways.

2. This job is one in which a lot of people can be affected by how well the work gets done.

How accurate is the statement in describing your job?

1	2	3	4	5	6	7
Very inaccurate	Mostly inaccurate	Slightly inaccurate	Uncertain	Slightly accurate	Mostly accurate	Very accurate

3. The job itself is *not* very significant or important in the broader scheme of things.*

How accurate is the statement in describing your job?

1	2	3	4	5	6	7
Very inaccurate	Mostly inaccurate	Slightly inaccurate	Uncertain	Slightly accurate	Mostly accurate	Very accurate

Autonomy

1. How much *autonomy* is there in your job? That is, to what extent does your job permit you to decide *on your own* how to go about doing your work?

1	2	3	4	5	6	7
Very little; the job gives me almost no personal "say" about how and when the work is done.			Moderate autonomy; many things are standardized and not under my control, but I can make some decisions about the work.			Very much; the job gives me almost complete responsibility for deciding how and when the work is done.

2. The job gives me considerable opportunity for independence and freedom in how I do the work.

How accurate is the statement in describing your job?

1	2	3	4	5	6	7
Very inaccurate	Mostly inaccurate	Slightly inaccurate	Uncertain	Slightly accurate	Mostly accurate	Very accurate

3. The job denies me any chance to use my personal initiative or judgment in carrying out the work.*

How accurate is the statement in describing your job?

1	2	3	4	5	6	7
Very inaccurate	Mostly inaccurate	Slightly inaccurate	Uncertain	Slightly accurate	Mostly accurate	Very accurate

Feedback

1. To what extent does *doing the job itself* provide you with information about your work performance? That is, does the actual *work itself* provide clues about how well you are doing—aside from any "feedback" coworkers or supervisors may provide?

1	2	3	4	5	6	7
Very little; the job itself is set up so I could work forever without finding out how well I am doing.			Moderately; sometimes doing the job provides "feedback" to me; sometimes it does not.			Very much; the job is set up so that I get almost constant "feedback" as I work about how well I am doing.

2. Just doing the work required by the job provides many chances for me to figure out how well I am doing.

How accurate is the statement in describing your job?

1	2	3	4	5	6	7
Very inaccurate	Mostly inaccurate	Slightly inaccurate	Uncertain	Slightly accurate	Mostly accurate	Very accurate

3. The job itself provides very few clues about whether or not I am performing well.*

How accurate is the statement in describing your job?

1	2	3	4	5	6	7
Very inaccurate	Mostly inaccurate	Slightly inaccurate	Uncertain	Slightly accurate	Mostly accurate	Very accurate

Scoring: Responses to the three items for each core characteristic are averaged to yield an overall score for that characteristic. Items marked with an asterisk (*) should be scored as follows: 1 = 7; 2 = 6; 3 = 5; 6 = 2; 7 = 1

$$\text{Motivating potential score} \times \left(\frac{\text{Skill variety} \times \text{Task identity} \times \text{Task significance}}{3}\right) \times \text{Autonomy} \times \text{Feedback}$$

OB Online

1. Find the website of a company that appears to promote job flexibility.
2. Visit the websites of the companies listed in the text that have used alternative approaches to job design, and try to find evidence of what job design practices, if any, they are promoting now.
3. Develop a framework that illustrates how the Internet might affect participation in the workplace. Use the Internet to find some evidence to support your framework.
4. Find the websites of at least four companies that discuss alternative work arrangements as part of their human resources recruiting process.

Building Managerial Skills

Exercise Overview: Conceptual skills involve a person's ability to think in the abstract. This exercise will help you develop your conceptual skills as they relate to designing jobs.

Exercise Background: Begin by thinking of three different jobs: one that appears to have virtually no enrichment, one that seems to have moderate enrichment, and one that appears to have a great deal of enrichment. These might be jobs you have personally held or jobs you have observed and about which you can make some educated or informed judgments.

Evaluate each job along the five dimensions described in the job characteristics theory. Next, see if you can identify ways to improve each dimension for each job; that is, try to determine how to enrich the jobs using the job characteristics theory as a framework.

Finally, meet with a classmate and share results. See if you can improve your job enrichment strategy based on the critique your classmate offers.

Exercise Task: Using the background information about the three jobs you examined as context, answer the following questions.

1. What job qualities make some jobs easier to enrich than others?
2. Can all jobs be enriched? Why or why not?
3. Even if a particular job can be enriched, does that always mean it *should* be enriched?
4. Under what circumstances might an individual prefer to have a routine and unenriched job?

TEST PREPPER

ACE self-test

You have read the chapter and studied the key terms, and the exam is any day now. Think you're ready to ace it? Take this sample test to gauge your comprehension of chapter material. You can check your answers at the back of the book. Want more test questions? Visit the student website at http://college.hmco.com/business/students/ (select Griffin/Moorhead, Fundamentals of Organizational Behavior 1e) and take the ACE quizzes for more practice.

1. **T F** Job flexibility can help employees reduce an imbalance between their work and their families.
2. **T F** Unmet employee needs typically translate into increased job performance without management intervention.
3. **T F** In job specialization, employees become skilled at as many tasks as possible.
4. **T F** The greatest problems with job specialization are employee boredom and monotony.
5. **T F** In job rotation, the employee searches for new ways to complete the same task.
6. **T F** Job enlargement is also known as horizontal job loading.
7. **T F** Giving employees control over their tasks is called vertical loading.
8. **T F** Virtually all job enrichment programs have failed to increase productivity.
9. **T F** According to job characteristics theory, one critical psychological state employees must experience to feel good about themselves and respond favorably to their jobs is experienced meaningfulness of the work.
10. **T F** Employees with the lowest need for personal growth and development will be the most easily motivated by the five core job dimensions.
11. **T F** A quality circle is defined by the links between the customer and the organization.
12. **T F** Efforts at increasing empowerment seem to work best if the organization is committed to maintaining participation and empowerment.
13. **T F** In a compressed workweek, all employees work on the same days and the business closes one extra day each week.
14. **T F** Employees on a "nine-eighty" schedule take one extra day off every two weeks.
15. **T F** One cost benefit to the organization of job sharing is that two part-time employees may not receive full-time benefits.
16. **T F** Organizations that use telecommuting save money on facilities such as parking spaces because fewer people are at work on any given day.
17. **T F** Telecommuting seems to be decreasing in popularity among many organizations.
18. To cope with the uncertainty accompanying today's economy, many firms have increased their
    - a. job flexibility.
    - b. long-term debt.
    - c. hiring quotas.
    - d. union membership.
    - e. capital expenses.
19. Lower costs, less need for rehiring and retraining after a downsizing, and greater ease in scheduling staff are all benefits of
    - a. equal employment opportunity.
    - b. self-employment.
    - c. regulated competition.
    - d. flexible job arrangements.
    - e. the baby boomer generation.
20. The framework in this chapter for linking motivation theories and operational methods is based on the idea that motivated behavior can be induced by _____ or _____ circumstances.
    - a. specific, general
    - b. need-based, process-based
    - c. new, old
    - d. individual, collective
    - e. work-related, family-related
21. Megan likes to set up her subordinates' jobs by scientifically studying the work, breaking it down into small component tasks, and then standardizing the procedures for completing those tasks across all workers. Megan follows which approach to job design?
    - a. Job rotation
    - b. Job enlargement
    - c. Job specialization
    - d. Job enrichment
    - e. Job characteristics
22. Kyle works in a machine shop. Every two weeks he moves to a different machine. Two weeks ago, he was stationed at the drill press; for the next two weeks, he

will work at the lathe; and two weeks from now, he will operate the metal press. Kyle's job is based on
   a. rotation.
   b. enlargement.
   c. specialization.
   d. enrichment.
   e. facets.

23. According to the job characteristics theory, employees are most highly motivated when they achieve critical psychological states. Which of the following is not one of these critical psychological states?
   a. Experienced meaningfulness of the work
   b. Experienced satisfaction with pay for the work
   c. Experienced responsibility for work outcomes
   d. Knowledge of results
   e. All of the above are critical psychological states in the job characteristics theory.

24. Bill is a general automotive mechanic. He fixes virtually every aspect of cars, from body work to engine repairs to interior and electronics. According to the job characteristics theory, Bill's job entails a high level of
   a. autonomy.
   b. feedback.
   c. job specialization.
   d. job rotation.
   e. skill variety.

25. Job characteristics theory can be put into practice by implementing all of the following except
   a. forming natural work units.
   b. combining existing tasks into more complex ones.
   c. establishing direct relationships between workers and clients.
   d. increasing worker autonomy through vertical loading.
   e. eliminating open feedback channels.

26. During the human relations movement (1930s–1950s), managers tended to view participation primarily as a way to
   a. reduce employee theft.
   b. increase job satisfaction.
   c. eliminate unions.
   d. close feedback channels.
   e. reduce managers' workloads.

27. Which of the following best illustrates the relationship between participation and expectancy theory?
   a. Employees who participate in making decisions will perceive they are being treated fairly.
   b. Employees who participate in making decisions will better understand the linkage between their performance and the rewards they want most.
   c. Employees who participate in making decisions will be absent less often.
   d. Employees who participate in making decisions will be less likely to join unions.
   e. Employees who participate in making decisions will be more committed to the organization.

28. Using work teams is a fairly common way to
   a. build power for managers.
   b. enlarge jobs.
   c. empower workers.
   d. increase job specialization.
   e. limit participation.

29. For empowerment to enhance organizational effectiveness, all of the following conditions must exist except
   a. the organization must be sincere in its efforts to spread power and autonomy.
   b. the organization must be committed to maintaining participation and empowerment.
   c. The organization must be systematic and patient in its efforts to empower workers.
   d. The organization must be well established and engage in free-market practices.
   e. All of the above are necessary conditions for empowerment to enhance organizational effectiveness.

30. Madison and Kennedy both want to work at The Fundamentals Group, a consulting firm that is looking to hire a new receptionist. However, neither wants to work a full forty-hour week. Which of the following alternative work schedules might solve this problem?
   a. Flextime
   b. Core time
   c. Job sharing
   d. Compressed workweek
   e. Job enrichment

31. Organizations are increasingly using telecommuting because
   a. telecommuters can be paid less.
   b. telecommuters arrive at work when there is less traffic.
   c. telecommuters need less training.
   d. telecommuters require less empowerment.
   e. telecommuters don't need to take as much "formal" time off.

CHAPTER 6

Goal Setting, Performance Management, and Rewards

MANAGEMENT PREVIEW

This chapter continues our discussion of how managers can use various strategies and techniques to enhance employee motivation and performance. Essentially, this chapter follows a logical progression of discrete activities that, taken together, provide an integrated, systematic approach to motivating employee performance. This sequence involves setting goals, evaluating performance, and providing rewards. We begin by examining the role of goal setting in employee motivation. Next, we look at performance management and measurement. Then we discuss in more detail how a good performance management system contributes to total quality management. We subsequently turn to reward systems and their role in motivation. Finally, we identify important types of rewards and explore perspectives on managing reward systems.

After you have studied this chapter, you should be able to:
- ☐ *Describe goal setting and relate it to motivation.*
- ☐ *Discuss performance management in organizations.*
- ☐ *Identify the key elements in an effective organizational reward system.*
- ☐ *Describe the issues and processes involved in managing reward systems.*

We begin by describing how Honda is using access to training as a meaningful reward for employees.

Employees often welcome the chance to obtain additional training, particularly if their employer is willing to foot the bill. Training is legitimately viewed as a means to increase workers' skills; these new skills, in turn, can lead to enhanced opportunities for promotion and advancement. Training also provides some protection against job loss because skilled workers can more easily find new employment if their current jobs are eliminated. Employers also appreciate the benefit training offers them: a more skilled and flexible workforce.

But have you ever heard of a company paying to train employees *before* they are hired? That's exactly what's happening at Honda's new minivan factory in Lincoln, Alabama. The automaker has built a $10 million pretraining facility, which includes replicas of Honda production equipment and multimedia classrooms. Andy Ritter, a Honda human resources manager, was chosen to lead the innovative project. He explains, "I knew I would need to find and train about 1,500 employees... The clock was ticking." Ritter brought a staff of experienced Honda managers to the new facility. Jim Willman became part of Ritter's training team. Willman says, "Everything in Ohio [Honda's first U.S. plant], I had inherited. The systems were in place; anyone could have done it. Andy [Ritter] gave me license to come down here and do it my way. He said, 'If it worked well in Ohio, we'll take it, but we don't have to use anything we're not comfortable with.'" Ken Pyo, who became the quality manager, maintains, "I saw an opportunity to live out a vision in quality that I had. It would have been very difficult for me to change things in Ohio because they're so instilled." As a result of Ritter's team effort, the Alabama plant opened six months earlier than scheduled.

In the program, applicants for production work are screened for education, experience, and residency requirements. Those who pass the screening then participate in a six-week training course that meets in the evenings. Trainees learn many different types of information about working at Honda, including viewing a video of a Honda assembly line and discussing how to get along with Japanese coworkers. Hands-on training requires applicants to perform basic production tasks while a team of assessors grades their performance.

During the training, "[Honda explains everything] up front, so there's no surprise. About 15 percent drop out," according to Lee Hammett, training project manager for Alabama Industrial Development Training. Even after applicants successfully complete the training course, there is no job guarantee, just the chance to apply for open positions. Furthermore, applicants may even have to risk their current jobs to take the training; some local businesses reportedly have fired employees who sign up for the sessions. Hammett says, "99 percent of the people who participate in the training have full-time jobs. They commit to the time and effort of the program with no guarantees. If they survive until the end, it tells Honda something special about them." Thus far, 2,600 trainees have completed the course, with another 1,400 waiting. Feedback about the program has been positive. Wendy Curvin, now a quality administrator, explains, "They taught you how to do things over and over so you'd see what it was like, and I'm using things I learned in the classroom... every day."

"[Applicants] commit to ... the program with no guarantees. If they survive until the end, it tells Honda something special about them."—Lee Hammett, training manager, Alabama Industrial Development Training

References: Hiroyuki Yoshino, "Remarks: 2003 Year-End Press Conference," Honda website, www.hondanews.com on April 29, 2004; Robert J. Grossman, "Made from Scratch," *HR Magazine*, April 2002, pp. 44–48 (quotation, p. 48); "The Top 25 Managers of the Year: Hiroyuki Yoshino of Honda Motor," *BusinessWeek*, January 14, 2002.

For years, management experts have advocated the importance of providing meaningful rewards for employees. But until recently, most firms focused primarily on pay as the basic reward offered to employees. As the opening case illustrates, however, some forward-looking companies are realizing the benefit of offering new and innovative reward opportunities, including valuable job skills training. Of course, both the companies and the employees they seek to reward have important goals they hope to achieve. Goals, then, play an important foundational role in motivating employee behavior. As you will see, goals provide context and direction for assessing performance and allocating rewards.[1]

Goal Setting and Motivation

LEARNING OBJECTIVE
Describe goal setting and relate it to motivation.

A **goal** is a desirable objective.

Goal setting is a very useful method of enhancing employee performance. From a motivational perspective, a **goal** is a desirable objective. Goals are used for two purposes in most organizations. First, they provide a useful framework for managing motivation. Managers and employees can set goals for themselves and then work toward them. Thus, if the organization's goal is to increase sales by 10 percent, a manager can use individual goals to help attain the overall goal. Second, goals are an effective control device; control is the monitoring by management of how well the organization is performing. Comparing people's short-term performances with their goals can be an effective way to monitor the organization's long-run performance.

Social learning theory perhaps best describes the role of goal setting in organizations.[2] This perspective suggests that feelings of pride or shame about performance are a function of the extent to which people achieve their goals. A person who achieves a goal will be proud of having done so, whereas a person who fails to achieve a goal will feel personal disappointment and perhaps even shame. Individuals' degree of pride or disappointment is affected by their **self-efficacy,** the extent to which they believe they can still meet their goals even if they failed to do so in the past.

Self-efficacy is the extent to which people believe they can accomplish their goals even if they failed to do so in the past.

Goal-Setting Theory

Social learning theory provides insights into why and how goals can motivate behavior. It also helps us understand how different people cope with failure to reach their goals. The research of Edwin Locke and his associates most clearly established the utility of goal-setting theory in a motivational context.[3]

Locke's goal-setting theory of motivation assumes behavior is a result of conscious goals and intentions. Therefore, by setting goals for people in the organization, a manager should be able to influence their behavior. Given this premise, the challenge is to develop a thorough understanding of the processes by which people set goals and then work to reach them. In the original version of goal-setting theory, two specific goal characteristics, goal difficulty and goal specificity, were expected to shape performance.

Goal difficulty is the extent to which a goal is challenging and requires effort.

Goal Difficulty **Goal difficulty** is the extent to which a goal is challenging and requires effort. If people work to achieve goals, it is reasonable to assume they will work harder to achieve more difficult goals. However, a goal must not be so difficult that it is unattainable. If a new manager asks her sales force to increase sales by 300 percent, the group may actually ignore her charge because they regard it as impossible to reach. A more realistic but still difficult goal—perhaps a 20 percent increase in sales—would probably be a better incentive. A substantial body of research supports the importance of goal difficulty.[4] In one study, managers at Weyerhauser set difficult goals for truck drivers hauling loads of timber from cutting sites to wood yards. Over a nine-month period, the drivers increased the quantity of wood they delivered by an amount that would have required $250,000 worth of new trucks at the previous per-truck average load.[5] Reinforcement also fosters motivation toward difficult goals. A person who is rewarded for achieving a difficult goal will be more inclined to strive toward the next difficult goal than will someone who received no reward for reaching the first goal.

Chapter 6 Goal Setting, Performance Management, and Rewards 145

Goals, or desirable objectives, play two important roles in organizations: They provide a framework for managing motivation, and they are effective control devices. Dr. Taryn Rose started her career as an orthopedic surgeon. But since one of her earliest interests was fashion, she was motivated to create fashionable women's footwear that was comfortable and less damaging to feet than traditional designer shoes. Motivated by her sense of style and her understanding of bone structures, she launched a line of designer shoes in 1997. Today the pricey shoes are sold in her two boutiques (in Beverly Hills and New York City), as well as in more than 200 other retail outlets, such as Neiman Marcus and Nordstrom. She still practices medicine, but spends most of her time running her growing shoe empire.

Goal specificity is the clarity and precision of a goal.

Goal acceptance is the extent to which a person accepts a goal as his or her own.

Goal commitment is the extent to which an individual is personally interested in reaching a goal.

Goal Specificity **Goal specificity** is the clarity and precision of a goal. A goal of "increasing productivity" is not very specific; a goal of "increasing productivity by 3 percent in the next six months" is quite specific. Some goals, such as those involving costs, output, profitability, and growth, can easily be stated in clear, precise terms. Other goals, such as improving employee job satisfaction and morale, company image and reputation, ethical behavior, and social responsibility, are much harder to state in specific terms.

Like difficulty, specificity has been shown to be consistently related to performance. The study of timber truck drivers previously mentioned also examined goal specificity. The initial loads the truck drivers were carrying were found to be 60 percent of the maximum weight each truck could haul. The managers set a new goal for drivers of 94 percent, which the drivers were soon able to reach. Thus, the goal was quite specific as well as difficult.

Locke's theory attracted much widespread interest and support from both researchers and managers. Thus, Locke, together with Gary Latham, eventually proposed an expanded model of the goal-setting process. The expanded model, shown in Figure 6.1, attempts to capture more fully the complexities of goal setting in organizations.

The expanded theory argues that goal-directed effort is a function of four goal attributes: difficulty and specificity (which we already discussed), acceptance, and commitment. **Goal acceptance** is the extent to which a person accepts a goal as his or her own. **Goal commitment** is the extent to which an individual is personally interested in reaching the goal. The manager who vows to take whatever steps are necessary to cut costs by 10 percent has made a commitment to achieving the goal. Factors that can foster goal acceptance and commitment include participating in the goal-setting process, making goals challenging but realistic, and believing that goal achievement will lead to valued rewards.[6]

The interaction of goal-directed effort, organizational support, and individual abilities and traits determines actual performance. Organizational support is everything the organization does to help or hinder performance. Positive support might mean providing whatever resources are needed to meet the goal; negative support might mean failing to provide such resources, perhaps due to cost considerations or staff reductions. Individual abilities and traits are the skills and other personal

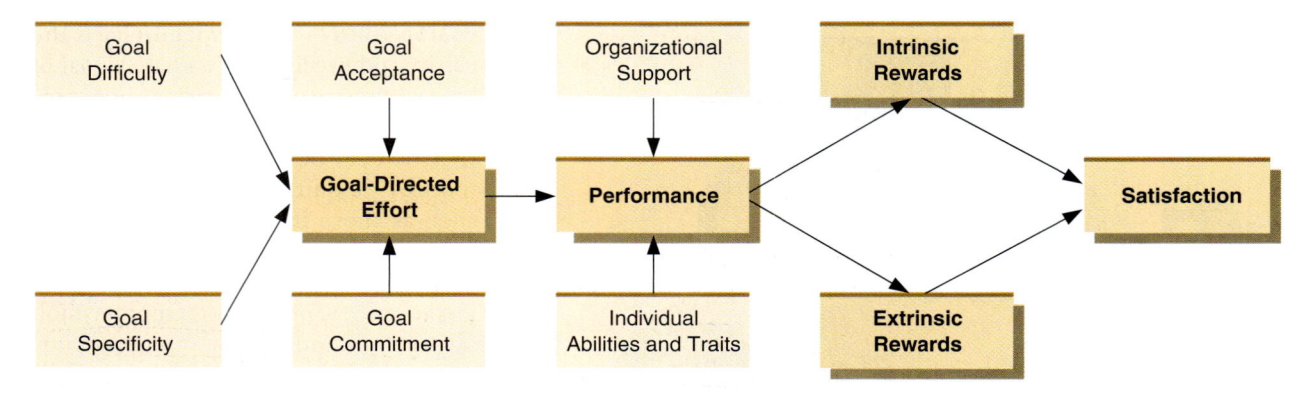

FIGURE 6.1

The Goal-Setting Theory

The goal-setting theory of motivation provides an important means of enhancing employees' motivation. As illustrated here, appropriate goal difficulty, specificity, acceptance, and commitment contribute to goal-directed effort. This effort, in turn, has a direct impact on performance.

Source: From *Organizational Dynamics*, Vol. 8, No. 2, Gary P. Latham et al., "Goal Setting—A Motivational Technique That Works," pp. 68–80, 1979, with permission from Elsevier.

characteristics necessary to do a job. As a result of performance, a person receives various intrinsic and extrinsic rewards that, in turn, influence satisfaction. Note that the latter stages of this model are quite similar to those of the Porter-Lawler expectancy model discussed in Chapter 4.

Broader Perspectives on Goal Setting

Some organizations undertake goal setting from the somewhat broader perspective of **management by objectives,** or **MBO.** MBO is essentially a collaborative goal-setting process through which organizational goals systematically cascade down through the organization. Our discussion describes a generic approach, but many organizations adapt MBO to suit their own purposes.

A successful MBO program starts with top managers establishing overall goals for the organization. After these goals have been set, managers and employees throughout the organization collaborate to set subsidiary goals. First, the overall goals are communicated to everyone. Then each manager meets with each subordinate. During these meetings, the manager explains the unit goals to the subordinate, and the two together determine how the subordinate can contribute to the goals most effectively. The manager acts as a counselor and helps ensure that the subordinate develops goals that are verifiable. For example, a goal of "cutting costs by 5 percent" is verifiable, whereas a goal of "doing my best" is not. Finally, manager and subordinate ensure that the subordinate has the resources needed to reach his or her goals. The entire process spirals downward as each subordinate meets with his or her own subordinates to develop their goals. Thus, as we noted earlier, the initial goals set at the top cascade down through the entire organization.

During the time frame set for goal attainment (usually one year), the manager periodically meets with each subordinate to check progress. It may be necessary to modify goals in light of new information, provide additional resources, or take some other action. At the end of the specified time period, managers hold a final evaluation meeting with each subordinate. At this meeting, manager and subordinate assess how well goals were met and discuss why. This meeting often

Management by objectives (MBO) is a collaborative goal-setting process through which organizational goals cascade down throughout the organization.

serves as the annual performance review as well, determining salary adjustments and other rewards based on reaching goals. This meeting may also serve as the initial goal-setting meeting for the next year's cycle.

Evaluation and Implications

Goal-setting theory has been widely tested in a variety of settings. Research has demonstrated fairly consistently that goal difficulty and specificity are closely associated with performance. Other elements of the theory, such as acceptance and commitment, have been studied less frequently. A few studies have shown the importance of acceptance and commitment, but little is currently known about how people accept and become committed to goals. Goal-setting theory may also focus too heavily on the short run at the expense of long-term considerations. Despite these questions, however, goal setting is clearly an important way for managers to convert motivation into actual improved performance.

From the broader perspective, MBO remains a very popular technique. Alcoa, Tenneco, Black & Decker, General Foods, and Du Pont, for example, have used versions of MBO with widespread success. The technique's popularity stems in part from its many strengths. For one thing, MBO clearly has the potential to motivate employees because it helps implement goal-setting theory on a systematic basis throughout the organization. It also clarifies the basis for rewards, and it can stimulate communication. Performance appraisals are easier and more clear-cut under MBO. Further, managers can use the system for control purposes.

However, using MBO also presents pitfalls, especially if a firm takes too many shortcuts or inadvertently undermines how the process is supposed to work. Sometimes, for instance, top managers do not really participate; that is, the goals are actually established at the middle levels of the organization and may not reflect the real goals of top management. If employees believe this situation to be true, they may become cynical, interpreting the lack of participation by top management as a sign that the goals are not important and their own involvement is therefore a waste of time. MBO also has a tendency to overemphasize quantitative goals to enhance verifiability. Another potential liability is that an MBO system requires a great deal of paperwork and recordkeeping, since every goal must be documented. Finally, some managers do not really let subordinates participate in goal setting but instead merely assign goals and order subordinates to accept them.

On balance, MBO is often an effective and useful system for managing goal setting and enhancing performance in organizations. Research suggests that it can actually do many of the things its advocates claim, but must also be handled carefully. In particular, most organizations need to tailor MBO to their own unique circumstances. When properly used, MBO can also be an effective approach to managing an organization's reward system. It requires, however, one-on-one interactions between each supervisor and each employee, which are often difficult because of the time they take and the likelihood that at least some of these interactions will involve critical assessments of unacceptable performance.

Performance Management in Organizations

LEARNING OBJECTIVE
Discuss performance management in organizations.

As described earlier, most goals are oriented toward some element of performance. Managers can do a variety of things to enhance employee motivation and performance, including redesigning jobs, allowing greater participation, creating alternative work arrangements, and setting goals. They may also fail to take steps that might have improved motivation and performance, and they may even inadvertently do things that reduce motivation and performance. Thus, it is clearly important that performance be approached as something that can and should be managed.

The Nature of Performance Management

The core of performance management is the actual measurement of the performance of an individual or a group. **Performance measurement,** or **performance appraisal,** is the process by which a manager (1) evaluates an employee's work behaviors by measurement and comparison with previously established standards, (2) documents the results, and (3) communicates the results to the employee.[7] A **performance management system (PMS)** comprises the processes and activities involved in performance appraisals, as shown in Figure 6.2.

Simple performance appraisal involves a manager and an employee, whereas a PMS incorporates the total quality management context along with the organizational policies, procedures, and resources that support the activity being approved. The timing and frequency of evaluations, choice of who appraises whom, measurement procedures, methods of recording the evaluations, and storage and distribution of information are all aspects of the PMS.

Purposes of Performance Measurement

Performance measurement may serve many purposes. The ability to provide valuable feedback is one critical purpose. Feedback, in turn, tells the employee where she or he stands in the eyes of the organization. Appraisal results, of course, are also used to decide and justify reward allocations. Performance evaluations may be used as a starting point for discussions of training, development, and improvement. Finally, the data produced by the performance appraisal system can be used to forecast fu-

Performance measurement, or **performance appraisal,** is the process by which a manager (1) evaluates an employee's work behaviors by measurement and comparison with previously established standards, (2) documents the results, and (3) communicates the results to the employee.

A **performance management system (PMS)** comprises the processes and activities involved in performance appraisals.

FIGURE 6.2

The Performance Management System

An organization's performance management system plays an important role in determining its overall level of effectiveness. This is especially true when the organization is attempting to employ total quality management. Key elements of a performance management system, as shown here, include timing and frequency of evaluations, choice of who does the evaluation, choice of measurement procedures, storage and distribution of performance information, and recording methods. These elements are used by managers and employees in most organizations.

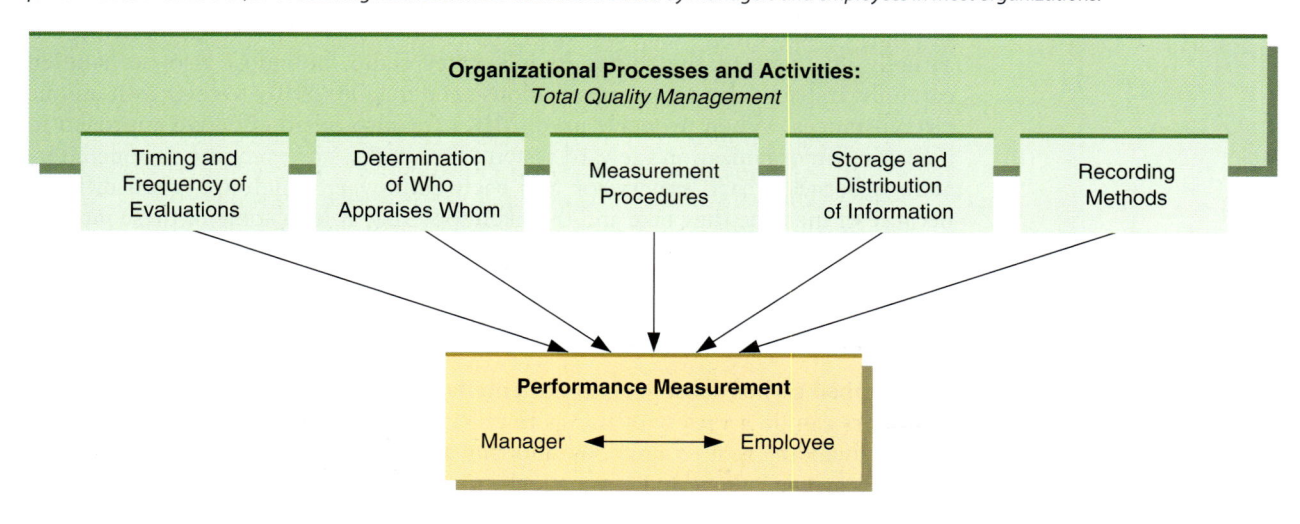

Organizational Processes and Activities: *Total Quality Management*

- Timing and Frequency of Evaluations
- Determination of Who Appraises Whom
- Measurement Procedures
- Storage and Distribution of Information
- Recording Methods

Performance Measurement

Manager ↔ Employee

Figure 6.3

Basic Purpose of Performance Measurement: Provide Information About Work Performance

Judgment of Past Performance
- Provide a basis for reward allocation
- Provide a basis for promotions, transfers, layoffs, and so on
- Identify high-potential employees
- Validate selection procedures
- Evaluate previous training programs

Development of Future Performance
- Foster work improvement
- Identify training and development opportunities
- Develop ways to overcome obstacles and performance barriers
- Establish supervisor-employee agreement on expectations

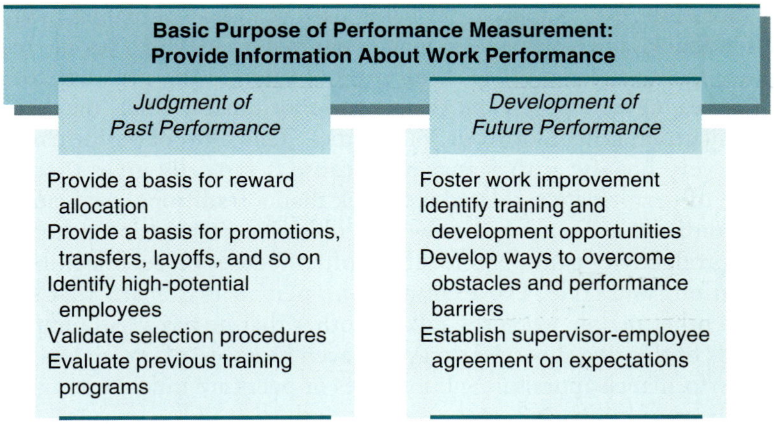

FIGURE 6.3

Purposes of Performance Measurement

Performance measurement plays a variety of roles in most organizations. This figure illustrates that these roles can help managers judge an employee's past performance and help managers and employees improve future performance.

ture human resource needs, plan management succession, and guide other human resource activities such as recruiting, training, and development programs.

Providing job performance feedback is the primary use of appraisal information. Performance appraisal information can indicate that an employee is ready for promotion or that he or she needs additional training to gain experience in another area of company operations. It may also show that a person lacks the skills for a certain job and that another person should be recruited to fill that particular role. Other purposes of performance appraisal can be grouped into two broad categories, judgment and development, as shown in Figure 6.3.

Performance appraisals with a judgmental orientation focus on past performance and deal mainly with measuring and comparing performance and with the uses of the information generated. Appraisals with a developmental orientation focus on the future and use information from evaluations to improve performance. If improved future performance is the intent of the appraisal process, the manager may focus on goals or targets for the employee, on eliminating obstacles or problems that hinder performance, and on future training needs.

Performance Measurement Basics

Employee appraisals are common in every type of organization, but how they are performed may vary. Many issues must be considered in determining how to conduct an appraisal. Three important issues are who does the appraisals, how often they are conducted, and how performance is measured.

The Appraiser In most appraisal systems, the employee's primary evaluator is the supervisor. This stems from the obvious fact that the supervisor is presumably in the best position to be aware of the employee's day-to-day performance. Further, it is the supervisor who has traditionally provided performance feedback to employees and determined performance-based rewards and sanctions. Problems often arise, however, if the supervisor has incomplete or distorted information about the employee's performance. For example, the supervisor may have little firsthand knowledge of the performance of an employee who works alone outside the company premises, such as a salesperson who makes solo calls on clients or a maintenance person who handles equipment problems in the field. Similar problems may arise when the supervisor has a limited understanding of the technical knowledge involved in an employee's job.

One solution to these problems is a multiple-rater system that incorporates the ratings of several people familiar with the employee's performance. One alternative is to use the employee as an evaluator. Although they may not actually do so, most employees are actually very capable of evaluating themselves in an unbiased manner.

360-degree feedback is a performance management system in which people receive performance feedback from those on all sides of them in the organization: their boss, their colleagues and peers, and their own subordinates.

One of the more interesting approaches being used in many companies today is **360-degree feedback,** a performance management system in which people receive performance feedback from those on all sides of them in the organization: their boss, their colleagues and peers, and their own subordinates. Thus, the feedback comes from all around them, or from 360 degrees. This form of performance evaluation can be very beneficial to managers because it typically gives them a much wider range of performance-related feedback than a traditional evaluation provides. That is, rather than focusing narrowly on objective performance, such as sales increases or productivity gains, 360 feedback often focuses on such factors as interpersonal relations and style. For example, one person may learn that she stands too close to other people when she talks, another that he has a bad temper. These are the kinds of things a supervisor may not even be aware of, much less report as part of a performance appraisal. Subordinates or peers are much more willing to provide this sort of feedback.

Of course, to benefit from 360-degree feedback, a manager must have a thick skin. The manager is likely to hear some personal comments on sensitive topics, which may be threatening. Thus, a 360-feedback system must be carefully managed so that its focus remains on constructive rather than destructive criticism.[8] Because of its potential advantages and despite its potential shortcomings, many companies today are using this approach to performance feedback. AT&T, Nestlé, Pitney Bowes, and Chase Manhattan Bank are just a few major companies using 360-degree feedback to help managers improve a wide variety of performance-related behaviors.[9]

Frequency of the Appraisal Another important issue is the frequency of appraisals. Regardless of the employee's level of performance, the type of task, or the employee's need for information on performance, the organization usually conducts performance appraisals on a regular basis, typically once a year. Annual performance appraisals are convenient for administrative purposes such as recordkeeping and scheduling. Some organizations also conduct appraisals semiannually.[10] Several systems for monitoring employee performance on an as-needed basis have been proposed as an alternative to the traditional annual system.

Managers in international settings must take care to incorporate cultural factors in their performance appraisal strategies. For example, in highly individualistic cultures such as the United States, appraising performance at the individual level is both common and accepted. In collectivistic cultures such as Japan, however, performance appraisals almost always need to focus more on group performance and feedback. In countries where people put a lot of faith in destiny, fate, or some form of divine control, employees may be strongly unreceptive to performance feedback, believing their actions are irrelevant to the results that follow.

Measuring Performance The cornerstone of a good PMS is the method for measuring performance. Detailed descriptions of the many different methods for measuring performance are beyond the scope of this book; they are more appropriately covered in a course in human resource management or a specialized course in performance appraisal. However, we present a few general comments about how to measure performance. The Mastering Change box provides some useful insights into recent approaches to measuring performance.

The measurement method provides the information managers use to make decisions about salary adjustment, promotion, transfer, training, and discipline. The courts and Equal Employment Opportunity Commission guidelines have

MASTERING CHANGE

High-Tech Performance Measurement: Workers' Friend or Foe?

Advances in technology have enabled companies to gather, analyze, report, and use information in ways that would have been impossible a decade ago. One area in great need of improved accuracy and objectivity is worker performance measurement. "[W]hat was once a smushy, subjective effort by finger-in-the-wind managers is hitting new levels of scientific precision," says *BusinessWeek* writer Michelle Conlin. British Airways manager Steven Pruneau claims that the productivity of his airline's physical and financial capital can be measured precisely with indicators such as the hours planes spend in the air versus on the ground, but he explains, "[We don't have] a fraction of that kind of information about the productivity of our other assets—our human capital."

Consider the effects of the technology revolution on performance measurement at household goods retailer Pier 1 Imports. In the past, daily sales reports could be calculated only at the end of the day; thus, employees didn't know how well they were doing until it was too late to do anything about it. Now Pier 1 Imports uses information technology to tabulate sales continuously. In cities where Pier 1 has multiple stores, the same technology pits one store against the others because employees see their store's results as well as those of other stores. Employees check the sales performance data regularly and set improvement goals that enable the firm to boost sales and employees to increase their bonuses.

At British Airways, software monitors employees' every action, ensuring their time in the break room or on a personal phone call doesn't get charged to the company. Progress toward corporate goals such as increased

> *"[Worker performance measurement] was once a smushy, subjective effort by finger-in-the-wind managers, [but now it] is hitting new levels of scientific precision."* —Michelle Conlin, writer for BusinessWeek

ticket sales and complaint resolutions is also tracked. Workers have instant access to their performance scores and can see the impact of incentive compensation on their daily pay.

Some firms are employing even more intrusive technologies, such as recording entry card data to determine what time workers arrive and leave and using security cameras—sometimes without notifying employees of their presence—in cubicles, hallways, and even restrooms. Software now enables managers to receive reports of every website their workers have accessed and also records employees' keystrokes. Many workers see the benefits of accurate and objective performance measurement, but others claim the systems invade workers' privacy. As technology continues to evolve, this debate is sure to persist.

References: James C. Cooper and Kathleen Madigan, "The Surprise Economy," *BusinessWeek*, March 18, 2002; "The Software Says You're Just Average," *BusinessWeek*, February 25, 2002 (quotation); "Making Performance Reviews Pay Off," *BusinessWeek*, February 6, 2002; Eric Wahlgren, "Have Investors Missed the Boat on Pier 1?" *BusinessWeek*, December 21, 2001.

---

mandated that performance measurements be based on job-related criteria rather than on some other factor such as age, sex, religion, or national origin. In addition, to provide useful information for the decision maker, performance appraisals must be valid, reliable, and free of bias. They must not produce ratings that are consistently too lenient, too severe, or clustered in the middle. They must also be free of perceptual and timing errors.

Some of the most popular methods for evaluating individual performance are graphic rating scales, checklists, essays or diaries, behaviorally anchored rating scales, and forced-choice systems. These systems are easy to use and familiar to most managers. However, two major problems are common to all individual methods: a tendency to rate most individuals at about the same level and the inability to discriminate among variable levels of performance.

Comparative methods evaluate two or more employees by comparing them with each other on various performance dimensions. The most popular comparative methods are ranking, forced distribution, paired comparisons, and the use of multiple raters. Comparative methods, however, are more difficult to use than the individual methods, are unfamiliar to many managers, and may require sophisticated development procedures and a computerized analytical system to extract usable information.

Individual Rewards in Organizations

> **LEARNING OBJECTIVE**
>
> Identify the key elements in understanding individual rewards in organizations.

As noted earlier, a primary purpose of performance management is to provide a basis for rewarding employees. We now turn to rewards and their impact on employee motivation and performance. The **reward system** consists of all organizational components—including people, processes, rules and procedures, and decision-making activities—involved in allocating compensation and benefits to employees in exchange for their contributions to the organization.[11] As we examine organizational reward systems, it is important to keep in mind their role in psychological contracts (discussed in Chapter 3) and employee motivation (discussed in Chapter 4). Rewards constitute many of the inducements organizations provide to employees as their part of the psychological contract, for example. Rewards also satisfy some of the needs employees attempt to meet through their choice of work-related behaviors.

The **reward system** consists of all organizational components, including people, processes, rules and procedures, and decision-making activities, involved in allocating compensation and benefits to employees in exchange for their contributions to the organization.

Roles, Purposes, and Meanings of Rewards

The purpose of the reward system in most organizations is to attract, retain, and motivate qualified employees. The organization's compensation structure must be equitable and consistent to ensure equality of treatment and compliance with the law. Compensation should also be a fair reward for the individual's contributions to the organization, although in most cases these contributions are difficult, if not impossible, to measure objectively. Given this limitation, managers should be as fair and equitable as possible. Finally, the system must be competitive in the external labor market so the organization can attract and retain competent workers in appropriate fields.[12]

Beyond these broad considerations, an organization must develop its philosophy of compensation based on its own conditions and needs, and this philosophy must be defined and built into the actual reward system. For example, Wal-Mart has a policy that none of its employees will be paid the minimum wage. Even though it may pay some people only slightly more than this minimum, the firm nevertheless attempts to communicate to all workers that it places a higher value on their contributions than just having to pay them the lowest wage possible.

The organization needs to decide what types of behaviors or performance it wants to encourage with a reward system, because what is rewarded tends to recur. Possible behaviors include performance, longevity, attendance, loyalty, contributions to the "bottom line," responsibility, and conformity. Performance measurement, as described earlier, assesses these behaviors, but the choice of which behaviors to reward is a function of the compensation system. A reward system must also take into account volatile economic issues such as inflation, market conditions, technology, labor union activities, and so forth.

Chapter 6 Goal Setting, Performance Management, and Rewards

It is also important for the organization to recognize that organizational rewards have many meanings for employees. Intrinsic and extrinsic rewards carry both surface and symbolic value. The **surface value** of a reward to an employee is its objective meaning or worth. A salary increase of 5 percent, for example, means an individual has 5 percent more spending power than before, whereas a promotion, on the surface, means new duties and responsibilities. Managers must recognize that rewards also carry **symbolic value.** If a person gets a 3 percent salary increase when everyone else gets 5 percent, one plausible meaning is that the organization values other employees more. But if the same person gets 3 percent and all others get only 1 percent, the meaning may be just the opposite: the individual is seen as the most valuable employee. Thus, rewards convey to people not only how much the organization values them but also their importance relative to others. Managers need to tune in to the many meanings rewards can convey—not only to the surface messages but to the symbolic messages as well.

> The **surface value of a reward** to an employee is its objective meaning or worth.
>
> The **symbolic value of a reward** to an employee is its subjective and personal meaning or worth.

Types of Rewards

Most organizations use several types of rewards. The most common forms are base pay (wages or salary), incentive systems, benefits, perquisites, and awards. These rewards are combined to create an individual's **compensation package.**

> An individual's **compensation package** is the total array of money (wages, salary, or commission), incentives, benefits, perquisites, and awards provided by the organization.

Base Pay   For most people, the most important reward for work is the pay they receive. Obviously money is important because of the things it can buy, but as we just noted, it can also symbolize an employee's worth. Pay is very important to an organization for a variety of reasons. For one thing, an effectively planned and managed pay system can improve motivation and performance. For another, employee compensation is a major cost of doing business—as much as 50 to 60 percent in many organizations; thus, a poorly designed system can be an expensive proposition. Finally, since pay is considered a major source of employee dissatisfaction, a poorly designed system can result in problems in other areas, such as turnover and low morale.

Incentive Systems   **Incentive systems** are plans that allow employees to earn additional compensation in return for certain types of performance. Examples of incentive programs include the following:

> An **incentive system** is a plan in which employees can earn additional compensation in return for certain types of performance.

1. *Piecework programs*, which tie a worker's earnings to the number of units produced
2. *Gain-sharing programs*, which grant additional earnings to employees or work groups for cost reduction ideas
3. *Bonus systems*, which provide managers with lump-sum payments from a special fund based on the financial performance of the organization or a unit
4. *Long-term compensation*, which gives managers additional income based on stock price performance, earnings per share, or return on equity
5. *Merit pay plans*, which base pay raises on the employee's performance
6. *Profit-sharing plans*, which distribute a portion of the firm's profits to all employees at a predetermined rate
7. *Employee stock option plans*, which set aside stock in the company for employees to purchase at a reduced rate

Plans oriented mainly toward individual employees may cause increased competition for the rewards and some possibly disruptive behaviors, such as sabotaging a coworker's performance, sacrificing quality for quantity, or competing for

Anne Mulcahy is CEO of Xerox. Her compensation includes a combination of base salary plus incentives. Mulcahy's base salary is $2.5 million. However, she can also earn a considerable bonus plus receive potentially lucrative stock options if the firm meets and then exceeds the performance expectations of its board of directors.

customers. A group incentive plan, on the other hand, requires employees to trust one another and work together. Of course, incentive systems have advantages and disadvantages.

Long-term compensation for executives is particularly controversial because of the large sums of money involved and the basis for the payments. Indeed, executive compensation is one of the most controversial issues to challenge U.S. businesses in recent years. News reports and the popular press are quick to report stories about how this or that executive just received a huge windfall from his or her organization. Clearly, successful top managers deserve significant rewards. The job of a senior executive, especially a CEO, is grueling and stressful, and takes talent and decades of hard work to reach. Only a small handful of managers ever attain a top position in a major corporation. The question is whether some companies are overrewarding such managers for their contributions to the organization.[13]

When a firm is growing rapidly, and its profits are also growing rapidly, few would object to paying the CEO well. However, objections arise when an organization is laying off workers, its financial performance is less than expected, and the CEO is still earning a huge amount of money. Such a situation dictates that the company's board of directors take a close look at the appropriateness of its actions.[14]

Indirect Compensation Another major component of the compensation package is **indirect compensation,** also commonly referred to as the *employee benefits plan*. Typical benefits provided by businesses include the following:

Indirect compensation, or *benefits,* refers to non wage or salary compensation such as paid time off and insurance coverage.

1. *Payment for time not worked,* both on and off the job. On-the-job free time includes lunch, rest, coffee breaks, and wash-up or get-ready time. Off-the-job time not worked includes vacation, sick leave, holidays, and personal days.
2. *Social security contributions.* The employer contributes half the money paid into the system established under the Federal Insurance Contributions Act (FICA). The employee pays the other half.
3. *Unemployment compensation.* People who have lost their jobs or are temporarily laid off get a percentage of their wages from an insurance-like program.
4. *Disability and workers' compensation benefits.* Employers contribute funds to help workers who cannot work due to occupational injury or ailment.
5. *Life and health insurance programs.* Most organizations offer insurance at a cost far below what individuals would pay to buy insurance on their own.
6. *Pension or retirement plans.* Most organizations offer plans to provide supplementary income to employees after they retire.

A company's social security, unemployment, and workers' compensation contributions are set by law. How much to contribute for other kinds of benefits is up to each company. Some organizations contribute more to the cost of these benefits

Chapter 6 Goal Setting, Performance Management, and Rewards 155

than others. Some companies pay the entire cost; others pay a percentage of the cost of certain benefits, such as health insurance, and bear the entire cost of other benefits. Offering benefits beyond wages became a standard component of compensation during World War II as a way to increase employee compensation when wage controls were in effect. Since then, competition for employees and employee demands (expressed, for instance, in union bargaining) have caused companies to increase these benefits. In many organizations today, benefits account for 30 to 40 percent of the payroll.

The burden of providing employee benefits is growing heavier for firms in the United States than for organizations in other countries, especially among unionized firms. For example, consider the problem General Motors faces. Workers at GM's brake factory in Dayton, Ohio, earn an average of $27 an hour in wages. They also earn another $16 an hour in benefits, including full health care coverage with no deductibles, full pension benefits after thirty years of service, life and disability insurance, and legal services. Thus, GM's total labor costs per worker at the factory average $43 an hour. Meanwhile a German rival, Robert Bosch GmbH, has a nonunionized brake plant in South Carolina. It pays its workers an average of $18 an hour in wages, and its hourly benefit cost is around $5. Bosch's benefits include medical coverage with a $2,000 deductible, 401-K retirement plans with employee participation, and life and disability coverage. Bosch's total hourly labor costs per worker, therefore, are only $23. Toyota, Nissan, and Honda buy most of their brakes for their U.S. factories from Bosch, whereas General Motors must use its own factory to supply brakes. Thus, foreign competitors realize considerable cost advantages over GM in the brakes they use, and this pattern runs across a variety of other component parts as well.[15]

> **Perquisites** are special privileges awarded to selected members of an organization, usually top managers.

Perquisites Perquisites are special privileges awarded to selected members of an organization, usually top managers. For years, the top executives of many businesses were allowed privileges such as unlimited use of the company jet, motor home, vacation home, and executive dining room. In Japan, a popular perquisite is a paid membership in an exclusive golf club; a common perquisite in England is first-class travel. In the United States, the Internal Revenue Service has recently ruled that some "perks" constitute a form of income and thus can be taxed. This decision has substantially changed the nature of these benefits, but they have not entirely disappeared, nor are they likely to. Today, however, many perks tend to be more job related. For example, popular perks currently include a car and driver (so the executive can conduct business while being transported to and from work) and cellular telephones (so the executive can conduct business anywhere). More than anything else, though, perquisites seem to add to their recipients' status and thus may increase job satisfaction and reduce turnover.[16]

Awards At many companies, employees receive awards for everything from seniority to perfect attendance, from zero defects (quality work) to cost reduction suggestions. Award programs can be costly in the time required to run them and in money if cash awards are given. But award systems can improve performance under the right conditions. In one medium-size manufacturing company, careless work habits were pushing up the costs of scrap and rework (the cost of scrapping defective parts or reworking them to meet standards). Management instituted a zero-defects program to recognize employees who did perfect or near-perfect work. During the first month, two workers in shipping caused only one defect in more than two thousand parts handled. Division management called a meeting in the lunchroom and recognized each worker with a plaque and a

Organizations often seek to recognize, reward, and motivate their best employees by giving them various awards. One long-standing tradition is to provide awards to long-term employees at key anniversary dates to reward their loyalty and dedication and to recognize their value or seniority. For such programs to be effective, the awards and prizes themselves must have value to the employees being recognized. For example, as illustrated here, although some employees might regard extra time with their boss as a reward, others clearly see it a different way.
DILBERT reprinted by permission of United Feature Syndicate, Inc.

ribbon. The next month, the same two workers had two defects, so there was no award. The following month, the two workers had zero defects, and once again top management called a meeting to give out plaques and ribbons. Elsewhere in the plant, defects, scrap, and rework decreased dramatically as workers evidently sought recognition for quality work. What succeeded in this particular plant may or may not work in others. And, of course, as the cartoon illustrates, managers and workers sometimes have very different perceptions of the value of different awards!

Managing Reward Systems

LEARNING OBJECTIVE

Describe the issues and processes involved in managing reward systems.

Much of our discussion on reward systems has focused on general issues. As Table 6.1 shows, however, the organization must address other issues when developing organizational reward systems. The organization must consider its ability to pay employees at certain levels, economic and labor market conditions, and the impact of the pay system on organizational financial performance. In addition, the organization must consider the relationship between performance and rewards, as well as the issues of reward system flexibility, employee participation in the reward system, pay secrecy, and expatriate compensation.

Linking Performance and Rewards

For managers to take full advantage of the symbolic value of pay, employees must perceive that their rewards are linked to their performance. For example, if everyone in an organization starts working for the same hourly rate and then receives a predetermined wage increase every six months or year, there is clearly no relationship between performance and rewards. Instead, the organization is indicating that all entry-level employees are worth the same amount, and pay increases are tied solely to the length of time worked in the organization. This holds true whether the employee is a top, average, or mediocre employee. The only requirement is that the employee works well enough to avoid being fired.

TABLE 6.1

Issues to Consider in Developing Reward Systems

Issue	Important Examples
Pay Secrecy	■ Open, closed, partial ■ Link with performance appraisal ■ Equity perceptions
Employee Participation	■ By human resource department ■ By joint employee/management committee
Flexible System	■ Cafeteria-style benefits ■ Annual lump sum or monthly bonus ■ Salary versus benefits
Ability to Pay	■ Organization's financial performance ■ Expected future earnings
Economic and Labor Market Factors	■ Inflation rate ■ Industry pay standards ■ Unemployment rate
Impact on Organizational Performance	■ Increase in costs ■ Impact on performance
Expatriate Compensation	■ Cost of living differentials ■ Managing related equity issues

At the other extreme, an organization might attempt to tie all compensation to actual performance. Thus, each new employee might start at a different wage as determined by his or her experience, education, skills, and other job-related factors. After joining the organization, the individual then receives rewards based on actual performance. One employee, for example, may start at $15 an hour because she has ten years of experience and a good performance record at her previous employer. Another may start the same job at a rate of $10.50 an hour because he has only four years' experience and an adequate but not outstanding performance record. If the first employee performs up to expectations, she may also get several pay increases, bonuses, and awards throughout the year, whereas the second employee may get only one or two small increases and no other rewards. Of course, organizations must ensure that pay differences are based strictly on performance-related factors (including seniority), not on factors unrelated to performance (such as gender, ethnicity, or other discriminatory factors).

In reality, most organizations attempt to develop a reward strategy somewhere between these two extremes. Because in reality it is difficult to differentiate all employees, most firms use some basic compensation level for everyone. For example, they may start all workers performing a specific job at the same rate, regardless of experience. They may also work to provide reasonable incentives and other inducements for high performers while taking care not to ignore the "average" employees. The key fact for managers to remember is simply that if they expect rewards to motivate performance, employees must see a clear, direct link between their own job-related behaviors and the attainment of those rewards.[17]

Flexible Reward Systems

A **flexible reward system** allows employees to choose the combination of benefits that best suits their needs.

Flexible, or cafeteria-style, reward systems are a recent and increasingly popular variation on the standard compensation system. A **flexible reward system** allows employees, within specified ranges, to choose the combination of benefits that best suits their needs. For example, a younger worker just starting out might prefer to have especially strong health care coverage with few deductibles, a worker with a few years of experience more child care benefits, a mid-career employee with greater financial security more time off with pay, and an older worker more rewards concentrated into his or her retirement plans.

Some organizations are starting to apply the flexible approach to pay. For example, employees sometimes have the option to take an annual salary increase in one lump sum rather than in monthly increments. General Electric recently implemented such a system for some of its managers. UNUM Corporation, a large insurance firm, allows all its employees the option to draw a full third of their annual compensation in the month of January. This makes it easier for them to handle such major expenses as purchasing a new automobile, buying a home, or covering college education costs for children. Obviously the administrative costs of providing this level of flexibility are greater, but many employees value this flexibility and may develop strong loyalty and attachment to an employer that offers such a compensation package.

Participative Pay Systems

In keeping with the current trend toward involving workers in organizational decision making, employee participation in the pay process is also increasing. A participative pay system may involve employees in the system's design, administration, or both. A pay system can be designed by staff members of the organization's human resources department, a committee of managers within the organization, an outside consultant, employees, or a combination of these sources. Organizations that have used a joint management employee task force to design the compensation system have generally succeeded in implementing a plan that is useful to managers and equitable to employees. Employee participation in administering the pay system is a natural extension of having employees participate in its design. Examples of companies that have involved employees in the administration of the pay system include Romac Industries, where employees vote on the pay of other employees; Graphic Controls, where each manager's pay is determined by a group of peers; and Friedman-Jacobs Company, where employees set their own wages based on their perceptions of their performance.[18]

Pay Secrecy

When a company has a policy of open salary information, the exact salary amounts for employees are public knowledge. State governments, for instance, make public the salaries of everyone on their payrolls. A policy of complete secrecy means no information is available to employees regarding other employees' salaries, average or percentage raises, or salary ranges. The National Labor Relations Board recently upheld an earlier ruling that an employer starting or enforcing a rule that forbids employees from discussing their salaries constitutes interference, restraint, and coercion of protected employee rights under the National Labor Relations Act. Although a few organizations have completely public or completely secret systems, most have systems somewhere in the middle.

Expatriate Compensation

Expatriate compensation is yet another important issue in managing reward systems.[19] Consider a manager living and working in Houston currently making $250,000 a year. That income allows the manager to live in a certain kind of home, drive a certain kind of car, have access to certain levels of medical care, and live a

Chapter 6   Goal Setting, Performance Management, and Rewards

certain kind of lifestyle. Now suppose the manager is asked to accept a transfer to Tokyo, Geneva, or London, cities where the cost of living is considerably higher than in Houston. The same salary cannot begin to support a comparable lifestyle in those cities. Consequently, the employer is almost certain to redesign the manager's compensation package so the employee's lifestyle in the new location will be comparable to that in the former one.

Now suppose the same manager is asked to accept a transfer to an underdeveloped nation. The cost of living in this nation may be quite low by U.S. standards. But there may also be relatively few choices in housing, poorer schools and medical care, a harsh climate, greater personal danger, or similar unattractive characteristics. The firm will probably have to pay the manager some level of additional compensation to offset the decrement in quality of lifestyle. Thus, developing rewards for expatriates is a complicated process.

Figure 6.4 illustrates the approach to expatriate compensation used by one major multinational corporation. The left side of the figure shows how a U.S.

FIGURE 6.4

The Expatriate Compensation Balance Sheet

Organizations that ask employees to accept assignments in foreign locations usually must adjust their compensation levels to account for differences in cost of living and similar factors. Amoco used the system shown here. The employee's domestic base salary is first broken down into the three categories shown on the left. Then adjustments are made by adding compensation to the categories on the right until an appropriate, equitable level of compensation is achieved.

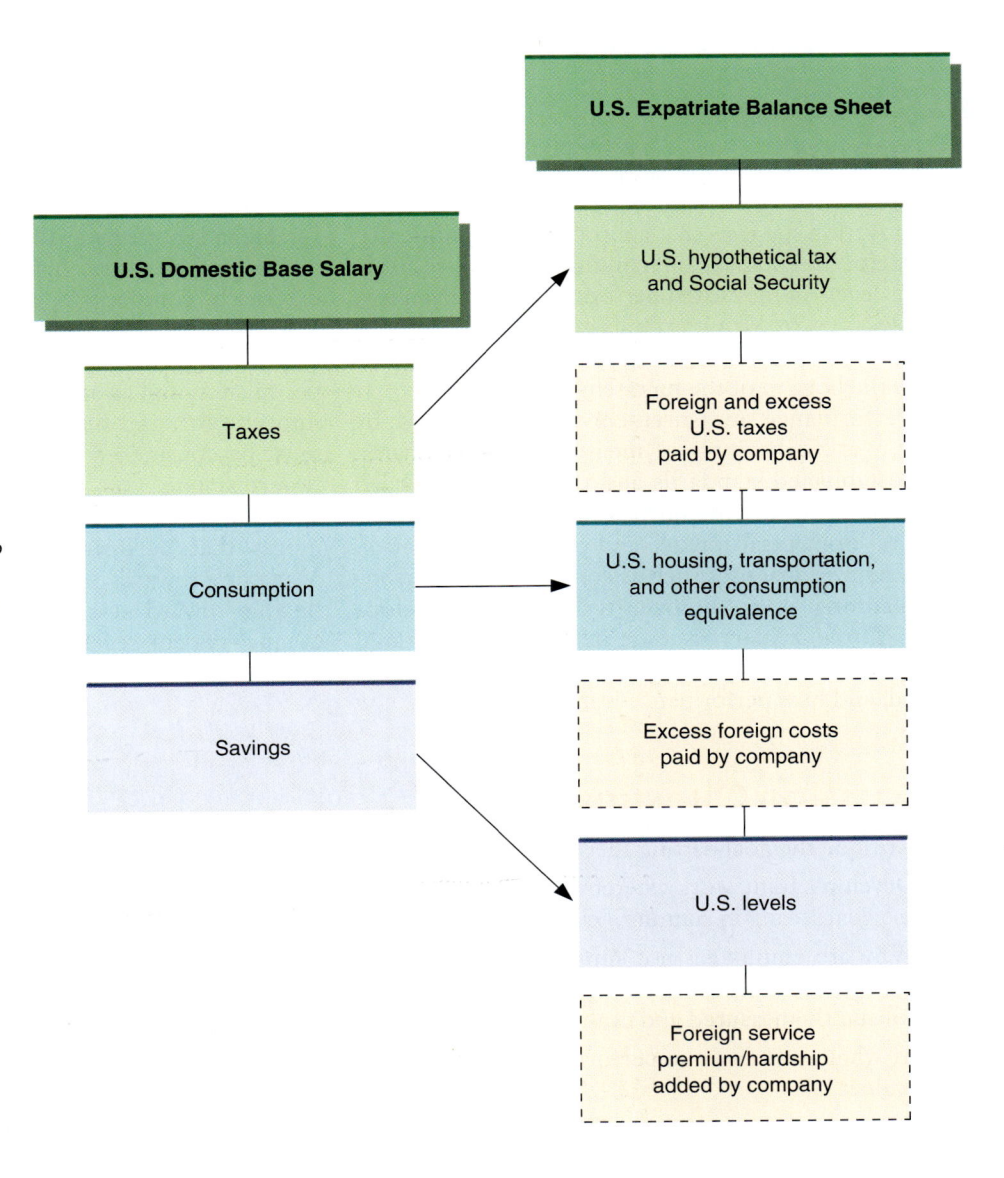

employee currently uses her or his salary: Part of it goes for taxes, part is saved, and the rest is consumed. When a person is asked to move abroad, a human resource manager works with the employee to develop an equitable balance sheet for the new compensation package. As shown on the right side of the figure, the individual's compensation package will potentially consist of six components. First, the individual will receive income to cover what his or her taxes and social security payments in the United States would have been. The employee may also have to pay foreign taxes and additional U.S. taxes as a result of the move, so the company covers these as well.

Next, the firm pays an amount adequate for the employee's current consumption levels in the United States. If the cost of living is greater in the foreign location than at home, the firm pays the excess foreign costs. The employee also receives income for saving comparable to what she or he is currently saving. Finally, if the employee faces a hardship because of the assignment, the firm provides an additional foreign service premium or hardship allowance. Not surprisingly, then, expatriate compensation packages can be very expensive for an organization and must be carefully developed and managed.[20]

Synopsis

A goal is a desirable objective. The goal-setting theory of motivation suggests that appropriate goal difficulty, specificity, acceptance, and commitment will result in higher levels of motivated performance. Management by objectives, or MBO, extends goal setting throughout an organization by cascading goals down from the top to the bottom of the hierarchy.

Performance measurement is the process by which work behaviors are measured and compared with established standards and the results recorded and communicated. Its purposes are to evaluate employees' work performance and provide information for organizational uses such as compensation, personnel planning, and employee training and development. Three primary issues in performance appraisal are who does the appraisals, how often they are conducted, and how performance is measured.

The purpose of the reward system is to attract, retain, and motivate qualified employees and to maintain a pay structure that is internally equitable and externally competitive. Rewards have both surface and symbolic value. Rewards take the form of monetary incentives, indirect compensation or benefits, perquisites, and awards. Factors such as motivational impact, cost, and fit with the organizational system must be considered when designing or evaluating a reward system.

Effective management of a reward system requires that performance be linked with rewards. Managing rewards entails dealing with issues such as flexible reward systems, employee participation in the pay system, secrecy of pay systems, and expatriate rewards.

Discussion Questions

1. Critique the goal-setting theory of motivation.
2. Develop a framework whereby an instructor could use goal setting in running a class such as this one.
3. Why are employees not simply left alone to do their jobs instead of having their performance constantly measured and evaluated?
4. In what ways is your performance as a student evaluated?
5. How is the performance of your instructor measured? What are the limitations of this method?
6. Can performance on some jobs simply not be measured? Why or why not?
7. What conditions make it easier for an organization to achieve continuous improvement in performance? What conditions make it more difficult?

8. As a student in this class, what "rewards" do you receive in exchange for your time and effort? What are the rewards for the professor who teaches this class? How do your contributions and rewards differ from those of one of your classmates?

9. Do you expect to obtain the rewards you discussed in question 8 on the basis of your intelligence, your hard work, the number of hours you spend in the library, your height, your good looks, your work experience, or some other personal factor?

10. What rewards are easiest for managers to control? What rewards are more difficult to control?

11. Institutions in federal and state governments often give the same percentage pay raise to all their employees. What do you think is the effect of this type of pay raise on employee motivation?

Organizational Behavior Case for Discussion

Rewarding the Hourly Worker

Hourly workers, people who are paid a set dollar amount for each hour they work, have long been the backbone of the U.S. economy. But times are changing, and with them the lot of the hourly worker. As with most employment conditions, organizations are able to take a wider variety of approaches to managing compensation for hourly workers. And nowhere are these differences more apparent than in the contrasting conditions for hourly workers at General Motors and Wal-Mart.

General Motors is an old, traditional industrial company that until recently was the nation's largest employer. For decades, its hourly workers have been protected by strong labor unions such as the United Auto Workers (UAW). These unions, in turn, have forged contracts and established working conditions that seem almost archaic in today's economy. Consider the employment conditions of Tim Philbrick, a forty-two-year-old plant worker and union member at the firm's Fairfax plant near Kansas City who has worked for GM for twenty-three years. Philbrick makes almost $20 an hour in base pay. With a little overtime, his annual earnings top $60,000. But even then, he is far from the highest-paid factory worker at GM. Skilled-trade workers such as electricians and toolmakers make $2.00 to $2.50 an hour more and, with greater overtime opportunities often make $100,000 or more per year. Philbrick also gets a no-deductible health insurance policy that allows him to see any doctor he wants. He gets four weeks of vacation per year, plus two weeks off at Christmas and at least another week off in July. He gets two paid twenty-three-minute breaks and a paid thirty-minute lunch break per day. He also has the option to retire after thirty years with full benefits.

GM estimates that, with benefits, its average worker makes more than $43 an hour. Perhaps not surprisingly, then, the firm is always looking for opportunities to reduce its workforce through attrition and cutbacks, with the goal of replacing production capacity with lower-cost labor abroad. The UAW, of course, is staunchly opposed to further workforce reductions and cutbacks. And long-standing work rules strictly dictate who gets overtime, who can be laid off and who can't, and myriad other employment conditions for Tim Philbrick and his coworkers.

The situation at Wal-Mart differs sharply in many ways from those at GM. Along many different dimensions, Wal-Mart is slowly but surely supplanting General Motors as the quintessential U.S. corporation. For example, it is growing rapidly, is becoming more and more ingrained in the American lifestyle, and now employs more people than GM did in its heyday. But the hourly worker at Wal-Mart has a much different experience than the hourly worker at GM. Consider Nancy Handley, a twenty-seven-year-old Wal-Mart employee who oversees the men's department at a big store in St. Louis. Jobs like Handley's pay between $9 and $11 an hour, or about $20,000 a year. About $100 a month is deducted from Handley's paycheck to help cover the costs of benefits. Her health insurance has a $250 deductible; she then pays 20 percent of her health care costs as long as she uses a set of approved physicians. During her typical workday, Handley gets two 15-minute breaks and an hour for lunch, which are unpaid. Some believe the compensation plan is inadequate. Barbara Ehrenreich, author of *Nickel and Dimed: On (Not) Getting By in America*, worked at a Wal-Mart while researching her book and now says, "Why would anybody put up with the wages we were paid?"

But Nancy Handley doesn't feel mistreated by Wal-Mart. Far from it—she says she is appropriately compensated for what she does. She has received three merit raises in the last seven years and has ample job security. Moreover, if she decides to try for advancement, Wal-Mart seems to offer considerable potential, promoting thousands of hourly workers a year to the ranks of management. And Handley clearly isn't unique in her views: Wal-Mart employees have routinely rejected most overtures from labor unions.

In the twenty-first century, the gap between "Old Economy" and "New Economy" workers, between unionized manufacturing workers and nonunion or service workers, may be shrinking. Unions are losing their power in the auto industry, for example, as foreign-owned plants within the United States give carmakers such as Toyota and BMW, which are nonunion, a cost advantage over the "big three" U.S. automakers. U.S. firms are telling the UAW and other unions, "We're becoming noncompetitive, and unless you organize the [foreign-owned firms], we're going to have to modify the proposals we make to you." At the same time, Wal-Mart is facing lawsuits from employees who claim the retailer forced them to work unpaid overtime, among other charges. And a recent class-action lawsuit charges that the retailer has discriminated against women in hundreds of different settings. At a Las Vegas store, the firm faces its first union election. In a world where Wal-Mart now employs three times as many workers as GM, it may be inevitable that the retailer's labor will organize. On the other hand, will labor unions continue to lose their power to determine working conditions for America's workforce?

Case Questions

1. Compare and contrast hourly working conditions at General Motors and Wal-Mart.
2. Describe the most likely role the hourly compensation at these two companies plays in motivating employees.
3. Discuss how goal setting might be used for each of the two jobs profiled in this case.

References: Joann Muller, "Can the UAW Stay in the Game?" *BusinessWeek*, June 10, 2002; Mark Gimein, "Sam Walton Made Us a Promise," *Fortune*, March 18, 2002; Barbara Ehrenreich, *Nickel and Dimed: On (Not) Getting By in America* (New York: Metropolitan Books, 2001); "I'm Proud of What I've Made Myself Into—What I've Created," *Wall Street Journal*, August 28, 1997, pp. B1, B5; "That's Why I Like My Job . . . I Have an Impact on Quality," *Wall Street Journal*, August 28, 1997, pp. B1, B8.

Experiencing Organizational Behavior

Using Compensation to Motivate Workers

Purpose: The purpose of this exercise is to illustrate how compensation can be used to motivate employees.

Format: You will be asked to review eight managers and make salary adjustments for each.

Procedure: Listed below are your notes on the performance of eight managers who work for you. You (either individually or as a group, depending on your instructor's choice) have to recommend salary increases for eight managers who have just completed their first year with the company and are now to be considered for their first annual raise. Keep in mind that you may be setting precedents and that you need to keep salary costs down. However, there are no formal company restrictions on the kind of raises you can give. Indicate the sizes of the raise that you would like to give each manager by writing a percentage next to each name.

Variations: The instructor might alter the situation in one of several ways. One way is to assume that all of the eight managers entered the company at the same salary, say $30,000, which gives a total salary expense of $240,000. If upper management has allowed a salary raise pool of 10 percent of the current salary expenses, then you as the manager have $24,000 to give out as raises. In this variation, students can deal with actual dollar amounts rather than just percentages for the raises. Another interesting variation is to assume that all of the managers entered the company at different salaries, averaging $30,000. (The instructor can create many interesting possibilities for how these salaries might vary.) Then, the students can suggest salaries for the different managers.

_____ % Abraham McGowan. Abe is not, as far as you can tell, a good performer. You have checked your view with others, and they do not feel that he is effective either. However, you happen to know he has one of the toughest work groups to manage. His subordinates have low skill levels, and the work is dirty and hard. If you lose him, you are not sure whom you could find to replace him.

Chapter 7 Communication in Organizations 185

The **gatekeeper** has a strategic position in the network that allows him or her to control information moving in either direction through a channel.

The **liaison** serves as a bridge between groups, tying groups together and facilitating the communication flow needed to integrate group activities.

The **cosmopolite** links the organization to the external environment and may also be an opinion leader in the group.

communicate with one another; the firm's CEO, for example, communicates most often with employee 5. (This does not mean individuals not linked in the communication network never communicate; rather, their communications are relatively infrequent.) Perhaps the CEO and the employee interact frequently outside of work, in church, in service organizations such as Kiwanis, or at sporting events. Such interactions may lead to close friendships that carry over into business relationships. The figure also shows that the group managers do not have important roles in the communication network, contrary to commonsense expectations.

The roles people play in organizational communication networks can be analyzed in terms of their contribution to the functioning of the network.[16] The most important roles are labeled in the bottom portion of Figure 7.5. A **gatekeeper** (employee 5) has a strategic position in the network that allows him or her to control information moving in either direction through a channel. A **liaison** (employee 15) serves as a bridge between groups, tying groups together and facilitating the communication flow needed to integrate group activities. Employee 13 performs the interesting function of **cosmopolite**, who links the organization to the external environment by, for instance, attending conventions and trade shows, keeping up with outside technological innovations, and having more frequent contact with sources outside the organization. This person may also be an opinion leader in the group. Finally, the **isolate** (employee 3) and the **isolated dyad** (employees 2 and 9) tend to work alone and to interact and communicate little with others.

Each of these roles and functions plays an important part in the overall functioning of the communication network and in the organization as a whole. Understanding these roles can help both managers and group members facilitate communication. For instance, the manager who wants to ensure that the CEO receives certain information is well advised to go through the gatekeeper. If the employee who has the technical knowledge necessary for a particular project is an isolate, the manager can take special steps to integrate the employee into the communication network for the duration of the project.

Recent research indicates some possible negative impacts of communication networks. Employee turnover has been shown to occur in clusters related to employee communication networks.[17] That is, employees who communicate regularly in a network may share feelings about the organization and thus influence one another's intentions to stay or quit. Communication networks therefore may have both positive and negative consequences.

As we discuss in Chapter 13, a primary function of organizational structure is to coordinate the activities of many people doing specialized tasks. Organizational communication networks provide

Communication networks are a common element in organizations. Some firms ignore them, a few try to get rid of them, but some successful firms capitalize on their advantages. Techline, a custom furniture manufacturer, actively seeks to create communication networks among groups such as this one, in order to expedite the diffusion of information and enhance overall organizational performance.

The **isolate** and the **isolated dyad** tend to work alone and to interact and communicate little with others.

this much-needed integration. In fact, in some ways communication patterns influence organizational structure. Some companies are finding that the need for better communication forces them to create smaller divisions. The fewer managerial levels and improved team spirit of these divisions tend to enhance communication flows.

Managing Communication

LEARNING OBJECTIVE

Discuss how communication can be managed in organizations.

Communication fidelity is the degree of correspondence between the message intended by the source and the message understood by the receiver.

As simple as the process of communication may seem, messages are not always understood. The degree of correspondence between the message intended by the source and the message understood by the receiver is called **communication fidelity**. Fidelity can be diminished anywhere in the communication process, from the source to the feedback. Moreover, organizations may have characteristics that impede the flow of information.

Improving the Communication Process

To improve organizational communication, one must understand potential problems. Using the basic communication process, we can identify several ways to overcome typical problems.

Source The source may intentionally withhold or filter information on the assumption that the receiver does not need it to understand the communication. Withholding information, however, may render the message meaningless or cause an erroneous interpretation. For example, during a performance appraisal interview, a manager may not tell the employee all the sources of information being used to make the evaluation, thinking the employee does not need to know them. If the employee knew, however, he or she might be able to explain certain behaviors or otherwise alter the manager's perspective of the evaluation and thereby make it more accurate. Filtering may be more likely to occur in electronic communication such as email or voicemail, since they usually call for brevity and conciseness. Selective filtering may cause a breakdown in communication that cannot be repaired, even with good follow-up communication.

To avoid filtering, the communicator needs to understand why it occurs. Filtering can result from a lack of understanding of the receiver's position, from the sender's need to protect his or her own power by limiting the receiver's access to information, or from doubts about what the receiver might do with the information. The sender's primary concern, however, should be the message. In essence, the sender must determine exactly what message he or she wants the receiver to understand, send the receiver enough information to understand the message but not enough to create an overload, and trust the receiver to use the information properly.

Encoding and Decoding Encoding and decoding problems occur as the message is translated into or from the symbols used in transmission. Such problems can relate to the meanings of the symbols or to the transmission itself. Encoding and decoding problems include lack of common experience between source and receiver, problems related to semantics and the use of jargon, and difficulties with the medium. The cartoon illustrates another potential problem.

Clearly the source and the receiver must share a common experience with the symbols that express the message if they are to encode and decode them in exactly the same way. People who speak different languages or come from different cultural

"I thought you said I should take the ball and slowly meander around with it."

Encoding and decoding are critical parts of the communication process. But all too often, errors and mistakes in one or both of these processes can lead to problems. For instance, in the situation shown here the boss apparently meant for his subordinate to "take the ball and run with it." But the subordinate heard something else altogether!

© The New Yorker Collection 2003 Bruce Eric Kaplan from cartoonbank.com. All Rights Reserved.

Semantics is the study of language forms.

Jargon is the specialized or technical language of a trade, field, profession, or social group.

backgrounds may experience problems of this sort. However, even people who speak the same language can misunderstand each other.

Semantics is the study of language forms, and semantic problems occur when people attribute different meanings to the same words or language forms. For example, J. Edgar Hoover, the legendary former director of the FBI, once jotted "watch the borders" on a memo he had received and sent it back to the senior agency manager who had written it. Only after dispatching several dozen agents to guard the border between the United States and Mexico did the agency manager learn what Hoover had actually meant: The margins on the memo were too narrow! Similarly, suppose that when discussing a problem employee, a division head tells her assistant, "We need to get rid of this problem." The division head means the employee should be scheduled for more training or transferred to another division. However, the assistant may interpret the statement differently and fire the employee.

Jargon is the specialized or technical language of a trade, field, profession, or social group. Jargon may be a hybrid of standard language and specialized language. For example, experts in the computer field use terms, such as *gigs*, *megs*, *RAM*, and *bandwidth*, that have little or no meaning to those unfamiliar with computers. The use of jargon makes communication within a close group of colleagues more efficient and meaningful, but outside the group it has the opposite effect. Sometimes a source person comfortable with jargon inadvertently uses it while communicating with a receiver who does not understand it; the result is a communication breakdown. In other cases, the source may use jargon intentionally to obscure meaning or to show outsiders that he or she belongs to the group that uses the language.

The use of jargon is acceptable if the receiver is familiar with it; otherwise, it should be avoided. Repeating a jargon-filled message in clearer terms should help the receiver understand it. In general, both source and receiver should clarify the set of symbols to be used before they communicate. Also, the receiver can ask questions frequently and, if necessary, ask the source to repeat all or part of the message. The source must send the message through a medium appropriate for the message itself and for the intended receiver. For example, a commercial run on an AM radio station will miss its intended effect if the people in the desired market segment listen only to FM radio.

Largely influenced by the Enron debacle, investors are increasingly beginning to scrutinize the financial reporting systems of larger companies. Coca-Cola, for instance, recently saw its own accounting practices criticized in the media. These critics contend that the firm is using increasingly complex reporting methods to make its earnings seem higher than if simpler and more straightforward accounting practices had been used.[18]

Receiver Several communication problems originate in the receiver, including problems with selective attention, value judgments, source credibility, and overload. Selective attention exists when the receiver attends only to selected parts of a message—a frequent occurrence with oral communication. For example, in a college class, some students may hear only part of the professor's lecture as their minds wander to other topics. To focus receivers' attention on the message, senders often engage in attention-getting behaviors such as varying the volume, repeating the message, and offering rewards.

Value judgments are influenced by the degree to which a message reinforces or challenges the receiver's basic personal beliefs. If a message reinforces the receiver's beliefs, she may pay close attention and believe it completely, without examination. On the other hand, if the message challenges those beliefs, the receiver may entirely discount it. Thus, if a firm's sales manager predicts that the demand for new baby-care products will increase substantially over the next two years, he may ignore reports that the birthrate is declining.

The receiver may also judge the credibility of the source of the message. If the source is perceived to be an expert in the field, the listener may pay close attention to the message and believe it. Conversely, if the receiver has little respect for the source, he or she may disregard the message. The receiver considers both the message and the source in making value judgments and determining credibility. An expert in nuclear physics may be viewed as a credible source if the issue is building a nuclear power plant; however, the same person's evaluation of the birthrate may be disregarded, perhaps correctly. This is one reason trial lawyers ask expert witnesses about their education and experience at the beginning of their testimony: to establish credibility.

A receiver experiencing communication overload is receiving more information than she or he can process. In organizations, this can happen very easily; a receiver can be bombarded with computer-generated reports and messages from superiors, peers, and sources outside the organization. It is not unusual for middle managers or telecommuters to receive one hundred email messages per day. Unable to take in all the messages, decode them, understand them, and act on them, the receiver may use selective attention and value judgments to focus on the messages that seem most important. Although this type of selective attention is necessary for survival in an information-glutted environment, the result may be that vital information is lost or overlooked.[19]

Feedback The purpose of feedback is **verification,** in which the receiver sends a message to the source indicating receipt of the message and the degree to which it was understood. Lack of feedback can cause at least two problems. First, the source may need to send another message that depends on the response to the first; if the source receives no feedback, he may not send the second message or may be forced to send the original message again. Second, the receiver may act on the unverified message; if she misunderstood the message, the resulting act may be inappropriate.

Because feedback is so important, the source must actively seek it and the receiver must supply it. Often it is appropriate for the receiver to repeat the original message as an introduction to the response, although the medium or symbols used may be different. Nonverbal cues can provide instantaneous feedback. These include body language and facial expressions such as anger and disbelief.

The source needs to be concerned with the message, the symbols, the medium, and the feedback from the receiver. Of course, the receiver is concerned with these things too, but from a different point of view. In general, the receiver

---

Verification is the feedback portion of communication in which the receiver sends a message to the source indicating receipt of the message and the degree to which he or she understood it.

Focus	Source Question	Source Corrective Action	Receiver Question	Receiver Corrective Action
Message	What idea or thought are you trying to get across?	Give more information. Give less information. Give entire message.	What idea or thought does the sender want you to understand?	Listen carefully to the entire message, not just to part of it.
Symbols	Does the receiver use the same symbols, words, jargon?	Say it another way. Employ repetition. Use receiver's language or jargon. Before sending, clarify symbols to be used.	What symbols are being used—for example, foreign language, technical jargon?	Clarify symbols before communication begins. Ask questions. Ask sender to repeat message.
Medium	Is this a channel that the receiver monitors regularly? Sometimes? Never?	Use multiple media. Change medium. Increase volume (loudness).	What medium or media is the sender using?	Monitor several media.
Feedback	What is the receiver's reaction to your message?	Pay attention to the feedback, especially nonverbal cues. Ask questions.	Did you correctly interpret the message?	Repeat message.

TABLE 7.1

Improving the Communication Process

needs to be source oriented just as the source needs to be receiver oriented. Table 7.1 gives specific suggestions for improving the communication process.

Improving Organizational Factors in Communication

Organizational factors that can create communication breakdowns or barriers include noise, status differences, time pressures, and overload. As previously stated, disturbances anywhere in the organization can distort or interrupt meaningful communication. Thus, the noise created by a rumored takeover can disrupt the orderly flow of task-related information. Kmart's stock recently dropped precipitously based on rumors that the company planned to file bankruptcy. Although the retailer did eventually take this step, rumor alone caused great damage to the company in the eyes of the investment community.[20]

Status differences between source and receiver can cause some of the communication problems just discussed. For example, a firm's chief executive officer may pay little attention to communications from employees far lower on the organization chart, and employees may pay little attention to communications from the CEO. Both are instances of selective attention prompted by the organization's status system. Time pressures and communication overloads are also detrimental to communication. When the receiver is not allowed enough time to understand incoming messages, or when there are too many messages, he or she may misunderstand or ignore some of them. Effective organizational communication provides the right information to the right person at the right time and in the right form.

*The **grapevine** is an informal system of communication that coexists with the formal system.*

Reduce Noise Noise is a primary barrier to effective organizational communication. A common form of noise is the rumor **grapevine,** an informal system of communication that coexists with the formal system. The grapevine usually transmits information faster than official channels do. Because the accuracy of this information is often quite low, however, the grapevine can distort organizational communication. Management can reduce the effects of the distortion by using the grapevine as an additional channel for disseminating information and constantly monitoring it for accuracy.

Foster Informal Communication Communication in well-run companies was once described as "a vast network of informal, open communications."[21] Informal communication fosters mutual trust, which minimizes the effects of status differences. Open communication can also contribute to better understanding between diverse groups in an organization. Monsanto Company created fifteen-member teams in its Agricultural Group, the primary objective being to increase communication and awareness among various diverse groups. Its Chemical Group set up diversity pairs of one supervisor and one worker to increase communication and awareness. In both cases, Monsanto found that increasing communication between people who were different paid handsomely for the organization.[22] Open communication also allows information to be communicated when it is needed rather than when the formal information system allows it to emerge. Thomas Peters and Robert Waterman further describe communication in effective companies as chaotic and intense, supported by the reward structure and the physical arrangement of the facilities. This means the performance appraisal and reward system, offices, meeting rooms, and work areas are designed to encourage frequent, unscheduled, and unstructured communication throughout the organization.

Develop a Balanced Information Network Many large organizations have developed elaborate formal information networks to cope with the potential problems of information overload and time pressures. In many cases, however, the networks have created problems instead of solving them. Often they produce more information than managers and decision makers can comprehend and use in their jobs. The networks also often use only formal communication channels and ignore various informal lines of communication. Furthermore, they frequently provide whatever information the computer is set up to provide—information that may not apply to the most pressing problem at hand. The result of all these drawbacks is loss of communication effectiveness.

Organizations need to balance information load and information processing capabilities. In other words, they must take care not to generate more information than people can handle. It is useless to produce sophisticated statistical reports that managers have no time to read. Furthermore, the new technologies that are making more information available to managers and decision makers must be unified to produce usable information. Information production, storage, and processing capabilities must be compatible with one another and, equally important, with the needs of the organization.

Some companies—for example, General Electric, Anheuser-Busch, and McDonald's—have formalized an upward communication system that uses a corporate "ombudsperson" position. A highly placed executive who is available outside the formal chain of command to hear employees' complaints usually holds this position. The system provides an opportunity for disgruntled employees to complain without fear of losing their jobs and may help some companies achieve a balanced communication system.

Chapter 7 Communication in Organizations

Synopsis

Communication is the process by which two parties exchange information and share meaning. It plays a role in every organizational activity. The purposes of communication in organizations are to achieve coordinated action, share information, and express feelings and emotions.

People in organizations communicate through written, oral, and nonverbal means. Written communications include letters, memos, email, reports, and the like. Oral communication is the type most commonly used. Personal elements, such as facial expressions and body language, and environmental elements, such as office design, are forms of nonverbal communication.

Communication among individuals, groups, or organizations is a process in which a source sends a message and a receiver responds. The source encodes a message into symbols and transmits it through a medium to the receiver, who decodes the symbols. The receiver then responds with feedback, an attempt to verify the meaning of the original message. Noise—anything that distorts or interrupts communication—may interfere in virtually any stage of the process.

The fully integrated communication-information office system—the electronic office—links personnel in a communication network through a combination of computers and electronic transmission systems. The full range of effects of such systems has yet to be fully realized.

Communication networks are systems of information exchange within organizations. Patterns of communication emerge as information flows from person to person in a group. Typical small-group communication networks include the wheel, chain, circle, and all-channel networks. The organizational communication network, which constitutes the real communication links in an organization, usually differs from the arrangement on an organization chart. Roles in organizational communication networks include those of gatekeeper, liaison, cosmopolite, and isolate or isolated dyad.

Managing communication in organizations involves understanding the numerous problems that can interfere with effective communication. Problems may arise from the communication process itself and from organizational factors such as status differences, time pressures, and information overload.

Discussion Questions

1. How is communication in organizations an individual process as well as an organizational process?
2. Discuss the three primary purposes of organizational communication.
3. Describe a situation in which you tried to carry on a conversation when no one was listening. Were any messages sent during the "conversation"?
4. A college classroom is a forum for a typical attempt at communication as the professor tries to communicate the subject to students. Describe classroom communication in terms of the basic communication process outlined in the chapter.
5. Is there a communication network (other than professor-to-student) in the class in which you are using this book? If so, identify the specific roles people play in the network. If not, why has no network developed? What would be the benefits of having a communication network in this class?
6. Why might educators typically focus most communication training on written and oral methods and pay little attention to nonverbal methods? Do you think more training emphasis should be placed on nonverbal communication? Why or why not?
7. Is the typical classroom means of transferring information from professor to student an effective form of communication? If not, where does it break down? What are the communication problems in the college classroom?
8. Who is responsible for solving classroom communication problems: the students, the professors, or the administrations?
9. Have you ever worked in an organization in which communication was a problem? If so, what were some causes of the problem?
10. What methods were used, or should have been used, to improve communication in the situation you described in question 9?
11. Would the use of advanced computer information processing or telecommunications have helped solve the communications problem you described in question 9?

12. What types of communication problems are new telecommunications methods expected to help solve? Why?
13. What types of communications would *not* be appropriate to send by email? By voicemail?
14. Which steps in the communication process are usually left out, or at least poorly done, when email and voicemail are used for communication?

Organizational Behavior Case for Discussion
A Tale of Two Companies

To quote Charles Dickens's *A Tale of Two Cities*, "It was the best of times[;] it was the worst of times." With apologies to Dickens, this description handily sums up the current state of affairs in the communications industry. Firms that are able to take advantage of technological developments prosper, whereas firms that have remained in traditional markets are losing sales and profits. Agilent, an electronics component manufacturer, described the situation in its 2001 annual report: "The dramatic slowdown in the communications and semiconductor markets defined Agilent's second year as an independent company. After very strong growth in 1999 and 2000, the decline in demand in these markets was unprecedented in its speed and severity . . . The downturn worsened as we moved through 2001."

EchoMail provides software that automatically processes, responds, stores, and tracks email correspondence, reducing the time users spend on these chores. Founded by MIT scientists and headquartered in Cambridge, Massachusetts, home of Harvard and MIT, EchoMail's clients include many large organizations such as AT&T, Compaq, Nike, and the U.S. Senate. EchoMail was used to create the controversial Calvin Klein advertisements that allowed consumers to email the "characters" in television or print ads and receive customized, scripted emails in response. EchoMail is the oldest firm (at seven years) in the intelligent-email response industry, which is predicted to grow to $500 million in sales by 2005. Thus, the firm is poised to take advantage of the expected flood of intelligent software users over the next decade, and it recently hired sales and technical professionals.

Agilent, in contrast, was created as a spinoff from Hewlett-Packard (HP) when that company refocused its businesses on computing and printing. The November 1999 initial public offering was the largest in Silicon Valley history, valued at $2.1 billion. With 43,000 employees in 40 countries, Agilent is a leader in developing and manufacturing electrical components and testing equipment, as well as in installation and maintenance services for its equipment. Agilent customers compete in a wide variety of industries, including agricultural chemicals; pharmaceuticals; petrochemicals; semiconductors; wireless communications; PCs; foods; appliances; and automotive, aerospace, and consumer products. Therefore, Agilent is vulnerable to economic downturns in which manufacturers reduce their purchases of equipment and services. Agilent has instituted pay cuts; in 2001 the firm laid off 4,000 workers. Since then another 4,000 jobs have been eliminated.

Although Agilent seems to be facing a host of problems because of its dependence on a currently lackluster segment of the communications industry, there is also a bright side. Agilent considers itself the true heir of Hewlett-Packard founders Dave Packard and Bill Hewlett, who used participatory management, open-door policies, and decision making by consensus to keep HP employees working together as a team. Agilent, which carefully built on the foundation of HP's culture, also carefully worked to maintain its culture when things got tough. Initially the company tried everything within its power to avoid layoffs: cost cutting, hiring freezes, and even pay cuts. Then, when layoffs became inevitable, CEO Ned Barnholt asked each manager to choose from among the employees known personally to them and insisted that workers be told face to face. Barnholt made the announcement himself, ensuring that employees heard the news from him and not from reporters. He described exactly how employees would be evaluated and how the layoffs would occur. In a rough, emotional tone of voice, he intoned, "This is the toughest decision of my career, but we've run out of alternatives."

As a result of his honest and sincere communication, most Agilent employees did not blame the firm or their supervisors. "I knew that this isn't the HP Way, and it's not what Bill and Dave [Hewlett and Packard] would have wanted, but if they were faced with the same situation, they would have had to do the exact same thing. I know Ned [CEO Barnholt] probably lost a lot [of sleep] having to get up there in front of everybody and make this announcement and have to let go people in his family," said Benjamin Steers, an Agilent employee.

While EchoMail is prospering as its new technology enables the firm to increase sales, profitability, and personnel, Agilent is facing declining markets for many of its traditional products. Its hope for the future depends on its ability to innovate and develop new products. However, as Agilent is demonstrating, appropriate communication, especially of bad news, can be key to building a culture of responsibility, loyalty, and empathy.

Case Questions

1. How did Agilent's communication choices lead to an effective employee response to the firm's downsizing?
2. Both Agilent and EchoMail are international firms, with production and sales locations in multiple countries. What are some potential problems or challenges that these firms' international involvement present?
3. Communication is described as reflecting the organization culture and as having the power to change the culture. How does the communication taking place in your Management classroom reflect your school's culture? Has communication at your school changed its culture? If so, how?

References: "About Agilent," "History," "Industries," "2003 Annual Report," Agilent corporate website, www.agilent.com on May 10, 2004; "About EchoMail," corporate website; Daniel Roth, "How to Cut Pay, Lay Off 8,000 People, and Still Have Workers Who Love You. It's Easy: Just Follow the Agilent Way," *Fortune*, February 4, 2002; Erin Allday, "Agilent Cuts 600 More Local Jobs," *Press Democrat* (Santa Rosa, CA), December 11, 2001, p. A1; John Evan Frook, "Technology Leads Prospects to Sales," *BtoB Magazine*, October 10, 2002; Deborah Shapley, "Dr. E-Mail Will See You Now," *Technology Review*, January–February 2000, pp. 42–47; Roberta Fusaro, "E-Mail Adds Aura to Calvin Klein Campaign," *Computerworld*, November 30, 1998, p. 103.

Experiencing Organizational Behavior
The Importance of Feedback in Oral Communication

Purpose: This exercise demonstrates the importance of feedback in oral communication.

Format: You will be an observer or play the role of either a manager or an assistant manager trying to tell a coworker where a package of important materials is to be picked up. The observer's role is to make sure the other two participants follow the rules and to observe and record any interesting occurrences.

Procedure: The instructor will divide the class into groups of three. (Any extra members can be roving observers.) The three people in each group will take the roles of manager, assistant manager, and observer. In the second trial, the manager and the assistant manager will switch roles.

Trial 1: The manager and assistant manager should turn their backs to each other so that neither can see the other. Here is the situation: The manager is in another city that he or she is not familiar with but the assistant manager knows quite well. The manager needs to find the office of a supplier to pick up drawings of a critical component of the company's main product. The supplier will be closing for the day in a few minutes; the drawings must be picked up before closing time. The manager has called the assistant manager to get directions to the office. However, the connection is faulty; the manager can hear the assistant manager, but the assistant manager can hear only enough to know the manager is on the line. The manager has redialed once, but the connection was still poor. Now there is no time to lose. The manager has decided to get the directions from the assistant without asking questions.

Just before the exercise begins, the instructor will give the assistant manager a detailed map of the city that shows the locations of the supplier's office and the manager. The map will include a number of turns, stops, stoplights, intersections, and shopping centers between these locations. The assistant manager can study it for no longer than a minute or two. When the instructor gives the direction to start, the assistant manager describes to the manager how to get from his or her present location to the supplier's office. As the assistant manager gives the directions, the manager draws the map on a piece of paper.

The observer makes sure no questions are asked, records the beginning and ending times, and notes how the assistant manager tries to communicate particularly difficult points (including points about which the manager obviously wants to ask questions) and any other noteworthy occurrences.

After all pairs have finished, each observer "grades" the quality of the manager's map by comparing it with the original and counting the number of obvious mistakes. The instructor will ask a few managers who believe they have drawn good maps to tell the rest of the class how to get to the supplier's office.

Trial 2: In trial 2, the manager and assistant manager switch roles, and a second map is given to the new assistant managers. The situation is the same as in the first trial except the telephones are working properly and the manager can ask questions of the assistant manager. The observer's role is the same as in trial 1: recording the beginning and ending times, the methods of communication, and other noteworthy occurrences.

After all pairs have finished, the observers grade the maps, just as in the first trial. The instructor then selects a few managers to tell the rest of the class how to get to the supplier's office. The subsequent class discussion should center on the experiences of the class members and the follow-up questions.

Follow-up Questions

1. Which trial resulted in more accurate maps? Why?
2. Which trial took longer? Why?
3. How did you feel when a question needed to be asked but could not be asked in trial 1? Was your confidence in the final result affected differently in the two trials?

Self-Assessment Exercise
Diagnosing Your Listening Skills

Introduction: Good listening skills are essential for effective communication and are often overlooked when communication is analyzed. This self-assessment questionnaire examines your ability to listen effectively.

Instructions: Go through the following statements, checking "Yes" or "No" next to each one. Mark each question as truthfully as you can in light of your behavior in the last few meetings or gatherings you attended.

Yes No

____ ____ 1. I frequently attempt to listen to several conversations at the same time.

____ ____ 2. I like people to give me only the facts and then let me make my own interpretation.

____ ____ 3. I sometimes pretend to pay attention to people.

____ ____ 4. I consider myself a good judge of nonverbal communications.

____ ____ 5. I usually know what another person is going to say before he or she says it.

____ ____ 6. I usually end conversations that don't interest me by diverting my attention from the speaker.

____ ____ 7. I frequently nod, frown, or in some other way let the speaker know how I feel about what he or she is saying.

____ ____ 8. I usually respond immediately when someone has finished talking.

____ ____ 9. I evaluate what is being said while it is being said.

____ ____ 10. I usually formulate a response while the other person is still talking.

____ ____ 11. The speaker's "delivery" style frequently keeps me from listening to content.

____ ____ 12. I usually ask people to clarify what they have said rather than guess at the meaning.

____ ____ 13. I make a concerted effort to understand other people's point of view.

____ ____ 14. I frequently hear what I expect to hear rather than what is said.

____ ____ 15. Most people feel that I have understood their point of view when we disagree.

Scoring

The correct answers according to communication theory are as follows:

No for statements 1, 2, 3, 5, 6, 7, 8, 9, 10, 11, 14.
Yes for statements 4, 12, 13, 15.

If you missed only one or two responses, you strongly approve of your own listening habits, and you are on the right track to becoming an effective listener in your role as manager. If you missed three or four responses, you have uncovered some doubts about your listening effectiveness, and your knowledge of how to listen has some gaps. If you missed five or more responses, you probably are not satisfied with the way you listen, and your friends and coworkers may not feel you are a good listener, either. Work on improving your active listening skills.

Reference: "Diagnosing Your Listening Skills," from Ethel C. Glenn and Elliott A. Pond, "Listening Self-Inventory," *Supervisory Management*, January 1989, pp. 12–15. Copyright © 1989 by American Management Association. Reproduced with permission of American Management Association in the format Textbook via Copyright Clearance Center.

OB Online

1. Find the country-specific websites of a single large company, such as Coca-Cola, IBM, or Toyota, for at least three different countries. Then identify the similarities and differences among the websites.
2. Compare electronic communication with the three basic methods of communication. For example, can nonverbal messages be sent via email?
3. Identify how several attributes of electronic communication can serve as noise. For example, cell phone static may make it difficult for the receiver to hear the sender.
4. Use the Internet to research the most frequently used methods of communicating in organizations.

Building Managerial Skills

Exercise Overview: Communication skills involve a manager's ability both to convey ideas and information effectively to others and to receive ideas and information effectively from others. This exercise focuses on communication skills in deciding how to best convey information.

Exercise Background: Assume you are a middle manager for a large electronics firm. People in your organization generally use one of three means for communicating with one another. The most common way is oral communication, accomplished either face to face or by telephone. Electronic mail is also widely used. Finally, a surprisingly large amount of communication is still done on paper, such as through memos, reports, and letters.

During the course of a typical day, you receive and send a variety of messages and other communications. You generally use some combination of all the communication methods previously noted during the day. The things you need to communicate today include the following:

1. You need to schedule a meeting with five subordinates.
2. You need to congratulate a coworker who just had a baby.
3. You need to reprimand a staff assistant who has been coming to work late for the last several days.
4. You need to inform the warehouse staff that several customers have recently complained because their shipments were not properly packed.
5. You need to schedule a meeting with your boss.
6. You need to announce two promotions.
7. You need to fire someone who has been performing poorly for some time.
8. You need to inform several individuals about a set of new government regulations that will soon affect them.
9. You need to inform a supplier that your company will soon be cutting back on its purchases because a competing supplier has lowered its prices, and you plan to shift more of your business to that supplier.
10. You need to resolve a disagreement between two subordinates who want to take their vacation at the same time.

Exercise Task: Using the information just presented, do the following:

1. Indicate which methods of communication would be appropriate for each situation.
2. Rank-order the methods for each communication situation from best to worst.
3. Compare your rankings with those of a classmate, and discuss any differences

TEST PREPPER

ACE self-test

You have read the chapter and studied the key terms, and the exam is any day now. Think you're ready to ace it? Take this sample test to gauge your comprehension of chapter material. You can check your answers at the back of the book. Want more test questions? Visit the student website at http://college.hmco.com/business/students/ (select Griffin/Moorhead, Fundamentals of Organizational Behavior 1e) and take the ACE quizzes for more practice.

1. **T F** Gestures and facial expressions usually mean the same things across cultures.
2. **T F** The most common form of organizational written communication is the annual report.
3. **T F** The mouth is the most expressive component of the face.
4. **T F** The arrangement and nature of furniture in an office is a form of communication.
5. **T F** When a receiver gets a message from a source, he or she must encode it.
6. **T F** A face-to-face communication has a greater carrying capacity than does an email.
7. **T F** Feedback occurs when a message doesn't reach its destination and cycles back to the sender.
8. **T F** Telecommuting may increase productivity, personal freedom, and social interactions in the office.
9. **T F** The real increases in organizational productivity due to information technology may come from the ability to communicate in new and different ways rather than from simply speeding up existing communication patterns.
10. **T F** Roger works in an informal group without a designated leader. He is likely to be part of a chain communication network.
11. **T F** Latisha has a strategic position in the organization because she can control information moving in either direction through a channel. Latisha occupies a gatekeeper role.
12. **T F** Filtering is more likely to occur in electronic communication, such as email, than in face-to-face interactions.
13. **T F** Jargon can make the communication of a close group of colleagues more efficient.
14. **T F** Communication overload exists when a sender transmits more information than he or she is allowed to.
15. **T F** To establish the most effective communication, the source should actively seek feedback and the receiver should actively send it.
16. **T F** Information transmitted through the grapevine is often more accurate than information transmitted through official channels.
17. The primary purpose of organizational communication is to
    a. manage uncertainty.
    b. identify low performers.
    c. reward high performers.
    d. achieve coordinated action.
    e. make a profit.
18. Which of the following statements best captures the issues regarding communication across cultures?
    a. Colors and body language have universal meanings across nearly all cultures.
    b. Direct translations of messages ensure the clearest communication across cultures.
    c. Technology has overcome most of the problems involved in communicating across cultures.
    d. Managers should avoid attempting to communicate across cultures.
    e. Verbal and nonverbal messages may have different meanings in different cultures.
19. The most common form of written communications is the
    a. termination slip.
    b. application form.
    c. paycheck.
    d. work schedule.
    e. memo.
20. The most prevalent form of organizational communication is
    a. oral.
    b. nonverbal.
    c. written.
    d. body language.
    e. colors and symbols.
21. Which of the following is not an example of nonverbal communication?
    a. Eye contact
    b. Sitting on the edge of a chair during a discussion
    c. Facial expressions
    d. Office furniture
    e. Email

22. During the complete communication process, the receiver responds with a message to the source to verify the communication. This portion of the communication process is known as
    a. decoding.
    b. transmission.
    c. the medium of communication.
    d. the feedback loop.
    e. noise control.

23. Ronald has an idea he wants to communicate to his boss, so he writes it down on a piece of paper. Ronald has just completed which portion of the communication process?
    a. Source
    b. Encoding
    c. Medium
    d. Feedback
    e. Transmission

24. Which medium has the largest carrying capacity?
    a. Voicemail
    b. Email
    c. Letter
    d. Telephone
    e. Face-to-face conversation

25. After Josh received a letter communicating a job offer, he responded immediately by sending a letter indicating his acceptance. Josh's response is an example of which portion of the communication process?
    a. Noise reduction
    b. Decoding
    c. Feedback
    d. Receiver
    e. Verbal communication

26. Effective communication occurs when
    a. the sender encodes the message.
    b. the receiver decodes the message.
    c. the sender and the receiver share the same meaning.
    d. all noise has been eliminated.
    e. the appropriate transmission medium is used.

27. Which of the following is a disadvantage of telecommuting?
    a. Reduced personal freedom
    b. Decreased productivity
    c. Reduced social interactions
    d. Increased air pollution
    e. Increased fatigue

28. Electronic information technology not only speeds up existing communication but also
    a. eliminates obsolete communications.
    b. reduces unnecessary social interactions.
    c. reduces personal freedom.
    d. forces managers to spend more time at work.
    e. allows for communication in new and different ways.

29. An organization structured as a narrow vertical hierarchy likely follows which communication pattern?
    a. Wheel
    b. Chain
    c. Circle
    d. All-channel
    e. Spiral

30. Randy's work position requires him to relay information to many of his coworkers. This position is likely to affect which of the following for Randy?
    a. His level in the organizational hierarchy
    b. His organizing skills
    c. His technical skills
    d. His organizational commitment
    e. His opportunity for informal leadership

31. Which of the following generally provides directions rather than feedback to top management?
    a. Upward communication
    b. Downward communication
    c. Horizontal communication
    d. Lateral communication
    e. Informal communication

32. Lisa serves as the communication "go-between" for two manufacturing groups in the organization. Which communication role is she filling?
    a. Gatekeeper
    b. Liaison
    c. Cosmopolite
    d. Isolate
    e. Dyad

33. Carlos frequently leaves very short instructions for his subordinates because he believes they do not need to understand the extra information to complete their tasks. Carlos would improve his communications if he stopped
    a. encoding.
    b. decoding.
    c. sourcing.
    d. isolating.
    e. filtering.

34. Tammy heard about the company layoffs from James, who heard about them from Vince, who heard about them even before the official plans were announced by the company president. This is an example of the speed of
    a. dyadic interchanges.
    b. selective perception.
    c. vertical communication.
    d. the grapevine.
    e. a wheel network.

CHAPTER 8

Group Dynamics

MANAGEMENT PREVIEW

Just about everyone can identify several groups to which she or he belongs. Some groups are based on friendships and personal relationships; others are more formally established and may be part of a larger organization. All organizations have numerous groups that do some part of the organization's work. The performance and productivity of an organization is the total of the output and productivity of all of the individuals and groups that work within it. Large companies around the world are restructuring their organizations around work groups and teams to increase productivity and innovation and to improve customer service.

This chapter is the first of a two-chapter sequence on groups and teams in organizations: groups such as the traditional work groups to which most people belong in their work organizations, pit crews at stock-car races, the Zebra teams that reenergized the black-and-white photo processing unit at Eastman Kodak, a football team, an engineering work group, or a group of nurses working the night shift at a local hospital. In this chapter, we cover the basics of group dynamics: the reasons for group formation, the types of groups in organizations, group performance factors, and the potential for conflict in groups. In Chapter 9, we consider how today's organizations are using teams.

We begin this chapter by defining *group* and summarizing the importance of groups in organizations. We then describe different types of groups and discuss the stages in which they evolve from newly formed groups into mature, high-performing units. Next, we identify four key factors that affect group performance. We then move to a discussion of how groups interact with other groups in organizations and examine conflict among groups in organizations. Finally, we identify the important elements in managing groups in organizations.

After you have studied this chapter, you should be able to:
- ☐ *Define a group.*
- ☐ *Discuss the types of groups commonly found in organizations.*
- ☐ *Describe the general stages of group development.*

Chapter 8 Group Dynamics

- *Discuss the major group performance factors.*
- *Describe intergroup dynamics.*
- *Explain conflict in organizations.*
- *Discuss methods for managing group and intergroup dynamics.*

We start with some examples that underscore the importance of groups to the successful performance of a variety of businesses today.

At one time, many observers feared that recent advances in communications marked the end of face-to-face dialogues, collaboration, teamwork, and other human interactions. Instead companies today are finding technology can enhance and extend the use of traditional team interactions. "There's an opportunity for a whole new level of business-performance improvements in the collaborative redesign of processes, using the Internet," according to James A. Champy, chairman of consulting at Perot Systems.

Lockheed Martin uses a system of ninety web software tools to coordinate a $200 billion project for building the next-generation stealth fighters. The manufacturer brings together 40,000 users, 80 subcontractors, and 187 locations around the world. Lockheed uses the Web to exchange documents and designs and to monitor project progress. "We're getting the best people, applying the best designs, from wherever we need them," says Mark Peden, Lockheed information systems vice president.

At General Motors, web collaboration helps engineers and external parts suppliers work together on product design. Complex designs might involve fourteen worldwide sites in addition to the dozens of partner firms that create components and subsystems. By saving time, the engineers are able to complete three or four alternative designs instead of just one and still finish weeks sooner.

Prospective students at Yale University use an Internet-based system to investigate the school, complete an application, and apply for financial aid. Admissions staff around the country then share information about applicants, with online discussion and comments posted to documents. Nevertheless, James Stevens, director of admissions, still notifies accepted applicants with a phone call. He explains, "[They will] hear from me personally. It is very important to us for people to understand how personal the experience is here."

General Electric holds virtual company meetings, with speeches webcast to all of its locations simultaneously. Management shares financial results with all employees via the Internet. "There are no secrets. The whole organization has everything," says former CEO Jack Welch. He claims the shared data facilitate building employees' trust and allow everyone to have the same information, thereby improving teamwork.

"Without meaningful personal interaction …, it's hard to build understanding and accountability." —Jon Katzenbach, consultant and author of The Discipline of Teams

The Children's Hospital at Montefiore has integrated a patient information system throughout the facility. Patients and family members use smart cards for customized access to information about illnesses and treatments, video games or movies on demand, and the Internet. "It's about the patient's ability to control [his or her] environment," says Jeb Weisman, software designer. David Rockwell, a lead designer of the system, says the intent is "to provide information, insight, and a sense of wonder and delight." Patients and their families thus become team members in their own treatment.

The technology is helpful, but it doesn't manage itself. Paul R. Gudonis, chairman and CEO of Genuity, Inc., says that although managers have made a good start in encouraging teams to use technology, "[t]hey've now found that it's going to take more effort offline to integrate

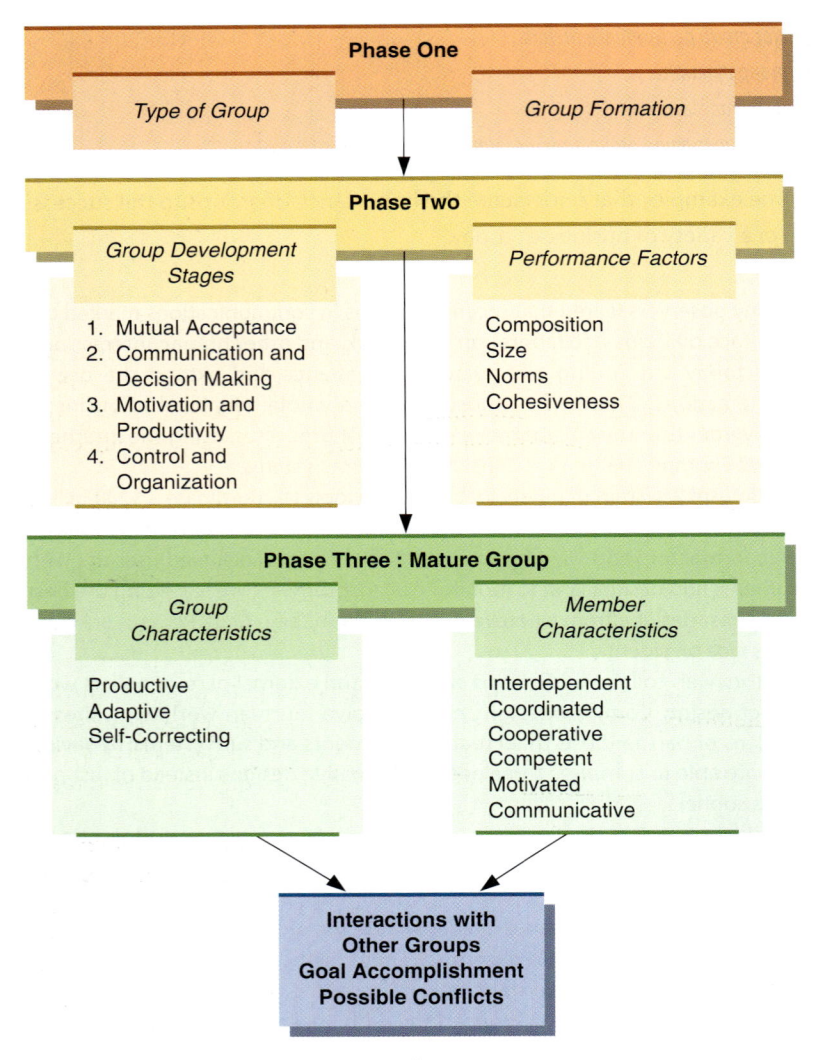

FIGURE 8.1

A General Model of Group Dynamics

This model serves as the framework for this chapter. In phase one, the reasons for group formation determine what type of group it will be. In the second phase, groups evolve through four stages under the influence of four performance factors. Finally, a mature group emerges that interacts with other groups and can pursue organizational goals; conflicts with other groups sometimes occur.

Phase One
- Type of Group
- Group Formation

Phase Two
- Group Development Stages
  1. Mutual Acceptance
  2. Communication and Decision Making
  3. Motivation and Productivity
  4. Control and Organization
- Performance Factors
  - Composition
  - Size
  - Norms
  - Cohesiveness

Phase Three: Mature Group
- Group Characteristics
  - Productive
  - Adaptive
  - Self-Correcting
- Member Characteristics
  - Interdependent
  - Coordinated
  - Cooperative
  - Competent
  - Motivated
  - Communicative

Interactions with Other Groups
Goal Accomplishment
Possible Conflicts

---

offline and online processes to get the kind of changed behavior and benefits that they're looking for." Jon Katzenbach, consultant and author of *The Discipline of Teams*, claims, "Without meaningful personal interaction and doing 'real' work together, it's hard to build understanding and accountability," reminding leaders of the continuing value of hands-on management and face-to-face meetings.

References: "Paul Gudonis, Chairman and CEO, Genuity, Inc." *Fast Company*, May 2002; Polly LaBarre, "Strategic Innovation: The Children's Hospital at Montefiore," *Fast Company*, May 2002; "The New Teamwork," *BusinessWeek*, February 18, 2002; Anne Fisher, "Virtual Teams and Long-Distance Meetings: More on Staying Grounded," *Fortune*, October 15, 2001 (quotation); "Giants Can Be Nimble," *BusinessWeek Biz*, September 18, 2000; "Meet Yale's Admissions Director," *BusinessWeek*, December 15, 1999.

Understanding how and why people interact with one another is a complex process, whether the interaction occurs in a sports team, a work group, or a school committee. This is especially true when those individuals are members of the same group. Figure 8.1 presents a three-phase model of group dynamics. In the first phase, the reasons for forming the group determine what type of group it will be. A four-step process of group development occurs during the second stage; the precise nature of these steps depends on four primary group performance factors. In the final phase, a mature, productive, adaptive group has evolved. As the model shows, mature groups interact with other groups, meet goals, and sometimes have conflicts with other groups. This model serves as the framework for our discussion of groups in this chapter.

The Nature of Groups

LEARNING OBJECTIVE
Define a group.

Definitions of *group* are as abundant as studies of groups. Groups can be defined in terms of perceptions, motivation, organization, interdependencies, and interactions. We define a **group** as two or more people who interact with one another such that each person influences and is influenced by each other person.[1] Two people who are physically near each other are not a group unless they interact and

Chapter 8   Group Dynamics

A **group** is two or more people who interact with one another such that each person influences and is influenced by each other person.

have some influence on each other. Coworkers may work side by side on related tasks, but if they do not interact, they are not a group.

Although groups often have goals, our definition does not state that group members must share a goal or motivation. This omission implies that members of a group may identify little or not at all with the group's goal. People can be a part of a group and enjoy the benefits of group membership without wanting to pursue any group goal. Members may satisfy needs just by being members, without pursuing anything. Of course, the quality of the interactions and the group's performance may be affected by members' lack of interest in the group goal. Our definition also suggests a limit on group size. A collection of people so large that its members cannot interact with and influence one another does not meet this definition. Furthermore, in reality, the dynamics of large assemblies of people usually differ significantly from those of small groups. Our focus in this chapter is on small groups in which the members interact with and influence one another.

Understanding the behavior of people in organizations requires that we understand the forces that affect individuals as well as how individuals affect the organization. The behavior of individuals both affects and is affected by the group. The accomplishments of groups are strongly influenced by the behavior of their individual members. For example, adding one key all-star player to a basketball team may make the difference between a losing season and a league championship. At the same time, groups have profound effects on the behaviors of their members. Group pressure, for instance, is often cited as a reason for lying or cheating, activities members claim they would not have chosen on their own.

Groups form to meet individual and organizational needs. For example, each year the National Black MBA Association holds a meeting for its members. Attendees make contacts, get acquainted with their peers, and form numerous groups in response to similar goals, aspirations, interests, and experiences. Both the overall organization and the various groups formed help satisfy a variety of needs and offer networking and other support for their members.

From a managerial perspective, the work group is the primary means by which managers coordinate individuals' behavior to achieve organizational goals. Managers direct the activities of individuals, but they also direct and coordinate interactions within groups. For example, efforts to boost salespeople's performance have been shown to have both individual and group effects.[2] Therefore, the manager must pay attention to both the individual and the group when trying to improve employee performance. Managers must be aware of individual needs and interpersonal dynamics to manage groups effectively and efficiently because the behavior of individuals is key to the group's success or failure.[3] The Mastering Change box underscores this point, showing how creating Innovation Teams made up of employees from various divisions, levels, and geographical regions has helped boost innovation at Whirlpool.

MASTERING CHANGE

Ongoing Innovation at Whirlpool

The appliance industry has long been considered one of the most predictable areas of business, with the same types of products—refrigerators, dishwashers, washers, and dryers—sold to the same types of consumers. Competitors such as Whirlpool, General Electric, and Maytag have always competed by offering lower-cost and higher-quality products while reducing manufacturing and distribution costs. However, managers at Whirlpool found that using that proven strategy left the company stagnant, with little room to grow and change, so the company adopted a new strategy.

Today Whirlpool uses its own employees, as well as consumers, to supply new, innovative ideas built around current lifestyles. Nancy Snyder, a Whirlpool vice president, says, "We had this internal market of people we weren't tapping into. We wanted to get rid of the 'great man' theory that only one person . . . is responsible for innovation." To encourage creativity, the firm created a seventy-five-member Innovation Team of employees from every division, level, and geographical region to search the company for new ideas.

The change has been dramatic. One employee suggestion led to the creation of Whirlpool's Inspired Chef division. The business uses home-based parties that feature chefs cooking gourmet meals for paying guests in the hope of selling them the kitchenware used to prepare the meals. A pilot program, with sixty chefs in six states, was a success, and a national rollout began in 2002. Listening to customers and workers has led to innovations such as a juicer that rotates more slowly to reduce frothing and

"[T]his time, it feels like innovation has become a part of us . . ."—Nancy Snyder, Whirlpool vice president for Strategic Competency Creation

an oven that cooks from the top and bottom simultaneously to enhance baking results. Other employee suggestions have resulted in the development of specialized washing machines for international customers, such as a washer that specializes in cleaning white clothes for the Indian market, in which whiteness is associated with good hygiene and purity.

Whirlpool's challenge is to sustain such creative efforts over the long term. J. D. Rapp, an Innovation Team leader, says, "With the constant pressure to innovate and change, creative ideas can end up being one-hit wonders." Nancy Snyder believes the firm can extend its creative streak:" [T]his time, it feels like innovation has become a part of us, that it's bigger than a specific project."

References: "Whirlpool's 2003 Annual Report: Chairman's Letter," "Whirlpool North America," Whirlpool website, www.whirlpool.com on May 20, 2004; Fara Warner, "Recipe for Growth," *Fast Company*, October 2001, pp. 40–41 (quotation, p. 41); "Whirlpool Announces First Stage of Global Restructuring," *Appliance Manufacturer*, February 26, 2001.

Types of Groups

LEARNING OBJECTIVE

Discuss the types of groups commonly found in organizations.

Our first task in understanding group processes is to develop a typology of groups that provides insight into their dynamics. Groups may be loosely categorized according to their degree of formalization (formal or informal) and permanence (relatively permanent or relatively temporary).

Formal Groups

A **formal group** is formed by an organization to do its work.

Formal groups are established by the organization to do its work. Formal groups include command (or functional) groups, task groups, and affinity groups. A **command** group is relatively permanent and is characterized by functional reporting relationships, such as a group manager and those who report to the manager. Command groups are usually included in the organization chart. A **task,** or **special-project, group** is created to perform a specific task, such as solving a

A **command group** is a relatively permanent, formal group with functional reporting relationships and is usually included in the organization chart.

A **task,** or **special-project, group** is a relatively temporary, formal group established to do a specific task.

An **affinity group** is a collection of employees from the same level in the organization who meet on a regular basis to share information, capture emerging opportunities, and solve problems.

particular quality problem, and is relatively temporary. An **affinity group** is a relatively permanent collection of employees from the same level in the organization who meet on a regular basis to share information, capture emerging opportunities, and solve problems.[4]

In business organizations, most employees work in command groups, as typically specified on an official organization chart. The size, shape, and organization of a company's command groups can vary considerably. Typical command groups in organizations include the quality assurance department, the industrial engineering department, the cost accounting department, and the personnel department. Other types of command groups include work teams organized as in the Japanese style of management, in which subsections of manufacturing and assembly processes are each assigned to a team of workers. The team members decide among themselves who will perform each task.

Teams are becoming widespread in automobile manufacturing. For instance, General Motors has organized most of its highly automated assembly lines into work teams of five to twenty workers. Although participative teams are becoming more popular, command groups, whether entire departments or sophisticated work teams, are the dominant type of work group in organizations. Federal Express organizes its clerical workers into teams that manage themselves.

Task groups are typically temporary and are often established to solve a particular problem. The group usually dissolves once it solves the problem or makes recommendations. People typically remain members of their command groups, or functional departments, while simultaneously serving in a task group and continuing to carry out their normal job duties. Members' command group duties may be temporarily reduced if the task group requires a great deal of time and effort. Task groups exist in all types of organizations around the world. For example, the Pope once established a special task force of cardinals to study the financial condition of the Vatican and develop new ways to raise money.[5]

Affinity groups are a special type of formal group: They are set up by the organization, yet are not part of the formal organization structure. They are not really command groups because they are not part of the organizational hierarchy, and they are not task groups because they endure longer than any one task. Affinity groups are groups of employees who share roles, responsibilities, duties, and interests, and represent horizontal slices of the normal organizational hierarchy. Because members share important characteristics such as roles, duties, and levels, they are said to have an affinity for one another. Members of affinity groups usually have very similar job titles and similar duties, but work in different divisions or departments within the organization.

Affinity groups meet regularly, and members have assigned roles such as recorder, reporter, facilitator, and meeting organizer. Members follow simple rules such as communicating openly and honestly, listening actively, respecting confidentiality, honoring time agreements, being prepared, staying focused, being individually accountable, and being supportive of one another and of the group. The greatest benefits of affinity groups are that they cross existing organizational boundaries and facilitate better communication among diverse departments and divisions across the organization.

Informal Groups

An **informal group** is established by its members.

Whereas formal groups are established by the organization, **informal groups** are formed by their members and consist of friendship groups, which are relatively

TABLE 8.1

Classification Scheme for Types of Groups

	Relatively Permanent	Relatively Temporary	
Formal	**Command Groups**	**Task Groups**	**Affinity Groups**
	Quality-assurance department	Search committee for a new school superintendent	New product development group
	Cost-accounting group	Task force on new-product quality	
Informal	**Friendship Groups**	**Interest Groups**	
	Friends who do many activities together (attend the theater, play games, travel)	Bowling group Women's network	

A **friendship group** is relatively permanent and informal, and draws its benefits from the social relationships among its members.

An **interest group** is relatively temporary and informal, and is organized around an activity or interest shared by its members.

permanent, and interest groups, which may be shorter lived. **Friendship groups** arise out of the cordial relationships among members and the enjoyment they get from being together. **Interest groups** are organized around a common activity or interest, although friendships may develop among members.

Good examples of interest groups are the recently developed networks of working women. Many of these groups began as informal social gatherings of women who wanted to meet with other women working in male-dominated organizations, but they soon developed into interest groups whose benefits went far beyond their initial social purposes. The networks became information systems for career counseling, job placement, and management training. Some networks were eventually established as formal, permanent associations; some remained informal groups based more on social relationships than on any specific interest; others were dissolved. These groups may be partly responsible for the dramatic increase in the percentage of women in managerial and administrative jobs.

Table 8.1 provides examples of the various formal and informal groups in organizations.

Stages of Group Development

LEARNING OBJECTIVE

Describe the general stages of group development.

Groups are not static; they typically develop through a four-stage process: (1) mutual acceptance, (2) communication and decision making, (3) motivation and productivity, and (4) control and organization.[6] Figure 8.2 shows the stages and the activities that typify them. We treat the stages as separate and distinct. It is difficult to pinpoint exactly when a group moves from one stage to another, however, because the activities in each phase tend to overlap.

Mutual Acceptance

In the **mutual acceptance** stage of group development, members share information about themselves and get to know one another.

In the **mutual acceptance** stage of group development, the group forms and members get to know one another by sharing information about themselves. They often test one another's opinions by discussing subjects that have little to do with

Chapter 8 Group Dynamics

```
New Group Formation  --→  Mutual Acceptance
New Task / New Members  --→

Mutual Acceptance:
  Making Acquaintances
  Sharing Information
  Discussing Subjects Unrelated to Task
  Testing One Another
  Being Defensive, Quibbling

Communication and Decision Making:
  Expressing Attitudes
  Establishing Norms
  Establishing Goals
  Openly Discussing Tasks

Motivation and Productivity:
  Cooperating
  Working Actively on Tasks
  Being Creative

Control and Organization:
  Working Interdependently
  Assigning Tasks Based on Ability
  Acting Spontaneously
  Being Flexible
  Self-Correcting
```

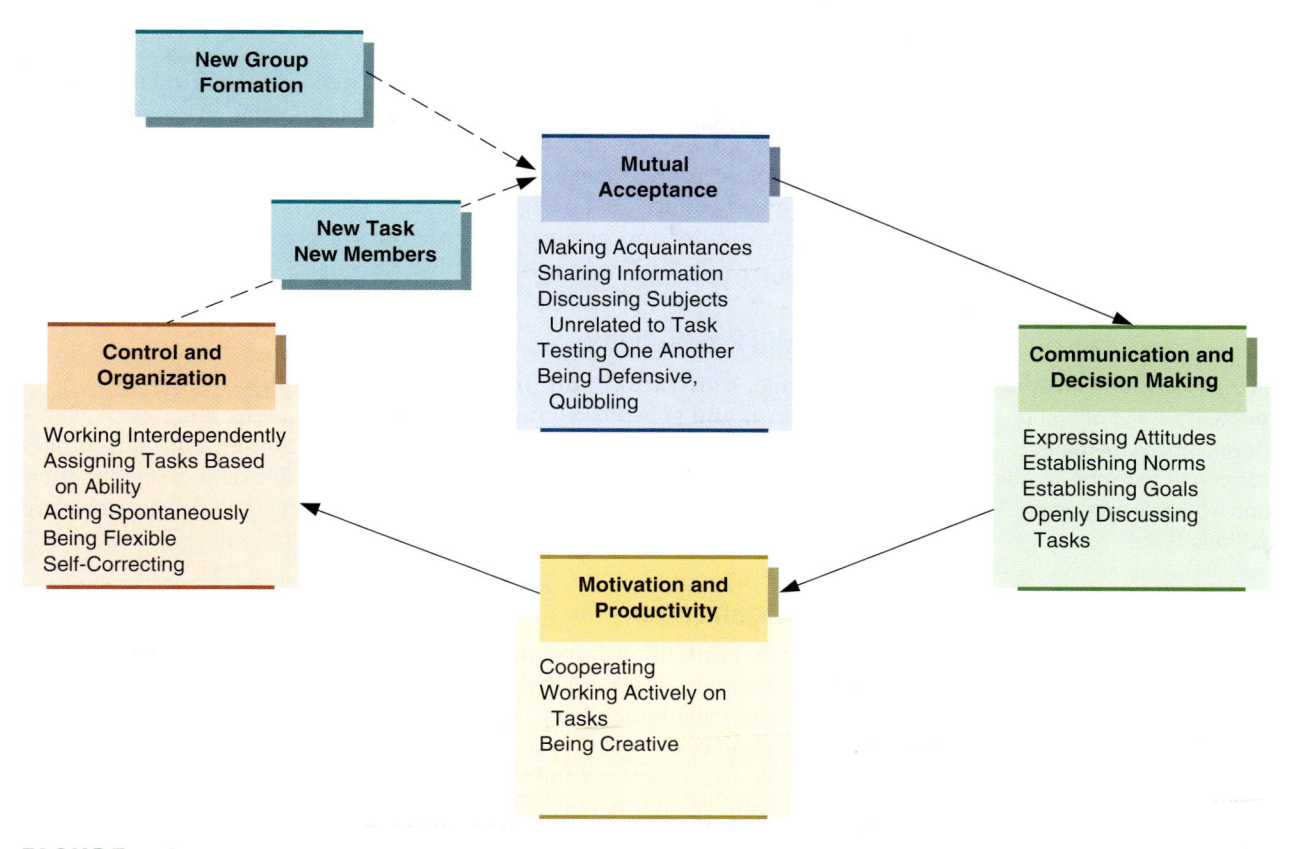

FIGURE 8.2

Stages of Group Development

This figure shows the stages of evolution from a newly formed group to a mature group. Note that as new members are added or an existing group gets a new task, the group needs to go through the stages again.

the group, such as the weather, sports, or recent events within the organization. Some aspects of the group's task, such as its formal objectives, may also be discussed at this stage. However, such discussion probably will not be very productive because members are usually unfamiliar with one another and do not know how to evaluate one another's comments. If members happen to know one another already, this stage may be brief, but it is unlikely to be skipped altogether because this is a new group with a new purpose. In addition, there are likely to be a few members whom the others do not know well or at all.

As the members get to know one another, discussion may turn to more sensitive issues, such as the organization's politics or recent controversial decisions. At this stage, members may have minor arguments as they explore one another's views on various issues, reactions, knowledge, and expertise. From their discussion, members come to understand the similarity among their beliefs and values and the extent to which they can trust one another. Members may discuss their expectations about the group's activities in terms of their previous group and organizational experience.[7] Eventually the conversation turns to the business of the group. When this discussion becomes serious, the group is moving to the next stage of development, communication and decision making.

Communication and Decision Making

In the **communication and decision-making stage** of group development, members discuss their feelings more openly and agree on group goals and individual roles in the group.

The group progresses to the **communication and decision-making** stage once group members have begun to accept one another. In this stage, members discuss their feelings and opinions more openly; they may show more tolerance for opposing viewpoints and explore different ideas to bring about a reasonable solution or decision. The membership usually begins to develop norms of behavior during this stage. Members discuss and eventually agree on the group's goals. Then they assign one another roles and tasks to accomplish the goals.

Motivation and Productivity

In the **motivation and productivity stage** of group development, members cooperate, help one another, and work toward accomplishing tasks.

In the next stage, **motivation and productivity,** the emphasis shifts away from personal concerns and viewpoints to activities that will benefit the group. Members perform their assigned tasks, cooperate with one another, and help others accomplish their goals. Members are highly motivated and may carry out their tasks creatively. In this stage, the group is accomplishing its work and moving toward the final stage of development.

Control and Organization

In the **control and organization stage** of group development, the group is mature; members work together and are flexible, adaptive, and self-correcting.

In the final stage, **control and organization,** the group works effectively toward accomplishing its goals. Tasks are assigned by mutual agreement and according to ability. In a mature group, members' activities are relatively spontaneous and flexible rather than subject to rigid structural restraints. Mature groups evaluate their activities and potential outcomes and take corrective actions if necessary. The characteristics of flexibility, spontaneity, and self-correction are very important for the group to remain productive over an extended period.

Not all groups go through all four stages. Some groups disband before reaching the final stage. Others fail to complete a stage before moving on to the next. Rather than spending the time necessary to get to know one another and build trust, for example, a group may cut short the first stage of development because of pressure from its leader, from deadlines, or from an outside threat (such as the boss).[8] If members are forced into activities typical of a later stage while the work of an earlier stage remains incomplete, they are likely to become frustrated; the group may not develop completely and may be less productive than it could be.[9] Group productivity depends on successful development at each stage. A group that evolves fully through the four stages of development usually becomes a mature, effective group.[10] Its members are interdependent, coordinated, cooperative, competent at their jobs and motivated to do them, self-correcting, and in active communication with one another.[11] The group formation process is not lengthy if the group makes a solid effort and stays on track toward its goals.

Finally, as working conditions and relationships change, either through a change in membership or when a task is completed and a new task begun, groups may need to reexperience one or more of the stages of development to maintain the cohesiveness and productivity characteristic of a well-developed group. The San Francisco Forty-Niners, for example, returned from an NFL strike to an uncomfortable and apprehension-filled period. Their coach, Bill Walsh, conducted rigorous practices, but also allowed time for players to get together to air their feelings. Slowly team unity returned, and players began joking and socializing again as they prepared for the rest of the season.[12] Their redevelopment as a mature group resulted in two subsequent Super Bowl victories.

Chapter 8   Group Dynamics

Communication and decision making are key stages of group development, but it looks like this team may have skipped an early stage like mutual acceptance. Groups need to openly discuss and agree on their goals, motivations, and individual roles before they can successfully accomplish tasks. It is essential that groups go through all four stages of development to become a mature, productive group.

Copyright 2001 by Randy Glasbergen.
www.glasbergen.com

"My team is having trouble thinking outside the box. We can't agree on the size of the box, what materials the box should be constructed from, a reasonable budget for the box, or our first choice of box vendors."

Although these stages are not separate and distinct in all groups, many groups make fairly predictable transitions in activities at about the midpoint of the period available to complete a task.[13] A group may begin with its own distinctive approach to the problem and maintain it until about halfway through the allotted time. The midpoint transition is often accompanied by a burst of concentrated activity, reexamination of assumptions, dropping old patterns of activity, adopting new perspectives on the work, and making dramatic progress. Following these midpoint activities, the new patterns of activity may be maintained until close to the end of the period allotted for the task. Another transition may occur just before the deadline. At this point, groups often go into the completion stage, launching a final burst of activity to finish the job.

Group Performance Factors

LEARNING OBJECTIVE

Discuss the major group performance factors.

Group performance factors—composition, size, norms, and cohesiveness—affect the success of the group in fulfilling its goals.

Group composition is the degree of similarity or difference among group members on factors important to the group's work.

The performance of any group is affected by several factors other than the group's reasons for forming and the stages of its development. In a high-performing group, a group synergy often develops in which the group's performance is more than the sum of its members' individual contributions. Several additional factors may account for this accelerated performance.[14] The four basic **group performance factors** are composition, size, norms, and cohesiveness.

Composition

The composition of a group plays an important role in group productivity.[15] **Group composition** is most often described in terms of the homogeneity or heterogeneity of the members. A group is *homogeneous* if members are similar in one or several ways that are critical to the work of the group, such as in age, work experience, education, technical specialty, or cultural background. In *heterogeneous* groups, members differ in one or more ways critical to the group's work. Homogeneous groups are often created when people are assigned to command groups

Group composition is an important factor in understanding group dynamics. These women attended a Women in Business seminar for women holding key executive positions in major corporations. The fact that they are all female gave them a shared frame of reference and common perspectives from which to identify key issues that will help shape the future of their respective businesses.

based on a similar technical specialty. Although the people who work in such command groups may differ in some ways, such as in age or work experience, they are homogeneous in terms of a critical work performance variable: technical specialty.

Much research has explored the relationship between a group's composition and its productivity. The group's heterogeneity in terms of age and tenure with the group has been shown to be related to turnover: Groups with members of different ages and experiences with the group tend to undergo frequent changes in membership.[16] Table 8.2 summarizes task variables that make a homogeneous or heterogeneous group more effective. A homogeneous group is likely to be more productive when the group task is simple, cooperation is necessary, group tasks are sequential, or quick action is required. A heterogeneous group is more likely to be productive when the task is complex, requires a collective effort (that is, each member performs a different task, and the sum of these efforts constitutes the group output), and demands creativity, and when speed is less important than thorough deliberations. For example, a group asked to generate ideas for marketing a new product probably needs to be heterogeneous to develop as many different ideas as possible.

The link between group composition and type of task is explained by the interactions typical of homogeneous and heterogeneous groups. A homogeneous group tends to have less conflict, fewer differences of opinion, smoother communication, and more interactions. When a task requires cooperation and speed, a homogeneous group is therefore more desirable. If, however, the task requires complex analysis of information and creativity to arrive at the best possible solution, a heterogeneous group may be more appropriate because it generates a wide range of viewpoints. More discussion and more conflict are likely, both of which can enhance the group's decision making.

TABLE 8.2

Task Variable and Group Composition

A homogeneous group is more useful for:	A heterogeneous group is more useful for:
Simple tasks	Complex tasks
Sequential tasks	Collective tasks
Tasks that require cooperation	Tasks that require creativity
Tasks that must be done quickly	Tasks that need not be done quickly

Reference: Based on discussion in Bernard M. Bass and Edward C. Ryterband, *Organizational Psychology*, 2nd ed. (Allyn & Bacon, 1979). Reprinted by permission.

Chapter 8 Group Dynamics

Group composition becomes especially important as organizations become increasingly diverse.[17] Cultures differ in the importance they place on group membership and in how they view authority, uncertainty, and other important factors. Increasing attention is being focused on how to deal with groups made up of people from different cultures.[18] In general, a manager in charge of a culturally diverse group can expect several things. First, members will probably distrust one another. Stereotyping will also present a problem, and communication difficulties are almost certain to arise. Thus, the manager needs to recognize that such groups will seldom function smoothly, at least at first. Managers may therefore need to spend more time helping a culturally diverse group through the rough spots as it matures, and they should allow a longer-than-normal time before expecting it to carry out its assigned task.

Many organizations are creating joint ventures and other types of alliances with organizations from other countries. Joint ventures have become common in the automobile and electronics industries, for example. However, managers from the United States tend to exhibit individualistic behaviors in a group setting, whereas managers from more collectivistic countries, such as the People's Republic of China, tend to exhibit more group-oriented behaviors. Thus, when these two different types of managers work together in a joint venture, they must be trained to be cautious and understanding in their interactions and in the types of behaviors they exhibit.

Size

Group size is the number of members of the group; group size affects the number of resources available to perform the task.

A group can have as few as two members or as many members as can interact and influence one another. **Group size** can have an important effect on performance. A group with many members has more resources available and may be able to complete a large number of relatively independent tasks. In groups established to generate ideas, those with more members tend to produce more ideas, although the rate of increase in the number of ideas diminishes rapidly as the group grows.[19] Beyond a certain point, the greater complexity of interactions and communication may make it more difficult for a large group to achieve agreement.

Social loafing is the tendency of some members of groups to put forth less effort in a group than they would when working alone.

Interactions and communication are much more likely to be formalized in larger groups. Large groups tend to set agendas for meetings and to follow a protocol or parliamentary procedure to control discussion. As a result, some time that otherwise would be available to work on tasks is taken up in administrative duties such as organizing and structuring the interactions and communications within the group. Also, the large size may inhibit participation by some members and increase absenteeism; some people may stop trying to make a meaningful contribution and may even stop coming to group meetings if their repeated attempts to contribute are thwarted by the sheer number of similar efforts by other members. Furthermore, large groups present more opportunities for interpersonal attraction, leading to more social interactions and fewer task interactions. **Social loafing** is the tendency of some members of groups not to put forth as much effort in a group situation as they would working alone. Social loafing often results from the assumption by some members that if they do not work hard, other members will pick up the slack. How serious this situation becomes depends on the nature of the task, the characteristics of the people involved, and the ability of the group leadership to recognize the potential problem and do something about it.

The most effective group size, therefore, is determined by the group members' ability to interact and influence one another effectively. The need for interaction is affected by the maturity of the group, the group's tasks, the maturity of individual members, and the ability of the group leader or manager to manage the communication, potential conflicts, and task activities. In some situations, the most effective group size is three or four; other groups can function effectively with fifteen or more members.

Norms

> A **norm** is a standard against which the appropriateness of a behavior is judged.

A **norm** is a standard against which the appropriateness of a behavior is judged. Thus, norms determine the behavior expected in a certain situation. Group norms are usually established during the second stage of group development (communication and decision making) and carried forward into the maturity stage. By providing a basis for predicting others' behaviors, norms enable people to behave in a manner consistent with and acceptable to the group. Without norms, the activities in a group would be chaotic.

Norms result from the combination of members' personality characteristics, the situation, the task, and the historical traditions of the group.[20] Lack of conformity to group norms may result in verbal abuse, physical threats, ostracism, or ejection from the group. Group norms are enforced, however, only for actions that are important to group members. For example, if the office norm is for employees to wear suits to convey a professional image to clients, a staff member who wears blue jeans and a sweatshirt violates the group norm and will hear about it quickly. But if the norm is that dress is unimportant because little contact with clients occurs in the office, the fact that someone wears blue jeans may not even be noticed.

Norms serve four purposes in organizations. First, they help the group survive. Groups tend to reject deviant behavior that does not help meet group goals or contribute to the group's survival if it is threatened. Accordingly, a successful group that is not under threat may be more tolerant of deviant behavior. Second, norms simplify and make more predictable the behaviors expected of group members. Because they are familiar with norms, members do not have to analyze each behavior and decide on a response; they can anticipate the actions of others on the basis of group norms, usually resulting in increased productivity and goal attainment. Third, norms help the group avoid embarrassing situations. Group members often want to avoid damaging other members' self-images and are likely to avoid certain subjects that might hurt a member's feelings. Finally, norms express the central values of the group and identify the group to others. Certain clothes, mannerisms, or behaviors in particular situations may be a rallying point for members and may signify to others the nature of the group.[21]

Cohesiveness

> **Group cohesiveness** is the extent to which a group is committed to staying together.

Group cohesiveness is the extent to which a group is committed to remaining together; it results from forces acting on the members to remain in the group. The forces that create cohesiveness are attraction to the group, resistance to leaving the group, and motivation to remain a member.[22] As Figure 8.3 shows, group cohesiveness is related to many aspects of group dynamics that we have already discussed: maturity, homogeneity, manageable size, and frequency of interactions.

The figure also shows that group cohesiveness can be increased by competition or by the presence of an external threat. Either factor can focus members' attention on a clearly defined goal and increase their willingness to work together. Finally, successfully reaching goals often increases the cohesiveness of a group because people are proud to be identified with a winner and to be thought of as com-

improve schools, and challenge people to commit themselves to the team. Jon Katzenbach and Douglas Smith studied more than thirty teams and found that demanding, high-performance goals often challenge members to create a real team—as opposed to being merely a group—because when goals are truly demanding, members must pull together, find resources within themselves, develop and use the appropriate skills, and take a common approach to reach the goals.[6]

Agreeing on a common approach is especially important for teams because it is often the approach that differentiates one team from others. The team's approach usually covers how work will be done, social norms regarding dress, attendance at meetings, tardiness, norms of fairness and ethical behavior, and what will and will not be included in team activities.

Finally, the definition states that teams hold themselves mutually accountable for results rather than merely meeting a manager's demands for results, as in the traditional approach. If the members translate accountability to an external manager into internal, or mutual, accountability, the group moves toward acting as a team. Mutual accountability is essentially a promise members make to one another to do everything possible to achieve their goals, and it requires the commitment and trust of all members. It is the promise of each member to take personal responsibility for the team's goals that earns that individual the right to express her or his views and expect them to get a fair and constructive hearing. With this promise, members maintain and strengthen the trust essential for the team to succeed. The clearly stated high-performance goals and the common approach serve as the standards to which the team holds itself. Because teams are mutually accountable for meeting performance goals, three other differences between groups and teams become important: job categories, authority, and reward systems. Table 9.1 summarizes these differences.

Teams have become an increasingly important mechanism for organizations to get things done. For example, some large companies are beginning to suggest that small suppliers work together as partners to win major contracts. To facilitate such partnerships, each supplier generally provides one or more team members who work together to coordinate their efforts. Woodrow Hall, owner of a plastic packaging business, Film Fabrications, Inc., and Robert Johnson, owner of Johnson-Bryce Corporation, a plastic bag manufacturer and printer, worked together as a team in pursuit of a major contract from Proctor & Gamble.

Job Categories

The work of conventional groups is usually described in terms of highly specialized jobs that require minimal training and moderate effort. Tens or even hundreds of people may have similar job descriptions and see little relationship between their effort and the end result or finished product. In teams, on the other hand, members have many different skills that fit into one or two broad job categories. Neither workers nor managers worry about who does what job as long as the team puts out the finished product or service and meets its performance goals.[7]

TABLE 9.1

Differences Between Teams and Traditional Work Groups

Issue	Conventional Work Groups	Teams
Job Categories	Many narrow categories	One or two broad categories
Authority	Supervisor directly controls daily activities	Team controls daily activities
Reward System	Depends on the type of job, individual performance, and seniority	Based on team performance and individual breadth of skills

Reference: Adapted from Jack D. Osburn, Linda Moran, and Ed Musselwhite, with Craig Perrin, *Self-Directed Work Teams: The New American Challenge* (Homewood, Ill.: Business One Irwin, 1990), p. 11.

Authority

As Table 9.1 shows, in conventional work groups the supervisor directly controls workers' daily activities. In teams, members discuss what activities need to be done and determine who has the necessary skills and who will do each task. The team, rather than the supervisor, makes the decisions. If a "supervisor" remains on the team, the person's role usually changes to that of coach, facilitator, or one who helps the team make decisions rather than the traditional role of decision maker and controller.

Reward Systems

How employees are rewarded is vital to the long-term success of an organization. The traditional reward and compensation systems suitable for individual motivation (discussed in Chapter 4) are not appropriate in a team-based organization. In conventional settings, employees are usually rewarded on the basis of their individual performance, seniority, or job classification. In a team-based situation, team members are rewarded for mastering a range of skills needed to meet team performance goals, and rewards are sometimes based on team performance. Such a pay system tends to promote the flexibility teams need to be responsive to changing environmental factors. Three types of reward systems are common in a team environment: skill-based pay, gain-sharing systems, and team bonus plans.

Skill-Based Pay   Skill-based pay systems require team members to acquire a set of the core skills needed for their particular team plus additional special skills, depending on career tracks or team needs. Some programs require all members to acquire the core skills before any member receives additional pay. Usually employees can increase their base compensation by some fixed amount—say, $0.30 per hour for each additional skill acquired—up to some fixed maximum. Companies using skill-based pay systems include Eastman Chemical Company, Colgate-Palmolive Company, and Pfizer.

Gain-Sharing Systems   Gain-sharing systems usually reward all team members from all teams based on the performance of the organization, division, or plant. Such a system requires a baseline performance that team members must exceed to receive some share of the gain over the baseline measure. Westinghouse gives equal one-time, lump-sum bonuses to everyone in the plant based on improvements in productivity, cost, and quality. Employee reaction is usually positive because when employees work harder to help the company, they share in the profits they helped generate. On the other hand, when business conditions or other factors beyond their control make it impossible to generate improvements over the preset baseline, employees may feel disappointed and even disillusioned with the process.

Team Bonus Plans Team bonus plans are similar to gain-sharing plans except that the unit of performance and pay is the team rather than a plant, a division, or the entire organization. For the plan to be effective, each team must have specific performance targets or baseline measures that it considers realistic. Companies using team bonus plans include Milwaukee Insurance Company, Colgate-Palmolive, and Harris Corporation.

Changes in an organizational compensation system can be traumatic and threatening to most employees. However, matching the reward system to the way work is organized and accomplished can have very positive benefits. The three types of team-based reward systems presented can be used in isolation for simplicity or in some combination to address different types of issues for each organization.

Benefits and Costs of Teams in Organizations

LEARNING OBJECTIVE
Discuss the benefits and costs of teams in organizations.

Given the increasing use of teams worldwide, some organizations may be starting to use teams simply because everyone else is doing it, which is obviously the wrong reason. The reason for creating teams should be that teams make sense for that particular organization. The best reason to start teams in any organization is to recap the potential benefits of a team-based environment: enhanced performance, employee benefits, reduced costs, and organizational enhancements. Table 9.2 shows four categories of benefits and examples of each.

Enhanced Performance

Enhanced performance can take many forms, including improved productivity, quality, and customer service. Working in teams enables workers to avoid wasted effort, reduce errors, and respond better to customers, resulting in more output for each unit of employee input.

Such enhancements result from pooling individual efforts in new ways and continuously striving to improve for the benefit of the team. For example, a General Electric plant in North Carolina experienced a 20 percent increase in productivity after team implementation.[8] K Shoes reported a 19 percent increase in productivity and significant reductions in rejects in the manufacturing process. The Mastering Change box discusses how technological advances mandated that scientists at Roche Group begin working in collaborative groups to best utilize their new knowledge.

Employee Benefits

Employees tend to benefit as much as organizations in a team environment. Much attention has focused on the differences between the baby boom generation and the "postboomers" in their attitudes toward work, its importance to their lives, and what they want from it. In general, younger workers tend to be less satisfied with their work and the organization, to have lower respect for authority and supervision, and to want more than a paycheck every week. Teams can provide the sense of self-control, human dignity, identification with work, and sense of self-worth and self-fulfillment for which current workers seem to strive. Rather than relying

TABLE 9.2

Benefits of Teams in Organizations

Type of Benefit	Specific Benefit	Organizational Examples
Enhanced Performance	• Increased productivity • Improved quality • Improved customer service	Ampex: On-time customer delivery rose 98%. K Shoes: Rejects per million dropped from 5,000 to 250. Eastman: Productivity rose 70%.
Employee Benefits	• Quality of work life • Lower stress	Milwaukee Mutual: Employee assistance program usage dropped to 40% below industry average.
Reduced Costs	• Lower turnover, absenteeism • Fewer injuries	Kodak: Reduced turnover to one-half the industry average. Texas Instruments: Reduced costs more than 50%. Westinghouse: Costs down 60%.
Organizational Enhancements	• Increased innovation, flexibility	IDS Mutual Fund Operations: Improved flexibility to handle fluctuations in market activity. Hewlett-Packard: Innovative order-processing system.

References: Adapted from Richard S. Wellins, William C. Byham, and George R. Dixon, *Inside Teams* (San Francisco: Jossey-Bass, 1994); Charles C. Manz and Henry P. Sims Jr., *Business Without Bosses* (New York: Wiley, 1993).

on the traditional, hierarchical, manager-based system, teams give employees the freedom to grow and to gain respect and dignity by managing themselves, making decisions about their work, and making a genuine difference in the world around them.[9] As a result, employees have a better work life, face less stress at work, and make less use of employee assistance programs.

Reduced Costs

As empowered teams reduce scrap, make fewer errors, file fewer worker compensation claims, and reduce absenteeism and turnover, organizations based on teams are showing significant cost reductions. Team members believe they have a stake in the outcomes, want to make contributions because they are valued, and do not want to let their team down. Wilson Sporting Goods reported saving $10 million per year for five years thanks to its teams. Colgate-Palmolive reported that technician turnover was extremely low—more than 90 percent of technicians were retained after five years—once it changed to a team-based approach.

Organizational Enhancements

Other improvements in organizations that result from moving from a hierarchically based, directive culture to a team-based culture include increased innovation, creativity, and flexibility.[10] Use of teams can eliminate redundant layers of bureaucracy and flatten the hierarchy in large organizations. Employees feel closer and more in

MASTERING CHANGE

Technology Changes the Culture at Roche

Conducting 1 million genomics* experiments a day? Testing more than 3 million new compounds annually? It sounds impossible, but it's the new reality for pharmaceutical firms. Of the myriad technological developments and applications of the last fifteen years, perhaps none are as rapid in their evolution or startling in their outcomes as the recent advances in bioengineering. Industries as diverse as agriculture and petrochemicals are feeling the impact as the pharmaceutical industry is experiencing an unprecedented upheaval.

The technological revolution began with the decoding of human DNA. Innovative equipment now uses that knowledge to match compounds with their affected genes. Promising compounds are then tested to ensure their effectiveness against cancer-causing genes and determine whether they have adverse effects on other body organs.

Before these advances, Swiss drug manufacturer Roche Group had a competitive culture that pitted development teams against one another. The system worked when the firm was occupied with finding ideas for new blockbuster drugs. However, breakthroughs in technology made that culture obsolete, pushing the firm to adopt a more collaborative team approach. One incentive for more teamwork is to reduce the number of experiments given their cost in computer capacity and researcher time. One Roche scientist explains, "Back when we were working on one gene, we could do fishing experiments. [However, w]hen you get [information] from 12,000 genes, you need to be careful ... If it isn't useful, you can waste a lot of time looking at it." Teams found they needed members from all parts of the organization to access specialized knowledge. Roche researcher Barry Goggin recalls, "We'd just get together in the corridors and design all sorts of small projects." At first, team members had trouble communicating, but they learned how to share information effectively. "It was almost as if two different languages were being spoken by the geneticists and the oncologists," Goggin says. "We had to bridge the gap."

Although the increase in collaboration and cross-specialty communication is good for the firm, some workers are suffering. The changing technology and increased capacity of robotic equipment have caused Roche to lay off some R&D staff. Although this move will reduce costs, Roche must proceed cautiously to avoid upsetting its new and effective collaborative organization culture.

*Genomics is the study of DNA nucleotide sequences.

References: "Roche in the Sciences and Medicine," "Innovative R & D," Roche website, www.roche.com on May 24, 2004; Jesse Eisinger, "Roche's Planned Job Cuts Look Desperate, Not Smart," *Wall Street Journal*, June 1, 2001; interactive.wsj.com/archive on May 11, 2002; George Anders, "Roche's New Scientific Method," *Fast Company,* January 2002, pp. 60–67 (quotation p. 64).

---

touch with top management. Employees who think their efforts are important are more likely to make significant contributions. In addition, the team environment constantly challenges teams to innovate and solve problems creatively. If the "same old way" does not work, empowered teams are free to throw it out and develop a new way. With increasing global competition, organizations must constantly adapt to keep abreast of changes. Teams provide the flexibility to react quickly. One of Motorola's earliest teams challenged a long-standing top-management policy regarding supplier inspections to reduce cycle times and improve delivery of crucial parts.[11] After several attempts, management finally allowed the team to change the system and consequently reaped the expected benefits.

Costs of Teams

The costs of teams are usually expressed in terms of the difficulty of changing to a team-based organization. Managers have expressed frustration and confusion about their new roles as coaches and facilitators, especially if they developed their managerial skills under the traditional hierarchical management philosophy. Some managers have felt they were working themselves out of a job as they turned over more and more of their old directing duties to a team.[12]

Employees may also feel like losers during the change to a team culture. Some traditional staff groups, such as technical advisory staffs, may fear their jobs are in jeopardy as teams do more and more of the technical work formerly done by technicians. New roles and pay scales may need to be developed for the technical staff in these situations. Often technical people have been assigned to a team or a small group of teams and become members who fully participate in team activities.

Another cost associated with teams is the slowness of the process of full team development. As discussed earlier, it takes a long time for teams to go through the full development cycle and become mature, efficient, and effective. If top management balks at the slow progress, teams may be disbanded, returning the organization to its original hierarchical form with significant losses for employees, managers, and the organization.

Probably the most dangerous cost is premature abandonment of the change to a team-based organization. If top management gets impatient with the team change process and cuts it short, never allowing teams to develop fully and realize benefits, all the hard work of employees, middle managers, and supervisors is lost. As a result, employee confidence in management in general and in the decision makers in particular may suffer for a long time.[13] The losses in productivity and efficiency will be very difficult to recoup. Management must therefore be fully committed before initiating a change to a team-based organization.

Types of Teams

LEARNING OBJECTIVE
Describe various types of teams.

Many different types of teams exist in organizations today. Some evolved naturally in organizations that permit various types of participative and empowering management programs. Others were formally created at the suggestion of enlightened management. One easy way to classify teams is by what they do; for example, some teams make or do things, some teams recommend things, and some teams run things. The most common types of teams are quality circles, work teams, and problem-solving teams; management teams are also quite common.

Quality Circles

Quality circles (QCs) are small groups of employees from the same work area who meet regularly (usually weekly or monthly) to discuss and recommend solutions to workplace problems.[14] QCs were the first type of team created in U.S. organizations, becoming most popular during the 1980s in response to growing Japanese competition. QCs had some success in reducing rework and cutting defects on the shop floors of many manufacturing plants. Some attempts have been made to use QCs in offices and service operations. They exist alongside the traditional management structure and are relatively permanent. The role of QCs is to investigate a variety of quality problems that might come up in the workplace. They do not replace the work group or make decisions about how the work is done. Interest in QCs has dropped somewhat, although many companies still have them.[15] QCs are teams that make recommendations.

Quality circles (QCs) are small groups of employees from the same work area who regularly meet to discuss and recommend solutions to workplace problems.

Work teams include all the people working in an area, are relatively permanent, and do the daily work, making decisions regarding how the team's work is done.

Work Teams

Like quality circles, **work teams** tend to be permanent, but they, rather than auxiliary committees, are the teams that do the daily work.[16] The nurses, orderlies, and various technicians responsible for all patients on a floor or wing in a hospital comprise a work team. Rather than investigate a specific problem, evaluate alternatives, and recommend a solution or change, a work team does the actual daily work of the unit. The difference between a traditional work group of nurses and the patient care team is that the latter has the authority to decide how the work is done, in what order, and by whom; the entire team is responsible for all patient care. When the team decides how the work is to be organized or performed, it becomes a self-managing team that accrues all of the benefits described in this chapter. Work teams are teams that make or do things.

Problem-Solving Teams

Problem-solving teams are temporary teams established to tackle specific problems in the workplace. Teams can use any number of methods to solve the problem, as discussed in Chapter 12. After solving the problem, the team is usually disbanded, allowing members to return to their normal work. One survey found that 91 percent of U.S. companies utilize problem-solving teams regularly.[17] High-performing problem-solving teams are often cross-functional, meaning team members come from many different functional areas. Crisis teams are problem-solving teams created only for the duration of an organizational crisis and are usually composed of people from many different areas. Problem-solving teams are teams that make recommendations for others to implement.

> **Problem-solving teams** are temporary teams established to attack specific problems in the workplace.

Management Teams

Management teams consist of managers from various areas and coordinate work teams. They are relatively permanent because their work does not end with the completion of a particular project or resolution of a problem. Management teams must concentrate on the teams that have the most impact on overall corporate performance. The primary job of management teams is to coach and counsel other teams to be self-managing by making decisions within the team. The second most important task of management teams is to coordinate work between work teams that are interdependent in some manner. Digital Equipment Corporation abandoned its team matrix structure because the matrix of teams was poorly organized and coordinated. Team members at all levels reported spending endless hours in meetings trying to coordinate among teams, leaving too little time to get the real work done.[18]

> **Management teams** consist of managers from various areas and coordinate work teams.

Top-management teams may have special problems. First, the work of the top-management team may not be conducive to teamwork. Vice presidents or heads of divisions may be in charge of different sets of operations that are unrelated and do not need to be coordinated. Forcing that type of top-management group to be a team may be inappropriate. Second, top managers often have reached high levels in the organization because they have certain characteristics or abilities to get things done. For successful managers to alter their style, pool resources, and sacrifice their independence and individuality can be very difficult.[19]

Product Development Teams

Product development teams are combinations of work teams and problem-solving teams that create new designs for products or services that will satisfy customer needs. They are similar to problem-solving teams in that when the product is fully developed and in production, the team may be disbanded. As global com-

> **Product development teams** are combinations of work teams and problem-solving teams that create new designs for products or services that will satisfy customer needs.

Product development teams are commonly used in organizations today. Apple hardware chief Jon Rubenstein and industrial designer Jonathan Ive worked with a group of other specialists to help create the Apple iPod. The team designed the product and got it into production in just eight months.

petition and electronic information storage, processing, and retrieving capabilities increase, companies in almost every industry are struggling to cut product development times. The primary organizational means of accomplishing this important task is the "blue-ribbon" cross-functional team. Boeing's team that developed the 777 commercial airplane and the platform teams at Chrysler are typical examples.

The rush to market with new designs can lead to numerous problems for product development teams. The primary problems of poor communication and coordination of typical product development processes can be rectified by creating self-managing cross-functional product development teams.[20]

Virtual Teams

Virtual teams may never actually meet together in the same room; their activities take place on the computer via teleconferencing and other electronic information systems. Engineers in the United States can directly connect audibly and visually with their counterparts around the globe, sharing files via Internet, electronic mail, and other communication utilities. All participants can look at the same drawing, print, or specification; hence, decisions are made much faster. With electronic communication systems, team members can move in or out of a team or a team discussion as the issues warrant.

Implementing Teams in Organizations

LEARNING OBJECTIVE

Explain how organizations implement the use of teams.

Implementing teams in organizations is not easy; it takes a lot of hard work, time, training, and patience. Changing from a traditional organizational structure to a team-based structure is much like other organizational changes (which we discuss in Chapter 15). It is a complete cultural change for the organization. Typically the organization is hierarchically designed to provide clear direction and control. However, many organizations need to be able to react quickly to a dynamic environment. Team procedures artificially imposed on existing processes are a recipe for disaster. In this section, we look at several essential elements specific to an organizational change to a team-based situation.

Virtual teams work together via computer and other electronic communication utilities; members move in and out of meetings and the team itself as the situation dictates.

Planning the Change

The change to a team-based organization requires a great deal of analysis and planning before it is implemented; the decision cannot be made overnight. It is such a drastic departure from the traditional hierarchy and authority-and-control orientation that significant planning, preparation, and training are prerequisites. The plan-

Chapter 9 Using Teams in Organizations

Organizations planning to implement teams are generally advised to follow a clear plan. Of course, too much bureaucracy in the process can quickly derail any effort. For instance, Dilbert's boss is making the implementation of his idea so onerous that he is likely to think twice before making future suggestions.

DILBERT reprinted by permission of United Feature Syndicate, Inc.

ning takes place in two phases, the first leading to the decision about whether to move to a team-based approach and the second while preparing for implementation.

Making the Decision Prior to making the decision, top management needs to establish the leadership for the change, develop a steering committee, conduct a feasibility study, and then make the go/no-go decision. Top management must be sure the team culture is consistent with its strategy, as we discuss in Chapter 14. Often the leadership for the change is the chief executive officer, the chief operating officer, or another prominent person in top management. Regardless of the position, the person leading the change must (1) have a strong belief that employees want to be responsible for their own work, (2) be able to demonstrate the team philosophy, (3) articulate a coherent vision of the team environment, and (4) have the creativity and authority to overcome obstacles as they surface.

The leader of the change needs to put together a steering committee to help explore the organization's readiness for the team environment and lead it through the planning and preparation for the change. The steering committee can be of any workable size, from two to ten people who are influential and know the work and the organization. Members may include plant or division managers, union representatives, human resource department representatives, and operational-level employees. The work of the steering committee includes visits to sites that might be candidates for utilizing work teams, visits to currently successful work teams, data gathering and analysis, low-key general discussions, and deliberating and deciding whether to use a consultant during the change process.

A feasibility study is critical before making the decision to use teams. The steering committee needs to know if the work processes are conducive to team use, if the employees are willing and able to work in a team environment, if the managers in the unit to be converted are willing to learn and apply the hands-off managerial style necessary to make teams work, if the organization's structure and culture are ready to accommodate a team-based organization, if the market for the unit's products or services is growing or at least stable enough to absorb the increased productive capacity the teams will be putting out, and if the community will support the transition teams. Without answers to these questions, management is merely guessing and hoping that teams will work, and may be destined for many surprises that could doom the effort.

After the leadership has been established, the steering committee set up, and a feasibility study conducted, the go/no-go decision can be made. The committee and top management will need to decide jointly to go ahead if conditions are right. On the other hand, if the feasibility study indicates that the organizational unit's readiness is questionable, the committee can decide to postpone implementation while changes are made in personnel, organizational structure, organizational policies, or market conditions. The committee may also decide to implement training and acculturation for employees and managers in the unit in preparation for later implementation.

Preparing for Implementation   Once the decision is made to change to a team-based organization, much needs to be done before implementation can begin. Preparation consists of the following five steps: clarifying the mission, selecting the site for the first work teams, preparing the design team, planning the transfer of authority, and drafting the preliminary plan.

The mission statement is simply an expression of purpose that summarizes the long-range benefits the company hopes to gain by moving to a team environment. It must be consistent with the organization's strategy as it establishes a common set of assumptions for executives, middle managers, support staff, and the teams. In addition, it sets the parameters or boundaries within which the change will take place. It may identify which divisions or plants will be involved or what levels will be converted to teams. The mission statement attempts to stimulate and focus the energy of those people who will be involved in the change. The mission can focus on continuous improvement, employee involvement, increasing performance, competition, customer satisfaction, and contributions to society. The steering committee should involve many people from several areas of the company to foster fuller involvement in the change.

Once the mission is established, the steering committee needs to decide where teams will be implemented first. Selection of the first site is crucial because it sets the tone for the success of the total program. The best initial site is one that includes workers from multiple job categories, where improving performance or reaching the targets set in the mission is feasible, and where workers accept the idea of using teams. Also valuable are a tradition or history of success and a staff that is receptive to training, especially training in interpersonal skills. One manufacturing company based its choice of sites for initial teams not on criteria such as these but on the desire to reward the managers of successful divisions or to "fix" areas performing poorly. Consequently team implementation in that company was very slow and not very successful.[21] Initial sites must also have a local "champion" of the team concept.

Once the initial sites have been identified, the steering committee needs to set up the team that will design the other teams. The design team is a select group of employees, supervisors, and managers who will work out the staffing and operational details to make the teams perform well. The design team selects the initial team members, prepares members and managers for teams, changes work processes for use with the team design, and plans the transition from the current state to the new self-managed team structure. The design team usually spends the first three months learning from the steering committee, visiting sites where teams are being used successfully, and spending a significant amount of time in classroom training. Considering the composition of the teams is one of the most important decisions the design team has to make.

Planning the transfer of authority from management to teams is the most important phase of planning the implementation. It is also the most distinctive and difficult part of moving to a team-based organization. The planning is a gradual process, taking from two to five years in most situations. Teams must learn new skills and make new decisions related to their work, all of which take time. It is, essentially, a cultural change for the organization.

Chapter 9 Using Teams in Organizations

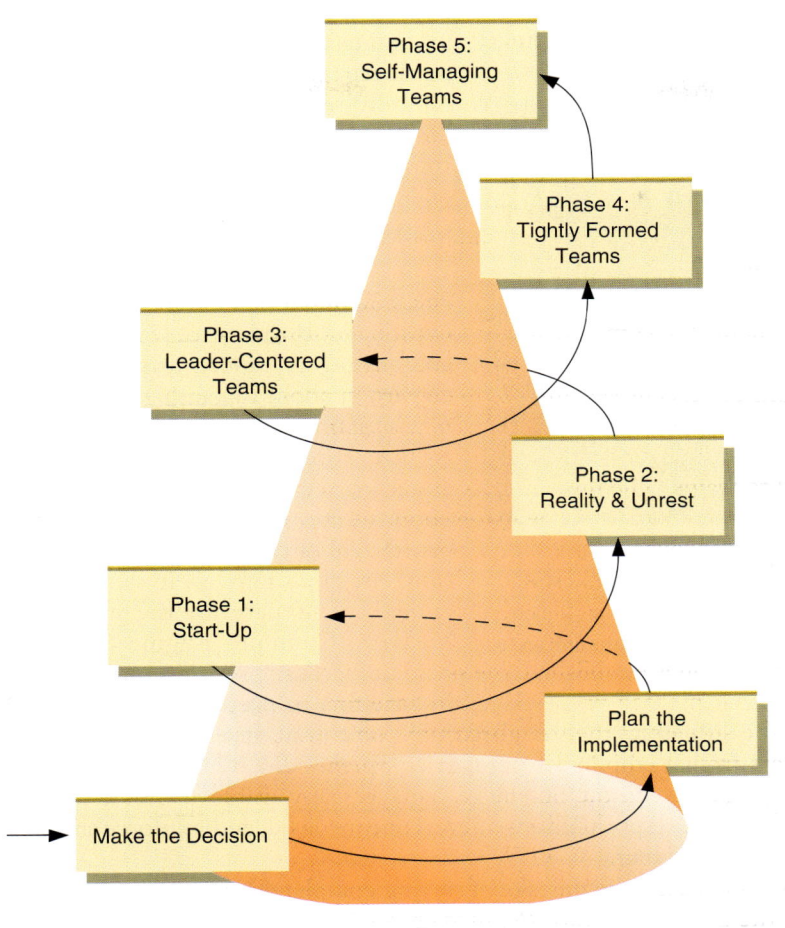

FIGURE 9.1

Phases of Team Implementation

Implementation of teams in organizations is a long, arduous process. After the decision is made to initiate teams, the steering committee develops plans for the design team, which plans the entire process. The goal is for teams to become self-managing. The time each stage takes varies with the organization.

The last stage of planning the implementation is to write the tentative plan for the initial work teams. The draft plan combines the work of the steering and design committees and becomes the primary working document that guides the continuing work of the design teams and the first work teams. The draft plan (1) recommends a process for selecting the people who will be on the first teams; (2) describes roles and responsibilities for all those who will be affected (team members, team leaders, facilitators, support teams, managers, and top management); (3) explains what training the various groups will need; (4) identifies specifically which work processes will be involved; (5) describes what other organizational systems will be affected; and (6) lays out a preliminary master schedule for the next two to three years. Once the steering committee and top management approve the preliminary plan, the organization is ready to start the implementation.

Phases of Implementation

As we just noted, implementation of self-managing work teams is a long and difficult process, often taking two to five years. During this period, the teams go through a number of phases (see Figure 9.1); these phases are not, however, readily apparent at the times the team is going through them.

Phase 1: Start-Up In phase 1, team members are selected and prepared to work in teams so the teams have the best possible chance of success. Much of the initial training is informational or "awareness" training sending the message that top management is firmly committed to teams and teams are not experimental. The steering committee usually starts the training at the top, and the training and information are passed down the chain to the team members. Training covers the rationale for moving to a team-based organization, how teams were selected, how they work, their roles and responsibilities, compensation, and job security. In general, training covers the technical skills necessary to do the team's work, the administrative skills the team needs to function within the organization, and the interpersonal skills necessary to work with people in the team and throughout the organization. Sometimes the interpersonal skills are important. Perhaps most important is establishing the idea that teams are not "unmanaged" but "differently managed." The difference is that the new teams manage themselves. Team

Implementing teams in organizations is a complex and multistep process. But if done well, the payoffs can be dramatic. India's Wipro Technologies moved to a team organization to compete more effectively with other international software solution companies such as EDS and IBM Global Solutions. Wipro's teams helped the firm win a major contract from Home Depot.

boundaries are also identified, and the preliminary plan is adjusted to fit the particular team situations. Employees typically sense that much is changing during the first few months, enthusiasm runs high, and employees' anticipation is quite positive. Performance by teams increases at start-up because of this initial enthusiasm for the change.

Phase 2: Reality and Unrest After perhaps six to nine months, team members and managers report frustration and confusion about the ambiguities of the new situation. For employees, unfamiliar tasks, more responsibility, and worry about job security replace hope for the opportunities presented by the new approach. All of the training and preparation, as important as it is, is never enough to prepare for the storm and backlash. Cummins Engine Company held numerous "prediction workshops" in an effort to prepare employees and managers for the difficulties that lay ahead—all to no avail. Its employees reported the same problems that employees of other companies did. The best advice is to perform phase 1 effectively and then make managers very visible, continue to work to clarify the roles and responsibilities of everyone involved, and reinforce the positive behaviors that do occur.

Some managers make the mistake of staying completely away from the newly formed teams, thinking the whole idea is to let teams manage themselves. In reality, managers need to be highly visible to provide encouragement, monitor team performance, act as intermediaries between teams, help teams acquire needed resources, foster the right type of communication, and, sometimes, protect teams from those who want to see them fail. Managers, too, feel the unrest and confusion. The change they supported results in more work for them. In addition, there is the real threat, at least initially, that work will not get done, projects will not get finished, or orders will not get shipped on time and that they will be blamed for these problems.[22] Managers also report that they still have to intervene and solve problems for the teams because the teams do not know what they are doing.

Phase 3: Leader-Centered Teams As the discomfort and frustrations of the previous phase peak, teams usually long for a system that resembles the old manager-centered organizational structure (see Figure 9.1). However, members are learning about self-direction and leadership from within the team and usually start to focus on a single member as the team leader. In addition, the team begins to think of itself as a unit as members learn to manage themselves. Managers begin to appreciate the potential benefits of organizing in teams and to withdraw slowly from the units' daily operations and begin focusing on standards, regulations, systems, and resources for the team.[23] This phase is not a setback to team development, although it may seem like one because development of and reliance on one internal leader is a move away from focusing on the old hierarchy and traditional lines of authority.

The design and steering committees need to be sure that two things happen during this phase. First, they need to encourage the rise of strong internal team leaders. The new leaders can be either company appointed or team appointed. Top managers sometimes prefer the additional control they get from appointing the team leaders, assuming production will continue through the team transition. On the other hand, if the company-appointed leaders are the former managers, team members have trouble believing that anything has really changed. Team-appointed leaders can be a problem if the leaders are not trained properly and oriented toward team goals.

If the team-appointed leader is ineffective, the team usually recognizes the problem and makes the adjustments necessary to get the team back on track. Another possibility for team leadership is a rotating system in which the position changes every quarter, month, week, or even day. A rotating system fosters professional growth of all members of the team and reinforces the strength of the team's self-management.

The second important issue for this phase is to help each team develop its own sense of identity. Visits to observe mature teams in action can be a good step for newly formed teams. Recognizing teams and individuals for good performance is always powerful, especially when the teams choose the recipients. Continued training in problem-solving steps, tools, and techniques is imperative. Managers need to push as many problem-solving opportunities as possible down to the team level. Finally, as team identity develops, teams develop social activities and display T-shirts, team names, logos, and other items that show off their identity. All of these events are a sure sign that the team is moving into phase 4.

Phase 4: Tightly Formed Teams   In the fourth phase of team implementation, teams become tightly formed to the point that their internal focus can become detrimental to other teams and to the organization as a whole. Such teams are usually extremely confident of their ability to do everything. They are solving problems, managing their schedule and resources, and resolving internal conflicts. However, communication with external teams begins to diminish, the team covers up for underperforming members, and interteam rivalries can turn sour, leading to unhealthy competition.

To avoid the dangers of the intense team loyalty and isolation inherent in phase 4, managers need to ensure that teams continue to do the things that have enabled them to prosper thus far. First, teams need to keep the communication channels with other teams open through councils of rotating team representatives who meet regularly to discuss what works and what does not; teams that communicate and cooperate with other teams should be rewarded. At the Digital Equipment plant in Connecticut, team representatives meet weekly to share successes and failures so that all can avoid problems and improve the ways their teams operate.[24] Second, management needs to provide performance feedback, either through computer terminals in the work area that give up-to-date information on performance or via regular feedback meetings. At TRW plants, management introduced peer performance appraisal at this stage of the team implementation process. It found that in phase 4, teams were ready to take on this administrative task but needed significant training in how to perform and communicate appraisals. Third, teams need to follow the previously developed plan to transfer authority and responsibility to the teams and ensure that all team members have followed the plan to get training in all of the skills necessary to do the team's work. By the end of phase 4, the team should be ready to take responsibility for managing itself.

Phase 5: Self-Managing Teams Phase 5 is the end result of the months or years of planning and implementation. Mature teams are meeting or exceeding their performance goals. Team members are taking responsibility for team-related leadership functions. Managers and supervisors have withdrawn from the daily operations, and are planning and providing counseling for teams. Probably most important, mature teams are flexible—taking on new ideas for improvement; making changes as needed to membership, roles, and tasks; and doing whatever it takes to meet the organization's strategic objectives. Although the teams are mature and functioning well, several things need to be done to keep them on track. First and foremost, individuals and teams need to continue their training in job skills and in team and interpersonal skills. Second, support systems need to be constantly improved to facilitate team development and productivity. Third, teams always need to improve their internal customer and supplier relationships within the organization. Partnerships among teams throughout the organization can help the internal teams continue to meet the needs of external customers.

Essential Team Issues

LEARNING OBJECTIVE

Discuss other essential team issues.

This chapter has described the many benefits of teams and the process of changing to a team-based organization. Teams can be utilized in small and large organizations, on the shop floor and in offices, and in countries around the world. Teams must be initiated for performance-based business reasons, and proper planning and implementation strategies must be used. In this section, we discuss two additional issues organizations face as they move to a team-based setup: team performance and starting at the top.

Team Performance

Organizations typically expect too much too soon when they implement teams. In fact, things often get worse before they get better.[25] Figure 9.2 shows how, shortly after implementation, team performance often declines and then rebounds to rise to the original levels and above. Management at Investors Diversified Services, the financial services giant in Minneapolis, expected planning for team start-up to take three or four months; the process took eight-and-a-half months.[26] It often takes a year or more before performance returns to at least before-team levels. If teams are implemented without proper planning, their performance may never return to prior levels. The long lead time for improving performance can be discouraging to managers who jumped on the team "bandwagon" and expected immediate returns.

The phases of implementation discussed in the previous sections correspond to key points on the team performance curve. At start-up, performance is at its normal levels, although sometimes the anticipation of and enthusiasm for teams cause a slight increase in performance. In phase 2, reality and unrest, teams are often confused and frustrated with the training and lack of direction from top management to the point that actual performance may decline. In phase 3, leader-centered teams become more comfortable with the team idea and refocus on the team's work. They once again have established leadership, although now with an internal leader rather than an external manager or supervisor. Thus, their performance usually returns to at least their former levels. In phase 4, teams are beginning to experience the real potential of teamwork and are producing above their prior levels. Finally, in phase 5, self-managing teams are mature, flexible, and usually setting new records for performance.

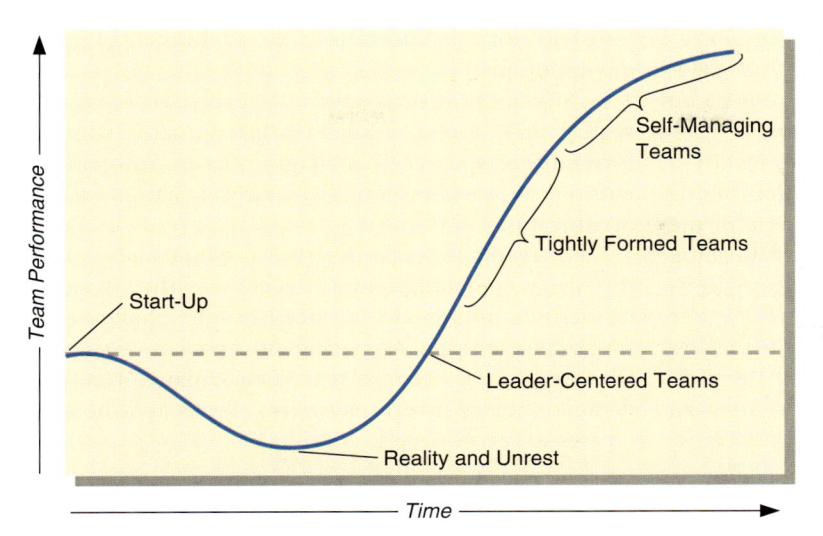

FIGURE 9.2
Performance and Implementation of Teams

The team performance curve shows that performance initially drops as reality sets in and team members experience frustration and unrest. However, performance soon increases and rises to record levels as the teams mature and become self-managing.

Reference: Reprinted by permission of Harvard Business School Publishing. From *The Wisdom of Teams: Creating the High Performance Organization* by Jon R. Katzenbach and Douglas K Smith. Boston, MA, 1993, p. 84. Copyright ©1993 McKinley & Company, Inc. All rights reserved.

Organizations changing to a team-based arrangement need to recognize the time and effort involved in making such a change. Hopes for immediate, positive results can lead to disappointment. The most rapid increases in performance occur between the leader-centered phase and the team-centered phase because teams have managed to get past the difficult, low-performance stages, have had a lot of training, and are ready to utilize their independence and freedom to make decisions about their own work. Team members are deeply committed to one another and to the success of the team. In phase 5, management needs to make sure teams are focused on the strategic goals of the organization.

Start at the Top

The question of where to start in team implementation is really not an issue. Change starts at the top in every successful team implementation. Top management has three important roles to play. First, top management must decide to go to a team-based organization for sound, business performance–related reasons. A major cultural change cannot be made simply because it is the fad, because the boss went to a seminar on teams, or because a quick fix is needed. Second, top management is instrumental in communicating the reasons for the change to the rest of the organization. Third, top management must support the change effort during the difficult periods. As discussed previously, performance usually goes down in the early phases of team implementation. Top-management support may involve verbal encouragement of team members, but organizational support systems for the teams are also needed. Examples of support systems for teams include more efficient inventory and scheduling systems, better hiring and selection systems, improved information systems, and appropriate compensation systems.

Synopsis

Teams are much different from work groups. A team is a small number of people with complementary skills who are committed to a common purpose, shared performance goals, and a common approach for which they hold themselves mutually accountable. Teams differ from traditional work groups in their job categories, authority, and reward systems.

Teams are used because they make sense for a specific organization. Organizational benefits include enhanced performance, employee benefits, and reduced costs, among others.

Many types of teams exist in organizations. Quality circles are small groups of employees from the same work area who meet regularly to discuss and recommend solutions to workplace problems. Work teams perform the daily operations of the organization and make decisions about how to do the work. Problem-solving teams are temporarily established to solve a particular problem. Management teams consist of managers from various areas; these teams are relatively permanent and coach and counsel the new teams. Product development teams are responsible for developing a new product or service for the organization. Members of virtual teams usually meet via teleconferencing, may never actually sit in the same room together, and often have a fluid membership.

Planning the change to a team-based organization entails all the activities leading to the decision to utilize teams and then preparing the organization for the initiation of teams. Essential steps include establishing leadership for the change, creating a steering committee, conducting a feasibility study, and making the go/no-go decision. After the decision to use teams has been made, preparations include clarifying the mission of the change, selecting the site for the first teams, preparing the design team, planning the transfer of authority, and drafting the preliminary implementation plan.

Implementation includes five phases: start-up, reality and unrest, leader-centered teams, tightly formed teams, and self-managing teams. Implementation of teams is essentially a cultural change for the organization.

For teams to succeed, the change must start with top management, who must decide why the change is needed, communicate the need for the change, and support the change. Management must not expect too much too soon because team performance tends to decrease before it returns to prior levels and then increases to record levels.

Discussion Questions

1. Why is it important to make a distinction between *group* and *team*? How might they differ in terms of behaviors?
2. Other than the obvious example of the strong presence of teams, what other organizational characteristics are different for a team-based organization?
3. Some say that changing to a team-based arrangement "just makes sense" for organizations. What are the four primary reasons this might be so?
4. If employees are happy working in a traditional hierarchical organization, why should management even consider changing to a team-based organization?
5. How are the six types of teams related to one another?
6. Under what circumstances is a cross-functional team useful in an organization?
7. Which type of team is the most common in organizations? Why?
8. Why is planning the change to a team-based structure important in the implementation process?
9. What can happen if an organization prematurely starts building a team-based organization by clarifying the mission and then selecting the site for the first work teams?
10. What are two primary issues facing team-based organizations?

Organizational Behavior Case for Discussion

None of Us Is as Smart as All of Us

Are you unhappy about your recent encounters with the medical profession? Do you think doctors are too rushed and impersonal, insurance companies have too much control, fees are too high, and procedures and tests are inadequately explained? If you do, you're not alone; national consumer surveys show a low level of satisfaction with health care. But at the Mayo Clinic in Rochester, Minnesota, patient satisfaction soars above the average. At the same time, costs are lower and the staff is happier than those at most other hospitals. Teamwork is the key to the clinic's remarkable success.

The Mayo Clinic was founded by Dr. William W. Mayo, a Minnesota physician, and his two sons, William J. and Charles, also physicians. After a catastrophic tornado in 1883, the doctors joined forces with nurses from the Sisters of St. Francis, and the arrangement was made permanent with the opening of St. Mary's Hospital in 1889. The Mayo brothers recruited more physicians, hiring technicians and business managers and creating one of the first group medical practices. The closeness of the two brothers, coupled with advances in medicine, helped guide the development of Mayo's team-based culture. Harry Harwick, its first business manager, claims, "The first and perhaps greatest lesson I learned from the Mayos was that of teamwork. For 'my brother and I' was no mere convenient term of reference, but rather the expression of a basic, indivisible philosophy of life." Dr. William J. Mayo said, "It has become necessary to develop medicine as a cooperative science; the clinician, the specialist, and the laboratory workers uniting for the good of the patient. Individualism in medicine can no longer exist."

The team approach permeates the culture of the entire organization. It begins with staff and physician recruiting. Mayo runs its own medical school and residency programs, and hires many of its own graduates. The clinic selects only those with the "right" attitude, the ones who are willing to put patients' needs first. All clinic medical staff, including doctors, nurses, and technicians, call one another "consultants," a term that emphasizes collaboration and reduces status barriers, enabling all workers to participate as equals in patient care decisions. The CEO is a physician; every committee is headed by medical personnel, with business staffers working as advisers only. The Mayo brothers turned their life savings into the Mayo Foundation, which funds the clinic's operation as well as medical education and research. Doctors at Mayo are employees, not owners, so they receive a salary, ensuring they will make decisions in the best interests of their patients rather than for personal gain. Without worries about turf battles, collaboration is the norm. Oncologist Lynn Hartman explains, "I take great comfort in the proximity of expertise. I feel much more confident in the accuracy of my diagnosis because I've got some very, very smart people next to me who have expertise that I don't have."

A typical patient's experience at Mayo goes something like this: A cancer patient would have multiple professionals involved in his or her care, from oncologists to nurses to radiologists to surgeons to social workers, and the group would meet as a team with the patient to work out a joint strategy for treatment. Cancer patients typically feel they have little control, but Mayo doctors know that getting patients actively involved in their own care dramatically increases the odds of successful treatment. Hartman claims, "Most patients today want a more interactive style . . . so [that] they can be part of the decision. They're on the Internet; they're doing their own research. What they're looking for is someone who can help them sort through that information." With help from the professionals, patients can work out a treatment that makes sense for their particular circumstances. When a patient's needs or questions change, the team adapts. "We work in teams, and each team is driven by the medical problems involved in a case and by the patient's preferences. Sometimes that means that a team must be expanded—or taken apart and reassembled," says Hartman.

Part of Mayo's success comes from past successes—for example, when its medical school graduates refer patients to the clinic. The foresight of William and Charlie Mayo in providing financially for the clinic is another factor. Mayo's reputation also creates opportunities, such as Mayo physician Donald D. Hensrud's recurring column for *Fortune* readers and the award-winning website mayoclinic.com. But most of Mayo's success is due to the passion for teamwork expressed in the founders' philosophy: "No one is big enough to be independent of others. None of us is as smart as all of us."

Case Questions

1. Would you consider the patient care groups at the Mayo Clinic to be teams? Explain your answer in terms of job categories, authority, and reward system. (Hint: See Table 9.1 for guidance.)
2. What team-related benefits does this case describe? What are the possible team-related costs?
3. What type of team are the patient care teams? Explain your answer.

References: 2003 Mayo Foundation Annual Report, www.mayoclinic.org on May 23, 2004; "History," "Mayo's Mission," "The Tradition," Mayo clinic website (quotation from "History"), www.mayoclinic.org on May 23, 2004; Paul Roberts, "The Agenda—Total Teamwork," *Fast Company*, April 1999.

Experiencing Organizational Behavior
Using Teams

Introduction: The use of groups and teams is becoming more common in organizations throughout the world. The following assessment surveys your beliefs about the effective use of teams in work organizations.

Instructions: You will agree with some of the statements and disagree with others. In some cases, you may find making a decision difficult, but you should force a choice. Record your answers next to each statement according to the following scale:

Chapter 10   Leadership Models and Concepts

The **least-preferred coworker (LPC) scale** presumes to measure a leader's motivation.

The degree of task or relationship motivation in a given leader is measured by the **least-preferred coworker** (**LPC**) **scale.** The LPC instructions ask respondents (i.e., leaders) to think of all the individuals with whom they have worked and then select their least-preferred coworker. Respondents then describe this coworker by marking a series of sixteen scales anchored at each end by a positive or negative quality or attribute.[19] For example, three of the items Fiedler uses in the LPC are

Pleasant	8 7 6 5 4 3 2 1	Unpleasant
Inefficient	1 2 3 4 5 6 7 8	Efficient
Unfriendly	1 2 3 4 5 6 7 8	Friendly

The higher numbers on the scales are associated with a positive evaluation of the least-preferred coworker. (Note that the higher scale numbers are associated with the more favorable term and that some items reverse both the terms and the scale values. The latter feature forces the respondent to read the scales more carefully and provide more valid answers.) Respondents who describe their least-preferred coworker in relatively positive terms receive a high LPC score, whereas those who use relatively negative terms receive a low LPC score.

Fiedler assumed these descriptions actually say more about the leader than about the least-preferred coworker. He believed, for example, that everyone's least preferred coworker is likely to be equally "unpleasant" and that differences in descriptions actually reflect differences in personality traits among the leaders responding to the LPC scale. Fiedler contended that high-LPC leaders are basically more concerned with interpersonal relations and low-LPC leaders with task-relevant problems. Not surprisingly, controversy has always surrounded the LPC scale. Researchers have offered several interpretations of the LPC score, arguing that it may be an index of behavior, personality, or some other unknown factor. Indeed, the LPC measure and its interpretation have long been among the most debated aspects of this theory.

Situational Favorableness

Fiedler also identified three factors that determine the favorableness of the situation. In order of importance (from most to least important), these factors are leader-member relations, task structure, and leader position power.

Leader-member relations refers to the personal relationship between subordinates and their leader. It is based on the extent to which subordinates trust, respect, and have confidence in their leader, and vice versa. A high degree of mutual trust, respect, and confidence obviously indicates good leader-member relations, and a low degree indicates poor leader-member relations.

Task structure is the second most important determinant of situational favorableness. A structured task is routine, simple, easily understood, and unambiguous. The LPC theory presumes that structured tasks are more favorable because the leader need not be closely involved in defining activities and can devote time to other matters. On the other hand, an unstructured task is nonroutine, ambiguous, and complex. Fiedler argues that this task is more unfavorable because the leader must play a major role in guiding and directing subordinates' activities.

Finally, *leader position power* is the power inherent in the leader's role itself. If the leader has considerable power to assign work, reward and punish employees, and recommend them for promotion, position power is high and favorable. If the leader must have job assignments approved by someone else, does not control rewards and punishment, and has no voice in promotions, position power is low and unfavorable; that is, many decisions are beyond the leader's control.

Leader Motivation and Situational Favorableness Fiedler and his associates conducted numerous studies examining the relationships among leader motivation, situational favorableness, and group performance. Table 10.2 summarizes the results of these studies.

To begin interpreting the results, let's first examine the situational favorableness dimensions shown in the table. The various combinations of these three dimensions result in eight different situations, as arrayed across the first three lines of the table. These situations, in turn, define a continuum ranging from very favorable to very unfavorable situations from the leader's perspective. Favorableness is noted in the fourth line of the table. For example, good relations, a structured task, and either high or low position power result in a very favorable situation for the leader; poor relations, an unstructured task, and either high or low position power create very unfavorable conditions for the leader.

The table also identifies the leadership approach intended to achieve high group performance in each of the eight situations. These linkages are shown in the bottom line of the table. A task-oriented leader is appropriate for very favorable as well as very unfavorable situations. For example, the LPC theory predicts that if leader-member relations are poor, the task is unstructured, and leader position power is low, a task-oriented leader will be effective. It also predicts that a task-oriented leader will be effective if leader-member relations are good, the task is structured, and leader position power is high. Finally, for situations of intermediate favorableness, the theory suggests that a person-oriented leader will be most likely to achieve high group performance.

Leader-Situation Match What happens if a person-oriented leader faces a very favorable or very unfavorable situation, or a task-oriented leader faces a situation of intermediate favorableness? Fiedler considers these leader-situation combinations to be "mismatches." Recall that a basic premise of his theory is that leadership behavior is a personality trait. Thus, the mismatched leader cannot readily adapt to the situation and achieve effectiveness. Fiedler contends that when a leader's style and the situation do not match, the only available course of action is to change the situation through "job engineering."[20]

For example, Fiedler suggests that if a person-oriented leader ends up in a very unfavorable situation, she or he should attempt to remedy matters by spending

TABLE 10.2

The LPC Theory of Leadership

Leader-Member Relations	Good				Poor			
Task Structure	Structured		Unstructured		Structured		Unstructured	
Position Power	High	Low	High	Low	High	Low	High	Low
Situational Favorableness	Very favorable		Moderately favorable				Very unfavorable	
Recommended Leader Behavior	↓ Task-oriented behavior			↓ Person-oriented behavior			↓ Task-oriented behavior	

more time with subordinates to improve leader-member relations and laying down rules and procedures to provide more task structure. Fiedler and his associates have also developed a widely used training program for supervisors on how to assess situational favorableness and change the situation, if necessary, to achieve a better match.[21] Weyerhauser and Boeing are among the firms that have experimented with Fiedler's training program.

Evaluation and Implications

The validity of Fiedler's LPC theory has been heatedly debated because of the inconsistency of the research results. Apparent shortcomings of the theory are that the LPC measure lacks validity, research does not always support the theory, and Fiedler's assumptions about the inflexibility of leader behavior are unrealistic.[22] The theory itself, however, represents an important contribution because it returned the field to a study of the situation and explicitly considered the organizational context and its role in effective leadership.

The Path-Goal Theory of Leadership

LEARNING OBJECTIVE
Discuss the path-goal theory of leadership.

Another important contingency approach to leadership is the path-goal theory. Developed jointly by Martin Evans and Robert House, the path-goal theory focuses on the situation and leader behaviors rather than on fixed traits of the leader.[23] In contrast to the LPC theory, the path-goal theory suggests that leaders can readily adapt to different situations.

Basic Premises

The path-goal theory has its roots in the expectancy theory of motivation discussed in Chapter 4. Recall that expectancy theory says that a person's attitudes and behaviors can be predicted from the degree to which the person believes job performance will lead to various outcomes (expectancy) and the value of those outcomes (valences) to the individual. The **path-goal theory of leadership** argues that subordinates are motivated by their leader to the extent that the leader's behaviors influence their expectancies. In other words, the leader affects subordinates' performance by clarifying the behaviors (paths) that will lead to desired rewards (goals). Ideally, of course, getting a reward in an organization depends on effective performance. Path-goal theory also suggests that a leader may behave in different ways in different situations.

The **path-goal theory of leadership** suggests that effective leaders clarify the paths (behaviors) that will lead to desired rewards (goals).

Leader Behaviors As Figure 10.2 shows, path-goal theory identifies four kinds of leader behavior: directive, supportive, participative, and achievement-oriented. With *directive leadership*, the leader lets subordinates know what is expected of them, gives specific guidance regarding how to accomplish tasks, schedules work to be done, and maintains definitive standards of performance for subordinates. A leader exhibiting *supportive leadership* is friendly and shows concern for subordinates' status, well-being, and needs. With *participative leadership*, the leader consults with subordinates about issues and takes their suggestions into account before making a decision. Finally, *achievement-oriented leadership* involves setting challenging goals, expecting subordinates to perform at their highest level, and showing strong confidence that subordinates will put forth effort and accomplish the goals. Unlike the LPC theory, path-goal theory assumes leaders can change their behavior and exhibit any or all of these leadership styles. The theory also predicts that

The path-goal theory of leadership encompasses four kinds of leader behavior. Andrea Jung, chair and CEO of Avon, uses each of these behaviors on a regular basis. For example, she occasionally uses directive behavior to set performance expectations and provide guidance. Jung demonstrates supportive behavior through her interest in those she works with. She frequently uses participative leadership by soliciting input from other executives in the firm. Finally, she uses achievement-oriented leadership by setting challenging goals and providing constant encouragement for everyone to work toward those goals.

the appropriate combination of leadership styles depends on situational factors.

Situational Factors The path-goal theory proposes two types of situational factors that influence how leader behavior relates to subordinate satisfaction: the personal characteristics of subordinates and the characteristics of the environment (see Figure 10.2).

Two important personal characteristics of subordinates are locus of control and perceived ability. Locus of control, discussed in Chapter 3, refers to the extent to which individuals believe that what happens to them results from their own behavior or from external causes. Research indicates that individuals who attribute outcomes to their own behavior may be more satisfied with a participative leader (since they believe their own efforts can make a difference), whereas individuals who attribute outcomes to external causes may respond more favorably to a directive leader (since they think their own actions are of little consequence). Perceived ability pertains to how people view their own ability with respect to the task. Employees who rate their own ability relatively high are less likely to feel a need for directive leadership (since they think they know how to do the job), whereas those who perceive their own ability as relatively low may prefer directive leadership (since they think they need someone to show them how to do the job).

Important environmental characteristics are task structure, the formal authority system, and the primary work group. The path-goal theory proposes that leader behavior will motivate subordinates if it helps them cope with environmental uncertainty created by those characteristics. In some cases, however, certain forms of leadership will be redundant, decreasing subordinate satisfaction. For example, when task structure is high, directive leadership is less necessary and therefore less effective; similarly, if the work group gives the individual plenty of social support, a supportive leader will not be especially attractive. Thus, the extent to which leader behavior matches the people and environment in the situation is presumed to influence subordinates' motivation to perform.

As another example, consider the success of Barbara Samson, founder of Intermedia, a Florida telephone company. To get her idea from the drawing board into the business world, Samson had to use directive leadership to organize her employees. However, she also had to use supportive leadership to help them get through the tough times during the early days of start-up. When she met with investors, she had to demonstrate achievement-oriented leadership to convey her goals and strategies. As her business has grown, she has increasingly used participative leadership to spread decision-making authority throughout the firm.[24]

FIGURE 10.2

The Path-Goal Theory of Leadership

The path-goal theory of leadership specifies four kinds of leader behavior: directive, supportive, participative, and achievement oriented. Leaders are advised to vary their behaviors in response to such situational factors as personal characteristics of subordinates and environmental characteristics.

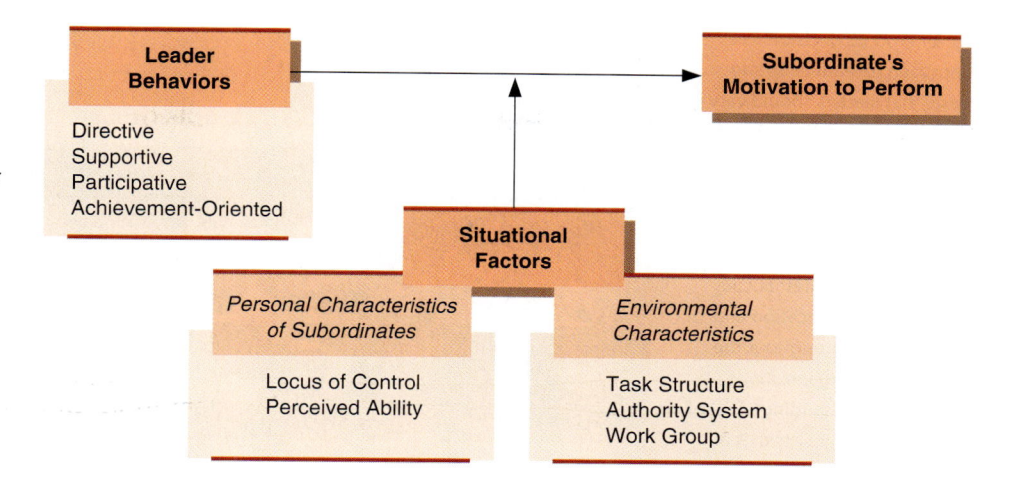

Leader Behaviors
- Directive
- Supportive
- Participative
- Achievement-Oriented

→ **Subordinate's Motivation to Perform**

Situational Factors

Personal Characteristics of Subordinates
- Locus of Control
- Perceived Ability

Environmental Characteristics
- Task Structure
- Authority System
- Work Group

Evaluation and Implications

The path-goal theory was designed to provide a general framework for understanding how leader behavior and situational factors influence subordinate attitudes and behaviors. The intention of path-goal theorists, however, was to stimulate research on the theory's major propositions, not to offer definitive answers. Researchers hoped a more fully developed, formal theory of leadership would emerge from continued study. Further work actually has supported the theory's major predictions, but it has not validated the entire model. Moreover, many of the theory's predictions remain overly general and have not been fully refined and tested.

Vroom's Decision Tree Approach to Leadership

LEARNING OBJECTIVE

Describe Vroom's decision tree approach to leadership.

Vroom's decision tree approach to leadership attempts to prescribe how much participation to allow subordinates in making decisions.

The third major contemporary approach to leadership is **Vroom's decision tree approach.** The earliest version of this model was proposed by Victor Vroom and Philip Yetton and later revised and expanded by Vroom and Arthur Jago.[25] Most recently, Vroom has developed yet another refinement of the original model.[26] Like the path-goal theory, this approach attempts to prescribe a leadership style appropriate to a given situation. It also assumes the same leader may display different leadership styles. Vroom's approach, however, concerns only a single aspect of leader behavior: subordinate participation in decision making.

Basic Premises

Vroom's decision tree approach assumes the degree to which subordinates should be encouraged to participate in decision making depends on the characteristics of the situation. In other words, no one decision-making process is best for all situations. After evaluating a variety of problem attributes (characteristics of the problem or decision), the leader determines an appropriate decision style that specifies the amount of subordinate participation.

Vroom's current formulation suggests that managers should use one of two different decision trees.[27] To do so, the manager first assesses the situation in terms of several factors. This assessment involves determining whether the given factor is "high" or "low" for the decision to be made. For instance, the first factor is

Victor Vroom's decision tree approach to leadership suggests that leaders should vary the degree of participation they provide to subordinates in making decisions. In the wake of one financial scandal after another, some top managers have begun to systematically increase communication and participation throughout the ranks of their organizations. Steve Odland (standing), CEO of AutoZone, now insists that all top managers fully participate in discussions and decisions regarding the firm's finances. Indeed, he requires that each top manager certify the accuracy of his or her unit's financial performance before submitting the results to him.

decision significance. If the decision is extremely important and may have a major impact on the organization (e.g., choosing a location for a new plant), its significance is high. But if the decision is routine and its consequences not very important (e.g., selecting a logo for the firm's softball team uniforms), its significance is low. This assessment guides the manager through the paths of the decision tree to a recommended course of action. One decision tree is to be used when the manager is interested primarily in making the decision on the most timely basis possible; the other is to be used when time is less critical and the manager is interested mainly in helping subordinates improve and develop their own decision-making skills.

The two decision trees appear in Figures 10.3 and 10.4. The problem attributes (situational factors) are arranged along the top of the decision tree. To use the model, the decision maker starts at the left side of the diagram and assesses the first problem attribute (decision significance). The answer determines the path to the second node on the decision tree, where the next attribute (importance of commitment) is assessed. This process continues until a terminal node is reached. In this way, the manager identifies an effective decision-making style for the situation.

The various decision styles reflected at the ends of the tree branches represent different levels of subordinate participation that the manager should attempt to adopt in a given situation. The five styles are defined as follows:

- *Decide:* The manager makes the decision alone and then announces or "sells" it to the group.
- *Delegate:* The manager allows the group to define for itself the exact nature and parameters of the problem and then develop a solution.
- *Consult (individually):* The manager presents the program to group members individually, obtains their suggestions, and then makes the decision.
- *Consult (group):* The manager presents the problem to group members at a meeting, gets their suggestions, and then makes the decision.
- *Facilitate:* The manager presents the problem to the group at a meeting, defines the problem and its boundaries, and then facilitates group member discussion as members make the decision.

Vroom's decision tree approach represents a very focused but quite complex perspective on leadership. To compensate for this difficulty, Vroom has developed elaborate expert system software to help managers assess a situation accurately and quickly and then make an appropriate decision regarding employee participation.

Chapter 10 Leadership Models and Concepts

Decision Significance	Importance of Commitment	Leader Expertise	Likelihood of Commitment	Group Support	Group Expertise	Team Competence	
H	H	H	H	-	-	-	Decide
H	H	H	L	H	H	H	Delegate
H	H	H	L	H	H	L	Consult (Group)
H	H	H	L	H	L	-	Consult (Group)
H	H	H	L	L	-	-	Consult (Group)
H	H	L	H	H	H	H	Facilitate
H	H	L	H	H	H	L	Facilitate
H	H	L	H	H	L	-	Consult (Individually)
H	H	L	H	L	-	-	Consult (Individually)
H	H	L	L	H	H	H	Facilitate
H	H	L	L	H	H	L	Facilitate
H	H	L	L	H	L	-	Consult (Group)
H	H	L	L	L	-	-	Consult (Group)
H	L	H	-	-	-	-	Decide
H	L	L	-	H	H	H	Facilitate
H	L	L	-	H	H	L	Facilitate
H	L	L	-	H	L	-	Consult (Individually)
H	L	L	-	L	-	-	Consult (Individually)
L	H	-	H	-	-	-	Decide
L	H	-	L	-	-	H	Delegate
L	H	-	L	-	-	L	Facilitate
L	L	-	-	-	-	-	Decide

FIGURE 10.3

Vroom's Time-Driven Decision Tree

This matrix is recommended for situations in which time is of the highest importance in making a decision. The matrix operates like a funnel. You start at the left with a specific decision problem in mind. The column headings denote situational factors that may or may not be present in that problem. You progress by selecting High or Low (H or L) for each relevant situational factor. Proceed down from the funnel, judging only those situational factors for which a judgment is called for, until you reach the recommended process.

Reference: "Vroom's Time-Driven Tree" from *A Model of Leadership Style* by Victor H. Vroom. Copyright © 1998. Reprinted by permission of Victor H. Vroom.

Vroom's Development-Driven Decision Tree

	Decision Significance	Importance of Commitment	Leader Expertise	Likelihood of Commitment	Group Support	Group Expertise	Team Competence	
P R O B L E M S T A T E M E N T	H	H	–	H	H	H	H	Decide
							L	Facilitate
						L	–	Consult (Group)
					L	–	–	Consult (Group)
				L	H	H	H	Delegate
							L	Facilitate
						L	–	Facilitate
					L	–	–	Consult (Group)
		L	–	–	H	H	H	Delegate
							L	Facilitate
						L	–	Consult (Group)
					L	–	–	Consult (Group)
	L	H	–	H	–	–	–	Decide
				L	–	–	–	Delegate
		L	–	–	–	–	–	Decide

FIGURE 10.4

Vroom's Development-Driven Decision Tree
This matrix is to be used when the leader is more interested in developing employees than in making the decision as quickly as possible. Just as with the time-driven tree shown in Figure 10.3, the leader assesses up to seven situational factors. These factors, in turn, funnel the leader to a recommended process for making the decision.

Reference: "Vroom's Development-Driven Decision Tree" from *A Model of Leadership Style* by Victor H. Vroom. Copyright © 1998. Reprinted by permission of Victor H. Vroom.

Many firms, including Halliburton Company, Litton Industries, and Borland International, have provided their managers with training in using the various versions of this model.

Evaluation and Implications

Because Vroom's current approach is relatively new, it has not been fully scientifically tested. The original model and its subsequent refinement, however, attracted a great deal of attention and were generally supported by research.[28] For example, there is some support for the idea that individuals who make decisions consistent with the model's predictions are more effective than those who make decisions inconsistent with it. The model therefore appears to be a tool managers can apply with some confidence in deciding how much subordinates should participate in the decision-making process.

Other Contemporary Approaches to Leadership

LEARNING OBJECTIVE

Discuss two other contemporary approaches to leadership.

Because leadership is such an important area, managers and researchers continue to study it. As a result, new ideas, theories, and perspectives are continuously evolving. Two of the better-known theories are the LMX model and the Hersey and Blanchard theory.

The Leader-Member Exchange Model

The **leader-member exchange (LMX) model of leadership** stresses the fact that leaders develop unique working relationships with each of their subordinates.

The **leader-member exchange (LMX) model** of leadership, conceived by George Graen and Fred Dansereau, stresses the importance of variable relationships between supervisors and each of their subordinates.[29] Each superior-subordinate pair is referred to as a *vertical dyad*. The model differs from earlier approaches in that it focuses on the differential relationship leaders often establish with different subordinates. Figure 10.5 shows the basic concepts of the leader-member exchange theory.

The model suggests that supervisors establish a special relationship with a small number of trusted subordinates referred to as the *in-group*. The in-group usually receives special duties requiring responsibility and autonomy; members may also receive special privileges. Subordinates who are not part of this group are called the *out-group*; they receive less of the supervisor's time and attention. Note in the figure that the leader has a dyadic, or one-to-one, relationship with each of the five subordinates.

Early in his or her interaction with a given subordinate, the supervisor initiates either an in-group or out-group relationship. It is not clear how a leader selects members of the in-group, but the decision may be based on personal compatibility and subordinates' competence. Research has confirmed the existence of in-groups and out-groups. In addition, studies generally have found that in-group members have a higher level of performance and satisfaction than out-group members.[30]

The Hersey and Blanchard Model

Another popular perspective among practicing managers is the Hersey and Blanchard model. Like some other leadership models not discussed here, this model

FIGURE 10.5

The Leader-Member Exchange (LMX) Model

The LMX model suggests that leaders form unique, independent relationships with each of their subordinates. As illustrated here, a key factor in this relationship is whether the individual subordinate is in the leader's out-group or in-group.

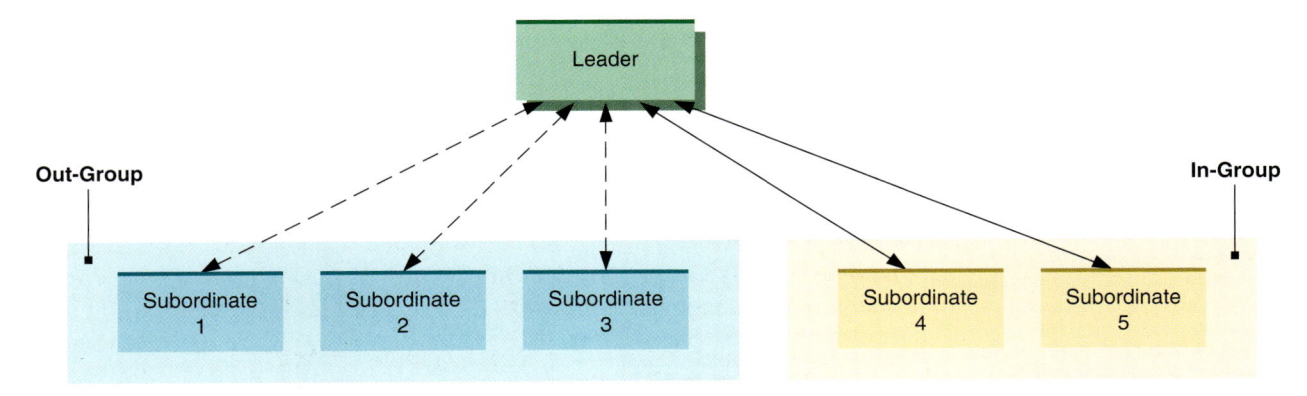

The **Hersey and Blanchard model** identifies different combinations of leadership presumed to work best with different levels of organizational maturity on the part of subordinates.

was developed as a consulting tool. The **Hersey and Blanchard model** is based on the notion that appropriate leader behavior depends on the readiness of the leader's subordinates.[31] In this instance, *readiness* refers to the subordinates' degree of motivation, competence, experience, and interest in accepting responsibility. Figure 10.6 shows the basic model.

The figure suggests that as subordinates' readiness increases, the leader's basic style should also change. When subordinate readiness is low, for example, the leader should rely on a "telling" style by providing direction and defining roles. When low to moderate readiness exists, the leader should use a "selling" style by offering direction and role definition accompanied by explanation and information. In a case of moderate-to-high subordinate readiness, the leader should use a "participating" style, allowing subordinates to share in decision making. Finally, when subordinate readiness is high, the leader is advised to use a "delegating" style by allowing them to work independently with little or no overseeing.

FIGURE 10.6

The Hersey and Blanchard Theory of Leadership

The Hershey and Blanchard theory suggests that leader behaviors should vary in response to the readiness of subordinates. This figure shows the nature of this variation. The curved line suggests that relationship leader behavior should start low, gradually increase, but then decrease again as subordinate readiness increases. Task behavior, however, shown by the straight line, should start high when subordinates lack readiness and then continuously diminish as they gain readiness.

Reference: The Situational Leadership Model is the registered trademark of the Center for Leadsership Studies, Escondido, CA. Excerpt from P. Hersey and K. Blanchard, *Management of Organizational Behavior: Utilizing Human Resources,* 3rd ed. (Englewood Cliffs, NJ: Prentice-Hall, 1977), p. 165.

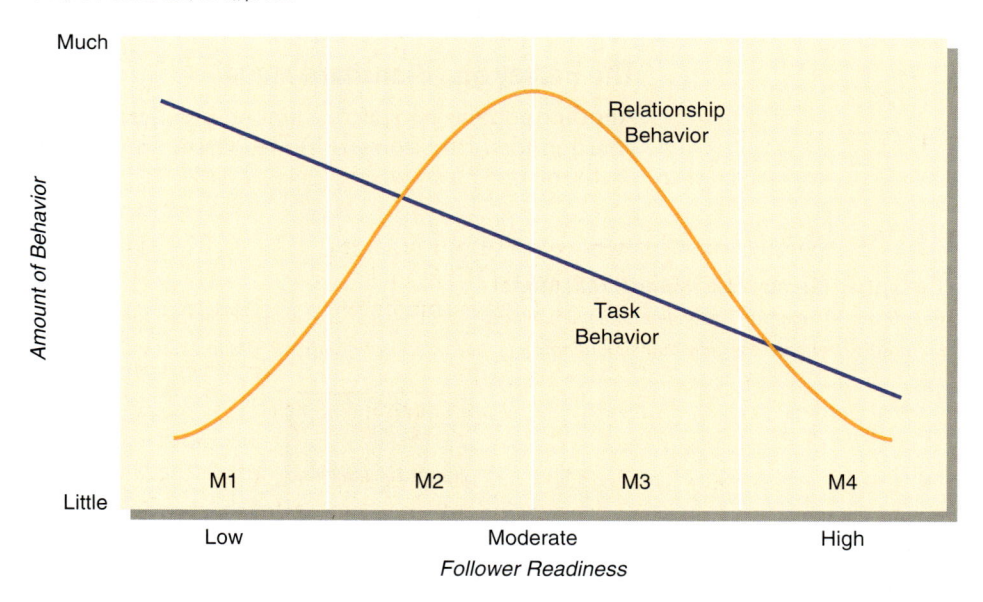

Synopsis

Leadership is both a process and a property. Leadership as a process is the use of noncoercive influence to direct and coordinate the activities of group members to meet goals. As a property, leadership is the set of characteristics attributed to those perceived to use such influence successfully. Leadership and management are related but distinct phenomena.

Early leadership research attempted primarily to identify important traits and behaviors of leaders. The Michigan and Ohio State studies each identified two kinds of leader behavior, one focusing on job factors and the other on people factors. The Michigan studies viewed these behaviors as points on a single continuum, whereas the Ohio State studies suggested they were separate dimensions.

Newer contingency theories of leadership attempt to identify appropriate leadership styles on the basis of the situation. Fiedler's LPC theory states that leadership effectiveness depends on a match between the leader's style (viewed as a trait of the leader) and the favorableness of the situation. Situation favorableness, in turn, is determined by task structure, leader-member relations, and leader position power. Leader behavior is presumed to reflect a constant personality trait and therefore cannot be easily changed.

The path-goal theory focuses on appropriate leader behavior for various situations. The path-goal theory suggests that directive, supportive, participative, or achievement-oriented leader behavior may be appropriate depending on the personal characteristics of subordinates and the characteristics of the environment. Unlike the LPC theory, this view presumes leaders can alter their behavior to best fit the situation.

Vroom's decision tree approach suggests appropriate decision-making styles based on situational characteristics. This approach focuses on deciding how much subordinates should participate in the decision-making process. Managers assess situational attributes and follow a series of paths through a decision tree that subsequently prescribes how they should make a particular decision.

Two recent perspectives not rooted in traditional leadership theories are the leader-member exchange (LMX) theory and the Hersey and Blanchard model. The LMX model focuses on specific relationships between a leader and individual subordinates. The Hersey and Blanchard model acknowledges that leader behavior toward a particular group needs to change as a function of subordinates' readiness.

Discussion Questions

1. How would you define *leadership*? Compare and contrast your definition with the one given in this chapter.
2. Cite examples of managers who are not leaders and leaders who are not managers. What makes them one and not the other? Cite examples of both formal and informal leaders.
3. What traits are presumed to characterize successful leaders? Do you think the trait approach has validity? Why or why not?
4. What other forms of leader behavior besides those cited in the chapter can you identify?
5. Critique Fiedler's LPC theory. Are other elements of the situation important? Do you think Fiedler's assertion about the inflexibility of leader behavior makes sense? Why or why not?
6. Do you agree or disagree with Fiedler's assertion that leadership motivation is basically a personality trait? Why?
7. Compare and contrast the LPC and path-goal theories of leadership. What are the strengths and weaknesses of each?
8. Of the three major leadership theories—the LPC theory, the path-goal theory, and Vroom's decision tree approach—which is the most comprehensive? Which is the narrowest? Which has the most practical value?
9. How realistic do you think it is for managers to attempt to use Vroom's decision tree approach as prescribed? Explain.
10. Which of the two contemporary theories of leadership—the LMX theory and the Hersey and Blanchard model—do you believe holds more promise? Why? Could either of these perspectives be integrated with any of the three major theories of leadership? If so, how?

Organizational Behavior Case for Discussion

How Do You Manage Magic?

According to science fiction writer Arthur C. Clarke, "Any significantly advanced technology is indistinguishable from magic." This statement aptly describes much of biotechnology. Manufacturing biotech pharmaceuticals is a complex, technical, and expensive process, with millions of pages of data, daily costs of $1 million, and an 80 percent failure rate. The entire process of getting a new product to market takes ten to twelve years, and numerous hurdles must be cleared along the way. The challenge for biotech managers, then, is how to manage complex processes as well as how to lead workers who are more knowledgeable and highly educated than their bosses.

The process begins with a test tube of cells being injected with a human gene. The gene creates a naturally occurring compound in the human body (interferon is one), but these cells have now been altered to make only that compound. The cells then reproduce and are moved into increasingly larger containers until the volume of the fluid is about 2,000 liters. The fluid is purified, yielding 2 liters of concentrated drug. All told, the procedure takes about five weeks, and if the batch has problems, they won't be discovered until the end. In spite of facilities more sterile than hospital operating rooms, bad batches can occur. The compounds are hundreds of times more complex than traditional drugs. For example, aspirin has a molecular weight (a crude measure of a compound's complexity) of about 180; biotech's average is 25,000.

The scientists who develop and manipulate this complicated process have M.D.s or Ph.D.s in subjects such as analytical chemistry, microbiology, or pharmacology. Biogen CEO James C. Mullen has a B.S. in chemical engineering and an M.B.A., has held engineering positions at pharmaceutical firms since 1980, and is an intellectual "heavyweight"; yet it's impossible for anyone to fully understand the firm's variety of specialized disciplines. Michael Gilman, Biogen's senior vice president of research, himself a research scientist, says, "I am completely ignorant about three-quarters of the stuff that goes on. And my colleagues on the senior management team? They are 98 percent ignorant."

Mullen is the right kind of person for the top job: open to debate, eager for input, yet decisive and tough-minded. He relies on objective data, asking, "Is this a fact, an opinion, or a guess?" "We're often making decisions in uncertainty," Mullen asserts. "If the organization is running correctly, the only decisions that get to my desk are the ones with high uncertainty." One development team couldn't answer Mullen's questions. Mullen says, "I was asking questions more from a commercial or a customer's point of view. I kept meeting resistance. Really, it was an attitude problem." Finally, in exasperation, Mullen demanded to see the raw data and analyzed it himself, finding trends the experts hadn't spotted. Mullen uses that experience as a lesson in how *not* to lead. He explains, "That group had the wrong values for this company. They no longer work at Biogen."

Another challenge is to focus on the end result while not losing track of the details. One team proposed a 180-day timetable for completing its FDA application; Mullen insisted it could be done in 90 days. According to Mullen, "Sometimes, you get more creativity when you're in a box than when you can do anything. In really difficult situations, sometimes you get the most interesting thinking." After Mullen pointed out to the scientists that an extra ninety days of drug sales might be worth $125 million, they completed the application in ninety-eight days. The ten-year development process is also a target. Mullen says, "People don't relate to ten-year product cycles. Half the people here haven't even worked for ten years. You have to break the time frames down so [that] a person can have an impact and see the impact."

Mullen wants more emphasis on the bottom line without sacrificing innovation. The CEO focuses intently on one thing at a time; he doesn't believe in multitasking. When teams are undisciplined, he ends the meeting by stating, "You aren't prepared. Call me when you're ready." Mullen reduced the number of people reporting to him from fifteen to nine to increase accountability. "The campfire culture doesn't work here anymore, with people sitting around telling each other what's going on," maintains Mullen, who is changing Biogen's culture. "We need to demand results."

Biogen's website's statement of corporate values claims, "Biogen's success is based on its people. Everyone here is a leader. The core of leadership is integrity and courage . . . These shared values describe how we aspire to lead and work together." Mullen's leadership at Biogen is moving the firm toward the accomplishment of that vision.

Case Questions

1. In what ways is James Mullen acting as a manager? In what ways is he acting as a leader? (Hint: For a good summary of the differences, see Table 10.1, "Distinctions Between Management and Leadership.")
2. Answer the following questions based on Fielder's LPC theory: Does Mullen seem to be motivated more by tasks or by relationships? Is the situation at Biogen more favorable or unfavorable? Considering the match or mismatch between leader motivation and situation favorableness, what outcomes would Fiedler predict?
3. Using the path-goal theory of leadership, explain whether you think Mullen is using the appropriate kind of leader behavior. Why or why not?

References: "Career Opportunities," "Our History," "Vision, Mission, Values," Biogen website, www.biogen.com on May 26, 2004; "Biogen Could Use This Shot in the Arm," *BusinessWeek*, May 16, 2002; "The Tech Outlook: Biotech," *BusinessWeek*, March 25, 2002; Charles Fishman, "Isolating the Leadership Gene," *Fast Company*, March 2002, pp. 83–90 (quotation, pp. 86–87).

Experiencing Organizational Behavior

Understanding Successful and Unsuccessful Leadership

Purpose: This exercise will help you better understand the behaviors of successful and unsuccessful leaders.

Format: You will be asked to identify contemporary examples of successful and unsuccessful leaders and then describe how these leaders differ.

Procedure:

1. With each student working alone, list the names of ten people you think of as leaders in public life. Note that the names should not be confined to "good" leaders but should also identify "strong" leaders.
2. Next, students will form small groups and compare their lists. This comparison should focus on common and unique names, as well as on the kinds of individuals listed (i.e., male or female, contemporary or historical, business or nonbusiness, and so on).
3. From all the lists, choose two leaders whom most people would consider very successful and two who would be deemed unsuccessful.
4. Identify similarities and differences between the two successful leaders and between the two unsuccessful leaders.
5. Relate the successes and failures to at least one theory or perspective discussed in the chapter.
6. Select one group member to report your findings to the rest of the class.

Follow-up Questions

1. What role does luck play in leadership?
2. Are there factors about the leaders you researched that might have predicted their success or failure before they achieved leadership roles?
3. What are some criteria of successful leadership?

Self-Assessment Exercise

Applying Vroom's Decision Tree Approach

This skill-builder will help you better understand your own leadership style regarding employee participation in decision making. Mentally play the role described in the following scenario; then make the comparisons suggested at the end of the exercise.

You are the southwestern U.S. branch manager of an international manufacturing and sales organization. The firm's management team is looking for ways to increase efficiency. As part of this effort, the company recently installed an integrated computer network linking sales representatives, customer service employees, and other sales support staff. Sales were expected to increase and sales expenses to drop as a result.

However, exactly the opposite has occurred: Sales have dropped a bit, and expenses are up. You have personally inspected the new system and believe the hardware is fine. However, you believe the software linking the various computers is less than ideal.

The subordinates you have quizzed about the system, on the other hand, think the entire system is fine. They attribute the problems to a number of factors, including inadequate training in how to use the system, a lack of incentive for using it, and generally poor morale. Whatever the reasons given, each worker queried had strong feelings about the issue.

Your boss has just called you and expressed concern about the problems. He has indicated he has confidence in your ability to solve the problem and will leave it in your hands. However, he wants a report on how you plan to proceed within one week.

First, think of how much participation you would normally allow your subordinates in making this decision. Next, apply Vroom's decision tree approach to the problem and see what it suggests regarding the optimal level of participation. Compare your usual approach with the recommended solution.

OB Online

1. Using your favorite search engine, do an Internet search using simply the word *leadership*. How many sites were identified? What conclusions can you draw based on this result?
2. Identify a historical figure whom you consider a highly effective leader. Use the Internet to find two or three sites that specifically address this individual as a leader.
3. Repeat the previous exercise for a contemporary figure.
4. Describe how a website might be created that would allow managers to input their situation and, using Vroom's tree diagram model, get advice on how much participation to allow their subordinates in making a decision. How popular do you think such a site would be? How much do you think managers might be willing to pay to use it?

Building Managerial Skills

Exercise Overview: Conceptual skills involve the manager's ability to think in the abstract. This exercise will enable you to apply your conceptual skills to better understand the distinction between leadership and management.

Exercise Task: Identify someone who currently occupies a management and/or leadership position. This individual can be a manager in a large business, the owner of a small business, the president of a campus organization, or any other similar position. Next, interview this individual and ask him or her the following questions:

1. Name three recent tasks or activities that were primarily managerial in nature, requiring little or no leadership.
2. Name three recent tasks or activities that primarily involved leadership, requiring little or no management.
3. Do you spend most of the time working as a manager or a leader?
4. How easy or difficult is it to differentiate activities based on their management versus leadership involvement?

After completing the interviews, the class breaks up into small groups. Discuss your results with your group. What have you learned about leadership from this activity?

TEST PREPPER

ACE self-test

You have read the chapter and studied the key terms, and the exam is any day now. Think you're ready to ace it? Take this sample test to gauge your comprehension of chapter material. You can check your answers at the back of the book. Want more test questions? Visit the student website at http://college.hmco.com/business/students/ (select Griffin/Moorhead, Fundamentals of Organizational Behavior 1e) and take the ACE quizzes for more practice.

1. **T F** Leadership was initially thought of as a process, but today it is studied primarily as a property.
2. **T F** Organizations are most effective once leadership has replaced traditional management.
3. **T F** Recently some researchers have reintroduced traits such as self-confidence and cognitive ability into the study of leadership.
4. **T F** A substantial amount of research and definitive conclusions have been reached regarding the differences between male and female leaders.
5. **T F** According to the University of Michigan leadership studies, an employee-centered leader attempts to build effective work groups with high performance goals.
6. **T F** A leader engaging in initiating-structure behavior is interested in forming new relationships with employees at work.
7. **T F** The major shortcoming of the behavioral theories of leadership is that they do not take into account important differences from situation to situation.
8. **T F** The LPC theory of leadership contends that a leader may be effective in one situation but not in another.
9. **T F** One element of situational favorableness in LPC theory is the potential performance of the group as a whole.
10. **T F** According to LPC theory, a task-oriented leader is most appropriate in highly favorable and highly unfavorable situations.
11. **T F** Fiedler suggested in his LPC theory that if a mismatch exists between the leader and the situation, the only thing that can be changed is the situation.
12. **T F** Path-goal theory is based in equity theory, the theory that emphasizes the universal desire to be treated fairly.
13. **T F** According to path-goal theory, subordinates who perceive their own ability as low prefer a nondirective leadership style so they can prove their worth to the leader.
14. **T F** Vroom's decision tree approach to leadership describes how leaders actually make decisions.
15. **T F** Recent developments in Vroom's decision tree approach to leadership are based on the question of whether time is a critical factor in the leader's decision-making process.
16. **T F** The basis of the leader-member exchange model of leadership is that leaders should treat all employees as similarly as possible.
17. **T F** According to the Hersey and Blanchard model of leadership, subordinates who are ready to perform the work should be led differently than those who are not ready to perform it.
18. An employee who follows a leader because he or she thinks the leader is intelligent subscribes to the _____ view of leadership.
    - a. process
    - b. property
    - c. coercion
    - d. influence
    - e. behavioral
19. A person who adopts a trait approach to studying leadership would argue which of the following?
    - a. Effective leaders build trust in their followers.
    - b. Effective leaders clarify the tasks subordinates must accomplish.
    - c. Effective leaders set effective goals.
    - d. Effective leaders are taller than ineffective leaders.
    - e. Effective leaders are successful because they are granted a position of authority.
20. According to the University of Michigan leadership studies, job-centered leaders do which of the following?
    - a. Respect subordinates' ideas
    - b. Build trust in subordinates
    - c. Make sure employees' needs are met
    - d. Explain work procedures
    - e. Build effective work groups
21. According to the Ohio State University leadership studies, a leader engaged in initiating-structure behaviors may do all of the following except
    - a. define the leader-subordinate roles.
    - b. establish channels of communication.
    - c. create a relationship of respect.
    - d. determine methods of accomplishing the group's task.
    - e. make sure subordinates know what is expected of them.

22. Unlike the researchers from the University of Michigan leadership studies, the Ohio State leadership researchers concluded that
    a. the most effective leaders also have the greatest number of subordinates.
    b. trait theories are as successful as behavioral theories in predicting leadership success.
    c. leaders of large companies are more effective than leaders of small companies.
    d. leaders usually come from inside the organization rather than from outside.
    e. leaders demonstrate concern for performance and concern for employee welfare simultaneously.

23. The basis of Fred Fiedler's LPC (least-preferred coworker) theory of leadership is that
    a. leaders are more effective with preferred coworkers.
    b. leaders are less effective with less-preferred coworkers.
    c. a leader's effectiveness depends on characteristics of the situation.
    d. a leader who engages in both employee-centered and job-centered behaviors is most effective.
    e. leaders must adapt their styles to meet certain conditions.

24. Which of the following factors does not affect the favorableness of the leader's situation as explained in Fiedler's LPC theory?
    a. Leadership motivation
    b. Leader-member relations
    c. Task structure
    d. Leader position power
    e. All of the above factors affect situational favorableness.

25. John is a leader whose primary motivation is to complete organizational tasks. In which of the following situations will John be most effective?
    a. High least-preferred coworker
    b. Weak relationship motivation
    c. Strong job-centered motivation
    d. Moderate situational favorableness
    e. Poor situational favorableness

26. Michael attempts to motivate his employees by reinforcing their expectation that good job performance will lead to valuable outcomes. Michael's approach is consistent with which theory of leadership?
    a. Trait theory
    b. Behavioral theory
    c. LPC theory
    d. Directive theory
    e. Path-goal theory

27. According to research based on the path-goal theory, individuals who attribute outcomes to their own behaviors may be most satisfied with which style of leadership?
    a. Directive
    b. Supportive
    c. Participative
    d. Achievement oriented
    e. Ability-control oriented

28. Victor Vroom and Philip Yetton's decision tree approach to leadership focuses on which aspect of leader behavior?
    a. Subordinate participation in decision making
    b. Improving leader-member relations
    c. Enhancing position power
    d. Clarifying task structure
    e. Broadening leadership styles

29. Vroom recently elaborated his decision tree approach to leadership by suggesting managers should use one of two different decision trees. The appropriate decision tree to use depends primarily on the
    a. cost of the decision.
    b. number of employees involved in the decision.
    c. impact of the decision on organizational effectiveness.
    d. decisions made by direct competitors of the organization.
    e. amount of time the manager has to make the decision.

30. The possible decision styles in Vroom's approach to leadership range from
    a. deciding alone to facilitating the group as members make the decision.
    b. consulting with individuals to consulting with the group as a whole.
    c. delegating the decision to consulting with the group.
    d. consulting with the group to letting the group make its own decision.
    e. delegating the decision to deciding alone.

31. Harold receives special duties that require responsibility and autonomy from his work leader. According to the leader-member exchange model of leadership, Harold is in the
    a. leadership dyad.
    b. LPC group.
    c. consulting group.
    d. in-group.
    e. out-group.

32. If Maria were to follow the Hersey and Blanchard model of leadership, she would use a delegating style only when
    a. all other approaches fail.
    b. leaders form dyadic relationships with subordinates.
    c. subordinates are ready and willing to do the work.
    d. situations are highly unfavorable.
    e. situations are highly favorable.

CHAPTER 11

Leadership and Influence Processes

MANAGEMENT PREVIEW

As we learned in Chapter 10, leadership is a powerful, complex, and often abstract concept. This chapter explores many of the skills and personal resources that affect leaders and leadership. First, we revisit the role of influence in leadership. We then introduce two contemporary influence-based perspectives on leadership: transformational and charismatic leadership. Next, we discuss various substitutes for leadership that may exist in organizations. We then describe power and political behavior in organizations, influence-based phenomena that often involve leadership. Finally, we explore impression management, a related but distinct concept.

After you have studied this chapter, you should be able to:
- ☐ *Characterize leadership as influence.*
- ☐ *Discuss influence-based approaches to leadership.*
- ☐ *Describe key leadership substitutes.*
- ☐ *Explain power in organizations.*
- ☐ *Discuss power and organizational politics.*
- ☐ *Describe impression management.*

We start with a discussion of the challenges facing some of today's newest business leaders.

The twenty-first century has thus far been quite challenging for corporate leaders, especially for new leaders, who must learn to lead while facing a very tough business environment. ABC Entertainment, Kinko's, and Southwest Airlines are among the major businesses whose new CEOs have had to weather the current business climate.

Susan Lyne, president of ABC Entertainment, assumes responsibility for the network's television programming. She first worked in print publishing—the *Village Voice* and *Premiere*—and later managed ABC's TV miniseries division. Her top priority is "getting the younger creative people at the network to feel comfortable speaking up." Lyne wants to change the television giant, which she says is "quick to blame and slow to celebrate." Also on her agenda are increasing managers' entrepreneurial spirit and focusing on unfilled market niches when choosing new shows.

When entrepreneur-turned-CEO Gary Kusin became leader of Kinko's, he knew store employees had the best information about the state of the firm. He visited with 2,500 associates and learned that business customers were demanding more services, more technology, and closer working partnerships. He spent time listening and learning about his new firm, but he also brought renewed attention to efficiency and costs. He says, "As far as running a tight operation is concerned, it's always good to play very defensively. When things are good, people become lax. We've taken this opportunity to get buttoned down. Then, even if the economy lifts[,] ... we will not lose that focus."

Southwest Airlines' James Parker has been with the airline since 1986, assuming the top position when Herb Kelleher stepped down. Three months after he became chief executive, the events of September 11 devastated the airlines. Unlike most of his competitors, Parker decided not to lay off any workers. He explains, "We have a lot of people who worked hard for more than thirty years so that they can have job security in hard times ... Cutting jobs should be the last thing a company does rather than the first thing." Parker cut costs elsewhere, such as by delaying aircraft purchases, and spent time reassuring employees.

The job of CEO is ever varied, requiring leaders to utilize their skills with both people and processes. Leaders need to build on their own strengths, but they also must be adaptable to successfully face the challenges in a variety of situations.

"Cutting jobs should be the last thing a company does rather than the first thing."
—James Parker, CEO of Southwest Airlines

References: Alison Overholt, "New Leaders, New Agendas," *Fast Company*, May 2002, pp. 52–62 (quotation, p. 62); "Who's Smiling Through This Recession?" *BusinessWeek*, October 26, 2001; "ABC's Next Hit Could Co-Star the Internet," *BusinessWeek*, March 26, 2001.

The leaders just described are dealing with one of the most significant challenges any leader can face: the need to transform an organization from one thing into something different. To have any chance for success, they must rely on power and political processes to facilitate key changes. In her or his own way, each leader is also attempting to influence the organization in new and profound ways—and influence, as we will see, is the foundation of effective leadership.

Leadership as Influence

LEARNING OBJECTIVE
Characterize leadership as influence.

Recall that in Chapter 10, we defined *leadership* (from a process perspective) as the use of noncoercive influence to direct and coordinate the activities of group members to meet goals. We then described a number of leadership models and theories based variously on leadership traits, behaviors, and contingencies. Unfortunately, most of these models and theories essentially ignore the influence component of leadership. That is, they tend to focus on the characteristics of the leader (traits, behaviors, or both) and the responses from followers (satisfaction and/or performance, for instance) with little regard for how the leader actually exercises influence to bring about the desired responses from subordinates.

Influence should actually be considered the cornerstone of the process. Regardless of the leader's traits or behaviors, leadership matters only if influence actually occurs; that is, a person's ability to affect the behavior of others through influence is the ultimate determinant of whether she or he is really a leader. No one can truly be a leader without the ability to influence others. Furthermore, a person who has the ability to influence others clearly has the potential to become a leader.

Influence can be defined as the ability to affect the perceptions, attitudes, or behaviors of others.[1] If a person can make another person recognize that her working conditions are more hazardous than she currently believes them to be (change in perceptions), influence has occurred. If an individual can convince someone else that the organization is a much better place to work than he currently believes it to be (change in attitude), influence has occurred. Finally, if a person can get others to work harder or to file a grievance against their boss (change in behavior), influence has occurred.[2] Note, too, that influence can be used in ways that are beneficial or harmful. A person can be influenced to help clean up a city park on the weekend as part of a community service program, for example, or be influenced to use or sell drugs.

Influence is the ability to affect the perceptions, attitudes, or behaviors of others.

Influence-Based Approaches to Leadership

LEARNING OBJECTIVE
Discuss influence-based approaches to leadership.

In recent years, influence has become a more significant component of some leadership models and concepts.[3] The two contemporary approaches to leadership discussed in this section, for example, are tied directly or indirectly to influence. These approaches are transformational leadership and charismatic leadership.

Transformational Leadership

Transformational leadership, a relative newcomer to the leadership literature, focuses on the basic distinction between leading for change and leading for stability.[4] According to this viewpoint, much of what a leader does occurs in the course of routine work-related transactions: assigning work, evaluating performance, making decisions, and so forth. Occasionally, however, the leader has to initiate and manage major change, such as managing a merger, creating a work group, or defining the organization's culture. The first set of issues involves transactional leadership, whereas the second entails transformational leadership.[5]

Recall from Chapter 10 the distinction between management and leadership. Transactional leadership is essentially the same as management in that it involves routine, regimented activities. Closer to the general notion of leadership, however, is **transformational leadership,** the set of abilities that allows the leader to recognize the need for change, create a vision to guide that change, and execute the change effectively. Only a leader with tremendous influence can hope to perform these functions successfully. Some experts believe change is such a vital organizational

Influence, the ability to affect the perceptions, attitudes, or behaviors of others, is a cornerstone of leadership. Childhood friends Rameck Hunt, Sampson Davis, and George Jenkins vowed to defy the limitations of their inner-city upbringing and became doctors together. Throughout the rigors of college and medical school, the friends pushed one another to do their best. And there is little doubt in any of their minds that their mutual influence was the catalyst for each one's success.

Transformational leadership is the set of abilities that allows the leader to recognize the need for change, create a vision to guide that change, and execute the change effectively.

function that even successful firms need to change regularly to avoid complacency and stagnation; accordingly, leadership for change is also important.[6]

Moreover, some leaders can adopt either transformational or transactional perspectives, depending on their circumstances. Others are able to do one or the other, but not both. Ron Canion, the first CEO of Compaq Computer, was clearly an excellent transactional leader. He built the firm from a single new idea and managed it efficiently and profitably for several years. However, the environment changed to the point where Compaq needed to change as well, and Canion apparently was unable to recognize the need for change, let alone lead the firm through those changes. His replacement, Eckhard Pfeiffer, evidently excelled at transformational leadership, as he led the firm through several very successful new initiatives and transformations. However, when this work was done and Compaq needed to refocus on efficient and effective operations best directed by a transactional leader, Pfeiffer faltered, and he too was replaced. The next CEO, Michael Capellas, then successfully negotiated a merger between Compaq and Hewlett-Packard.

Charismatic Leadership

Perspectives based on charismatic leadership, such as the trait theories discussed in Chapter 10, assume charisma is an individual characteristic of the leader. **Charisma** is a form of interpersonal attraction that inspires support and acceptance. **Charismatic leadership** is, accordingly, a type of influence based on the leader's personal charisma. All else being equal, then, someone with charisma is more likely to be able to influence others than someone without charisma. For example, a highly charismatic supervisor will be more successful in influencing subordinate behavior than a supervisor who lacks charisma. Thus, influence is again a fundamental element of this perspective.[7]

Charisma is a form of interpersonal attraction that inspires support and acceptance from others.

Charismatic leadership is a type of influence based on the leader's personal charisma.

Robert House first proposed a theory of charismatic leadership based on research findings from a variety of social science disciplines.[8] His theory suggests that charismatic leaders are likely to have a lot of self-confidence, firm confidence in their beliefs and ideals, and a strong need to influence people. They also tend to communicate high expectations about follower performance and to express confidence in their followers. Gordon Bethune, CEO of Continental Airlines, is an excellent example of a charismatic leader. Bethune possesses a unique combination of executive skill, honesty, and playfulness. These qualities have attracted a group of individuals at Continental who are willing to follow his lead without question and to dedicate themselves to carrying out his decisions and policies with unceasing passion.[9]

Figure 11.1 portrays the three elements of charismatic leadership in organizations that most experts acknowledge today.[10] First, the charismatic leader envisions the future, sets high expectations, and models behaviors consistent with meeting those expectations. Next, the charismatic leader is able to energize others by demonstrating personal excitement, personal confidence, and patterns of success. Finally, the charismatic leader enables others by supporting them, empathizing with them, and expressing confidence in them.[11]

Charismatic leadership ideas are quite popular among managers today and are the subject of numerous books and articles. Unfortunately, few studies have specifically attempted to test the meaning and impact of charismatic leadership. Lingering ethical concerns about charismatic leadership also trouble some people: Some

FIGURE 11.1

The Charismatic Leader

The charismatic leader is characterized by three fundamental attributes. As illustrated here, these are behaviors resulting in envisioning, energizing, and enabling. Charismatic leaders can be a powerful force in any organizational setting.

Reference: Reprinted from David A. Nadler and Michael L. Tushman, "Beyond the Charismatic Leader: Leadership and Organizational Change," *California Management Review,* Vol. 32, No. 2. Copyright © 1990 by The Regents of the University of California. By permission of The Regents.

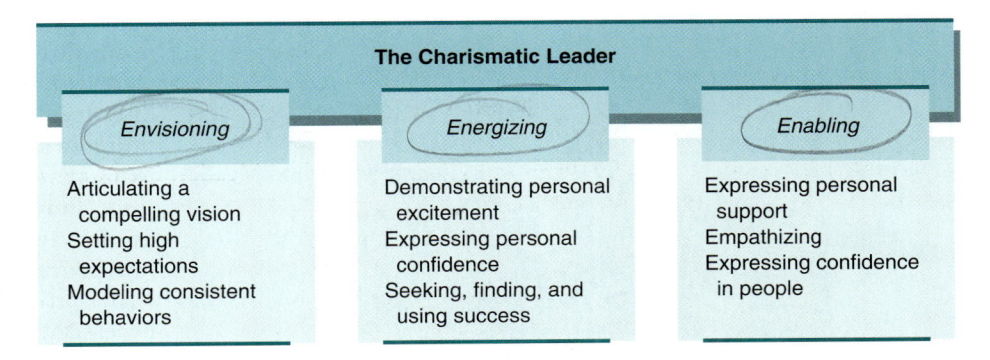

The Charismatic Leader

Envisioning	Energizing	Enabling
Articulating a compelling vision Setting high expectations Modeling consistent behaviors	Demonstrating personal excitement Expressing personal confidence Seeking, finding, and using success	Expressing personal support Empathizing Expressing confidence in people

charismatic leaders inspire such blind faith in their followers that they may engage in inappropriate, unethical, or even illegal behaviors merely because the leader instructed them to do so. Taking over a leadership role from someone with substantial personal charisma is also a challenge.

Leadership Substitutes: Can Leadership Be Irrelevant?

LEARNING OBJECTIVE

Describe key leadership substitutes.

Leadership substitutes are individual, task, and organizational characteristics that tend to outweigh the leader's ability to affect subordinates' satisfaction and performance.

Another interesting twist on leadership is the premise that it may sometimes be unnecessary or irrelevant. An implicit assumption made by each leadership and influence perspective described thus far is that the leader and the follower can be differentiated; That is, one person, the leader, is trying to influence or control another, the follower. However, the concept of leadership substitutes points out that in some situations, leadership may not be necessary.

Leadership substitutes are individual, task, and organizational characteristics that tend to outweigh the leader's ability to affect subordinates' satisfaction and performance.[12] In other words, if certain factors are present, the employee will perform his or her job capably without the direction of a leader. Unlike traditional theories, which assume hierarchical leadership is always important, the premise of the leadership substitutes perspective is that leader behaviors are irrelevant in many situations.

Workplace Substitutes

Ability, experience, training, knowledge, need for independence, professional orientation, and indifference to organizational rewards are individual characteristics that may neutralize leader behaviors. For example, an employee who has the skills and abilities to perform her job and a high need for independence may not need, and may even resent, a leader who tries to provide direction and structure.

A task characterized by routine, a high degree of structure, frequent feedback, and intrinsic satisfaction may also render leader behavior irrelevant. Thus, if the task gives the subordinate enough intrinsic satisfaction, he may not need support from a leader.

Explicit plans and goals, rules and procedures, cohesive work groups, a rigid reward structure, and physical distance between supervisor and subordinate are organizational characteristics that may substitute for leadership. For example, if job goals are explicit and there are many rules and procedures for task performance, a leader providing directions may not be necessary. Preliminary research lends support for the concept of leadership substitutes, but additional research is needed to identify other potential substitutes and their impact on leadership effectiveness.[13]

Superleadership

A relatively new addition to the literature on leadership substitutes is the notion of superleadership. **Superleadership** occurs when a leader gradually turns over power, responsibility, and control to a self-managing work group. As we discussed more fully in Chapter 9, many firms today are making widespread use of work teams that function without a formal manager. A big challenge these firms face is what to do with the existing group leader. Although some managers cannot handle this change and leave the firm, a superleader can alter his or her own personal style and become more of a coach or facilitator than a supervisor.

Leadership substitutes allow people to perform effectively without the direction of a leader. The Dragon Slayers, shown here, are a volunteer group of high school girls who provide the only round-the-clock emergency care available for 3,000 people in a region of Alaska that is the size of Maryland. The girls voluntarily undergo 200 hours of medical training and respond to about 450 calls a year. And they do all this without supervision and without a formal leader; they simply know what to do and then get it done to help people and save lives.

Superleadership occurs when a leader gradually and purposefully turns over power, responsibility, and control to a self-managing work group.

Power in Organizations

LEARNING OBJECTIVE

Explain power in organizations.

Influence is also closely related to the concept of power. Power is one of the most significant forces in organizations. Moreover, it can be an extremely important ingredient in organizational success—or organizational failure. In this section, we first describe the nature of power. Then we examine the types and uses of power.

The Nature of Power

Power has been defined in dozens of ways; no one definition is generally accepted. Drawing from the more common meanings of the term, we define **power** as the potential ability of a person or group to exercise control over another person or group.[14] Power is distinguished from influence due to the element of control: The

Power is the potential ability of a person or group to exercise control over another person or group.

Chapter 11 Leadership and Influence Processes

more powerful control the less powerful. Thus, power might be thought of as an extreme form of influence.

One obvious aspect of our definition is that it expresses power in terms of potential; that is, we may be able to control others but may choose not to exercise that control. Nevertheless, simply having the potential may be enough to influence others in some settings. Furthermore, power may reside in individuals (such as managers and informal leaders), in formal groups (such as departments and committees), and in informal groups (such as a clique of influential people). Finally, we should note the direct link between power and influence. If a person can convince another person to change his or her opinion on some issue, to engage in or refrain from some behavior, or to view circumstances in a certain way, that person has exercised influence—and used power.

Considerable differences of opinion exist about how thoroughly power pervades organizations. Some people argue that virtually all interpersonal relations are influenced by power; others believe exercise of power is confined to only certain situations. Whatever the case, power is undoubtedly a pervasive part of organizational life. It affects decisions ranging from the choice of strategies to the color of the new office carpeting. It makes or breaks careers. And it enhances or limits organizational effectiveness.

Types of Power

Within the broad framework of our definition, there obviously are many types of power. These types usually are described in terms of bases of power and position power versus personal power.

Bases of Power The most widely used and recognized analysis of the bases of power is the classic framework developed by John R. P. French and Bertram Raven.[15] French and Raven identified five general bases of power in organizational settings: legitimate, reward, coercive, expert, and referent power.

> **Legitimate power** is granted by virtue of one's position in the organization.

Legitimate power, essentially the same as authority, is granted by virtue of one's position in an organization. Managers have legitimate power over their subordinates. The organization specifies that it is legitimate for the designated individual to direct the activities of others. The bounds of this legitimacy are defined partly by the formal nature of the position involved and partly by informal norms and traditions. For example, it was once commonplace for managers to expect their secretaries not only to perform work-related activities such as typing and filing but also to run personal errands such as picking up laundry and buying gifts. In highly centralized, mechanistic, and bureaucratic organizations such as the military, the legitimate power inherent in each position is closely specified, widely known, and strictly followed. In less structured environments, such as research and development labs and software firms, the lines of legitimate power often are blurry. Employees may work for more than one boss at the same time, and leaders and subordinates may be on a nearly equal footing.

> **Reward power** is the extent to which a person controls rewards that another person values.

Reward power is the extent to which a person controls rewards that another values. The most obvious examples of organizational rewards are pay, promotions, and work assignments. A manager who has almost total control over the pay subordinates receive, can make recommendations about promotions, and has considerable discretion to make job assignments has a high level of reward power. Reward power can extend beyond material rewards. As we noted in our discussions of motivation theory in Chapter 4, people work for a variety of reasons in addition to pay. For instance, some people may be motivated primarily by a desire for

Coercive power is the extent to which a person has the ability to punish or physically or psychologically harm another.

Expert power is the extent to which a person controls information that is valuable to others.

Referent power exists when one person wants to be like or imitates someone else.

Position power resides in the position regardless of who is filling it.

recognition and acceptance. To the extent that a manager's praise and acknowledgment satisfy those needs, that manager has even more reward power.

Coercive power exists when someone has the ability to punish or physically or psychologically harm another person. For example, some managers berate subordinates in front of everyone, belittling their efforts and generally making their lives miserable. Certain forms of coercion may be subtle. In some organizations, a particular division may be notorious as a resting place for people who have no future with the company. Threatening to transfer someone to a dead-end branch or some other undesirable location is thus a form of coercion. Clearly the more negative the sanctions a person can bring to bear on others, the stronger is her or his coercive power. At the same time, the use of coercive power carries a considerable cost in terms of employee resentment and hostility.

Control over expertise or, more precisely, over information is another source of power, referred to as **expert power**. For example, to the extent that an inventory manager has information that a sales representative needs, the inventory manager has expert power over the sales representative. The more important the information and the fewer the alternative sources for getting it, the greater the power. Expert power can reside in many niches in an organization; it transcends positions and jobs. Although legitimate, reward, and coercive power may not always correspond exactly to formal authority, they often do. Expert power, on the other hand, may be associated much less with formal authority. Upper-level managers usually decide on the organization's strategic agenda, but individuals at lower levels in the organization may have the expertise those managers need to do the tasks. A research scientist may have crucial information about a technical breakthrough of great importance to the organization and its strategic decisions. Likewise, an assistant may take on so many of the boss's routine activities that the manager loses track of such details and comes to depend on the assistant to keep things running smoothly. In other situations, lower-level participants are given power as a way to take advantage of their expertise.

Referent power is power through identification. If José is highly respected by Adam, José has referent power over Adam. Like expert power, referent power does not always correlate with formal organizational authority. In some ways, referent power is similar to the concept of charisma in that it often involves trust, similarity, acceptance, affection, willingness to follow, and emotional involvement. Referent power usually surfaces as imitation. For example, suppose a new department manager is the youngest person in the organization to have reached that rank. Further, it is widely believed that she is being groomed for the highest levels of the company. Other people in the department may begin to imitate her, thinking they too may be able to advance. They may begin dressing like her, working the same hours, and trying to pick up as many work-related pointers from her as possible.

Position Versus Personal Power The French and Raven framework is only one approach to examining the origins of organizational power. Another approach categorizes power in organizations in terms of position or personal power.

Position power is power that resides in the position regardless of who holds it. Thus, legitimate, reward, and some aspects of coercive and expert power can all contribute to position power. Position power is thus similar to authority. In creating a position, the organization simultaneously establishes a sphere of power for the person filling that position. He or she will generally have the power to direct the activities of subordinates in performing their jobs, control some of their potential rewards, and have a say in their punishment and discipline. There are, however, limits to a manager's position power. A manager cannot order or control

Chapter 11 Leadership and Influence Processes

activities that fall outside his or her sphere of power—for instance, directing a subordinate to commit a crime, perform personal services, or take on tasks that clearly are not part of the subordinate's job.

Personal power is power that resides with an individual regardless of his or her position in the organization. Thus, the primary bases of personal power are referent and some traces of expert, coercive, and reward power. Charisma may also contribute to personal power. An individual usually exercises personal power through rational persuasion or by playing on followers' identification with him or her. An individual with personal power often can inspire greater loyalty and dedication in followers than someone who has only position power. The stronger influence stems from the fact that the followers are acting more from choice than from necessity (as dictated, for example, by their organizational responsibilities) and thus will respond more readily to requests and appeals. Of course, the influence of a leader who relies only on personal power is limited because followers may freely decide not to accept his or her directives or orders.

The distinctions between formal and informal leaders are also related to position and personal power. A formal leader will have, at minimum, position power, and an informal leader will have some degree of personal power. Just as a person may be both a formal and an informal leader, he or she can have both position and personal power simultaneously. Indeed, such a combination usually has the greatest potential influence on the actions of others. Figure 11.2 illustrates how personal and position power may interact to determine how much overall power a person has in a particular situation. An individual with both personal and position power will have the strongest overall power. Likewise, an individual with neither personal nor position power will have the weakest overall power. Finally, when either personal or position power is high but the other is low, the person will have a moderate level of overall power.

> **Personal power** resides in the person regardless of the position he or she holds.

FIGURE 11.2

Position Power and Personal Power

Position power resides in a job, whereas personal power resides in an individual. When these two types of power are broken down into high and low levels and related to each other, the two-by-two matrix shown here is the result. For example, the upper-right cell suggests that a leader with high levels of both position and personal power will have the highest overall level of power. Other combinations result in differing levels of overall power.

	Low Personal Power	High Personal Power
High Position Power	Moderate Overall Power	Strongest Overall Power
Low Position Power	Weakest Overall Power	Moderate Overall Power

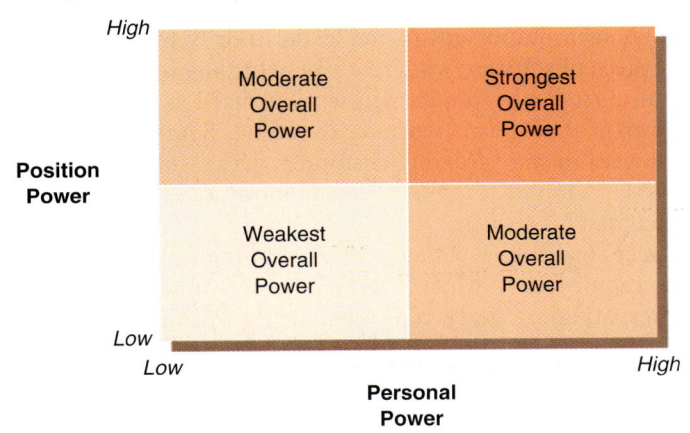

The Uses of Power in Organizations

Power can be used in many ways in an organization. Because of the potential for its misuse and concerns that it may engender, however, it is important that managers fully understand the dynamics of using power. Gary Yukl has presented a useful perspective for understanding how power may be wielded.[16] His perspective includes two closely related components. The first relates power bases, requests from individuals possessing power, and probable outcomes in the form of prescriptions for the manager. Table 11.1 indicates the three outcomes that may result when a leader tries to exert power. These outcomes depend on the leader's base of power, how that base is operationalized, and the subordinate's individual characteristics (for example, personality traits or past interactions with the leader).

TABLE 11.1

Uses and Outcomes of Power

Source of Leader Influence	Type of Outcome		
	Commitment	**Compliance**	**Resistance**
Referent Power	Likely	Possible	Possible
	If request is believed to be important to leader	If request is perceived to be unimportant to leader	If request is for something that will bring harm to leader
Expert Power	Likely	Possible	Possible
	If request is persuasive and subordinates share leader's task goals	If request is persuasive but subordinates are apathetic about leader's task goals	If leader is arrogant and insulting, or subordinates oppose task goals
Legitimate Power	Possible	Likely	Possible
	If request is polite and very appropriate	If request or order is seen as legitimate	If arrogant demands are made or request does not appear proper
Reward Power	Possible	Likely	Possible
	If used in a subtle, very personal way	If used in a mechanical, impersonal way	If used in a manipulative, arrogant way
Coercive Power	Very Unlikely	Possible	Likely
		If used in a helpful, nonpunitive way	If used in a hostile or manipulative way

Reference: From Dorwin P. Cartwright (ed.). *Studies in Social Power*, Copyright © 1959. Reprinted with permission from the Institute for Social Research, University of Michigan, Ann Arbor, Michigan.

Commitment will probably result from an attempt to exercise power if the subordinate accepts and identifies with the leader. Such an employee will be highly motivated by requests that seem important to the leader. For example, a leader might explain that a new piece of software will greatly benefit the organization if it is developed soon. A committed subordinate will work as hard as the leader to complete the project, even if that means working overtime. Sam Walton once asked all Wal-Mart employees to start greeting customers with a smile and an offer to help. Because Wal-Mart employees generally were motivated by and loyal to Walton, most of them accepted his request.

Compliance means the subordinate is willing to carry out the leader's wishes as long as doing so will not require extra effort. That is, the person will respond to normal, reasonable requests that are perceived to be clearly within the specified boundaries of the job. However, the person will not be inclined to do anything beyond the normal expectations for the job. Thus, the subordinate may work at a reasonable pace but refuse to work overtime, insisting that the job will still be there

the end of the year. (Some models of decision making do not start with a goal. We include it because it is the standard used to determine whether a decision is to be made.)

Identify the Problem   The purpose of problem identification is to gather information that bears on the goal. If a discrepancy exists between the goal and the actual state, action may be needed. In the marketing example, the group may gather information about the company's actual market share and compare it with the desired market share. A difference between the two represents a problem that necessitates a decision. Reliable information is very important in this step. Inaccurate information can lead to an unnecessary decision or no decision when one is required.

Determine the Decision Type   Next, the decision makers must determine if the problem represents a programmed or a nonprogrammed decision. If a programmed decision is needed, the appropriate decision rule is invoked, and the process moves on to the choice among alternatives. A programmed marketing decision may be called for if analysis reveals, for example, that competitors are outspending the company on print advertising. Because creating print advertising and buying space for it are well-established functions of the marketing group, the problem requires only a programmed decision.

Although it may seem simple to diagnose a situation as programmed, apply a decision rule, and arrive at a solution, mistakes can still occur. Choosing the wrong decision rule or assuming the problem calls for a programmed decision when it actually requires a nonprogrammed decision can result in a poor decision. The same caution applies to the determination that a nonprogrammed decision is called for. If the situation is wrongly diagnosed, the decision maker wastes time and resources seeking a new solution to an old problem, or "reinventing the wheel."

Generate Alternatives   The next step in making a nonprogrammed decision is to generate alternatives. The rational process assumes decision makers will generate all the possible alternative solutions to the problem. However, this assumption is unrealistic because even simple business problems can have scores of possible solutions. Decision makers may rely on education and experience as well as knowledge of the situation to generate alternatives. In addition, they may seek information from other people such as peers, subordinates, and supervisors. Decision makers may analyze the symptoms of the problem for clues or fall back on intuition or judgment to develop alternative solutions.[5] If the marketing department in our example determines that a nonprogrammed decision is required, it will need to generate alternatives for increasing market share.

Evaluate Alternatives   Evaluation involves assessing all possible alternatives in terms of predetermined decision criteria. The ultimate decision criterion is "Will this alternative bring us nearer to the goal?" In each case, the decision maker must examine each alternative for evidence that it will reduce the discrepancy between the desired state and the actual state. The evaluation process usually includes (1) describing the anticipated outcomes (benefits) of each alternative, (2) evaluating the anticipated costs of each alternative, and (3) estimating the uncertainties and risks associated with each alternative.[6] In most decision situations, the decision maker lacks perfect information regarding the outcomes of all alternatives. At one extreme, as shown earlier in Figure 12.2, outcomes may be known with certainty; at the other, the decision maker has no information whatsoever, so the outcomes are entirely uncertain. Risk, however, is the most common situation.

Choose an Alternative   Choosing an alternative is usually the most crucial step in the decision-making process. Choosing consists of selecting the alternative with the highest possible payoff based on the benefits, costs, risks, and uncertainties of all alternatives. In the PlayStation 2 promotion example, the decision maker evaluated the two alternatives by calculating their expected values. Following the rational approach, the manager would choose the alternative with the largest expected value.

Even with the rational approach, however, difficulties can arise in choosing an alternative. First, when two or more alternatives have equal payoffs, the decision maker must obtain more information or use some other criterion to make the choice. Second, when no single alternative will accomplish the objective, some combination of two or three alternatives may have to be implemented. Finally, if no alternative or combination of alternatives will solve the problem, the decision maker must obtain more information, generate more alternatives, or change the goals.[7]

An important part of the choice phase is the consideration of **contingency plans,** alternative actions that can be taken if the primary course of action is unexpectedly disrupted or rendered inappropriate.[8] Planning for contingencies is part of the transition between choosing the preferred alternative and implementing it. In developing contingency plans, the decision maker usually asks such questions as "What if something unexpected happens during the implementation of this alternative?" or "If the economy goes into a recession, will the choice of this alternative ruin the company?" or "How can we alter this plan if the economy suddenly rebounds and begins to grow?"

Contingency plans are alternative actions to take if the primary course of action is unexpectedly disrupted or rendered inappropriate.

Implement the Plan   Implementation puts the decision into action. It builds on the commitment and motivation of those who participated in the decision-making process (and may actually bolster individual commitment and motivation). To succeed, implementation requires the proper use of resources and good management skills. Following the decision to heavily promote the new PlayStation 2 game, for example, the marketing manager must implement the decision by assigning the project to a work group or task force. The success of this team depends on the leadership, the reward structure, the communications system, and group dynamics. Sometimes the decision maker begins to doubt a choice already made. This doubt is called *postdecision dissonance* or, more generally, **cognitive dissonance.**[9] To reduce the tension created by the dissonance, the decision maker may seek to rationalize the decision further with new information.

Cognitive dissonance is doubt about a choice that has already been made.

Control: Measure and Adjust   In the final stage of the rational decision-making process, the outcomes of the decision are measured and compared with the desired goal. If a discrepancy remains, the decision maker may restart the decision-making process by setting a new goal (or reiterating the existing one). The decision maker, dissatisfied with the previous decision, may modify the subsequent decision-making process to avoid another mistake. Changes can be made in any part of the process, as Figure 12.3 illustrates by the arrows leading from the control step to each of the other steps. Decision making therefore is a dynamic, self-correcting, and ongoing process in organizations.

Suppose a marketing department implements a new print advertising campaign. After implementation, it constantly monitors market research data and compares its new market share with the desired market share. If the advertising has the desired effect, no changes will be made in the promotion campaign. If, however, the data indicate no change in market share, additional decisions and imple-

Chapter 12 Decision Making and Negotiation

The decision-making process is supposed to be logical and rational, but often it is affected by behavioral, practical, and personal considerations. Consider Gabrielle Melchionda, a Maine native whose skin care product business is booming. She was recently offered a lucrative contract to begin exporting her products to Turkey. But she turned it down when she learned the exporter also sold weapons. Had rational decision making prevailed, she would have jumped on the idea. But her own personal values kept her focused on what was important to her as a person—and it wasn't just the money!

Bounded rationality is the idea that decision makers cannot deal with information about all aspects and alternatives pertaining to a problem and therefore choose to tackle some meaningful subset of it.

The **behavioral approach** uses rules of thumb, suboptimizing, and satisficing in making decisions.

mentation of a contingency plan may be necessary. In a classic example, when Nissan introduced its luxury car line Infiniti, it relied on a Zen-like series of ads that featured images of rocks, plants, and water—but no images of the car. At the same time, Toyota was featuring pictures of its new luxury car line, Lexus, which quickly established itself as a market leader. When Infiniti managers realized their mistake, they quickly pulled the old ads and started running new ones centered around images of the car.[10]

Strengths and Weaknesses of the Rational Approach

The rational approach has several strengths. It forces the decision maker to consider a decision in a logical, sequential manner, and the in-depth analysis of alternatives enables the decision maker to choose on the basis of information rather than emotion or social pressure. However, the rigid assumptions of this approach are often unrealistic.[11] The amount of information available to managers is usually limited by either time or cost constraints, and most decision makers have limited ability to process information about the alternatives. In addition, not all alternatives lend themselves to quantification in terms that will allow for easy comparison. Finally, because they cannot predict the future, decision makers are unlikely to know all possible outcomes of each alternative.

The Behavioral Approach

Whereas the rational approach assumes managers operate logically and rationally, the behavioral approach acknowledges the importance of human behavior in the decision-making process. In particular, a crucial assumption of the behavioral approach is that decision makers operate with bounded rationality rather than with perfect rationality as assumed by the rational approach. **Bounded rationality** is the idea that although individuals may seek the best solution to a problem, the demands of processing all the information bearing on the problem, generating all possible solutions, and choosing the single best solution are beyond the capabilities of most decision makers. Thus, they accept less than ideal solutions based on a process that is neither exhaustive nor entirely rational. For example, one study found that under time pressure, groups usually eliminate all but the two most favorable alternatives and then process the remaining two in great detail.[12] Thus, decision makers operating with bounded rationality limit the inputs to the decision-making process and base decisions on judgment and personal biases as well as on logic.[13]

The **behavioral approach** is characterized by (1) the use of procedures and rules of thumb, (2) suboptimizing, and (3) satisficing. Uncertainty in decision making can initially be reduced by relying on procedures and rules of thumb. If, for example, increasing print advertising has boosted a company's market share in the past, managers may use that linkage as a rule of thumb in decision making. When the previous month's market share drops below a certain level, the company might increase its print advertising expenditures by 25 percent during the following month.

Suboptimizing is knowingly accepting less than the best possible outcome. Frequently it is not feasible to make the ideal decision in a real-world situation given organizational constraints. The decision maker often must suboptimize to avoid unintended negative effects on other departments, product lines, or decisions.[14] An automobile manufacturer, for example, can cut costs dramatically and increase efficiency if it schedules the production of one model at a time. Thus, the production group's optimal decision is single-model scheduling. However, the marketing group, seeking to optimize its sales goals by offering a wide variety of models, may demand the opposite production schedule: short runs of entirely different models. The groups in the middle, design and scheduling, may suboptimize the benefits the production and marketing groups seek by planning long runs of slightly different models. This is the practice of large auto manufacturers such as General Motors and Ford, which make several body styles in numerous models on the same production line.

The final feature of the behavioral approach is **satisficing**: examining alternatives only until a solution that meets minimal requirements is found and then ceasing to look for a better one.[15] The search for alternatives is usually a sequential process guided by procedures and rules of thumb based on previous experiences with similar problems. The search often ends when the first minimally acceptable choice is encountered. The resulting choice may narrow the discrepancy between the desired and actual states, but it is not likely to be the optimal solution. As the process is repeated, incremental improvements slowly reduce the discrepancy between the actual and desired states.

> **Suboptimizing** is knowingly accepting less than the best possible outcome to avoid unintended negative effects on other aspects of the organization.

> **Satisficing** is examining alternatives only until a solution that meets minimal requirements is found.

The Practical Approach

Because of the unrealistic demands of the rational approach and the limited, short-run orientation of the behavioral approach, neither is entirely satisfactory. However, the worthwhile features of each can be combined into a **practical approach to decision making**, shown in Figure 12.4. The steps in this process are the same as in the rational approach; however, the conditions recognized by the behavioral approach are added to provide a more realistic process. For example, the practical approach suggests that rather than generating all alternatives, the decision maker should try to go beyond rules of thumb and satisficing limitations and generate as many alternatives as time, money, and other practicalities of the situation allow. In this synthesis of the other two approaches, the rational approach provides an analytical framework for making decisions, whereas the behavioral approach provides a moderating influence.

In practice, decision makers use some hybrid of the rational, behavioral, and practical approaches to make the tough day-to-day decisions in running organizations. Some decision makers use a methodical process of gathering as much information as possible, developing and evaluating alternatives, and seeking advice from knowledgeable people before making a decision. Others fly from one decision to another, making seemingly hasty decisions and barking out orders to subordinates. The second group would seem not to use much information or a rational approach to making decisions. Recent research, however, suggests that managers who make decisions very quickly probably are using just as much, or more, information and generating and evaluating as many alternatives as slower, more methodical decision makers.[16]

> The **practical approach to decision making** combines the steps of the rational approach with the conditions in the behavioral approach to create a more realistic approach for making decisions in organizations.

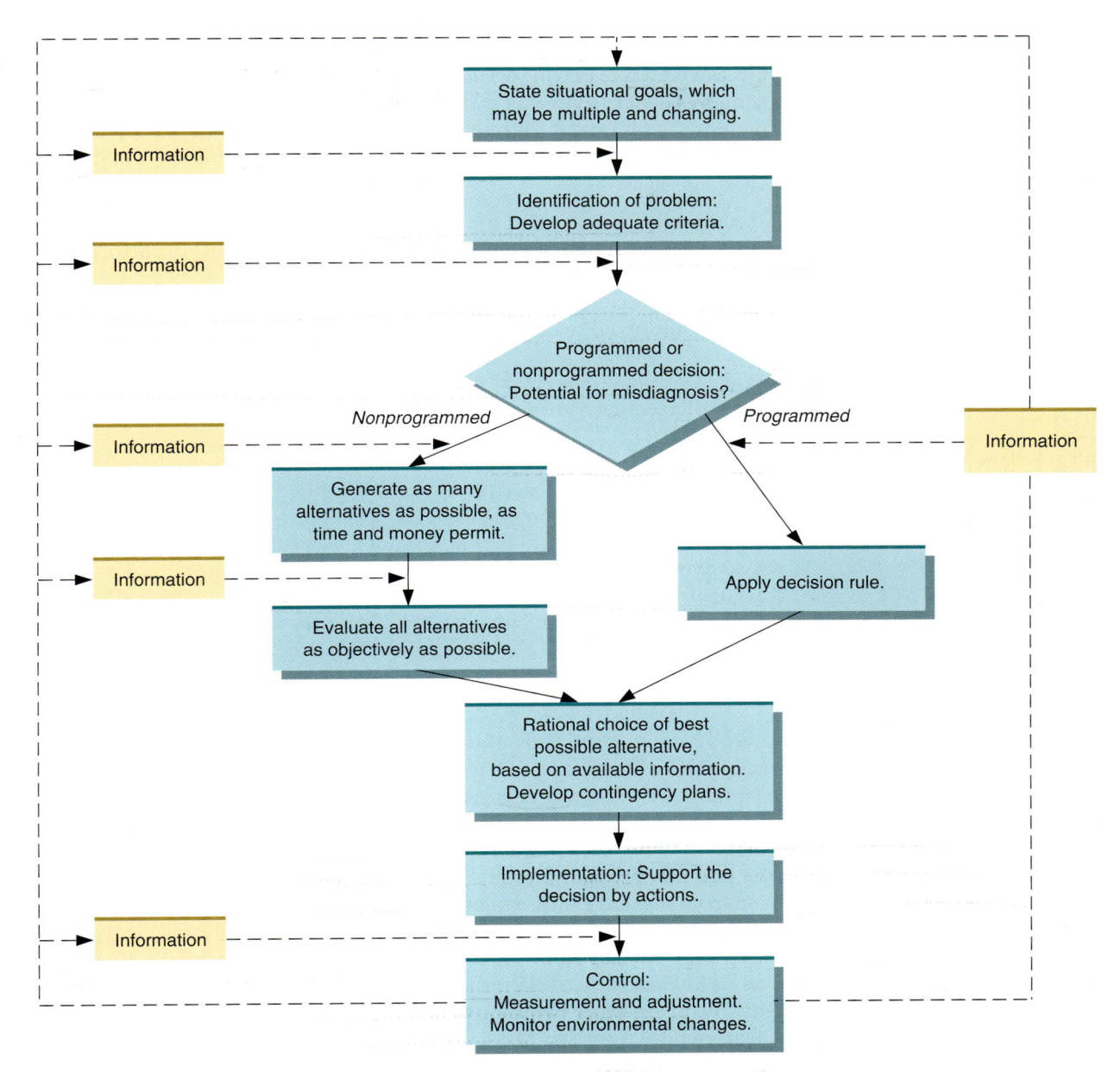

FIGURE 12.4

Practical Approaches to Decision Making with Behavioral Guidelines

The practical model applies some of the conditions recognized by the behavioral approach to the rational approach to decision making. Although similar to the rational model, the practical approach recognizes personal limitations at each point (or step) in the process.

The Personal Approach

Although the models just described have provided significant insight into decision making, they do not fully explain the processes people engage in when they are preoccupied and nervous about making a decision that has major implications for themselves, their organizations, or their families. In short, the models fail to capture all the conditions under which many decisions are made. One attempt to provide a more realistic view of individual decision making is the model presented by Irving Janis and Leon Mann.¹⁷ The Janis-Mann concept, called the **conflict model,** is based on research in social psychology and individual decision processes, and is a highly personal approach to decision making. Although the model may appear complex, if you examine it one step at a time and follow the example in this section, you should easily understand how it works. The model has five basic characteristics:

> The **conflict model** deals with the personal conflicts people experience in particularly difficult decision situations.

1. It deals only with important life decisions—marriage, schooling, career, and major organizational decisions—that commit the individual or the organization to a certain course of action following the decision.
2. It recognizes that procrastination and rationalization are mechanisms by which people avoid making difficult decisions and cope with the associated stress.
3. It explicitly acknowledges that some decisions probably will be wrong and that the fear of making an unsound decision can be a deterrent to making any decision at all.
4. It provides for **self-reactions,** comparisons of alternatives with internalized moral standards. Internalized moral standards guide decision making as much as economic and social outcomes do. A proposed course of action may offer many economic and social rewards, but if it violates the decision maker's moral convictions, it is unlikely to be chosen.
5. It recognizes that at times the decision maker is ambivalent about alternative courses of action; in such circumstances, it is very difficult to make a wholehearted commitment to a single choice. Major life decisions seldom allow compromise, however; usually they are either-or decisions that require commitment to one course of action.

> **Self-reactions** are comparisons of alternatives with internalized moral standards.

Figure 12.5 shows the Janis-Mann conflict model of decision making. A concrete example will help explain each step. Richard, a thirty-year-old engineer with a working wife and two young children, has been employed at a large manufacturing company for eight years. He keeps abreast of his career progress through visits with peers at work and in other companies, feedback from his manager and others regarding his work and future with the firm, the alumni magazine from his university, and other sources. At work one morning, Richard learns he has been passed over for a promotion for the second time in a year. He investigates the information, which can be considered negative feedback, and confirms it. As a result, he seeks out other information regarding his career at the company, the prospect of changing employers, and the possibility of going back to graduate school to get an MBA. At the same time, he asks himself, "Are the risks serious if I do not make a change?" If the answer is *no,* Richard will continue his present activities. In the model's terms, this option is called **unconflicted adherence.** If instead the answer is *yes* or *maybe,* Richard will move to the next question in the model.

> **Unconflicted adherence** entails continuing with current activities if doing so does not entail serious risks.

The second step asks, "Are the risks serious if I do make a change?" If Richard goes on to this step, he will gather information about potential losses from making a change. He may, for example, find out whether he would lose health insurance and pension benefits if he changed jobs or went back to graduate school. If he believes changing presents no serious risks, Richard will make the change, called an **unconflicted change.** Otherwise, he will move on to the next step.

> **Unconflicted change** involves making decisions in present activities if doing so presents no serious risks.

But suppose Richard has determined the risks are serious whether or not he makes a change. He believes he must make a change because he will not be pro-

Chapter 12 Decision Making and Negotiation

Antecedent Conditions — **Mediating Processes** — **Consequences**

Start: Challenging or negative feedback, or an opportunity

- Additional information about losses from continuing unchanged → Q. 1 Are the risks serious if I don't make a change? — No → Unconflicted Adherence
- Maybe or Yes ↓
- Information about losses from changing → Q. 2 Are the risks serious if I do make a change? — No → Unconflicted Change
- Maybe or Yes ↓
- Signs of more information available and of other unused resources → Q. 3 Is it realistic to hope to find a better solution? — No → Defensive Avoidance
- Maybe or Yes ↓
- Information about deadline and time pressures → Q. 4 Is there sufficient time to search and deliberate? — No → Hypervigilance
- Maybe or Yes ↓ → Vigilance

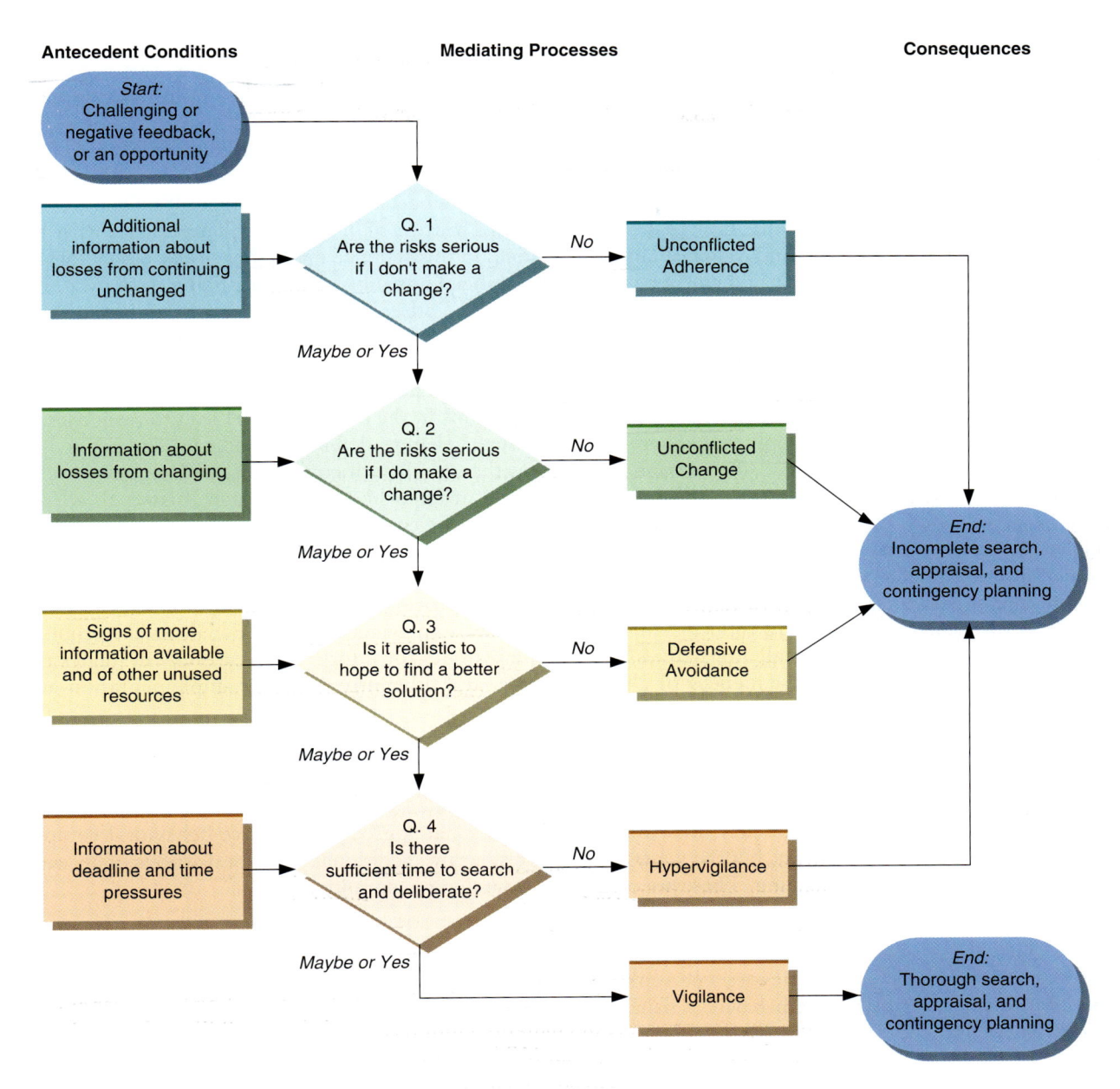

End: Incomplete search, appraisal, and contingency planning

End: Thorough search, appraisal, and contingency planning

FIGURE 12.5

Janis-Mann Conflict Model of Decision Making

A decision maker answering yes to all four questions will engage in vigilant information processing.

Reference: Adapted with the permission of The Free Press, a Division of Simon & Schuster Adult Publishing Group from *Decision Making: A Psychological Analysis of Conflict, Choice, and Commitment*, by Irving L. Janis and Leon Mann. Copyright © 1977 by the Free Press. All rights reserved.

moted further in his present company; yet serious risks are also associated with making a change—perhaps loss of benefits, uncertain promotion opportunities in another company, or lost income from going to graduate school for two years. In the third step, Richard wonders, "Is it realistic to hope to find a better solution?" He continues to look for information that can help him make the decision. If the

Defensive avoidance entails making no changes in present activities and avoiding further contact with associated issues because finding a better solution appears highly unlikely.

Hypervigilance is frantic, superficial pursuit of some satisficing strategy.

answer to this third question is *no*, Richard may give up hope of finding anything better and opt for what Janis and Mann call **defensive avoidance**; that is, he will make no change and avoid any further contact with the issue. A positive response, however, will move Richard onward to the next step.

At this point, Richard recognizes the serious risks involved but expects to find a solution, and asks himself, "Is there sufficient time to search and deliberate?" Richard now considers how quickly he needs to make a change. If he believes he has little time to deliberate, perhaps because of his age, he will experience what Janis and Mann call **hypervigilance.** In this state, he may suffer severe psychological stress and engage in frantic, superficial pursuit of some satisficing strategy. (This might also be called "panic"!) If, on the other hand, Richard believes he has two or three years to consider various alternatives, he will undertake vigilant information processing, in which he will thoroughly investigate all possible alternatives, weigh their costs and benefits before making a choice, and develop contingency plans.

Negative answers to the questions in the conflict model lead to responses of unconflicted adherence, unconflicted change, defensive avoidance, and hypervigilance. All are coping strategies that result in incomplete search, appraisal, and contingency planning. A decision maker who gives the same answer to all the questions will always engage in the same coping strategy. However, if the answers change as the situation alters, the individual's coping strategies may change as well. The decision maker who answers *yes* to each of the four questions is led to **vigilant information processing,** a process similar to that outlined in the rational decision-making model. The decision maker objectively analyzes the problem and all alternatives, thoroughly searches for information, carefully evaluates the consequences of all alternatives, and diligently plans for implementation and contingencies.

Vigilant information processing involves thoroughly investigating all possible alternatives, weighing their costs and benefits before making a decision, and developing contingency plans.

Related Behavioral Aspects of Decision Making

> **LEARNING OBJECTIVE**
>
> *Explain related behavioral aspects of decision making.*

The behavioral, practical, and personal approaches all have behavioral components, but the manager must consider two additional behavioral aspects of decision making. These are ethics and escalation of commitment.

Ethics and Decision Making

Ethics are a person's beliefs about what constitutes right and wrong behavior. Ethical behavior is behavior that conforms to generally accepted social norms; unethical behavior does not conform to these norms. Some decisions managers make may have little or nothing to do with their own personal ethics, but many other decisions are influenced by managers' ethics. For example, decisions involving such disparate issues as hiring and firing employees, dealing with customers and suppliers, setting wages and assigning tasks, and maintaining one's expense account are all subject to ethical influences.

In general, ethical dilemmas for managers may center on direct personal gain, indirect personal gain, or simple personal preferences. Consider a top executive contemplating a decision about a potential takeover. Her stock option package may result in enormous personal gain if the decision goes one way, even though stockholders may benefit more if the decision goes the other way. An indirect personal gain may result when a decision does not directly add value to a manager's personal worth but does enhance her or his career. Or the manager may face a choice about relocating a company facility in which one of the options is closest to his residence.

Ethics are an individual's personal beliefs about what is right and wrong behavior.

Managers should carefully and deliberately consider the ethical context of every one of their decisions. The goal, of course, is for the manager to make the decision that is in the best interest of the firm as opposed to the best interest of the manager. Doing so requires personal honesty and integrity. Managers also find it helpful to discuss potential ethical dilemmas with colleagues. Peers can often provide an objective view of a situation that may help a manager avoid unintentionally making an unethical decision. One recent situation concerning ethical decision making—Imclone's decision to present a cancer-fighting drug, Erbitux, for FDA approval—is discussed in the Business of Ethics box.

Ethics and decision making have become very visibly linked in recent times. Indeed, so critical are ethics today that some MBA programs have started screening potential students on the basis of their integrity. In the words of Rosemarie Martinelli, director of MBA admissions at the Wharton School, "Everyone has ethics on the mind right now."

Escalation of Commitment

Escalation of commitment is the tendency to persist in an ineffective course of action when evidence reveals that the project cannot succeed.

Sometimes people continue trying to implement a decision despite clear and convincing evidence that substantial problems exist. **Escalation of commitment** is the tendency to persist in an ineffective course of action when evidence indicates the project is doomed to failure. A good example is the decision by the government of British Columbia to hold a World's Fair in Vancouver. Originally the organizers expected the project to break even financially so the province would not have to increase taxes to pay for it. However, as work progressed, it became clear that expenses were far greater than projected. However, organizers considered it too late to call off the event, despite the huge losses that obviously would occur. Eventually the province conducted a $300 million lottery to try to cover the costs.[18] Similar examples abound in stock market investments, in political and military situations, and in organizations developing any type of new project.

There are several possible reasons for escalation of commitment.[19] Some projects require much front-end investment and offer little return until the end, requiring the investor to stay in all the way to get any payoff. These "all-or-nothing" projects require unflagging commitment. Furthermore, investors' or project leaders' egos often become so involved with the project that it consumes their identities. Failure or cancellation seems to threaten their reason for existence. They therefore continue to push the project as potentially successful despite strong evidence to the contrary. At other times, the social structure, group norms, and group cohesiveness support a project so strongly that cancellation is impossible. Organizational inertia also may force an organization to maintain a failing project. Thus, escalation of commitment is a phenomenon that has a strong foundation.

How can an individual or organization recognize that a project needs to be stopped before it results in throwing good money after bad? Several suggestions have been made; some are easy to put to use, and others are more difficult. Having good information about a project is always a first step in preventing the escalation problem. Usually it is possible to schedule regular sessions to discuss the project, its progress, the assumptions on which it was originally based, the current validity

BUSINESS OF ETHICS

How Fast Is Too Fast?

On one side are ill patients desperate for a wonder drug. On the other side are pharmaceutical companies, from tiny biotechnology start-ups to giant multinational corporations, eager to find blockbuster drugs. In the middle is the Food and Drug Administration (FDA), charged with ensuring drug safety but also aware of the urgent need for quick action. This mix stirs up plenty of potential for trouble.

Consider Erbitux, a cancer-fighting drug under development by small Imclone, Inc., working in partnership with giant Bristol-Myers Squibb. The drug showed promise in clinical trials, so much promise that the FDA gave it fast-track status to hasten its final approval. Dr. Robert J. Mayer, an oncologist, says, "There is no doubt that the compound works. We have had people who benefited quite dramatically."

In December 2001, however, the FDA rejected the Erbitux application, and the blaming started. Imclone and Bristol managers claim the rejection was unexpected. Industry observers note that sometimes the federal agency has abruptly changed the rules for approval, causing expensive delays. The approval process itself is cumbersome and complex, and requires input from many different constituencies. Drug approval decisions are poorly structured and nonprogrammed, with both sides facing significant uncertainties.

On their side, FDA officials claim Imclone managers received warnings but did not heed them. Imclone managers seemed to be in a hurry and failed to send complete data to the FDA. Imclone was not profitable, and financial pressure may have caused management to push too hard for quick approval of the drug. FDA officials emphasize

"A lot of biotech companies get into survival mode instead of success mode."—Richard B. Brewer, CEO of Scios, Inc.

that the decision stakes in such a situation are high, with many lives at risk, and an incorrect decision can be lethal.

Richard B. Brewer, CEO of small drug manufacturer Scios, Inc., understands the ethical issues all too well—his company had a heart medication rejected by the FDA in 2003—but he believes it's up to Imclone executives to ensure that the process stays on track. "A lot of biotech companies get into survival mode instead of success mode. They forget that the FDA is not here to get your drug approved. It's here to protect patients." Hopefully the two sides can come to an agreement soon because those cancer patients are waiting for a resolution.

References: Andrew Serwer, "Bristol's Bad Medicine," *Fortune*, April 29, 2002; Andrew Serwer, "The Socialite Scientist," *Fortune*, April 15, 2002; "The Trials of Erbitux," *Fortune*, April 15, 2002; "Where Imclone Went Wrong," *BusinessWeek*, February 18, 2002, pp. 68–71 (quotation, p. 68).

---

of these assumptions, and any problems with the project. An objective review is necessary to maintain control.

Some organizations have begun to make separate teams responsible for the development and implementation of a project to reduce ego involvement. Often, however, the people who initiate a project are those who know the most about it, and their expertise can be valuable in the implementation process. Experts suggest that a general strategy for avoiding the escalation problem is to try to create an "experimenting organization" in which every program and project is reviewed regularly and managers are evaluated on their contribution to the total organization rather than to specific projects.[20]

Group Decision Making

LEARNING OBJECTIVE
Describe group decision making in organizations.

People in organizations work in a variety of groups: formal or informal, permanent or temporary. Most of these groups make decisions that affect the welfare of the organization and its people. In this section, we discuss several issues surrounding how groups make decisions, including group polarization, groupthink, and group problem solving.

Group Polarization

Members' attitudes and opinions with respect to an issue or a solution may change during group discussion. Some studies of this tendency show the change to be a fairly consistent movement toward a riskier solution, called "risky shift."[21] Other studies and analyses have revealed that the group-induced shift is not always toward more risk; the group is just as likely to move toward a more conservative view.[22] Generally, **group polarization** occurs when the average of the group members' postdiscussion attitudes tends to be more extreme than the average prediscussion attitudes.[23]

Group polarization is the tendency for a group's average postdiscussion attitudes to be more extreme than its average prediscussion attitudes.

Several features of group discussion contribute to polarization. When individuals discover during group discussion that others share their opinions, they may become more confident about their opinions, resulting in a more extreme view. Persuasive arguments can also encourage polarization. If members who strongly support a particular position are able to express themselves cogently in the discussion, less avid supporters may become convinced that the position is correct. In addition, members may believe that because the group is deciding, they are not individually responsible for the decision or its outcomes. This diffusion of responsibility may enable them to accept and support a decision more radical than those they would make as individuals.

Polarization can profoundly affect group decision making. If group members are known to lean toward a particular decision before a discussion, their postdecision position will likely be even more extreme. Understanding this phenomenon may be useful for an individual who seeks to affect their decision.

Groupthink

As discussed in Chapters 8 and 9, highly cohesive groups and teams are often very successful at meeting their goals, although they sometimes have serious difficulties as well. One problem that can occur is groupthink. According to Irving L. Janis, **groupthink** is "a mode of thinking that people engage in when they are deeply involved in a cohesive in-group, when the members' strivings for unanimity override their motivation to realistically appraise alternative courses of action."[24] When groupthink occurs, then, the group unknowingly makes unanimity rather than the best decision its goal. Individual members may perceive that raising objections is not appropriate. Groupthink can occur in many decision-making situations in organizations. The current trend toward increasing use of teams in organizations may increase instances of groupthink because self-managing teams tend to be susceptible to this type of thought.[25]

Groupthink is a mode of thinking that occurs when members of a group are deeply involved in a cohesive in-group and their desire for unanimity offsets their motivation to appraise alternative courses of action.

Symptoms of Groupthink   The three primary conditions that foster the development of groupthink are cohesiveness, the leader's promotion of his or her preferred solution, and insulation of the group from experts' opinions. Based on analysis of the disaster associated with the explosion of the space shuttle *Challenger*, the original set of groupthink symptoms was expanded to include (1) the effects of increased time pressure and (2) the role of the leader in not stimulating critical thinking in developing the symptoms of groupthink.[26] Figure 12.6 outlines the revised groupthink process.

A group that has succumbed to groupthink exhibits eight well-defined symptoms:

1. An *illusion of invulnerability*, shared by most or all members, that creates excessive optimism and encourages extreme risk taking

FIGURE 12.6

The Groupthink Process

Groupthink can occur when a highly cohesive group with a directive leader is under time pressure. It can result in a defective decision process and a low probability of successful outcomes.

Reference: Gregory Moorhead, Richard Ference, and Chris P. Neck, "Group Decision Fiascoes Continue: Space Shuttle Challenger and a Revised Groupthink Framework," *Human Relations*, vol. 44 (1991), pp. 539–550.

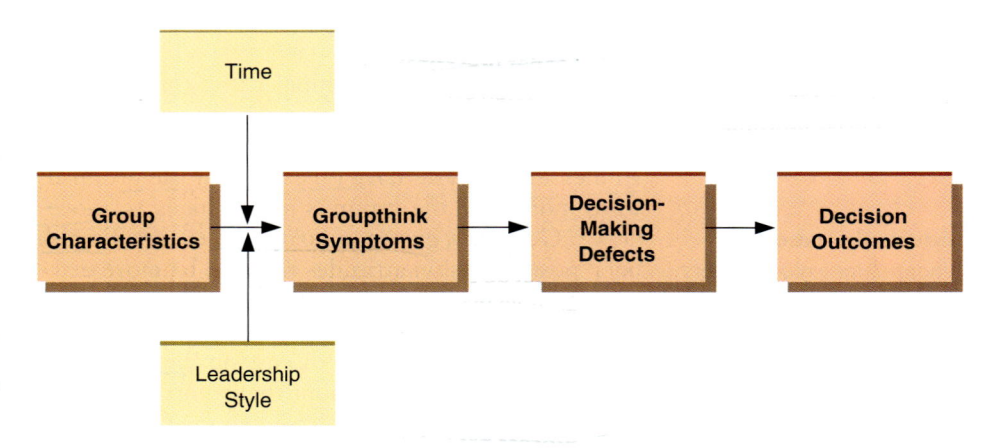

2. *Collective efforts to rationalize or discount warnings* that might lead members to reconsider assumptions before recommitting themselves to past policy decisions
3. An *unquestioned belief in the group's inherent morality*, inclining members to ignore the ethical and moral consequences of their decisions
4. *Stereotyped views of "enemy" leaders* as too evil to warrant genuine attempts to negotiate or as too weak or stupid to counter whatever risky attempts are made to defeat their purposes
5. *Direct pressure on a member* who expresses strong arguments against any of the group's stereotypes, illusions, or commitments, making clear that such dissent is contrary to what is expected of loyal members
6. *Self-censorship of deviations* from the apparent group consensus, reflecting each member's inclination to minimize the importance of his or her doubts and counterarguments
7. A *shared illusion of unanimity*, resulting partly from self-censorship of deviations, augmented by the false assumption that silence means consent[27]
8. *The emergence of self-appointed "mindguards,"* members who protect the group from adverse information that could shatter their shared complacency about the effectiveness and morality of their decisions[28]

Janis contends that the members of the group involved in the Watergate cover-up—Richard Nixon, H. R. Haldeman, John Ehrlichman, and John Dean—may have been victims of groupthink. Evidence of most of the groupthink symptoms appears in the unedited transcripts of the group's deliberations.[29]

Decision-Making Defects and Decision Quality   When groupthink dominates group deliberations, the likelihood that decision-making defects will occur increases. The group is less likely to survey a full range of alternatives and may focus on only a few, often one or two. In discussing a preferred alternative, the group may fail to examine it for obscure risks and drawbacks. Similarly, the group may not reexamine previously rejected alternatives for overlooked gains or some means of reducing apparent costs, even when it receives new information. The group may reject expert opinions that run counter to its own views and may choose to consider only information that supports its preferred solution. The decision to launch the space shuttle *Challenger* may have been a product of groupthink because due to the increased time pressure to make a decision and the leaders' style, negative information was ignored by the group that made the decision. Finally, the group may not

TABLE 12.2

Prescriptions for Preventing Groupthink

> **A. Leader prescriptions**
>   1. Assign everyone the role of critical evaluator.
>   2. Be impartial; do not state preferences.
>   3. Assign the devil's advocate role to at least one group member.
>   4. Use outside experts to challenge the group.
>   5. Be open to dissenting points of view.
>
> **B. Organizational prescriptions**
>   1. Set up several independent groups to study the same issue.
>   2. Train managers and group leaders in groupthink prevention techniques.
>
> **C. Individual prescriptions**
>   1. Be a critical thinker.
>   2. Discuss group deliberations with a trusted outsider; report back to the group.
>
> **D. Process prescriptions**
>   1. Periodically break the group into subgroups to discuss the issues.
>   2. Take time to study external factors.
>   3. Hold second-chance meetings to rethink issues before making a commitment.

consider any potential setbacks or countermoves by competing groups and therefore may fail to develop contingency plans. We should note that Janis contends these six defects may arise from other common problems as well, such as fatigue, prejudice, inaccurate information, information overload, or ignorance.[30]

Defects in decision making do not always lead to bad outcomes or defeats. Even if its own decision-making processes are flawed, one side can win a battle because of the poor decisions made by the other side's leaders. Nevertheless, decisions produced by defective processes are less likely to succeed.

Although the arguments for the existence of groupthink are convincing, the hypothesis has not been subjected to rigorous empirical examination. Research supports parts of the model but leaves some questions unanswered.[31]

Prevention of Groupthink Several suggestions have been offered to help managers reduce the probability of groupthink in group decision making. Summarized in Table 12.2, these prescriptions fall into four categories based on whether they apply to the leader, the organization, the individual, or the process. All are designed to facilitate critical evaluation of alternatives and discourage single-minded pursuit of unanimity.

Participation

A major issue in group decision making is the degree to which employees should participate in the process. Early management theories, such as those of the scientific management school, advocated a clear separation between the duties of managers and workers: Management was to make the decisions, and employees were to implement them.[32] Other approaches have urged that employees be allowed to participate in decisions to increase their ego involvement, motivation, and satisfaction.[33] Numerous research studies have shown that whereas employees who seek responsibility and challenge on the job may find participation in the decision-making process both motivating and enriching, other employees may regard such participation as a waste of time and a management imposition.[34]

Whether employee participation in decision making is appropriate depends on the situation. In tasks that require an estimation, a prediction, or a judgment of accuracy—usually referred to as *judgmental tasks*—groups typically are superior to individuals simply because more people contribute to the decision-making process. However, one especially capable individual may make a better judgment than a group.

In problem-solving tasks, groups generally produce more and better solutions than do individuals. However, groups take far longer than individuals to develop solutions and make decisions. An individual or a very small group may be able to accomplish some things much faster than a large, unwieldy group or organization. In addition, individual decision making avoids the special problems of group decision making such as groupthink or group polarization. If the problem to be solved is fairly straightforward, it may be more appropriate to have a single capable individual concentrate on solving it. On the other hand, complex problems are more appropriate for groups. Such problems can often be divided into parts and the parts assigned to individuals or small groups that bring their results back to the larger group for discussion and decision making.

An additional advantage of group decision making is that it often creates greater interest in the task. Heightened interest may increase the time and effort given to the task, resulting in more ideas, a more thorough search for solutions, better evaluation of alternatives, and improved decision quality.

The Vroom decision tree approach to leadership (discussed in Chapter 10) is one popular way of determining the appropriate degree of subordinate participation.[35] The model includes decision styles that vary from "decide" (the leader alone makes the decision) to "delegate" (the group makes the decision, with each member having an equal say). The choice of style rests on seven considerations that concern the characteristics of the situation and the subordinates.

Participation in decision making is also related to organization structure. For example, decentralization involves delegating some decision-making authority throughout the organizational hierarchy. The more decentralized the organization, the more its employees tend to participate in decision making. Whether one views participation in decision making as pertaining to leadership, organization structure, or motivation, it remains an important aspect of organizations that continues to occupy managers and organizational scholars.[36]

Brainstorming is a popular technique used in group decision making when the objective is to identify a variety of different alternatives. This team, for example, is enthusiastically brainstorming in their effort to come up with some creative new ideas.

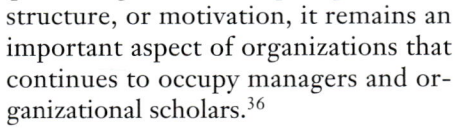

Group Problem Solving

A typical interacting group may have difficulty with any of several steps in the decision-making process. One common problem arises in the generation-of-alternatives phase: The search may be arbitrarily ended before all plausible alternatives have been identified. Several types of group interactions can have this effect. If members immediately express their reactions to the alternatives as they are first proposed, potential contributors may begin to censor their ideas to avoid embarrassing criticism from the group.

Less confident group members, intimidated by members who have more experience, higher status, or more power, may also censor their ideas for fear of embarrassment or sanctions. In addition, the group leader may limit idea generation by enforcing requirements concerning time, appropriateness, cost, feasibility, and the like.

To improve the generation of alternatives, managers may employ any of three techniques to stimulate the group's problem-solving capabilities: brainstorming, the nominal group technique, or the Delphi technique.

Brainstorming Brainstorming is most often used in the idea generation phase of decision making and is intended to solve problems that are new to the organization and have major consequences. In brainstorming, the group convenes specifically to generate alternatives. The members present ideas and clarify them with brief explanations. Each idea is recorded in full view of all members, usually on a flip chart. To avoid self-censoring, no attempts to evaluate the ideas are allowed. Group members are encouraged to offer any ideas that occur to them, even those that seem too risky or impossible to implement. (The absence of such ideas, in fact, is evidence that group members are engaging in self-censorship.) In a subsequent session, after the ideas have been recorded and distributed to members for review, the alternatives are evaluated.

The intent of brainstorming is to produce totally new ideas and solutions by stimulating the creativity of group members and encouraging them to build on the contributions of others. Brainstorming does not provide the resolution to the problem, an evaluation scheme, or the decision itself. Instead, it should produce a list of alternatives that is more innovative and comprehensive than one developed by the typical interacting group.

The Nominal Group Technique The nominal group technique is another means of improving group decision making. Whereas brainstorming is used primarily to generate alternatives, this technique may be used in other phases of decision making, such as identification of the problem and of appropriate criteria for evaluating alternatives. To use the **nominal group technique,** a group of individuals convenes to address an issue. The issue is described to the group, and each individual writes a list of ideas; no discussion among members is permitted. Following the five-to-ten-minute idea generation period, individual members take turns reporting their ideas, one at a time, to the group. The ideas are recorded on a flip chart, and members are encouraged to add to the list by building on the ideas of others. After all ideas have been presented, the members may discuss them and continue to build on them or proceed to the next phase. This part of the process can also be carried out without a face-to-face meeting or by mail, telephone, or computer. A meeting, however, helps members develop a group feeling and puts interpersonal pressure on the members to do their best in developing their lists.

After the discussion, members privately vote on or rank the ideas or report their preferences in some other agreed-on way. Reporting is private to reduce feelings of intimidation. After voting, the group may discuss the results and continue to generate and discuss ideas. The generation-discussion-vote cycle can continue until an appropriate decision is reached.

The nominal group technique has two principal advantages. It helps overcome the negative effects of power and status differences among group members, and it can be used to explore problems to generate alternatives or to evaluate them. Its primary disadvantage lies in its structured nature, which may limit creativity.

Brainstorming is a technique used in the idea generation phase of decision making that assists in developing numerous alternative courses of action.

In the nominal group technique, group members follow a generate-discussion-vote cycle until they reach an appropriate decision.

The **Delphi technique** is a method of systematically gathering judgments of experts for use in developing forecasts.

The Delphi Technique The **Delphi technique** was originally developed by Rand Corporation as a method to systematically gather the judgments of experts for use in developing forecasts. It is designed for groups that do not meet face to face. For instance, the product development manager of a major toy manufacturer might use the Delphi technique to probe the views of industry experts to forecast developments in the dynamic toy market.

The manager who wants the input of a group is the central figure in the process. After recruiting participants, the manager develops a questionnaire for them to complete. The questionnaire is relatively simple, containing straightforward questions that deal with the issue, trends in the area, new technological developments, and other factors that interest the manager. The manager summarizes the responses and reports back to the experts with another questionnaire. This cycle may be repeated as many times as necessary to generate the information the manager needs.

The Delphi technique is useful when experts are physically dispersed, anonymity is desired, or the participants are known to have trouble communicating with one another because of extreme differences of opinion. This method also avoids the intimidation problems that may exist in decision-making groups. On the other hand, the technique eliminates the often fruitful results of direct interaction among group members.

Negotiation in Organizations

LEARNING OBJECTIVE
Discuss negotiation in organizations.

During **negotiation**, two or more parties (people or groups) reach agreement despite having different preferences.

One special way decisions are made in organizations is through negotiation. **Negotiation** is the process in which two or more parties (people or groups) reach agreement even though they have different preferences. In its simplest form, the parties may be two individuals trying to decide who will pay for lunch. A somewhat more complex form occurs when two people, such as an employee and a manager, sit down to decide on personal performance goals for the next year against which the employee's performance will be measured. Even more complex are negotiations that take place between labor unions and a company's management or between two companies as they negotiate the terms of a joint venture. The key issues in such negotiations are that at least two parties are involved, their preferences differ, and they need to reach agreement.

Approaches to Negotiation

Interest in negotiation has grown steadily in recent years.[37] Four primary approaches to negotiation have dominated this study: individual differences, situational characteristics, game theory, and cognitive approaches. The following sections briefly describe each approach.

Individual Differences Early psychological approaches concentrated on the personality traits of the negotiators.[38] Traits investigated have included demographic characteristics and personality variables. Demographic characteristics have included age, gender, and race, among others. Personality variables have included risk taking, locus of control, tolerance for ambiguity, self-esteem, authoritarianism, and Machiavellianism. The assumption of this type of research was that the key to successful negotiation is selecting the right person to do the negotiating, one who has the appropriate demographic characteristics or personality. This assumption seemed to make sense because negotiation is such a personal and interactive process. However,

Negotiation can take place in many different settings. A key to any successful negotiation, however, is careful preparation. For instance, this antelope probably made a mistake by not learning more about the likely behavior of lions.
© Stu Rees

the research rarely showed the positive results expected because situational variables negated the effects of the individual differences.[39]

Situational Characteristics Situational characteristics are the context within which negotiation takes place. They include such things as the types of communication between negotiators, the potential outcomes of the negotiation, the relative power of the parties (both positional and personal), the time frame available for negotiation, the number of people representing each side, and the presence of other parties. Some of this research has contributed to our understanding of the negotiation process. However, the shortcomings of the situational approach are similar to those of the individual characteristics approach. Many situational characteristics are external to the negotiators and beyond their control. Often the negotiators cannot change their relative power positions or the setting within which the negotiation occurs. Hence, although we have learned a lot from research on situational issues, we still need to learn much more about the process.

Game Theory Game theory was developed by economists using mathematical models to predict the outcomes of negotiation situations (as illustrated in the Academy Award–winning movie *A Beautiful Mind*). It requires that every alternative and outcome be analyzed with probabilities and numerical outcomes reflecting the preferences for each outcome. In addition, the order in which different parties can make choices and every possible move are predicted, along with associated preferences for outcomes. The outcomes of this approach are exactly what negotiators want: a predictive model of how negotiation should be conducted. One major drawback is that it requires the ability to describe all possible options and outcomes for every possible move in every situation before the negotiation starts—an often tedious process, if possible at all. Another problem is that this theory assumes negotiators are rational at all times. Other research on negotiation has shown that negotiators often do not act rationally. Therefore, this approach, although elegant in its prescriptions, is usually unworkable in a real negotiation situation.

Cognitive Approaches The fourth approach to negotiation consists of several cognitive approaches, which recognize that negotiators often depart from perfect rationality during negotiation; they try to predict how and when negotiators will make these departures. Howard Raiffa's decision analytic approach focuses on providing advice to negotiators actively involved in negotiation.[40] K. H. Bazerman and M. A. Neale have added to Raiffa's work by specifying eight ways in which negotiators systematically deviate from rationality.[41] The types of deviations they describe include escalation of commitment to a previously selected course of action, overreliance on readily available information, assuming the negotiations can produce fixed-sum outcomes, and anchoring negotiations in irrelevant information. These cognitive approaches have advanced the study of negotiation a long way beyond the early individual and situational approaches.

Win-Win Negotiation

In addition to the approaches to negotiation previously described, a group of approaches proposed by consultants and advisers aims to give negotiators a specific model to use in carrying out difficult negotiations. One of the best of these models is the "Win-Win Negotiator" developed by Ross Reck and his associates.[42] The Win-Win approach does not treat negotiation as a game resulting in winners and losers. Instead, it approaches negotiation as an opportunity for both sides to be winners, to get what they want out of the agreement. The focus is on both parties reaching agreement such that both are committed to fulfilling their own end of the agreement and to returning for more agreements in the future. In other words, both parties want to have their needs satisfied. In addition, this approach does not advocate either a "tough guy" or a "nice guy" approach to negotiation, both of which are popular in the literature. It assumes both parties work together to find ways to satisfy each other at the same time.

The Win-Win approach is a four-step approach illustrated in the **PRAM model** shown in Figure 12.7. The PRAM four-step approach proposes that proper planning, building relationships, getting agreements, and maintaining the relationships are the key steps to successful negotiation.

Planning requires that each negotiator set his or her own goals, anticipate the goals of the other, determine areas of probable agreement, and develop strategies for reconciling areas of probable disagreement. Developing Win-Win *relationships* requires that negotiators plan activities that enable positive personal relationships to develop, cultivate a sense of mutual trust, and allow relationships to evolve fully before discussing business in earnest. The development of trust between the parties is probably the single most important key to success in negotiation. Forming Win-Win *agreements* requires that each party confirm the other's goals, verify areas of agreement, propose and consider positive solutions to reconcile areas of disagreement, and jointly resolve any remaining differences. The key in reaching agreement is to realize that both parties share many of the goals. The number of areas of disagreement is usually small. Finally, Win-Win *maintenance* entails providing meaningful feedback based on performance, each party holding up his or her end of the agreement, keeping in contact, and reaffirming trust between the parties. The assumption is that both parties want to keep the relationship going so that future mutually beneficial transactions can occur. Both parties must uphold their ends of the agreement and do what they said they would do. Finally, keeping in touch is as easy as making a telephone call or meeting for lunch.

In summary, the PRAM model provides straightforward advice for conducting negotiations. The four steps are easy to remember and carry out as long as tactics employed by other parties do not distract the negotiator. The focus is on planning, agreeing on goals, trust, and keeping commitments.

The **PRAM model** guides the negotiator through the four steps of planning for agreement, building relationships, reaching agreements, and maintaining relationships.

FIGURE 12.7

The Pram Model of Negotiation

The PRAM model shows the four steps in setting up negotiation so that both parties win.

Reference: From *Win-Win Negotiator* by Ross R. Reck and Brian G. Long. Reprinted with permission of Simon & Schuster Adult Publishing Group, Copyright © 1985, 1987 by Brian G. Long and Ross R. Reck.

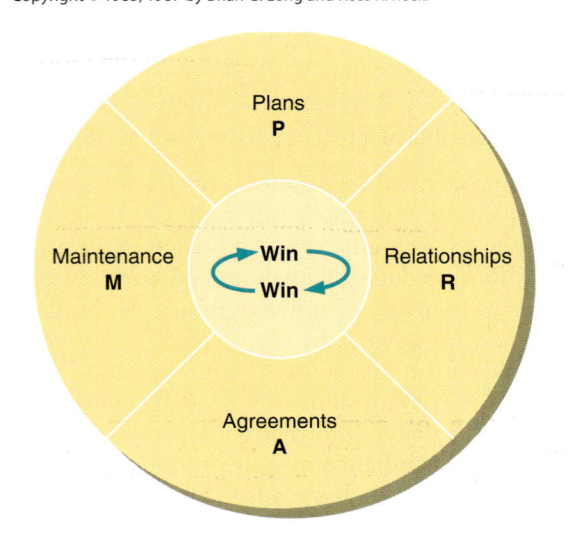

- Plans (P)
- Relationships (R)
- Agreements (A)
- Maintenance (M)
- Win-Win (center)

Synopsis

Decision making is the process of choosing one alternative from among several. The basic elements of decision making include choosing a goal; considering alternative courses of action; assessing potential outcomes of the alternatives, each with its own value relative to the goal; and choosing one alternative based on an evaluation of the outcomes. Information is available regarding the alternatives, outcomes, and values.

Programmed decisions are well-structured, recurring decisions made according to set decision rules. Nonprogrammed decisions involve nonroutine, poorly structured situations with unclear sources of information; these decisions cannot be made according to existing decision rules. Decision making may also be classified according to the information available. The classifications—certainty, risk, and uncertainty—reflect the amount of information available regarding the outcomes of alternatives.

The rational approach views decision making as a completely rational process in which goals are established, a problem is identified, alternatives are generated and evaluated, a choice is made and implemented, and control is exercised. The use of procedures and rules of thumb, suboptimizing, and satisficing characterize the behavioral model. The rational and behavioral views can be combined into a practical model. The Janis-Mann conflict model recognizes the personal anxiety individuals face when they must make important decisions.

Two related behavioral aspects of decision making are ethics and escalation of commitment. Ethics play an important role in both individual and managerial decisions. Escalation of commitment to an ineffective course of action occurs in many decision situations often caused by psychological, social, ego, and organizational factors. Group decision making involves problems as well as benefits. One possible problem is group polarization, the shift of members' attitudes and opinions to a more extreme position following group discussion. Another difficulty is groupthink, a mode of thinking in which the urge toward unanimity overrides critical appraisal of alternatives. Yet another concern involves employee participation in decision making. The appropriate degree of participation depends on the characteristics of the situation. Brainstorming, the nominal group technique, and the Dephi technique are three popular methods for managing group problem solving.

Negotiation is the process through which two or more parties (people or groups) reach agreement even though they have different preferences. Research on negotiation has examined individual differences, situational characteristics, game theory, and cognitive approaches. The Win-Win approach provides a simple four-step model to successful negotiation: planning, relationships, agreement, and maintenance.

Discussion Questions

1. Some have argued that people, not organizations, make decisions and that the study of "organizational" decision making is therefore pointless. Do you agree with this argument? Why or why not?
2. What information did you use in deciding to enter the school you now attend?
3. When your alarm goes off each morning, you have a decision to make: whether to get up and go to school or work or to stay in bed and sleep longer. Is this a programmed or nonprogrammed decision? Why?
4. Describe at least three points in the decision-making process at which information plays an important role.
5. How does the role of information in the rational model of decision making differ from its role in the behavioral model?
6. Why does it make sense to consider several different models of decision making?
7. Think of a time when you satisfied when making a decision. Recall a time when you suboptimized during decision making. How might your decision have differed had you used a different approach in each case?
8. Describe a situation in which you experienced escalation of commitment to an ineffective course of action. What did you do about it? Do you wish you had handled it differently? Why or why not?

9. How are group polarization and groupthink similar? How do they differ?
10. Describe a situation in which you negotiated an agreement, perhaps when buying a car or a house. How did the negotiation process compare with the PRAM approach? How did it differ? Were you satisfied with the result of the negotiation?

Organizational Behavior Case for Discussion
The Most Stressful Conditions

How can effective choices be made when there is no time, when your employees, your company, and your community are in imminent danger? Decision making under these conditions takes on a different character, as shown in the response of Sidley Austin Brown & Wood to the tragic events of September 11, 2001.

The giant law firm was formed in May 2001 when Brown & Wood merged its Wall Street financial law offices with those of Chicago-based Sidley & Austin, corporate law specialists, creating the nation's fourth-largest practice, with 1,400 lawyers worldwide. Many of the firm's lawyers are headquartered in New York City, with 600 formerly housed at 1 World Trade Center on floors 52 to 57 and another 100 seven miles away in midtown Manhattan. On September 11, the first plane struck overhead. Workers noticed the explosion's tremors and the smell of jet fuel. Director of Administration John Connelly asked workers to evacuate, helping the frightened, confused employees to the stairs. Being unaware of the extent of the danger, Connelly and others went from floor to floor to ensure that everyone was safely out, then left the building just as it collapsed. Only one company employee perished in the attack.

In the aftermath, with damaged facilities and workers in shock, Sidley Austin employees faced the most trying circumstances of their careers. When their attempts to contact the midtown building failed because cell phone towers had been destroyed, many employees walked to the site. At the midtown location, partner Alan S. Weil anticipated the need for additional office space and called his landlord, who granted immediate leases on two floors and also got another law firm to give up two newly leased floors. By the end of the day, hundreds of desks, computers, and cell phones were arriving, and contractors were installing computer cables. "It's just amazing what you can get in New York overnight," says partner Thomas R. Smith, Jr. According to *New York Times* writer John Schwartz, "The normal rules of business engagement—deliberate negotiation, adversarial wrangling and jockeying for advantage—were swept away. The infamously in-your-face New York attitude was nowhere to be found."

The partnership's directors were supposed to meet in Los Angeles on September 12 but were stranded elsewhere as airlines ceased operations. The executives used conference calls to begin "issue-spotting," according to Thomas Cole, partner. He explained, "The lawyers who assembled that day and in the days thereafter were people who had spent their entire working lives engaged in solving complex problems for clients. . . . But that was under normal conditions. Would we succeed under the most stressful conditions . . . ?" Issues involving people, insurance, and communications were complex; for example, the people issue covered such items as payroll continuity, trauma counseling, and safety and security. The organization pulled together; staffers from the Chicago headquarters drove all night to assist. When the firm's backup data tapes needed transport from a New Jersey warehouse to Chicago, the storage companies offered to have their employees drive overnight because no planes were flying. Dennis J. O'Donovan, head of the firm's technology section, says, "[Disaster recovery seminars] always prepare you for the worst—people not being available, people not being cooperative; the opposite has happened."

On September 17, firm employees met, and partner Charles W. Douglas told the crowd, "The assets of the law firm are not the desks in the offices, the woodwork that's on the walls or the paintings that are hung in the corridors. The assets of the law firm are its people." Smith agreed: "Being able to keep the business going is great, but it's the people that count." Employees and partners at Sidley Austin have taken on the added work with few complaints; many say that work is therapeutic. The lawyers have completed many financial deals on time, believing it's their patriotic duty to continue working as before. Employees claim the tragedy drew them closer together, creating intimate friendships. Others still suffer from stress, and some may choose paid disability leave. Nancy L. Karen, chief information officer, says the firm has learned a lot about crisis conditions. "We ought to be able to recover in less than a day next time," she says, adding with a nervous laugh, "God forbid!" Perhaps Thomas Cole best sums up the firm's response: "I have been asked . . . if the disaster has been a setback to the full realization of the anticipated benefits of our merger. I answer that because of the way we have risen to this challenge together, the most important yet most elusive goal in any merger integration, namely the creation of a true partnership, occurred overnight."

Case Questions

1. Using the rational approach to decision making, describe the ways in which these crisis conditions affected each step of the decision-making process.

2. Based on your answer to question 1, what are some potential problems firms should be aware of when they must make decisions during a crisis? What are some steps firms can take to avoid those problems or to minimize their negative impact?

3. Due to the extraordinary circumstances in New York City during and just after September 11, many individuals and firms changed their behavior, acting more altruistically and ethically. In your opinion, why did this occur? Do you think the change is likely to endure for a long time, or is it only temporary?

References: "About Sidley," "Our Offices," "Our Practices," Sidley Austin Brown & Wood website, www.sidley.com on May 25, 2002; Thomas Cole, "Our Test," *American Lawyer*, November 2001; John Schwartz, "Rebuilding a Day at a Time: Law Firm Pushes 2 Steps Forward for Every Step Back, Rebuilds a Day at a Time," *New York Times*, December 14, 2001; John Schwartz, "Up from the Ashes: *N.Y. Times* Profile of Sidley Austin Brown & Wood's Response to the World Trade Center Tragedy," *New York Times*, September 16, 2001 (quotation).

Experiencing Organizational Behavior

Programmed and Nonprogrammed Decisions

Purpose: This exercise will allow you to take part in making a hypothetical decision and help you understand the difference between programmed and nonprogrammed decisions.

Format: You will be asked to perform a task both individually and as a member of a group.

Procedure: A list of typical organizational decisions follows. Your task is to determine whether they are programmed or nonprogrammed. Number your paper, and write *P* for programmed or *N* for nonprogrammed next to each number.

Your instructor will divide the class into groups of four to seven. All groups should have approximately the same number of members. Your task as a group is to make the determinations just outlined. In arriving at your decisions, do not use techniques such as voting or negotiating ("Okay, I'll give in on this one if you'll give in on that one.") The group should discuss the difference between programmed and nonprogrammed decisions and each decision situation until all members at least partly agree with the decision.

Decision List

1. Hiring a specialist for the research staff in a highly technical field
2. Assigning workers to daily tasks
3. Determining the size of dividend to be paid to shareholders in the ninth consecutive year of strong earnings growth
4. Deciding whether to officially excuse an employee's absence for medical reasons
5. Selecting the location for another branch of a 150-branch bank in a large city
6. Approving the appointment of a new law school graduate to the corporate legal staff
7. Making annual assignments of graduate assistants to faculty
8. Approving an employee's request to attend a local seminar in his or her special area of expertise
9. Selecting the appropriate outlets for print advertisements for a new college textbook
10. Determining the location for a new fast-food restaurant in a small but growing town on the major interstate highway between two very large metropolitan areas

Follow-up Questions

1. To what extent did group members disagree about which decisions were programmed and which were nonprogrammed?

2. What primary factors did the group discuss in making each decision?

3. Were there any differences between the members' individual lists and the group lists? If so, discuss the reasons for the differences.

Self-Assessment Exercise
Rational Versus Practical Approaches to Decision Making

Managers need to recognize and understand the different models they use to make decisions. They also need to understand to what extent they tend to be relatively autocratic or relatively participative in making decisions. To develop your skills in these areas, perform the following activity.

First, assume you are the manager of a firm that is rapidly growing. Recent sales figures strongly suggest the need for a new plant to produce more of your firm's products. Key issues include where the plant might be built and how large it might be (for example, a small, less expensive plant to meet current needs that could be expanded in the future versus a large, more expensive plant that may have excess capacity today but could better meet long-term needs).

Using the rational approach diagrammed in Figure 12.3, trace the process the manager might use to make the decision. Note the kinds of information it may require and the extent to which other people may need to participate in making a decision at each point.

Next, go back and look at various steps in the process where behavioral processes might intervene and affect the overall process. Will bounded rationality come into play? What about satisficing?

Finally, use the practical approach shown in Figure 12.4 and trace through the process again. Again note where other input may be needed. Try to identify points in the process where the rational and practical approaches are likely to result in the same outcome and points where differences are most likely to occur.

OB Online

1. Assume you need to make decisions about where to locate a new plant. The options have been narrowed down to Madison, Wisconsin; Columbia, Missouri; and Bryan, Texas. You now need to find information about tax rates, unemployment statistics, and airport access for each community. Use the Internet to search for this information.
2. In what ways do you think the emergence of the Internet has affected how managers make decisions? Give concrete examples to support your ideas.
3. Describe ways in which information technology might be used to manage brainstorming, the nominal group technique, and the Delphi technique more efficiently than using these techniques in more traditional ways.
4. Pair up with a classmate and conduct a hypothetical negotiation via email. Then discuss the pros and cons of electronic negotiation versus face-to-face negotiation based on your experience.

Building Managerial Skills

Exercise Overview: Interpersonal skills involve the manager's ability to understand and motivate individuals and groups. This exercise will allow you to practice your interpersonal skills in a role-playing exercise.

Exercise Background: You supervise a group of six employees who work in an indoor facility in a relatively isolated location. The company you work for recently adopted an ambiguous policy regarding smoking. Essentially the policy states that all company work sites are to be smoke free unless employees at a specific site choose differently and at the discretion of the site supervisor.

Four members of the work group you supervise are smokers. They have come to you with the argument that since they constitute the majority, they should be allowed to smoke at work. The other two members, both nonsmokers, have heard about this

Chapter 12 Decision Making and Negotiation

request and have also discussed the situation with you. They argue that the health-related consequences of secondary smoke should outweigh the preferences of the majority.

To compound the problem, your boss wrote the new policy and is quite defensive about it; numerous individuals have already criticized the policy. You know your boss will get very angry with you if you also raise concerns about the policy. Finally, you are personally indifferent to the issue. You do not smoke yourself, but your spouse smokes. Secondary smoke does not bother you, and you do not have strong opinions about it. Still, you have to make a decision about what to do. You see that your choices are to (1) mandate a smoke-free environment, (2) allow smoking in the facility, or (3) ask your boss to clarify the policy.

Exercise Task: Based on the background previously presented, assume you are the supervisor and do the following:

1. Assume you have chosen option 1. Write an outline that you will use to announce your decision to the four smokers.
2. Assume you have chosen option 2. Write an outline that you will use to announce your decision to the two nonsmokers.
3. Assume you have chosen option 3. Write an outline that you will use when you meet with your boss.
4. Are there other alternatives?
5. What would you do if you were actually the group supervisor?

TEST PREPPER

ACE self-test

You have read the chapter and studied the key terms, and the exam is any day now. Think you're ready to ace it? Take this sample test to gauge your comprehension of chapter material. You can check your answers at the back of the book. Want more test questions? Visit the student website at http://college.hmco.com/business/students/ (select Griffin/Moorhead, Fundamentals of Organizational Behavior 1e) and take the ACE quizzes for more practice.

1. **T F** A decision rule tells a decision maker to consider multiple alternatives before making a decision.
2. **T F** The choice of what to do when the organization faces a major lawsuit is a nonprogrammed decision.
3. **T F** Managers prefer to operate in conditions of uncertainty rather than in conditions of risk.
4. **T F** Evaluating alternatives in the rational decision-making process involves describing anticipated outcomes, evaluating the expected costs of the alternatives, and estimating the risks associated with each alternative.
5. **T F** A contingency plan is a plan developed for temporary employees.
6. **T F** One strength of the rational decision-making model is that it forces the decision maker to consider a decision in a logical, sequential manner.
7. **T F** Managers who satisfice in making decisions attempt to maximize the satisfaction of their employees.
8. **T F** According to the Janis-Mann conflict model, decision makers who believe they have little time to deliberate over a decision experience hypervigilance.
9. **T F** A group whose members lean toward a particular decision before a discussion is likely to make an even more extreme decision following a discussion.
10. **T F** Self-censorship of deviations from the apparent group consensus is a symptom of groupthink.
11. **T F** The basic rule in the brainstorming technique is to evaluate alternatives as quickly as possible to generate more useful alternatives later.
12. **T F** The nominal group technique is used specifically to help newly formed groups determine their purpose.
13. **T F** The Delphi technique is a way to systematically gather the judgments of experts.
14. **T F** Picking the right person to do the negotiating, as suggested by early psychological approaches, has proven widely successful.
15. **T F** Game theory teaches managers the tricks and tips of how to win in negotiations.
16. **T F** In a Win-Win negotiation, managers are encouraged to adopt either a "tough" style or a "nice" style.
17. **T F** The PRAM model of negotiation assumes that negotiators want to keep the relationship going to enable future mutually beneficial transactions.
18. Each time inventory levels drop to a certain point, Rachel orders replacement items. Rachel is making a(n) _____ decision.
    - a. programmed
    - b. nonprogrammed
    - c. artificial
    - d. planning
    - e. leadership
19. _____ decisions require the decision maker to exercise judgment and creativity.
    - a. Programmed
    - b. Nonprogrammed
    - c. Artificial
    - d. Planning
    - e. Leadership
20. Jennifer believes there is a 60 percent chance she can successfully market a new athletic shoe by pricing it at $90 but an 80 percent chance by pricing it at $75. Jennifer's decision of which price to choose occurs in a condition of
    - a. certainty.
    - b. risk.
    - c. uncertainty.
    - d. rationality.
    - e. irrationality.
21. The first step in the rational decision making-model is
    - a. identify the problem.
    - b. determine the decision type.
    - c. generate alternatives.
    - d. evaluate alternatives.
    - e. state the situational goal.
22. Managers in Pentry Corporation have adopted a clear strategy to compete in a given market. However, they also have a secondary plan ready to implement should their intended strategy fail. This secondary plan is called a(n)
    - a. programmed plan.
    - b. nonprogrammed plan.
    - c. rational plan.
    - d. contingency plan.
    - e. uncertainty plan.
23. What typically happens when decision makers experience cognitive dissonance?
    - a. They immediately reverse their decision.
    - b. They ignore it and move on to the next decision.
    - c. They postpone future decisions.

Chapter 12 Decision Making and Negotiation 337

- d. They attempt to identify decision rules for future decisions.
- e. They seek to rationalize the decision further with new information.

24. One assumption in the rational decision-making model is that
    - a. decisions will be made in a condition of uncertainty.
    - b. decision makers, being human, have limits on their rationality.
    - c. decision makers can generate all possible alternative solutions to a problem.
    - d. political processes inhibit effective decision making.
    - e. all decisions are permanent and cannot be changed.

25. Jack needs a new computer for his office. Rather than compare all possible alternatives in terms of processing speed, memory capacity, and so on, he chooses the first computer he finds that falls within his budget. This is an example of
    - a. satisficing.
    - b. suboptimizing.
    - c. programming.
    - d. rules of thumb.
    - e. bounded rationality.

26. According to the Janis-Mann conflict model, a decision maker who believes serious risks will not occur if no change is made will
    - a. make small, gradual changes.
    - b. make a sudden, large-scale change.
    - c. seek as much information as possible before making a change.
    - d. adopt a general decision rule and apply it to all situations.
    - e. continue his or her present activities.

27. Vigilant information processing, as described in the Janis-Mann conflict model of decision making, is similar to
    - a. generating alternatives.
    - b. the rational decision-making model.
    - c. cognitive dissonance.
    - d. transformational leadership.
    - e. groupthink.

28. A person's beliefs about what constitutes right and wrong behavior are called
    - a. decision rules.
    - b. rational bounds.
    - c. decision vigilance.
    - d. conditions of certainty.
    - e. ethics.

29. Which of the following is not a potential cause of escalation of commitment?
    - a. New information that contradicts the decision
    - b. Personal egos
    - c. Organizational inertia
    - d. Social structures that strongly support the decision
    - e. High front-end investment

30. Individually, the members of Kimberly's task force have fairly moderate views about an issue, but when they get together and discuss the issue, each member's views are reinforced and validated. By the end of the discussion, Kimberly's task force makes a more extreme decision than the individual members' initial views would have predicted. This effect is called
    - a. irrational decision making.
    - b. group polarization.
    - c. escalation of commitment.
    - d. cognitive dissonance.
    - e. nonprogrammed decision making.

31. Which of the following is not a symptom of groupthink?
    - a. An illusion of invulnerability
    - b. Stereotyped views of the "enemy"
    - c. A shared illusion of unanimity
    - d. A formally appointed "devil's advocate"
    - e. Unquestioned belief in the group's inherent morality

32. Brainstorming may help generate numerous creative ideas and solutions, primarily because the group avoids self-censorship; in other words,
    - a. the group believes in its inherent morality.
    - b. the group views its decisions as unanimous.
    - c. the group has formally appointed a "devil's advocate."
    - d. no attempts to evaluate the ideas are made.
    - e. the group believes it is invulnerable to failure.

33. A Win-Win negotiation includes all of the following elements except
    - a. opportunities for both sides to successfully reach their objectives.
    - b. jointly resolving differences.
    - c. a "nice guy" approach.
    - d. setting personal goals and anticipating the goals of the other party.
    - e. cultivating a sense of mutual trust.

PART FOUR VIDEO CASE

The Bakers' Best Story

In 1984, Michael Baker and his wife established Bakers' Best, a small take-out restaurant in a community near Boston. In its first year, the restaurant was simply a deli and grossed around $200,000. Today Bakers' Best is a well-known multipurpose restaurant serving the greater Boston area. It has 75 full-time and 50 part-time employees, brings in $7.5 million per year, and includes a café and restaurant along with a full-service catering department. How did Bakers' Best grow from a small start-up to a bustling midsize firm? Much of its success can be attributed to the management style and leadership skills of its founder, Michael Baker.

In building his restaurant, Baker decided early on to focus on his employees and to build a fun, caring workplace. He believed if his employees enjoyed their jobs and felt cared for, they would be more committed to serving a quality product and providing exemplary customer service. To maintain this environment, Baker frequently does things for his employees that most companies don't do. For example, during a recent Thanksgiving holiday, he called a number of his managers at home and personally thanked them for working so hard. He regularly buys tickets to Boston Red Sox games and distributes them to his staff, free of charge. Baker also models the behavior he wants his employees to demonstrate. For example, he walks through the kitchen daily to make sure the kitchen staff is using the best possible ingredients. "I've been here for about seven-and-a-half years, and he actually comes through the kitchen every single day, and he'll see the food and taste it, [and] make sure we're all using the best ingredients," comments Geoff Skillman, one of Baker's executive chefs.

Judging by the impressive growth of his business and employees' admiration for him, Baker's efforts are clearly paying off. "Michael is a salt-of-the-earth kind of guy, and you look around—the food—the environment—it's all a reflection of him," says Ken Gasse, an assistant manager. "He's such a people person, and really cares a lot about you, about the job you're doing and about how we deal with our clients," remarks Pamela Shaw, director of catering. Baker's positive attributes have clearly rubbed off on his staff. In describing how he manages the restaurant's kitchen, executive chef Skillman explains, "We try to create a really nice work environment for our staff. It's very important that we have people who work here that don't have attitude problems or big chips on their shoulder." Skillman works hard to try to accommodate employees in terms of scheduling. "We believe in the quality of life outside of work," he says. Along with maintaining a fun and caring workplace, Baker believes in compensating his employees fairly. The company pays well, offers a health insurance plan, and offers an IRA. Still, employee turnover is about 20 percent per year, largely due to the demanding nature of the work. This statistic is a daily reminder to Baker and his managers that the company must continually work hard to attract, motivate, and retain high-quality employees.

Looking back over the years, Baker is pleased with the way his restaurant has grown and the environment he has created for his employees. "It's exceeded anything we've expected," he says. "It's a team effort, and although that's said all the time, I think that if everyone's on the same page, and if [the employees] are looking to serve a quality product and make people feel comfortable in the store, that's what brings in business."

Case Questions

1. Do you believe Michael Baker is an effective or ineffective leader? Cite evidence from the case to support your claim.
2. Discuss several key traits of effective leaders. To what extent does Michael Baker demonstrate these traits?
3. In what ways does Michael Baker's leadership style influence his employees? Does he make effective use of power? Which types of power does he use and which types does he avoid to influence his employees?
4. Would you enjoy working at Bakers' Best? Why or why not?

Reference: Bakers' Best homepage, www.bakersbestcatering.com on June 25, 2004.

PART FIVE

Organizational Processes and Characteristics

CHAPTER 13

Organization Design

CHAPTER 14

Organization Culture

CHAPTER 15

Organization Change and Development

CHAPTER 13

Organization Design

MANAGEMENT PREVIEW

Why is it that when some companies' products mature, the economy changes, or low-cost foreign competition enters the market, some companies die whereas others adjust and become stronger than ever? One key reason is organization design. Within the organization, the structure sets up a system to coordinate the efforts of individuals, work groups, and departments. It seems as though organizations are always restructuring, rearranging the organization chart and having people report to different managers. What they are really doing is seeking the best way to design a system of task, reporting, and authority relationships that will lead to the efficient accomplishment of organizational goals. We begin this chapter with a description of the essential elements of organization structure. Next, we discuss decision making and authority. Then we examine and differentiate between the universal and contingency perspectives of organization design and discuss the factors that determine how an organization should be structured. Finally, we look at several commonly used organization designs.

After you have studied this chapter, you should be able to:
- ☐ Describe the essential elements of organization structure.
- ☐ Explain three classic views of organization structure.
- ☐ Discuss the primary contingency approaches to organization design.
- ☐ Identify the factors and several popular approaches that determine how an organization should be designed.

We begin with a look at some of the organizational challenges faced by AOL Time Warner following their merger.

Whether you call it *integration, synergy,* or *convergence,* the last being former Time Warner chairman Steve Case's favorite word, it is the driving force behind the organization structures of so-called "new economy" firms, based on the hypothetical benefits of owning a variety of related business units. Since the future of technology remains uncertain, it makes sense for firms to hedge their bets by owning many different technologies. Case, a visionary leader, says,

"We are moving into an era of convergence where the lines between industries will blur." However, it is clear that owning widely diversified businesses does not yet contribute to profitability, perhaps because an overly diversified corporate structure is difficult to manage.

Time Warner is still struggling with this issue today. The huge firm, with more than $40 billion in revenue in 2003, comprises dozens of major brands. An exhaustive, and exhausting, list of brands includes Internet businesses such as AOL, CompuServe, Road Runner, icq, Instant Messenger, Netscape, and Mapquest; cable networks HBO, Cinemax, CNN, the Cartoon Network, TNT, TBS Superstation, Turner Classic Movies, and the WB; movie studios Warner Brothers, Castle Rock Entertainment, and New Line Cinema; magazines such as *Time, People, Sports Illustrated, Fortune, InStyle, Money, Entertainment Weekly, marie claire, MAD* comics, and more than one hundred other specialty titles; the Time Warner cable provider and four local TV stations; the Atlanta Braves baseball team, the Atlanta Hawks basketball team, and the Atlanta Thrashers hockey team; several book publishers; the Looney Tunes animation studio; and Atlantic, Elektra, Rhino, and other recording companies.

Thus far, the much-hyped benefits of the merger between AOL and Time Warner have failed to materialize. According to Case, the slow start was to be expected: "I've always said this is a marathon, not a sprint." The firm is effectively cross-selling products, for example, by advertising its other products on its web portals and cable stations. But it could do more. Case maintains, "The merger was never about cross-divisional promotion. It was about cross-divisional innovation." The firm has taken the first step, adding divisions with responsibility for achieving synergies, but some obvious moves, such as offering movie sneak previews exclusively to AOL subscribers, have been widely discussed but never implemented.

The challenge for new Chairman and CEO Richard Parsons is to create an organization structure that will harness the power of these combined businesses, realizing synergies and sparking innovation while also maintaining control. Parsons, who assumed the CEO position in May 2002 and the Chairman position in 2003, began with a reorganization, asking some top executives who had previously reported to Case to report directly to him and changing other reporting relationships at the firm's top level. The changes will give more formal authority and public visibility to several top executives, mainly those in strategic planning, external communications, and technology development. Parsons also plans to concentrate on making each business unit successful on its own, downplaying the importance of convergence. According to a senior Time Warner executive, Parsons believes that "if we set convergence as a dramatic target, we set ourselves up for a fall because it's clearly going to take longer than we thought." The new CEO is also attempting to respond to investors, who are clamoring for a simplified, more easily understood structure.

The firm's missteps, along with the slump in the technology sector, have caused the company's stock price to fall, erasing more than $100 billion of shareholder value since the 2001 merger of AOL and Time Warner. Still, Case believes that a convergence strategy will ultimately yield the best results. He points out, "The Internet phenomenon, the trend toward more of a connected society, is unabated." Now it is up to Parsons to find a way to organize the entity to capture Case's vision and then to make that organization profitable.

> *"The merger was never about cross-divisional promotion. It was about cross-divisional innovation."*—Steve Case, former Time Warner chairman

References: Jill Goldsmith, "TV, AOL, knock Time Warner Stock," *Daily Variety*, January 29, 2004, v 282 i23 pl(2); "AOL Time Warner 2002 Factbook," "Corporate Information: Timeline," "Overview," AOL Time Warner website, www.aoltimewarner.com on June 5, 2002; Martin Peers, "AOL CEO Parsons Reorganizes Reporting Lines for Senior Aides," *Wall Street Journal*, May 24, 2002, online.wsj.com on June 5, 2002; Marc Gunther and Stephanie N. Mehta, "Can Steve Case Make Sense of This Beast?" *Fortune*, May 13, 2002 (quotation), www.fortune.com on April 30, 2002; Martin Peers, "In New Turn, AOL Time Warner Will De-Emphasize 'Convergence,'" *Wall Street Journal*, May 13, 2002, online.wsj.com on June 5, 2002.

AOL Time Warner faces the task of developing an organization structure that allows the synergies it expected when the two companies merged, yet still enables management to have some control over operations. This is not unusual in business and industry today as companies struggle to remain competitive in a rapidly changing world. This chapter describes the essential elements of organization structure and several different ways they can be combined into an organization design that will help the organization achieve its objectives.

Essential Elements of Organization Structure

LEARNING OBJECTIVE
Describe the essential elements of organization structure.

An **organization** is a group of people working together to attain common goals.

Organizational goals are objectives that management seeks to achieve in pursuing the firm's purpose.

In other chapters, we discuss key elements of the individual and the factors that tie the individual and the organization together. In a given organization, these factors must fit together within a common framework: the organization's structure. An **organization** is a group of people working together to achieve common goals. Top management determines the direction of the organization by defining its purpose, establishing goals to meet that purpose, and formulating strategies to achieve the goals. The definition of its purpose gives the organization reason to exist; in effect, it answers the question "What business are we in?" Establishing goals converts the defined purpose into specific, measurable performance targets. **Organizational goals** are objectives that management seeks to achieve in pursuing the firm's purpose. Finally, strategies are specific action plans that enable the organization to achieve its goals and thus its purpose. Pursuing a strategy involves developing an organization structure and the processes to do the organization's work.

Organization Structure

Organization structure is the system of task, reporting, and authority relationships within which the organization does its work.

Organization structure is the system of task, reporting, and authority relationships within which the work of the organization is done. Thus, structure defines the form and function of the organization's activities. Structure also defines how the parts of an organization fit together, as is evident from an organization chart.

The purpose of an organization's structure is to order and coordinate the actions of employees to achieve organizational goals. The premise of organized effort is that people can accomplish more by working together than they can separately. The work must be coordinated properly, however, to realize the potential gains of collective effort. Consider what might happen if the thousands of employees at Dell Computers worked without any kind of structure. Each person might try to build a computer that he or she thought would sell. No two computers would be alike, and each would take months or years to build. The costs of making the computers would be so high that no one would be able to afford them. To produce computers that are both competitive in the marketplace and profitable for the company, Dell must have a structure in which its employees and managers work together in a coordinated manner. Daimler-Chrysler faced similar coordination problems following its merger due to duplication of capabilities, facilities, and product lines, as discussed in the Mastering Change box.

An **organization chart** is a diagram showing all people, positions, reporting relationships, and lines of formal communication in the organization.

The structure of an organization is most often described in terms of its organization chart (see Figure 13.1 for an example). A complete **organization chart** shows all people, positions, reporting relationships, and lines of formal communication in the organization. For large organizations, several charts may be necessary to show all positions. For example, one chart may show top management, includ-

MASTERING CHANGE

DaimlerChrysler Revs Up

In 1999, German automaker Daimler, which manufactures Mercedes cars, merged with Chrysler, one of America's Big Three. The new firm, DaimlerChrysler, then purchased a 34 percent stake in Japan-based Mitsubishi Motors. Although the merger seemed like a brilliant move, combining powerhouses from three continents, the results have been weak thus far.

The German-born CEO, Jurgen Schrempp, is trying to combine the firm's disparate units into an integrated whole. "The chief executive should not be the one who just sort of guides the board on vision and strategy. You also have to know what you are talking about," Schrempp says. To advise him, Schrempp created a chairman's council of eleven outsiders, including IBM's Lou Gerstner. He also established an executive automotive committee whose members are the heads of Mercedes, Chrysler, and Mitsubishi; he hopes the group can improve coordination.

One problematic area is cost control. The merger resulted in duplication of capabilities, facilities, and product lines, consequently increasing expenses. Combined with the effect of slower sales and increased competition, the cost increase caused the firm to lose $589 million in 2001, compared with a 2000 gain of $7 billion. Three years after the merger, the firm is still seeking closer integration in some functions. Schrempp asks, "Why not combine parts departments, workshops and things like that?" Sharing components across the three major divisions could bring significant savings; for example, using the Mercedes gearbox in Chrysler sedans could save as much as $100 million.

Another problem is the potential dilution of DaimlerChrysler's brands. For example, Schrempp wants to avoid the perception that a Mercedes is just an expensive Chrysler. Garel Rhys, professor at Cardiff Business School, warns, "[Mercedes] is not doing as well as it was. It is widening its share with cars that have lower margins."

A third problem is the need to jump-start synergy and creativity across the divisions. The new Crossfire roadster is a Chrysler brand, engineered by Mercedes, that shares components with both Mitsubishi and Mercedes. The innovative Pacifica station wagon/minivan hybrid was introduced in 2003, and Schrempp promises a pipeline of new designs through 2005. The changes seem to be working as DaimlerChrysler reported net income of almost $5 billion in 2002 and over $500 million in 2003.

References: Alex Taylor III, "Schrempp Shifts Gears," *Fortune*, March 18, 2002 (quotation), www.fortune.com on June 6, 2002; Christine Tierney and Joann Muller, "DaimlerChrysler's Foggy Forecast," *BusinessWeek*, February 14, 2002, www.businessweek.com on June 6, 2002; "DaimlerChrysler Chief Seeks Greater Brand Integration," as reported in the *Financial Times*, reprinted in Wall Street Journal Online, May 21, 2002, online.wsj.com on June 6, 2002; Joann Muller, "Daimler and Chrysler Have a Baby," *BusinessWeek*, January 14, 2002, www.businessweek.com on June 6, 2002. *Hoover's Online*, December 11, 2004, http://www.hoovers.com/daimlerchrysler/—ID58357—/free-co-fin-factsheet.xhtml

---

ing the board of directors, the chief executive officer, the president, all vice presidents, and important headquarters staff units. Subsequent charts may show the structure of each department and staff unit. Figure 13.1 depicts two organization charts for a large firm; top management is shown in the upper portion of the figure and the manufacturing department in the lower portion. Notice that the structures of the different manufacturing groups are given in separate charts.

An organization chart depicts reporting relationships and work group memberships, and shows how positions and small work groups are combined into departments, which together make up the organization's **configuration,** or shape. The configuration of organizations can be analyzed in terms of how the two basic requirements of structure—division of labor and coordination of the divided tasks—are fulfilled.

> An organization's **configuration,** or shape, reflects the division of labor and the means of coordinating the divided tasks.
>
> The **division of labor** is the way the organization's work is divided into different jobs to be done by different people.

Division of Labor

Division of labor is the extent to which the organization's work is separated into different jobs to be done by different people. Division of labor is one of the seven

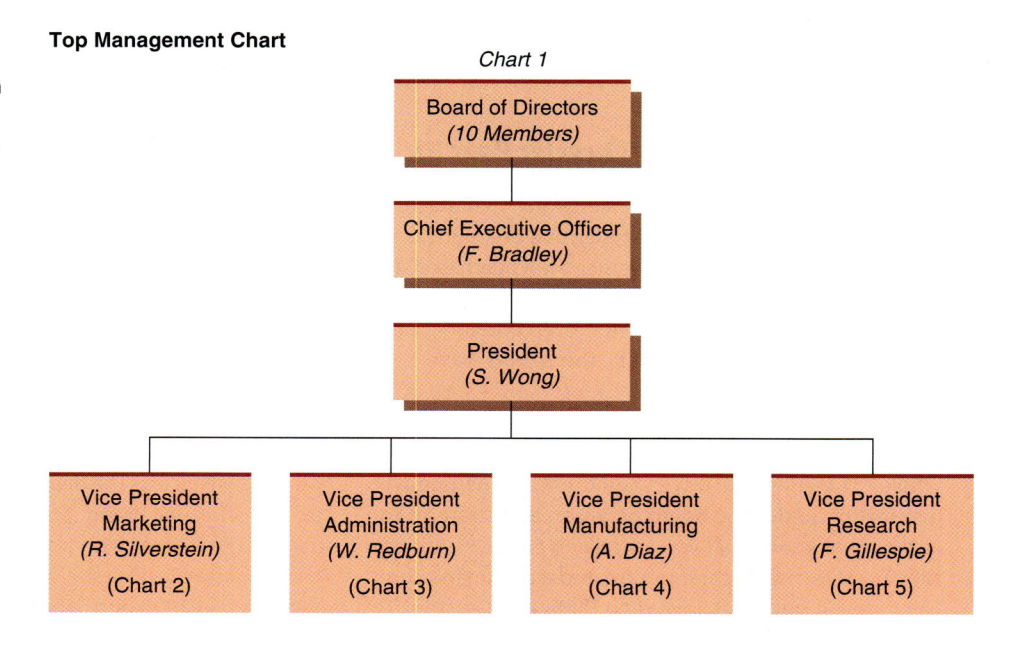

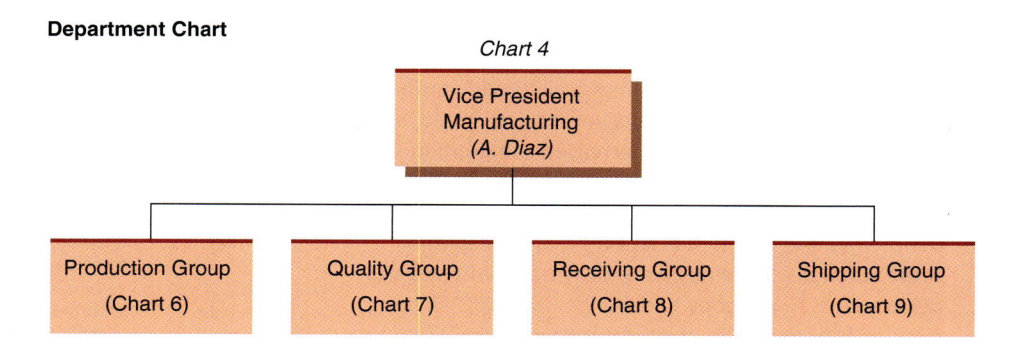

FIGURE 13.1

Examples of Organization Charts

These two charts show the similarities between a top management chart and a department chart. In each, managers have four other managers or work group reporting to them.

Top Management Chart

Chart 1

- Board of Directors (10 Members)
  - Chief Executive Officer (F. Bradley)
    - President (S. Wong)
      - Vice President Marketing (R. Silverstein) (Chart 2)
      - Vice President Administration (W. Redburn) (Chart 3)
      - Vice President Manufacturing (A. Diaz) (Chart 4)
      - Vice President Research (F. Gillespie) (Chart 5)

Department Chart

Chart 4

- Vice President Manufacturing (A. Diaz)
  - Production Group (Chart 6)
  - Quality Group (Chart 7)
  - Receiving Group (Chart 8)
  - Shipping Group (Chart 9)

primary characteristics of structuring described by Max Weber,[1] but the concept can be traced back to the eighteenth-century economist Adam Smith. Division of labor grew more popular as large organizations became more prevalent in a manufacturing society. This trend has continued, and most research indicates that large organizations usually have more division of labor than smaller ones.[2] Division of labor has been found to have both advantages and disadvantages (see Table 13.1). Modern managers and organization theorists still struggle with the primary disadvantage: Division of labor often results in repetitive, boring jobs that undercut worker satisfaction, involvement, and commitment.[3] In addition, extreme division of labor may be incompatible with new, integrated computerized manufacturing technologies that require teams of highly skilled workers.[4] However, division of labor need not result in boredom. Visualized in terms of a small organization such as a basketball team, it can be quite dynamic. On a successful basketball team, each of five players—typically a center, a power forward, a small forward, a shooting guard, and a point guard—play different roles and do different tasks.

Chapter 13 Organization Design

TABLE 13.1

Advantages and Disadvantages of Division of Labor

Advantages	Disadvantages
Efficient use of labor	Routine, repetitive jobs
Reduced training costs	Reduced job satisfaction
Increased standardization and uniformity of output	Decreased worker involvement and commitment
Increased expertise from repetition of tasks	Increased worker alienation
	Possible incompatibility with computerized manufacturing technologies

Coordinating the Divided Tasks

Three basic mechanisms are used to help coordinate the divided tasks: departmentalization, span of control, and administrative hierarchy. These mechanisms focus on grouping tasks in some meaningful manner, creating work groups of manageable size, and establishing a system of reporting relationships among supervisors and managers.

Departmentalization is the manner in which divided tasks are combined and allocated to work groups.

Departmentalization **Departmentalization** is the manner in which divided tasks are combined and allocated to work groups. It is a consequence of the division of labor. Because employees engaged in specialized activities can lose sight of overall organizational goals, their work must be coordinated to ensure that it contributes to the organization's welfare.

There are many possible ways to departmentalize tasks. The five groupings most often used are business function, process, product or service, customer, and geography. The first two, function and process, derive from the internal operations of the organization; the others are based on external factors. Most organizations tend to use a combination of methods, and departmentalization often changes as organizations evolve.[5] Departmentalization by business functions is based on traditional business functions such as marketing, manufacturing, and human resource administration (see Figure 13.2, *part a*). In this configuration, employees most frequently associate with others engaged in the same function, which enhances communication and cooperation. In a functional group, employees who do similar work can learn from one another by sharing ideas about opportunities and problems they encounter on the job. Unfortunately, functional groups lack an automatic mechanism for coordinating the flow of work through the organization.[6] In other words, employees in a functional structure tend to associate little with those in other parts of

Larger and fancier hotels have many employees providing services to guests, including bellhops, reception desk personnel, concierge, floor attendants, room service providers, and many more. These tasks are separated and usually assigned to different functional departments. As a result, these employees usually work somewhat independently from those in other departments. However, some hotels are finding that the work of these employees often needs to be better coordinated to improve guest service. One way they are doing this is by equipping all these employees with tiny two-way radios to improve coordination among them. One added feature is the ability to tell one another the name of each guest as she or he enters the facility. This bellhop is able to tell the reception desk the names of arriving guests so they can be greeted by name as they approach the desk. Hotels are finding that high-end guests love this personal touch.

FIGURE 13.2

Departmentalization by Business Function, by Process, and by Product

These charts compare departmentalization by business function, by process, and by product. "Functions" are the basic business functions, whereas "processes" are the specific categories of jobs people perform.

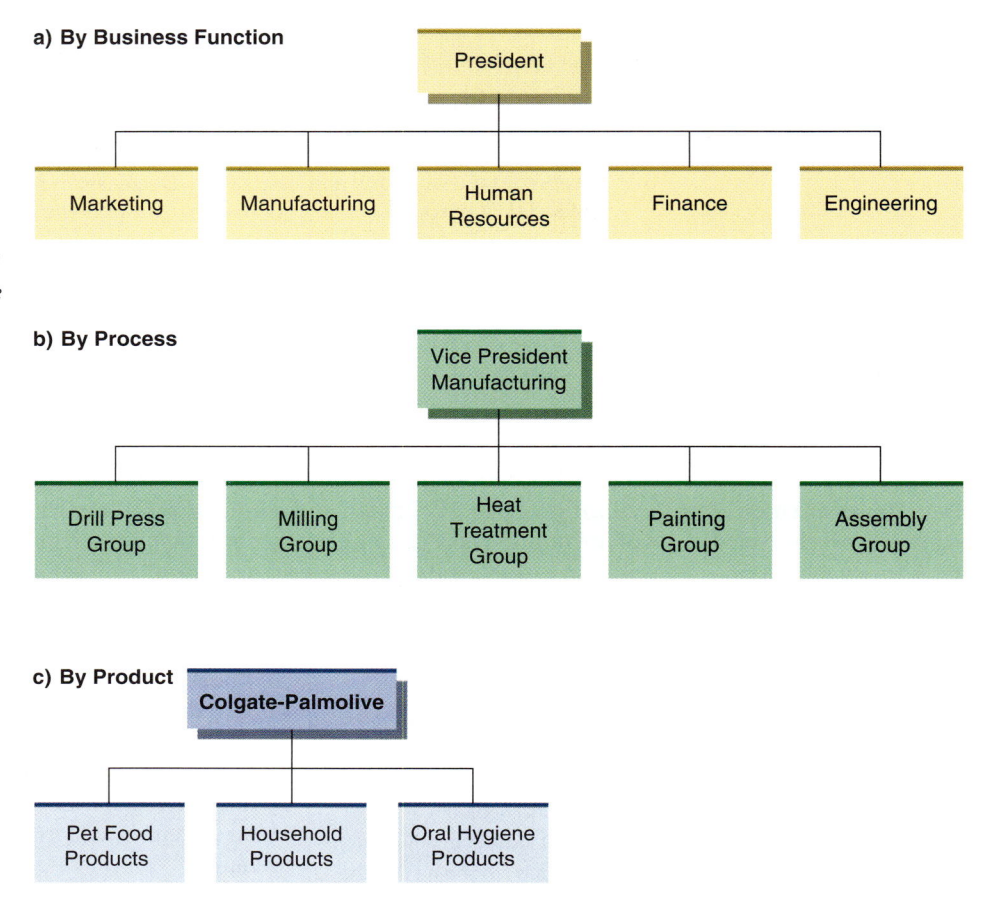

a) By Business Function

President
- Marketing
- Manufacturing
- Human Resources
- Finance
- Engineering

b) By Process

Vice President Manufacturing
- Drill Press Group
- Milling Group
- Heat Treatment Group
- Painting Group
- Assembly Group

c) By Product

Colgate-Palmolive
- Pet Food Products
- Household Products
- Oral Hygiene Products

---

the organization. The result can be a narrow focus that limits the coordination of work among functional groups, such as when the engineering department fails to provide marketing with product information because it is too busy testing materials to think about sales.

Departmentalization by process is similar to functional departmentalization except the focus is much more on specific jobs grouped according to activity. Thus, as Figure 13.2, *part b*, illustrates, the firm's manufacturing jobs are divided into certain well-defined manufacturing processes: drilling, milling, heat treatment, painting, and assembly. Hospitals often use process departmentalization, grouping the professional employees such as therapists according to the types of treatment they provide. Process groupings encourage specialization and expertise among employees, who tend to concentrate on a single operation and share information with departmental colleagues. A process orientation may develop into an internal career path and managerial hierarchy within the department. For example, a specialist might become the "lead" person for that specialty, such as the lead welder or lead press operator. As in functional grouping, however, narrowness of focus can be a problem in a process group. Employees may become so absorbed in the requirements and execution of their operations that they disregard broader considerations such as overall product flow.[7]

Departmentalization by product or service occurs when employees who work on a particular product or service are members of the same department regardless of their business function or the process in which they engage. Figure 13.2, *part c*, shows a partial product structure of Colgate-Palmolive. Departmentalization according to product or service obviously enhances interaction and communication among employees who produce the same product or service and may reduce coordination problems. In this type of configuration, there may be less process specialization but more specialization in the unique aspects of the specific product or service. The disadvantage is that employees may become so interested in their particular product or service that they miss technological improvements or innovations developed in other departments.

Departmentalization by customer is often called "departmentalization by market." Many lending institutions in Texas, for example, have separate departments for retail, commercial, agriculture, and petroleum loans similar to those shown in Figure 13.3. When significant groups of customers differ substantially from one another, organizing along customer lines may be the most effective way to provide the best product or service possible. This is why hospital nurses are often grouped by the type of illness they handle; the various maladies demand different treatment and specialized knowledge.[8] Deutsche Bank recently changed its organization structure from a regional structure to one based on client groups.[9] With customer departmentalization, there is usually less process specialization because employees must remain flexible to do whatever is necessary to enhance the relationship with customers. This configuration offers the best coordination of work flow to the customer. However, it may isolate employees from others in their special areas of expertise. For example, if each of a company's three metallurgical specialists is assigned to a different market-based group, these individuals are unlikely to have many opportunities to discuss the latest technological advances in metallurgy.

With departmentalization by geography, groups are organized according to a region of the country or world. Sales or marketing groups are often arranged by

FIGURE 13.3

Departmentalization by Customer and by Geographic Region

Departmentalization by customer and by geographic region is often used in marketing or sales departments in order to focus on specific needs or locations of customers.

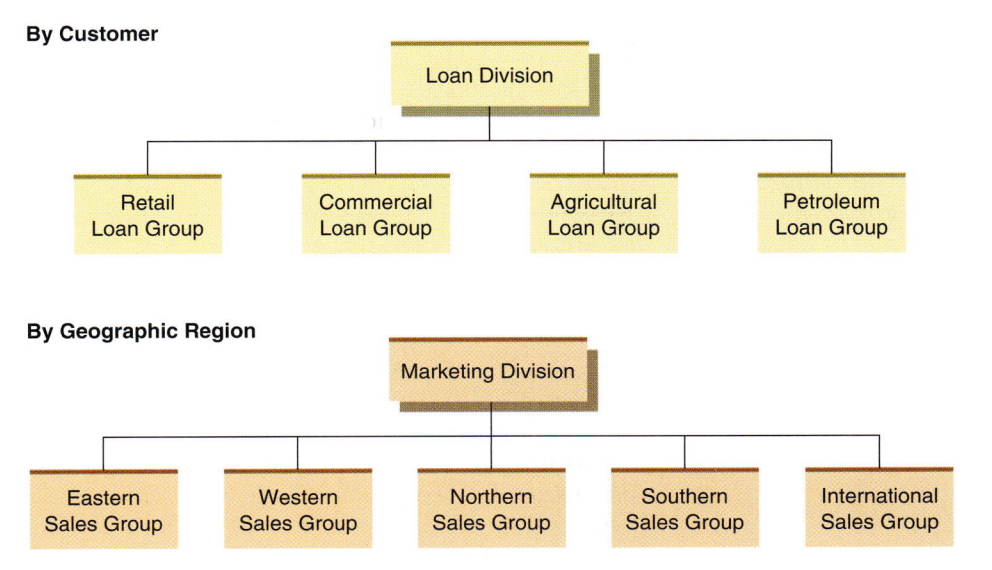

By Customer

- Loan Division
  - Retail Loan Group
  - Commercial Loan Group
  - Agricultural Loan Group
  - Petroleum Loan Group

By Geographic Region

- Marketing Division
  - Eastern Sales Group
  - Western Sales Group
  - Northern Sales Group
  - Southern Sales Group
  - International Sales Group

geographic region. As Figure 13.3 illustrates, the marketing effort of a large multinational corporation can be divided according to major geographical divisions. Using a geographically based configuration may result in significant cost savings and better market coverage. On the other hand, it may isolate work groups from activities in the organization's home office or in the technological community because the focus of the work group is solely on affairs within the region. Such a regional focus may foster loyalty to the work group that exceeds commitment to the larger organization. In addition, work-related communication and coordination among groups may be somewhat inefficient.

Many large organizations use a mixed departmentalization scheme. Such organizations may have separate operating divisions based on products, but within each division departments may be based on business function, process, customers, or geographic region (see Figure 13.4). Which methods work best depends on the organization's activities, communication needs, and coordination requirements. Another type of mixed structure often occurs in joint ventures, which are increasing in number.

Span of Control The second dimension of organizational configuration, **span of control** (or *span of management*), is the number of people reporting to a manager; thus, it defines the size of the organization's work groups. A manager who has a small span of control can maintain close control over workers and stay in contact with daily operations. If the span of control is large, close control is not possible. Figure 13.5 shows examples of large and small spans of control. Supervisors in the

> The **span of control** is the number of people who report to a manager.

FIGURE 13.4

Mixed Departmentalization

A mixed departmentalization scheme is often used in very large organizations with more complex structures. Headquarters is organized based on products. Industrial products and consumer products are departmentalized on the basis of function. The manufacturing department is based on process. Sales is based on customers. Marketing is based on geographical regions.

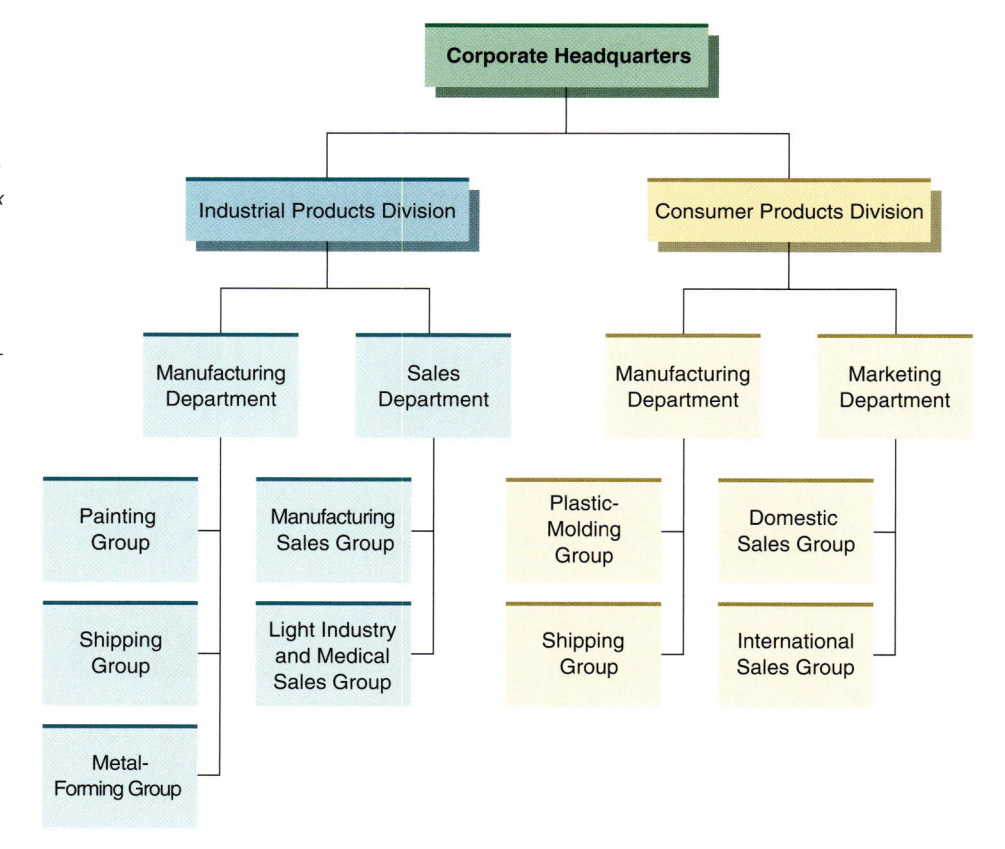

Chapter 13 Organization Design

Large Span of Control

Span of Control = 16
Number of Levels in the Hierarchy = 2

Small Span of Control

Span of Control = 8
Number of Levels in the Hierarchy = 3

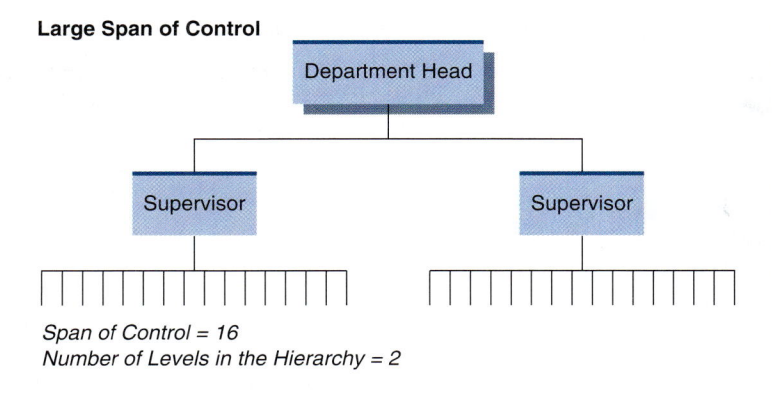

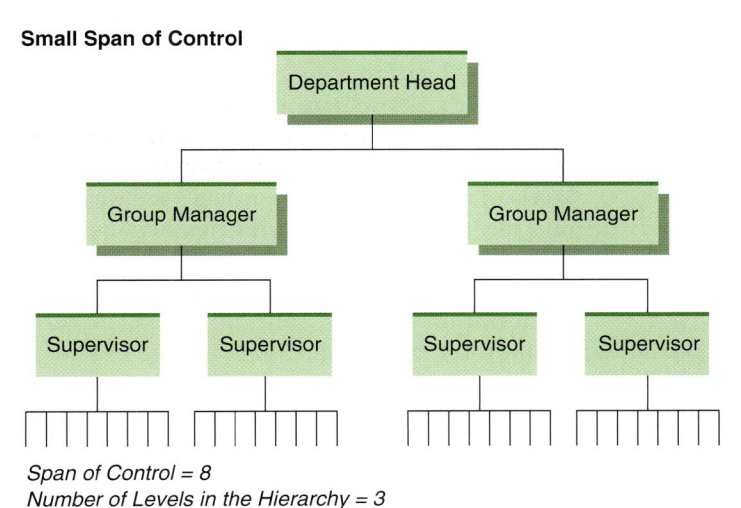

FIGURE 13.5

Span of Control and Levels in the Administrative Hierarchy

These charts show how span of control and the number of levels in the administrative hierarchy are inversely related. The thirty-two first-level employees are in two groups of sixteen in the top chart and in four groups of eight at the bottom chart. Either may be appropriate depending on the work situation.

The **administrative hierarchy** is the system of reporting relationships in the organization, from the lowest to the highest managerial levels.

upper portion of the figure have a span of control of sixteen, whereas those in the lower portion have a span of control of eight.

A number of formulas and rules have been offered for determining the optimal span of control in an organization, but research on the topic has not conclusively identified a foolproof method.[10] Henry Mintzberg concluded that the optimal unit size, or span of control, depends on five conditions:

1. The coordination requirements within the unit, including factors such as the degree of job specialization
2. The similarity of tasks in the unit
3. The type of information available or needed by unit members
4. Differences in members' need for autonomy
5. The extent to which members need direct access to the supervisor[11]

For example, a span of control of sixteen (Figure 13.5) may be appropriate for a supervisor in a typical manufacturing plant in which experienced workers do repetitive production tasks. On the other hand, a span of control of eight or fewer (Figure 13.5) may be suitable in a job shop or custom-manufacturing facility in which workers do many different things and the tasks and problems that arise are new and unusual.[12]

Administrative Hierarchy The **administrative hierarchy** is the system of reporting relationships in the organization, from the first level up through the president or CEO. It results from the need for supervisors and managers to coordinate the activities of employees. The size of the administrative hierarchy is inversely related to the span of control: Organizations with a small span of control have many managers in the hierarchy; those with a large span of control have a smaller administrative hierarchy. Companies often rearrange their administrative hierarchies to achieve more efficient operations. Using Figure 13.5 again, we can examine the effects of small and large spans of control on the number of hierarchical levels. The smaller span of control for the supervisors in the lower portion of the figure requires that there be four supervisors rather than two. Correspondingly, another management layer is needed to keep the department head's span of control at two. Thus, when the span of control is small, workers are under tighter supervision and more administrative levels exist. When the span of control is large, as in the upper portion of the figure, production workers are not closely supervised and fewer administrative levels exist. Because it measures the number of

Managing the organization culture requires attention to three factors. First, managers can take advantage of cultural values that already exist and use their knowledge to help subordinates understand them. Second, employees need to be properly socialized, or trained, in the organization's cultural values, either through formal training or by experiencing and observing the actions of higher-level managers. Third, managers can change the culture of the organization through managing the symbols, addressing the extreme difficulties of such a change, and relying on the durability of the new organization culture once the change has been implemented.

Discussion Questions

1. A sociologist or an anthropologist might suggest that the culture in U.S. firms simply reflects the dominant culture of the society as a whole. Therefore, to change the organization culture of a company, one must first deal with the inherent values and beliefs of the society. How would you respond to this claim?
2. Psychology has been defined as the study of individual behavior. Organizational psychology is the study of individual behavior in organizations. Many of the theories described in the early chapters of this book are based in organizational psychology. Why was this field not identified as a contributor to the study of organization culture along with anthropology, sociology, social psychology, and economics?
3. Describe the culture of an organization with which you are familiar—one in which you currently work, one in which you have worked, or one in which a friend or family member works. What values, beliefs, stories, and symbols are significant to employees of the organization?
4. Discuss the similarities and differences between the organization culture approaches of Ouchi and those of Peters and Waterman.
5. Describe how organizations use symbols and stories to communicate values and beliefs. Give some examples of how symbols and stories have been used in organizations with which you are familiar.
6. What is the role of leadership (discussed in Chapters 10 and 11) in developing, maintaining, and changing organization culture?
7. Review the characteristics of organization structure described in earlier chapters, and compare them with the elements of culture described by Ouchi and Peters and Waterman. Describe the similarities and differences, and explain how some characteristics of one may be related to characteristics of the other.
8. Discuss the role of organization rewards in developing, maintaining, and changing the organization culture.
9. Explain how culture and climate in organizations are similar and how they differ.
10. Describe how the culture of an organization can affect innovation.

Organizational Behavior Case for Discussion

Southwest Airlines: Flying High with Culture

It was a move that had been widely anticipated but dreaded: the resignation of a popular leader who had propelled his company to the forefront of its highly competitive industry. In June 2001, Southwest Airlines' founder, CEO, president, and chairman, seventy-year-old Herb Kelleher, stepped down, keeping only his chairman position. (Kelleher also maintains an active involvement in the firm by serving as a sort of "community ambassador.") In his place, Colleen Barrett assumed the roles of president and chief operating officer while James A. Parker tackled the CEO job. Although observers had confidence in the abilities of both Parker and Barrett—they have almost sixty years of combined experience at Southwest and were handpicked by Kelleher—there was concern that Southwest might lose its culture along with its flamboyant founder.

But such fears proved to be unfounded. Kelleher says, "We wanted to be sure the culture of Southwest Airlines would continue." Southwest has a strong culture that produces loyal and motivated employees, leading to high organization performance. The airline has worked to nurture its culture since Kelleher's resignation, starting with the appointment of the two insiders to the top positions. After the September 11, 2001, terrorist attacks, many airlines laid off workers, but Southwest chose not to do so. However, workers insisted on helping the company maintain profitability: some volunteered to mow lawns, while others worked "off the clock." When asked how the firm achieves such unity, Barrett answers, "It's a matter of getting buy-in from each new hire; making [ours] a culture they want to be part of. We want [employees] to start thinking in terms of 'we' immediately. You have a lot of mentoring going on, a lot of coaching, and a lot of storytelling."

Another Southwest value is "doing your own thing," even if that means overturning conventional wisdom. Kelleher's vision for the firm was a no-frills operation, with repetitive, short-haul flights and no seat assignments or food service. Unlike other airlines, Southwest sells tickets only on its own website. Parker claims, "Independence is the way we do things. Customers are not surprised when we do something different. They expect that." He adds that other airlines have tried to mimic Southwest's culture and practices but have failed. He explains, "They want to be Southwest, but they also want to assign seats, or offer a first class or serve hot meals. We've been very disciplined about what we are, and we stick to it, evolving with our vision." Barrett advises cultural copycats, "[Don't] mimic anybody. If you want a culture that's similar [to ours,] . . . you have to hold people accountable to whatever you want your core values to be."

Parker and Barrett will work together to help maintain the company, and the culture, that Herb Kelleher built. When asked if filling Kelleher's shoes will be difficult, Barrett replies, "Herb is who Herb is. Anyone who would even think they were going to emulate that would be crazy." Parker also acknowledges his indebtedness to Kelleher: "One thing I'll always think about is 'What would Herb do?' . . . This is a superb company that has been successful. My challenge is just [not to] screw it up."

Case Questions

1. Using the Ouchi framework, describe the organization culture of Southwest Airlines. (Hint: Use Table 14.2 of the chapter.) Address each of the seven cultural values. Is Southwest Airlines more like a Type Z firm or like a typical U.S. firm. Why?
2. What are the advantages of Southwest Airlines' culture for the firm? What are the disadvantages? In your opinion, is there anything that managers at Southwest Airlines can do to lessen or eliminate the disadvantages?
3. What have managers at Southwest Airlines done to make sure the culture continues since Herb Kelleher's departure? Do you think that is enough? What more, if anything, could they do?

References: Erika Rasmusson, "Flying High," *Sales and Marketing Management*, December 2001, p. 55 (quotation); Shaun McKinnon, "New Faces, Old Methods," *Arizona Republic* (Phoenix), July 29, 2001, pp. D1, D11 (see www.azcentral.com; Wendy Zellner, "Southwest: After Kelleher, More Blue Skies," *BusinessWeek*, April 2, 2001, p. 45 (see www.businessweek.com).

Experiencing Organizational Behavior
Culture of the Classroom

Purpose: This exercise will help you appreciate the fascination as well as the difficulty of examining culture in organizations.

Format: The class will divide into groups of four to six. Each group will analyze the organization culture of a college class. Students in most classes that use this book will have taken many courses at the college they attend and therefore should have several classes in common.

Procedure:

1. Each group first decides which class it will analyze. (Each person in the group must have attended the class.)
2. Each group lists the cultural factors to be discussed. Items to be covered should include
   a. Stories about the professor
   b. Stories about the exams
   c. Stories about the grading
   d. Stories about other students
   e. The use of symbols that indicate the students' values
   f. The use of symbols that indicate the instructor's values
   g. Other characteristics of the class as suggested by the frameworks of Ouchi and Peters and Waterman

3. Students carefully analyze the stories and symbols to discover their underlying meanings. They should seek stories from other members of the group to ensure that all aspects of the class culture are covered. Students should take notes as these items are discussed
4. After twenty to thirty minutes of work in groups, the instructor will reconvene the entire class and ask each group to share its analysis with the rest of the class.

Follow-up Questions

1. What was the most difficult part of this exercise? Did other groups experience the same difficulty?
2. How did your group overcome this difficulty? How did other groups overcome it?
3. Do you believe your group's analysis accurately describes the culture of the class you selected? Could other students who analyzed the culture of the same class come up with a very different result? How could that happen?
4. If the instructor wanted to try to change the culture in the class you analyzed, what steps would you recommend he or she take?

Self-Assessment Exercise

Assessing Your Preference for Organization Culture

Instructions: Using the 1–5 scale shown below, rate the extent to which you agree or disagree with each statement.

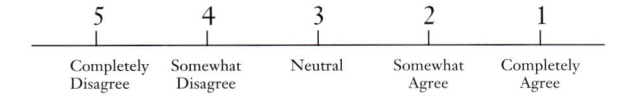

```
  5              4           3         2            1
Completely   Somewhat    Neutral   Somewhat   Completely
Disagree     Disagree              Agree      Agree
```

_____ 1. I want to work for a company that can guarantee me a job for the rest of my life.
_____ 2. I prefer to be evaluated very often on very measurable, or quantitative, factors.
_____ 3. I want a career in which I can stay in one area of the company and progress within that area.
_____ 4. I like a job where it is clear exactly what I am supposed to do and how to do it.
_____ 5. I want a job where I make the decisions without having to ask my work group or colleagues.
_____ 6. I want a job where I take personal and individual responsibility for work outcomes.
_____ 7. My ideal place to work would be where the only issue is whether I do my job and there is no concern for my personal life.
_____ = Total Score is the sum of your score on each of the seven items.

Interpretation: Total scores can range from 5 to 35 and are based on Ouchi's three types of firms. If your score is high (25–35), you prefer an organization culture that is most like the typical U.S. firms; if your score is low (5–15), you prefer an organization culture that is most like the Japanese companies; if your score is in the middle (15–25), you prefer an organization culture most like the Type Z U.S. firms.

Note: This brief instrument has not been scientifically validated and is to be used for classroom discussion purposes only.

OB Online

1. As you near graduation, you may become interested in interviewing for a job you can take after graduation. Pick several companies that appeal to you. Rank-order the companies in the sequence in which you would choose them (at least at this point). Then, starting from the top, search the Internet for articles on the management of each company, specifically for articles that describe something about the company's culture. Not all companies have articles describing their culture, so it may take several tries to find articles that do. Remember, an article that has a description of an organization's culture may not always use the word *culture*, so read carefully.
2. Describe the kinds of information you were able to locate. How much valuable information on culture did the articles provide?
3. What other information do you need to better understand the cultures of these companies?
4. Would you change your initial preference ranking based on the information you found? Why or why not?

Building Managerial Skills

Exercise Overview: Typically managers are promoted or selected to fill jobs in an organization with a given organization culture. As they begin to work, they must recognize the culture and either learn how to work within it or figure out how to change it. If the culture is a performance-reducing one, managers must figure out how to change it to a performance-enhancing culture. This exercise will give you a chance to develop your own ideas about changing organization culture.

Exercise Background: Assume you have just been appointed to head the legislative affairs committee of your local student government. As someone with a double major in business management and government, you are eager to take on this assignment and really make a difference. This committee has existed at your university for several years, but it has done little because members use the committee as a social group and regularly throw big parties. In all the years of its existence, the committee has done nothing to influence the local state legislature in relation to the issues important to university students, such as tuition. Since you know the issue of university tuition will come before the state legislature during the current legislative session, and you know many students could not afford a substantial raise in tuition, you are determined to use this committee to ensure that any tuition increase is as small as possible. However, you are worried that the party culture of the existing committee may make it difficult for you to use it to work for your issues. You also know you cannot "fire" any of the volunteers on the committee and can add only two people to the committee.

Exercise Task: Using this information as context, do the following:

1. Design a strategy for utilizing the existing culture of the committee to help you affect the legislature regarding tuition.
2. Assuming the existing culture is a performance-reducing culture, design a strategy for changing it to a performance-enhancing culture.

TEST PREPPER

ACE self-test

You have read the chapter and studied the key terms, and the exam is any day now. Think you're ready to ace it? Take this sample test to gauge your comprehension of chapter material. You can check your answers at the back of the book. Want more test questions? Visit the student website at http://college.hmco.com/business/students/ (select Griffin/Moorhead, Fundamentals of Organizational Behavior 1e) and take the ACE quizzes for more practice.

1. **T F** Microsoft's culture changed dramatically once Bill Gates resigned as chief executive officer.
2. **T F** Organization culture may be communicated through stories some authors call "myths" and "fairy tales."
3. **T F** The study of organization culture reflects the approaches of anthropology, sociology, social psychology, and economics.
4. **T F** An organization's history and traditions are apparent in its climate.
5. **T F** Basic beliefs about an organization's environment and its own capabilities form the organization's strategic values.
6. **T F** The formal reward system in an organization is probably not a good way to reinforce desired cultural behaviors.
7. **T F** In U.S. Type Z firms, individual managers are held responsible for decisions made by groups.
8. **T F** In their book *In Search of Excellence*, Peters and Waterman recommend valuing the customer over everything else.
9. **T F** Adding a digital camera to a cell phone is an example of a radical innovation.
10. **T F** The extent to which an organization's decision-making process is judged to be fair is becoming increasingly important to employees in the United States.
11. **T F** Most managers are in a position to create an organization's culture.
12. **T F** Socialization almost always changes the values of individual employees to match the organization's values.
13. **T F** All firms have cultural values that are consistent with high performance.
14. **T F** Changing a culture means changing stories and symbols, not changing people's basic assumptions about what is and what is not appropriate behavior in the organization.
15. **T F** One reason cultural values are difficult to change is that they are self-reinforcing.
16. When Bill Gates resigned as CEO of Microsoft and Steve Ballmer, who had been president, assumed the top role,
    - a. the company's culture remained essentially the same.
    - b. the company softened its aggressive, competitive stance.
    - c. hundreds of employees resigned with Gates.
    - d. the federal government dropped its antimonopoly lawsuit against Microsoft.
    - e. Ballmer made it his primary goal to change the company's vision and mission statement.
17. The set of shared values that help people understand which actions are considered acceptable and which unacceptable is called organization
    - a. strategy.
    - b. structure.
    - c. culture.
    - d. mission.
    - e. human resource management.
18. An organization's culture
    - a. is recorded in the company handbook.
    - b. has only a weak influence on organizational members.
    - c. can easily be copied from competitors.
    - d. starts to develop only after the company earns a profit.
    - e. is often taken for granted by organizational members.
19. Jim wants to communicate his company culture to a set of new employees. What approach would likely be most successful?
    - a. Have new employees read the company history.
    - b. Include a description of the culture in the new employee handbook.
    - c. Let the new employees learn the culture on their own.
    - d. Tell stories and give examples.
    - e. Offer a course in social psychology.
20. The current atmosphere in Tiffany's company is rather unpleasant. Despite a history of strong collaboration, for the past week union members have refused to speak with management representatives. This situation reflects the organization's
    - a. culture.
    - b. climate.
    - c. strategy.
    - d. departmentalization.
    - e. structure.

21. The basic beliefs about an organization's environment and its own capabilities are called
    a. cultural values.
    b. structural values.
    c. strategic values.
    d. organization climate.
    e. organizational myths.

22. Tim sees his small business becoming the leader in "providing affordable healthcare to the families of all military veterans by 2010." This represents the organization's
    a. culture.
    b. vision.
    c. climate.
    d. strategy.
    e. values.

23. All of the following will reinforce key cultural behaviors except
    a. formal rewards given for desired behaviors.
    b. stories told throughout the organization about employees who engaged in desired behaviors.
    c. treating all employees similarly regardless of their behaviors.
    d. ceremonies and rituals that emphasize the critical desired behaviors.
    e. All of the above will reinforce key cultural behaviors.

24. Japanese and Type Z U.S. firms have a strong cultural expectation that decision making will occur
    a. in groups.
    b. individually.
    c. by the senior manager.
    d. by the customer.
    e. by strategic partners.

25. Shannon often makes decisions before she has all the facts because she believes that for many important managerial decisions, all the facts will never be in. Which value of Peters and Waterman's approach does this demonstrate?
    a. Productivity through people
    b. Bias for action
    c. Autonomy and entrepreneurship
    d. Hands-on management
    e. Simultaneously loose and tight organization

26. Which of the following explains how managers simultaneously maintain tight and loose organizations?
    a. Competition is so fierce that employees know they must perform well.
    b. Higher pay will prevent employees from quitting.
    c. Human resource laws keep managers from making costly mistakes.
    d. Managers need to understand that most people are good self-managers.
    e. The organization's culture is a strong glue that holds the organization together.

27. Artificial hearts have been in use for more than twenty years, but newer models are self-adjusting. This improvement represents a(n)
    a. radical innovation.
    b. systems innovation.
    c. Type Z innovation.
    d. incremental innovation.
    e. new venture.

28. For managers to take advantage of an existing cultural system, they must first
    a. stick to their knitting.
    b. be fully aware of the culture's values and what behaviors those values support.
    c. maintain a simultaneously loose and tight organization.
    d. communicate their understanding of the culture to lower-level individuals.
    e. allow cultural values to guide their decisions.

29. The process through which employees learn about their firm's culture is called
    a. indoctrination.
    b. intrapreneurship.
    c. stratification.
    d. articulation.
    e. socialization.

30. What is the primary reason culture is so difficult to change?
    a. Culture is easy to change, but the process simply costs too much.
    b. Employees rarely want to change their organization's culture.
    c. Human resource management laws prevent significant cultural changes.
    d. Keeping culture stable almost always ensures better performance.
    e. People sometimes inadvertently revert to old patterns of behavior.

31. Once an organization successfully changes its culture and fully adopts new values, which of the following is likely to happen?
    a. Employees who previously left the organization will return.
    b. Competitors will change their cultures to match the new value system.
    c. Managers will focus on loosening organizational control.
    d. Performance is likely to decline.
    e. The new values will tend to be self-reinforcing.

CHAPTER 15

Organization Change and Development

MANAGEMENT PREVIEW

Companies constantly face pressures to change. Significant decreases in revenues and profits, forecasts of changing economic conditions, consumer purchasing patterns, technological and scientific factors, and competition, both foreign and domestic, can force top management to evaluate the organization and consider significant changes.

This chapter presents several perspectives on change in organizations. First, we examine the forces for change and discuss several approaches to planned organization change. Then we consider organization development processes and the resistance to change that usually occurs. We briefly cover several international and cross-cultural factors that affect organization change processes. Finally, we discuss how to manage organization change and development efforts.

After you have studied this chapter, you should be able to:
- ☐ *Summarize four dominant forces for change in organizations.*
- ☐ *Describe the process of planned organization change as a continuous process.*
- ☐ *Discuss several approaches to organization development.*
- ☐ *Explain organizational and individual sources of resistance to change.*
- ☐ *Identify six keys to managing successful organization change and development.*

We begin with a look at how one CEO has changed a small water company in France into a media and entertainment giant.

In 1996, when Jean-Marie Messier was named chairman of the French conglomerate Compagnie Générale des Eaux, the appointing board did not anticipate the wild ride of changes that were in store for the tradition-bound firm. CGE, which roughly translates as the "General Water Company," has a proud history. It was founded in 1853 by decree of Emperor Napoleon III, nephew of Napoleon I, to sell municipal water to Lyons. For more than one hundred years, the firm expanded slowly into other utilities, such as waste management and energy. It began to move into cable and other media ventures, and in 1988 changed its name to Vivendi to reflect its growing diversification.

Messier began with reorganization, creating two divisions—environment and communications—and selling all other assets. The CEO then made an aggressive series of acquisitions to move the company into the entertainment and consumer products industries, forming four divisions: music, publishing, TV and film, and Internet. The conglomerate soon had acquired more than three hundred companies and brands, artistic management and production enterprises, and entertainment products. Among the recognizable names on its roster were *American Pie, A Beautiful Mind,* Blink 182, Crash Bandicoot video games, Curious George children's books, *E.T.,* Elton John, Enrique Iglesias, George Strait, Houghton Mifflin Company (which publishes this textbook), the *Jerry Springer Show,* Jump Start educational software, *Jurassic Park, Law and Order,* Limp Bizkit, Mary J. Blige, MCA Records, Motown Records, mp3.com, tenor Placido Domingo, *Rolling Stone* magazine, the Sci-Fi Channel, Spencer Gifts, *The Mummy,* U2, Universal Studios and Theme Parks, the USA Network, and European web portal Vivazzi. Messier said, "For the first time in five years, we can now say that there are no parts missing in the strategy."

Some were skeptical of Vivendi's phenomenal growth during Messier's tenure as CEO. In spite of a $30.8 billion acquisition-related debt, synergies among units were slow to develop. European companies have a poor track record in American media. And the company's hands-off management style, promised as part of many of its acquisition deals, could lead to a problematic lack of corporate control. Messier tangled with the French government, refusing to pay particularly high telecom licensing fees. When Messier fired several low-performing but top-level managers, he was accused of ruining a French "national treasure" (Canal1, a French cable system). Messier also battled government labor regulations, including a mandatory 35-hour workweek.

Europeans resented what some regard as the "Americanization" of Messier and Vivendi. Ever since his public service days, when he championed privatization of French industries, Messier was accused of promoting "Anglo-Saxon capitalism." The contention is well founded. Vivendi shifted to American accounting principles to make the company more transparent and acceptable to American investors. Messier, who speaks perfect English, calls himself "the most un-French Frenchman you'll ever meet." When he received the French Legion of Honor, the typically elegant and dull event was transformed into a gaudy multimedia show. French society reacted with shock and outrage—exactly what Messier intended, his supporters said. Expressing a sentiment more American than French, Messier claimed, "It's rare to have a CEO who succeeds in expressing his personal emotions. That's the way I am, and it's too late to change myself." It is unclear how, or if, Messier will overcome his problems, which, according to *BusinessWeek* writer Ron Grover, include the fact that "he isn't American enough to satisfy U.S. investors[,] . . . and he isn't French enough to satisfy the hometown crew, who worry that he has gone Hollywood."

In 2002, Messier was forced to step down as head of Vivendi as his strategy collapsed around him and Vivendi posted a net loss of $18.8 billion in that year. Without Messier, and after selling off many of the acquisitions he had made (including Houghton Mifflin), Vivendi posted a net loss of $1.41 billion in 2003. The company continues to change rapidly and is likely to continue to make changes for several more years.

> *"It's rare to have a CEO who succeeds in expressing his personal emotions. That's the way I am, and it's too late to change myself."*—Jean-Marie Messier, former CEO of Vivendi

References: "2001—The Year in Brief," "Company Profile," "Executive Bio," "Our Leaders," "The Group History," "What We Do," Vivendi website, www.vivendiuniversal.com on June 22, 2002; Janet Guyon, "Getting Messier by the Minute," *Fortune*, June 10, 2002, www.fortune.com on June 22, 2002; Ron Glover, "A Loser's Race for Media Moguls," *BusinessWeek*, June 6, 2002, www.businessweek.com on June 22, 2002; Geoffrey Colvin, "Culture in Peril? Mais Oui!" *Fortune*, May 13, 2002, www.fortune.com on June 22, 2002; Richard Tomlinson, "The Nouveau CEO," *Fortune*, December 10, 2001, www.fortune.com on June 22, 2002; Devin Leonard, "Mr. Messier Is Ready for His Close-Up," *Fortune*, September 3, 2001 (quotation), www.fortune.com on June 22, 2002; "What Really Brought Messier Down," *BusinessWeek*, July 15, 2002, p. 106; "Vivendi Slowly Emerging from Two Years of Turmoil," *Amusement Business*, March 29, 2004, pp. 5–6.

Chapter 15 Organization Change and Development

Jean-Marie Messier made many changes at Vivendi that he thought were necessary given his vision of what the strategy for the company should be. This was not a turnaround situation for a company in trouble; rather, Messier's view of what the company should be to maximize shareholder wealth was the trigger for his changes. Undoubtedly, Messier saw opportunities in the environment that matched the capabilities of the organization and sought to exploit them. However, both the changes Messier made and the ways in which he made them met with great resistance. The situation at Vivendi illustrates many key issues regarding change in organizations.

Forces for Change

LEARNING OBJECTIVE

Summarize four dominant forces for change in organizations.

An organization faces pressures for change from numerous sources—far too many to cover in our discussion here. Moreover, it is difficult to predict what types of pressures for change will be most significant in the next decade because the complexity of events and the rapidity of change are increasing. In this section, we look at four broad categories of pressures most likely to have major effects on organizations: people, technology, information processing and communication, and competition. Table 15.1 gives examples of each category.

People

Approximately 56 million people were born between 1945 and 1960. These baby boomers differ significantly from previous generations with respect to education, expectations, and value systems.[1] As this group has aged, the median age of the U.S. population has gradually increased, passing 32 for the first time in 1988[2] and further increasing to 35.6 in 1999.[3] The special characteristics of baby boomers show up in distinct purchasing patterns that affect product and service innovation, technological change, and marketing and promotional activities.[4] Employment

TABLE 15.1

Pressures for Organization Change

Category	Examples	Type of Pressure for Change
People	Generation X Baby boomers Senior citizens Workforce diversity	Demands for different training, benefits, workplace arrangements, and compensation systems
Technology	Manufacturing in space Internet Artificial Intelligence	More education and training for workers at all levels, more new products, products move faster to market
Information Processing and Communication	Computer, satellite communications Videoconferencing	Faster reaction times, immediate responses to questions, new products, different office arrangements, telecommuting
Competition	Worldwide markets International trade agreements Emerging nations	Global competition, more competing products with more features and options, lower costs, higher quality

practices, compensation systems, promotion and managerial succession systems, and the entire concept of human resource management are also affected.

Other population-related pressures for change involve the generations that sandwich the baby boomers: the increasing numbers of senior citizens and those born after 1960. The parents of the baby boomers are living longer, healthier lives than previous generations, and today they expect to live the "good life" they missed when they were raising their children. The impact of the large number of senior citizens is already evident in part-time employment practices; in the marketing of everything from hamburgers to packaged tours of Asia; and in service areas such as health care, recreation, and financial services. The post-1960 generation of workers who are entering the job market also differ from the baby boomers. These changes in demographics extend to the composition of the workforce, family lifestyles, and purchasing patterns worldwide. The World View box depicts the makeover of Avon in response to changes in the population and workforce.

Technology

Not only is technology changing, but the rate of technological change is also increasing. In 1970, for example, all engineering students owned slide rules and used

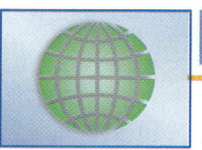

WORLD VIEW

A Makeover at Avon

What could possibly be more dated than the 1950s version of the Avon Lady, perfectly dressed down to her white gloves, ringing doorbells on weekday mornings to sell lipstick and perfume to stay-at-home moms? "Ding-dong. Avon calling." Yet today, thanks to savvy business moves by CEO Andrea Jung, the retailer is thriving, and so is the Avon Lady.

Today's Avon Lady is likely to be a young professional woman who supplements her income by selling products ranging from perfume and cosmetics to exercise equipment and vitamins to both men and women. She profits not only from sales but also from recruitment bonuses she earns for attracting new representatives, and she uses the Internet to find customers, place orders, and advertise. All of these changes were either introduced or advanced by Jung, who took the CEO role in 2000. Her other strategies for change include selling a new line of cosmetics in mall kiosks and at JCPenney under the brand name Becoming and focusing more on the international market, where 62 percent of the firm's sales occur.

Jung, the first woman to head Avon, has teamed with president Susan Kropf to improve back-office operations, reducing costs in R&D, purchasing, and logistics while also getting innovative products to market faster. Jung and Kropf agree that a female executive has only a minor advantage in the glamour industry. "You go home and try on a new mascara, and I guess a male CEO can't do that," Jung wryly notes. Kropf points out, "Maybe, on the periphery, there is a greater personal affinity for the products we sell. [But] in terms of leadership, the strategy, the disciplines, [and] the analytical rigor, it doesn't matter if you're a man, woman, dog, or cat. There is no gender consideration."

The two leaders do believe, however, that their gender allows them to relate well to the company's 500,000 representatives, the majority of whom are female. Jung asserts, "[Women] see that the glass ceiling has been broken at Avon."

References: "Let's Talk About Avon," Avon website, www.avoncompany.com on June 18, 2002; Diane Brady, "A Makeover Has Avon Looking Good," *BusinessWeek*, January 22, 2002, www.businessweek.com on June 18, 2002; Patricia O'Connell, "Meet the Avon Ladies-in-Chief," *BusinessWeek*, January 22, 2002, www.businessweek.com on June 18, 2002; Katrina Booker, "It Took a Lady to Save Avon," *Fortune*, October 15, 2001, pp. 202–208 (see www.fortune.com); Jennifer Pellet, "Ding-dong Avon Stalling?" *Chief Executive*, June 2000, pp. 26–31 (see www.chiefexecutive.net).

them in almost every class. By 1976, slide rules had given way to portable electronic calculators. In the mid-1980s, some universities began issuing microcomputers to entering students or assumed those students already owned one. In 1993, the Scholastic Aptitude Test (SAT), which many college-bound students take to get into college, allowed the use of calculators during the test. Today students cannot make it through college without owning or at least having ready access to a personal computer. At many universities, dorm rooms are wired for direct computer access for email and class assignments and for connection to the Internet. Now that buildings, hotels, and cafes are also wireless, anyone can hook up to the Internet just about anywhere. Technological development is increasing so rapidly in almost every field that it is quite difficult to predict which products will dominate ten years from now.

Interestingly, organization change is self-perpetuating. With the advances in information technology, organizations generate more information that circulates more quickly. Consequently employees can respond more rapidly to problems, enabling organizations to respond more quickly to demands from other organizations, customers, and competitors.[5]

Cell phone giants such as Nokia, Motorola, and Erikson have had a stranglehold on the worldwide cellular phone market. All three have major operations in China, manufacturing and selling in Asia as well as the rest of the world. That world is changing fast, however. The new competition may soon be from Chinese companies. More than thirty Chinese companies now manufacture cellular phones and work with software providers Microsoft and Qualcomm Inc. to develop much lower-priced handsets. Nokia and others had better watch out!

Information Processing and Communication

Advances in information processing and communication have paralleled each other. A new generation of computers, which will mark another major increase in processing power, is being designed. Satellite systems for data transmission are already in use. Today people carry their telephone, portable computer, music player, and pager all in one instrument.

In the future, people may not need offices as they work with computers and communicate through new data transmission devices. Workstations, both in and outside of offices, are more electronic than paper and pencil. For years the capability has existed to generate, manipulate, store, and transmit more data than managers could use, but the benefits were not fully realized. Now the time has come to utilize all of this information processing potential, and companies are making the most of it. Typically companies received orders by mail in the 1970s, by toll-free telephone numbers in the 1980s, by fax machine in the late 1980s and early 1990s, and by electronic data exchange in the mid-1990s. Orders used to take a week; now they are placed instantaneously, and companies must be able to respond immediately, because of advances in information processing and communication.[6]

Competition

Although competition is not a new force for change, competition today has some significant new twists. First, most markets are international because of decreasing transportation and communication costs and the increasing export orientation of business. The adoption of trade agreements such as the North American Free Trade Agreement (NAFTA) and the presence of the World Trade Organization (WTO) have changed the way business operates. Competition from industrialized countries such as Japan and Germany are taking a back seat to competition from the booming industries of developing nations. The Internet is creating new competitors overnight and in ways unimaginable just a decade ago. Companies in developing nations are offering different, newer, cheaper, or higher-quality products and services while enjoying the benefits of low labor costs, abundant supplies of raw materials, expertise in certain areas of production, and financial protection from their governments that may not be available to firms in older industrialized states.

Planned Organization Change

LEARNING OBJECTIVE
Describe the process of planned organization change as a continuous process.

External forces may impose change on an organization. Ideally, however, the organization will not only respond to change but will anticipate it, prepare for it through planning, and incorporate it in the organization strategy. Organization change can be viewed from a static point of view, such as that of Lewin (see the next section), or from a dynamic perspective.

Lewin's Process Model

Planned organization change requires a systematic process of movement from one condition to another. Kurt Lewin suggested that efforts to bring about planned change in organizations should approach change as a multistage process.[7] His model of planned change consists of three steps—unfreezing, change, and refreezing—as shown in Figure 15.1

Unfreezing is the process by which people become aware of the need for change. If people are satisfied with current practices and procedures, they may have little or no interest in making changes. The key factor in unfreezing is making employees understand the importance of a change and how it will affect their jobs. The employees who will be most affected by the change must be made aware of why it is needed, which in effect makes them dissatisfied enough with current operations to be motivated to change. **Change** itself is the movement from the old way of doing things to a new way. Change may entail installing new equipment, restructuring the organization, implementing a new performance appraisal system—anything that alters existing relationships or activities. **Refreezing** makes new behaviors relatively permanent and resistant to further change. Examples of refreezing techniques include repeating newly learned skills in a training session and role playing to teach how the new skill can be used in a real-life work situation. Refreezing is necessary because without it, the old ways of doing things may soon resurface while the new ways are forgotten. For example, many employees who attend special training sessions apply themselves diligently and resolve to change things in their organizations. When they return to the workplace, however, they find it easier to conform to the old ways than to make waves. There are usually few, if any, rewards for trying to

Unfreezing is the process of becoming aware of the need for change.

Change is the movement from an old way of doing things to a new way. This may be the adoption of any new idea, process, or procedure that requires organizational participants to alter how they do their jobs.

Refreezing is the process of making new behaviors relatively permanent and resistant to further change.

```
┌──────────┐   ┌──────────────┐   ┌──────────────┐   ┌──────────────┐   ┌──────────┐
│          │   │   Unfreeze   │   │    Change    │   │   Refreeze   │   │          │
│ Old State│ → │ (Awareness of│ → │(Movement from│ → │(Assurance of │ → │ New State│
│          │   │   Need for   │   │ Old State to │   │  Permanent   │   │          │
│          │   │   Change)    │   │  New State)  │   │   Change)    │   │          │
└──────────┘   └──────────────┘   └──────────────┘   └──────────────┘   └──────────┘
```

FIGURE 15.1

Lewin's Process of Organization Change

In Lewin's three-step model, change is a systematic process of transition from an old way of doing things to a new way. Inclusion of an unfreezing stage indicates the importance of preparing for the change. A refreezing stage reflects the importance of following up on the change to make it permanent..

change the organizational status quo; in fact, the personal sanctions against doing so may be difficult to tolerate. Learning theory and reinforcement theory (see Chapter 4) can play important roles in the refreezing phase.

The Continuous Change Process Model

Perhaps because Lewin's model is very simple and straightforward, virtually all models of organization change use his approach. However, it does not deal with several important issues. A more complex, and more helpful, approach is illustrated in Figure 15.2. This approach treats planned change from the perspective of top management and indicates that change is continuous. Although we discuss each step as if it were distinct from the others, it is important to note that as organization change becomes continuous, different steps probably occur simultaneously throughout the organization. The model incorporates Lewin's concept into the implementation phase.

In this approach, top management perceives that certain forces or trends call for change, and the issue is subjected to the organization's usual problem-solving and decision-making processes (see Chapter 12). Usually top management defines its goals in terms of what the organization or certain processes or outputs will be like after the change. Alternatives for change are generated and evaluated, and an acceptable one is selected.

Early in the process, the organization may seek the assistance of a **change agent,** a person who will be responsible for managing the change effort. The change agent may also help management recognize and define the problem or the need for the change, and may be involved in generating and evaluating potential plans of action. The change agent may be a member of the organization, an outsider such as a consultant, or even someone from headquarters whom employees view as an outsider. An internal change agent is likely to know the organization's people, tasks, and political situations, which may be helpful in interpreting data and understanding the system; however, an insider may also be too close to the situation to view it objectively. (In addition, a regular employee would have to be removed from normal duties to concentrate on the transition.) An outsider, then, is often received better by all parties because of his or her assumed impartiality. Under the direction and management of the change agent, the organization implements the change through Lewin's unfreeze–change–refreeze process.

A **change agent** is a person responsible for managing a change effort.

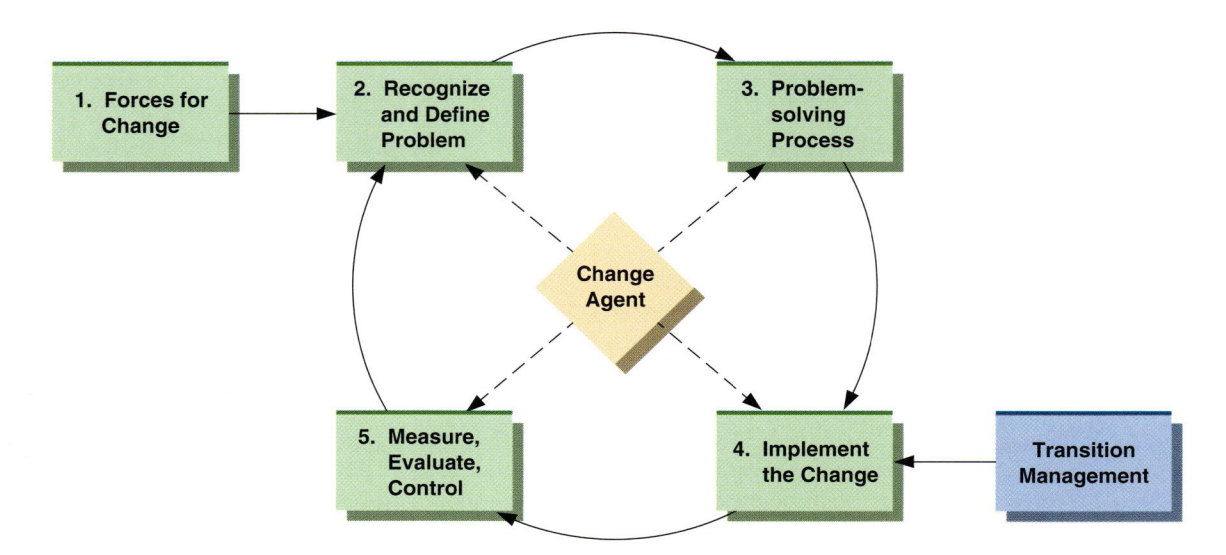

FIGURE 15.2

Continuous Change Process Model of Organization Change

The continuous change process model incorporates the forces for change, a problem-solving process, a change agent, and transition management. It takes a top management perspective and highlights the fact that in today's organizations change is a continuous process.

The final step is measurement, evaluation, and control. The change agent and the top management group assess the degree to which the change is having the desired effect; that is, they measure progress toward the goals of the change and make appropriate adjustments if necessary. The more closely the change agent is involved in the change process, the less distinct the steps become. The change agent becomes a "collaborator" or "helper" to the organization as she or he delves into defining and solving the problem with members of the organization. When this happens, the change agent may be working with many individuals, groups, and departments within the organization on different phases of the change process. When the change process is moving along from one stage to another, it may not be readily observable due to the total involvement of the change agent in every phase of the project. Throughout the process, however, the change agent brings in new ideas and viewpoints that help members look at old problems in new ways. Change often arises from the conflict that results when the change agent challenges the organization's assumptions and generally accepted patterns of operation.

Through the measurement, evaluation, and control phase, top management determines the effectiveness of the change process by evaluating various indicators of organizational productivity, effectiveness, and employee morale. It is hoped that the organization will be better after the change than before. However, the uncertainties and rapid change in all sectors of the environment make constant organization change a certainty for most organizations.

Transition management is the process of systematically planning, organizing, and implementing change, from the disassembly of the current state to the realization of a fully functional future state within the organization.[8] Once change begins, the organization is in neither the old state nor the new state, yet business must go on. Transition management ensures that business continues while the

Transition management is the process of systematically planning, organizing, and implementing change.

change is under way; therefore, it must begin before the change occurs. The members of the regular management team must take on the role of transition managers and coordinate organizational activities with the change agent. An interim management structure or interim positions may be created to ensure continuity and control of the business during the transition. Communication about the changes to all involved, from employees to customers and suppliers, plays a key role in transition management.[9]

Organization Development

LEARNING OBJECTIVE
Discuss several approaches to organization development.

Organization development is the process of planned change and improvement of an organization through the application of knowledge of the behavioral sciences. Three points in this definition make it simple to remember and use. First, organization development involves attempts to plan organization changes, which excludes spontaneous, haphazard initiatives. Second, the specific intention of organization development is to improve the organization. This point excludes changes that merely imitate those of another organization, are forced on the organization by external pressures, or are undertaken merely for the sake of changing. Third, the planned improvement must be based on knowledge of behavioral sciences such as organizational behavior, psychology, sociology, cultural anthropology, and related fields of study rather than on financial or technological considerations. The replacement of manual personnel records with a computerized system would not be considered an instance of organization development. Although such a change has behavioral effects, it is a technology-driven reform rather than a behavioral one. Likewise, alterations in recordkeeping to support new government-mandated reporting requirements are not a part of organization development because the change is obligatory and the result of an external force. The most basic types of organization development techniques are systemwide, task and technological, and group and individual.

Organization development is the process of planned change and improvement of the organization through application of knowledge of the behavioral sciences.

Systemwide Organization Development

The most comprehensive type of organization change involves a major reorientation or reorganization, usually referred to as **structural change** or a systemwide rearrangement of task division and authority and reporting relationships. A structural change affects performance appraisal and rewards, decision making, and communication and information processing systems. Reengineering and rethinking the organization are two contemporary approaches to systemwide structural change. Reengineering can be a difficult process, but it has great potential for organizational improvement. It requires that managers challenge long-held assumptions about everything they do, and set outrageous goals and expect they will be met.

Structural change is a systemwide organization development involving a major restructuring of the organization or instituting programs such as quality of work life.

An organization may change the way it divides tasks into jobs, combines jobs into departments and divisions, and arranges authority and reporting relationships among positions. It may move from functional departmentalization to a system based on products or geography, for example, or from a vertical, functional design to a matrix or a team-based design. Other changes may include dividing large groups into smaller ones or merging small groups into larger ones. In addition, the degree to which rules and procedures are written down and enforced, as well as the locus of decision-making authority, may be altered. Supervisors may become "coaches" or "facilitators" in a team-based organization.

Index

Scott, H. Lee, 17, 81
Scott, Larry, 350
Sears, 14, 15
Selective perception, 72
Self-efficacy, 68, 144
Self-esteem, 69
Self-reactions, 318
Semantics, 187
Senge, Peter, 65, 409
Sexual orientation, 45
Shaw, George Bernard, 90
Shell Oil, 45, 131, 409
Sherwood, Kaitlin Duck, 173
Short-term orientation, 41
Showtime, 307
Sidley & Austin, 332
Sidley Austin Brown & Wood, 332
Silicon Graphics, 31
Simon and Schuster, 307
Simond Rolling Machine Company, 6
Simple structure, 358
Sisters of St. Francis, 244
Situational approach, 12 and fig. 1.3
Situational favorableness, 263–264, 264, 265
Situational perspective, 11, 12 and fig. 1.3
Skill-based pay, 230
Skinner, B. F., 105
Small-group networks, patterns of, 181, 182 and fig. 7.4, 183
Smith, Adam, 122, 344
Smith, Debra, 292
Smith, Thomas R., Jr., 332
Snyder, Nancy, 202
Social learning, 109, 144
Social loafing, 209
Social psychology, 371, 372
Social responsibility
    definition of, 20. *See also* Ethics
Socialization, 381
Sociology, 371
Soldiering, 6
Solero, Carlos, 36
Sony, 259, 368
Soupata, Lea, 52
Source, 176, 186, 187
Southwest Airlines, 2, 3, 4, 114, 279, 280, 385, 386
Southwest Airlines: Flying High with Culture (Case study), 385, 386
Span of control
    administrative hierarchy and, 349 and fig. 13.5, 350
    conditions of, 349
    explanation of, 348, 349 and fig. 13.5
Special-project groups, 202, 203
Spencer Gifts, 392
Spokespersons, 16 and table 1.2
Sports Illustrated (magazine), 341
Springfield Remanufacturing, 113, 114
Stack, Jack, 114
Standard Oil of Ohio, 112
Stanford, 300
Starbucks, 300
Status differences, 189
Steers, Benjamin, 193
Stephens, Robertson, 171
Stereotypes
    definition and explanation of, 32
    managers and, 72

Stereotyping, 72
Stern, Carolyn, 126
Stevens, James, 199
Strait, George, 392
Strategic values, 373
Strategy, 354
Stress
    causes of, 74
    consequences of, 74, 75
    definition of, 73
    function of, 73
    general adaptation syndrome and, 73 and fig. 3.4
    managing, 75, 76
    personality profiles and, 73, 74
    stages of, 73 and fig. 3.4
Stressor
    definition of, 73
Stressors
    categories of work-related, 74
Stropki, John, 120
Structural change, 399
Structural imperatives approach
    explanation of, 354 and fig. 13.6
    size and, 354 and fig. 13.6, 355
    technology and, 354 fig. 13.6, 355, 356
Structural inertia, 405
Stuart, Spencer, 52
Suboptimizing, 316
Sun Microsystems, 90
Superleadership, 284
Superordinate goal, 217, 218
Surface value of a reward, 153
Survey feedback, 403–404 and fig. 15.3
Suttle, J. Lloyd, 400
Symbolic value of a reward, 153
Systems innovation, 379

Taco Bell, 254
Tale of Two Cities, A (Dickens), 192
Tale of Two Companies, A (case study), 192, 193
Task environment, 356
Task groups, 202, 203
Task redesign, 400, 401 and table 15.2
Tasks
    judgmental, 326
    problem-solving, 326
    types of, 208 and table 8.2
Taylor, Frederick W., 5, 6, 89, 122
TBS Superstation, 341
Team bonus plans, 231
Team building, 403
Team-level outcomes. *See* Group-level outcomes
Team performance, 242
Teams
    authority and, 230 and table 9.1
    commonalities of, 228, 229
    cost benefits of, 232 and table 9.2
    costs of, 233, 234
    definition of, 228
    employee benefits of, 231, 232 and table 9.2
    implementation phases for, 239 and fig. 9.1–241, 242
    issues of, 242, 243 and fig. 9.2
    job categories in, 229, 230 and table 9.1
    organizational enhancements and, 232 and table 9.2, 233
    organizations and implementing, 236–241, 242

    performance enhancements and, 231, 232 table 9.2
    performance of, 242, 243 and fig. 9.2
    planning for, 238, 239
    reward systems and, 230 and table 9.1
    top management and, 243
    types of, 234–235, 236
    types of skills in, 228
    work groups vs, 230 and table 9.1
Techline, 185
Technical skills, 17
Technology
    electronic information processing and, 179–180
    telecommunication and, 180, 181. *See also* Communication
Technology Changes the Culture at Roche, 233
Technology in organization design, 355, 356
Telecommuting, 133
Tenneco, 147
Texaco, 38
Texas Instruments, 91, 124, 125, 127, 232 table 9.2
Tharahirunchote, Wiwam, 44
Theme Parks, 392
Theory X, 9, 10 table 1.1
Theory Y, 9, 10 table 1.1
Theory Z (Ouchi), 371, 372
Thompson, Bill, 293
360-degree feedback, 150
3M, 31, 127
Time (magazine), 341
Time Warner, 340, 341
TNT, 341
Toshiba, 259
Total Quality Management, 148 fig. 6.2
Total Quality Management (TQM), 400
Toyota, 38, 155, 162, 315
Traditional approach (motivation), 89, 90
Training, 402
Trait approach, 258
Transformational leadership, 281, 282
Transition management, 398, 399
Transmission, 177, 178
Transportation, international business and, 37, 38 and fig. 2.3
Tricon, 255
TRW, 241
Turner Classic Movies, 341
Turnover, 21, 78, 133
Tyco, 20
Type A individuals, 73
Type B individuals, 73, 74
Type Z companies, 372, 375 and table 14.2, 376, 377, 383

U2, 392
UCLA, Anderson School at, 30
Uncertainty avoidance, 41
Unconflicted adherence, 318
Unconflicted change, 318
Unfreezing, 396
United Airlines, 3, 114
United Auto Workers (UAW), 161
United Food and Commercial Workers Union (UFCW), 114
United Parcel Service (UPS), 6, 51, 52
Universal approach, 7, 12 and fig. 1.3
Universal approach to organization

structure
  explanation of, 352
  human organization as, 353
  ideal bureaucracy, 352, 353
  principles of organizing as, 353
Universal Studios, 392
UNUM Corporation, 158
UPN, 307
UPS Delivers Diversity to a Diverse World (case study), 51, 52
Urwick, Lyndall, 6
U.S. Airways, 3
U.S. Civil Service, 124
U.S. Senate, 192
U.S. Steel (USX), 134
USA Network, 392
USA Today (newspaper), 48
Using Groups to Get Things Done (Case study), 219, 220

Valences, 102
Value customers, 377 and table 14.3
Valuing diversity, 35, 36
Valuing Employees at the World's Largest Firm (case study), 80–81
Vanderbilt University, 300
Vanderslice, Virginia, 114
Variable-interval reinforcement, 108 and table 4.1, 109
Ventures, new, 379
Verification, 77, 188
VH1, 307
Viacom, 307
Vigilant information processing, 320
Virtual teams, 236
Vivazzi, 392
Vivendi, 391
Vogelstein, Fred, 412
Volkswagen, 38
Volvo, 38, 127
Vroom, Victor, 100, 267
Vroom-Yetton-Jago model
  employee participation and, 128
Vroom's decision tree approach to leadership
  decision styles of, 268, 269 fig. 10.3, 270 fig. 10.4
  evaluation and implications of, 270
  explanation of, 267–268
  participation and, 326

W. R. Grace, 296

Wages, women and, 44
Wal-Mart, 17, 80, 81, 152, 161, 382, 409
Wall Street Journal, The (newspaper), 300
Wallace, Jennifer, 91, 92
Walsh, Bill, 206
Walton, Sam, 81, 382
Warner Brothers, 341
Warner-Lambert, 77
Waterman, Robert, 190, 371, 372, 377, 383
WB, 341
Weber, Max, 6, 19, 344, 352
Weil, Alan S., 332
Weisman, Jeb, 199
Welch, Jack, 90, 199, 350
Welch, James, 23
Welfare to Work program, 51
Wenig, Devin, 171
Wenning, Werner, 220
Western Electric, 7
Westinghouse, 91, 230, 232 table 9.2
Weyerhauser, 111, 144
Wharton School, 321
Wheel network, 181, 182 fig. 7.4, 183
When Employees Are Owners (case study), 113–114
Whirlpool, 202
Willard, Rick, 120
Willman, Jim, 143
Wilson Sporting Goods, 232
Win-win negotiation, 330 and fig. 12.7
Wipro Technologies, 240
Withdrawal behaviors, 78
Women
  as a dimension of diversity, 42–43, 44
  future workforce and, 33 and fig. 2.1, 34 fig. 2.2
  workforce diversity and, 30
Women in Business, 208
Work schedules
  compressed workweek, 131
  flexible, 131, 132 and fig. 5.4
  job sharing, 132, 133
  nine-eighty, 131
  telecommuting, 133
Work teams, 129, 234, 235
Workers
  consequences of stress and, 74, 75
  stress management and, 75, 76
  working conditions of, 7
Workforce
  composition of the, 33 and fig. 2.1
  diversity in, 30
  rightsizing, 18, 19

Workforce diversity
  benefits of, 47, 48 table 2.3
  definition and explanation of, 31–32
  global, 34, 35
  trends in, 31
Workforce (magazine), 220
Working conditions
  productivity and, 7
  of workers, 7
Working with Diversity, 382
Workplace behavior
  definition of, 78
  types of, 78, 79
Workplace substitutes, 283, 284
World View
  Equality for Asian Women in the Work-force, 44
  A Makeover at Avon, 394
  New Leadership Styles Propel Samsung Ahead, 259
World's Fair (Vancouver), 321
Wozniak, Steve, 17
Written communication, 174 and fig. 7.2, 175
WTA Tour, Inc., 350

Xerox, 43, 45, 47, 127, 154, 300, 379

Yale University, 199
Yellow Corporation, 23
Yellow Freight Corporation. See Yellow Corporation
Yellow Rules the Road (case study), 23, 24
Yetton, Philip, 267
Yong, Yun John, 259
YUM!, 254, 256, 262

Zemin, Jiang, 307
Zollars, Bill, 23